THE PURSUIT
OF JUSTICE

—◆—

KERMIT L. HALL
1944–2006

Oxford University Press mourns the loss of Kermit Hall, scholar, teacher, author, and friend. He completed work on this book just before his untimely death, and we gratefully dedicate it to him in recognition of his lifelong commitment to educating all Americans about the history of the U.S. Constitution and Supreme Court.

THE PURSUIT OF JUSTICE

Supreme Court Decisions that Shaped America

Kermit L. Hall & John J. Patrick

THE ANNENBERG
PUBLIC POLICY CENTER
OF THE UNIVERSITY OF PENNSYLVANIA

OXFORD
UNIVERSITY PRESS

Oxford University Press, Inc., publishes works that further
Oxford University's objective of excellence
in research, scholarship, and education.

Oxford New York
Auckland Cape Town Dar es Salaam Hong Kong Karachi
Kuala Lumpur Madrid Melbourne Mexico City Nairobi
New Delhi Shanghai Taipei Toronto

With offices in
Argentina Austria Brazil Chile Czech Republic France Greece
Guatemala Hungary Italy Japan Poland Portugal Singapore
South Korea Switzerland Thailand Turkey Ukraine Vietnam

Published by Oxford University Press, Inc.
198 Madison Avenue, New York, New York 10016
www.oup.com

Oxford is a registered trademark of Oxford University Press

Library of Congress Cataloging-in-Publication Data

Hall, Kermit.
  The Pursuit of Justice : Supreme Court decisions that shaped America / Kermit L. Hall and John J. Patrick. — 1st ed.
    p. cm.
  Includes bibliographical references and index.
  ISBN-13: 978-0-19-531189-1 (cloth)   ISBN-13: 978-0-19-532568-3 (paperback)
  ISBN-10: 0-19-531189-2 (cloth)   ISBN-10: 0-19-532568-0 (paperback)
 1. Constitutional law—United States—Cases. 2. United States. Supreme Court. I. Patrick, John J., 1935- II. Title.
  KF4549.H35 2006
  342.7300264—dc22

                                                                    2006021010

Printing number: 9 8 7 6 5 4 3 2 1

Printed in the United States of America
on acid-free paper

On the cover: The 1921 Supreme Court under Chief Justice William Howard Taft (seated, center).

Contents

Introduction

The Supreme Court as a Mirror of America

The Supreme Court of the United States seems a mysterious, distant institution. Its justices conduct their business in an imposing marble building; they don formal black robes to hear oral arguments and issue decisions; and they announce those decisions through the technical language of the law. On closer examination, however, this seemingly inscrutable institution of legal oracles turns out to be a uniquely human enterprise shaped by the personalities of its justices and by the disputes that constantly roil American society. Each case that comes before the Court is a unique slice of American life, not just an abstract legal matter, and the outcomes of these cases tell the story of the nation and its development. They also chronicle the institution's successful struggle to secure its power to review the actions of the other branches of government, to establish its independence, and to settle conclusively what the Constitution means.

The high court is simultaneously the least and the most accessible branch of government. Unlike the President and Congress, the Supreme Court invariably explains its actions through written opinions. Since the Court's founding in 1789 it has delivered enough opinions to fill more than five hundred fat volumes, known to us today as *United States Reports*. The justices reach those decisions through a process that involves open argument in court and intense media coverage. In almost every case, one justice speaks for the Court publicly, and his or her colleagues may concur or dissent with the decision, also publicly.

Still, the Court's reputation for mystery is well deserved. It reaches its decisions through highly confidential meetings, called conferences, in which the justices discuss the cases before them out of public earshot. Secrecy is so strict that the justices have adopted rules that preclude even their clerks from attending these meetings. The newest court appointee has the task of sending out messages and guarding access to the conference. We know about what transpires in these conference sessions only through the fragmentary notes that a few justices have left behind.

Even the well-known practice of an individual justice writing and signing an opinion gives way at times. The justices in some instances may decide to issue an opinion per curiam, or "for the court." Such an opinion is rendered either by the whole Court or a majority of it, rather than being attributed to an individual justice. This practice of issuing per curiam opinions means that the public cannot readily determine how the justices aligned themselves, adding to the mystery of the entire decision-making process. Early in the Court's history such opinions were used to dispose of minor cases in a terse, summary fashion; more recently, they have also become vehicles for major opinions. For example, the Court issued one of its great and controversial twentieth-century First Amendment decisions, *Brandenburg* v. *Ohio* (1969), per curiam. So, too, was *Bush* v. *Gore* (2000), in which the justices decided who would be the next President of the United States.

The framers of the Constitution intended just such a mix of secrecy and accessibility. They meant the justices to be judges, not politicians subject to direct public pressure. The justices serve during good behavior, a virtual grant of life tenure. The President appoints them with the advice and consent of the Senate; they can be removed only through impeachment by the House of Representatives and conviction by the Senate for "Treason, Bribery, or other high Crimes and Misdemeanors." Only one justice, Samuel Chase, has been impeached, but the vote to convict him fell short of the needed two-thirds majority.

The justices are insulated from politics in other ways as well. They do not have to stand for election. Their salaries cannot be diminished while they are in office. They alone decide when they will retire from the Court, even if they are infirm. They are, in the strongest sense of the term, agents of the law, whose ultimate responsibility is to uphold the Constitution without regard to political pressures or the standing of the people whose cases they decide. The words carved above the entrance of the Supreme Court building sum up its noblest ambitions: "Equal Justice under Law."

The Court is distinctively American and has been since it first opened its doors for business in 1789. Alexis de Tocqueville, a French visitor to the United States during the early nineteenth century, was astonished by the new nation's reliance on courts and judges. In his classic book *Democracy in America*, he wrote, "I am unaware that any nation on the globe has hitherto organized a judicial power in the same manner as the Americans....A more imposing judicial power was never constituted by a people." In more recent times, Chief Justice Charles Evans Hughes, who served during the Great Depression of the 1930s, explained the unique nature of the Court by pointing to the justicies' power to review acts of the other branches and, if necessary, overturn them. Only a few other courts in the world have powers in scope and operation similar to that of the U.S. Supreme Court; no other court figures so centrally in the life of its nation.

The Court was the most novel, yet least debated, institution to emerge from the Constitutional Convention of 1787. One reason that the delegates gathered in Philadelphia was to address the concern that rule of law—the concept that a nation should be governed by laws, not people—was under serious threat in the newly formed United States of America. The English government had a judiciary, but its judges did not hold tenure during good behavior; instead, they were effectively servants of the crown and, as a result, distrusted by many of the colonists. The colonies had courts of their own, but the final authority on legal matters rested with the distant Privy Council in London.

Moreover, under the Articles of Confederation, which were ratified in 1781 and represented the first attempt to establish a government for the new nation, there was no national judiciary; instead, state courts addressed almost all judicial matters, even those with national consequences. The framers of the Constitution, whose staunchest advocates were known as Federalists, wanted an independent judiciary capable of upholding standards of national law and restraining what they believed were the excesses of popular government. Thus, in Article 3 of the Constitution the delegates established a national judiciary, composed of one Supreme Court and as many lower federal courts as Congress wished.

This 1885 cartoon depicts an overworked Supreme Court. In 1891 the Judiciary Act relieved the Court's burden of deciding circuit court cases by establishing a new level of federal courts.

The framers granted the new Supreme Court limited original jurisdiction (the power to hear cases in the first instances as a trial court) and left Congress to sketch the boundaries of its appellate jurisdiction (the power to hear cases on appeal from other courts). Article 3 provided that the power of the federal courts in general and the Supreme Court in particular extended to "all Cases, in Law and Equity, arising under the Constitution, the Laws of the United States, and Treaties... to Controversies to which the United States shall be a Party;—to Controversies between two or more states; [between a State and Citizens of another State] between Citizens of different States...."

The framers chose the words in Article 3 carefully. Particularly important was their decision to merge the concepts of law and equity under one set of courts and judges, a practice that departed from the English system. Law constituted the formal rules adopted by legislatures and courts; equity, on the other hand, consisted of ideas about justice that rested on principles of fairness and that were administered in the English system by chancellors. Colonial Americans were deeply suspicious of equity courts because they operated under the control of English governors and were, therefore, often highly political, and they were able to defeat rights, especially property rights, that were otherwise protected through the law.

The crucial purpose of Article 3 was to empower, not limit, the courts in general and the Supreme Court in particular. The framers gave the Court a power of decision equal to that, in its appropriate sphere, of Congress. Article 6 established that the Constitution was "the Supreme law of the land," so by inference it followed that the Court, the nation's primary legal body, was to be its most important interpreter, one authorized to overturn an act of a state court or legislature and perhaps to set aside an act by another branch of the federal government.

It was left to Congress to determine how many justices were to exercise that power. In theory, the Supreme Court could function with only two justices—the chief justice and an associate justice. Today, the number of justices stands at nine, where it has remained since 1837 except for a brief period during the Civil War and Reconstruction, when it was as low as eight and as high as ten. At its inception, the Court had six justices, a number dictated in part by the requirement that each of these justices perform his duties in one of the six circuit courts of the United States. These circuit court duties included conducting trials, making the justices into republican teachers who brought through their circuit riding the authority of the federal government to the distant states. Circuit riding also exposed the justices to local political sentiments and legal practices. The justices continued to ride circuit until 1911, when Congress formally ended the practice.

Throughout the nineteenth and into the early twentieth century, Presidents tried to make sure that each of the circuits and the associated region had a representative on the bench. The number of justices was reduced briefly in 1801 to five, with the temporary abolition of circuit riding, but the number reverted to six with the passage of a new judiciary act in 1802. The number of justices grew to seven in 1807, and the eighth and ninth justices were added in 1837. That number remained constant until 1866, when Congress, in an attempt to deny President Andrew Johnson a chance to appoint any new justices, provided that the Court's number would decline by attrition to seven. The number dropped by one, to eight, and then the Judiciary Act of 1869 reestablished the number at nine. During the New Deal in the 1930s, President Franklin D. Roosevelt attempted unsuccessfully to expand the Court by as many as six new slots.

Whatever the number of justices, there is no constitutional requirement that they be lawyers, although all of them have been. Unlike the President, members of the Court can be foreign born, and several have been: James Wilson, James Iredell, David J. Brewer, George Sutherland, and Felix Frankfurter.

William Howard Taft (seated, center) was chief justice of the United States from 1921 to 1930. Although he wrote no landmark opinions, he influenced Congress to appropriate money for the Supreme Court Building and to pass the Judiciary Act of 1925, which gave the Court control over what cases it would decide. His distinguished Court included (seated) James McReynolds, Oliver Wendell Holmes Jr., Willis Van Devanter, and Louis D. Brandeis and (standing) Edward T. Sanford, George Sutherland, Pierce Butler, and Harlan Fiske Stone.

The Court has had several homes throughout its history. Until the Supreme Court moved into its present building in October 1935, it had always shared space with other government institutions. The Court held its first session at the Royal Exchange Building in New York City, which was also home to the lower house of the New York legislature. In December 1790 the nation's capital moved to Philadelphia and the justices had space in the newly constructed city hall of Philadelphia. Pierre Charles L'Enfant had designed a building for the Court in the new capital city of Washington, D.C., but it was never erected, in part because Congress never deemed a new home for the justices as particularly important. The justices moved in 1801 to an unfurnished chamber on the first floor of the Capitol. After the British burned the Capitol at the end of the War of 1812, the Court operated from a rented house on Capitol Hill for two years, but then went back to the Capitol, where the justices remained until moving to their current home in 1935. The tortured journey of the Court to its new magisterial home is a reminder of its growing prestige in the American scheme of government.

The new building was the singular triumph of Chief Justice William Howard Taft, the only justice also to have served as President of the United States. Following the design of architect Cass Gilbert, the building was constructed of white marble, with a central portico and matching wings. The imposing "White Palace" has come to symbolize the power and independence of not just the justices but the entire judicial branch.

The Court's most important business has always been exercised through its appellate jurisdiction. Again, this term simply means cases that have been heard and decided before they are brought—appealed—to the justices. For the first hundred years of the nation's history Congress was wary of giving the Court too much responsibility, fearing in part that the justices might become too powerful. For example, through the Judiciary Act of 1789, Congress granted the Court power to hear cases and controversies appealed to it based on diversity jurisdiction. This concept, contained in Article 3 of the Constitution, means that in order for a case to come to the Court, the parties to it must be from different, or diverse, states. Congress in 1789 could have granted the Court greater power by designating that it could hear any case—even if the parties were from the same state. The framers of the Constitution had also provided that Congress could specificy that the justices could hear cases "arising under" the Constitution, but the members of the First Congress decided not to invoke the broader power that these words in Article 3 conveyed.

Since then, Congress has not only significantly expanded the Court's jurisdiction but has also given it greater discretion in deciding which cases to hear. The Court has increasingly moved from one that decided cases it had to, to a court that decided those cases it wanted to. In the early years of the Court, the justices typically heard cases based on a mandatory writ of error, an assertion by a plaintiff that a lower court had made a mistake of law. The justices were required to hear these cases. Not surprisingly, as the nation expanded, the docket of the high court grew dramatically. In the first ten years of the new nation, the justices heard just one hundred cases, but by the 1880s they were drowning, hearing and deciding more than six hundred cases a year.

Beginning in the late 1890s and gaining momentum in the 1920s, Congress granted the justices far more discretion over their docket. One of the most important steps was the Judiciary Act of 1925, a measure for which Chief Justice Taft lobbied intensively. It broadened the use of the writ of certiorari and brought an immediate decline in the numbers of cases heard and decided by the justices.

The law often relies on Latin words to convey meaning. For example, the word "writ" means a formal written order by a court commanding someone to do something or to refrain from doing something. Certiorari is a Latin word that means "to ascertain" or, more liberally translated, "to make more certain."

The words are important because this particular writ, or order, is meant to bring cases to the Court that will make the law more certain in areas where there is conflict. But as Tocqueville so wisely reminded us, the resolution of conflicting legal interpretations almost always has political repercussions. Through this writ a petitioner comes to the Court and asks that the justices order a case to be heard. The writ is discretionary; the Court is not required to issue it or hear a case from anyone seeking such a writ. There are more than seven thousand petitions for "cert" sent to the Supreme Court annually. Only a handful—less than 2 percent—of these are accepted; the others are usually dismissed, almost always without written comment, leaving the parties to wonder why their plea for justice went unanswered. When that happens, the law stands as it was before. The denial of a writ of certiorari does not mean that the Court has decided that the lower court was correct; it only indicates that the justices are unwilling to make a decision, although as a matter of law the decision below stands.

The expanded use of the writ of certiorari and the declining use of the writ of error have helped the justices better manage their caseload. In recent years, the Court has decided as few as seventy cases a term, compared with the hundreds that it was deciding through most of the twentieth century. Moreover, with fewer cases to decide the justices are able to devote more time to the ones that they do decide. Throughout its history the Court has been important in resolving disputes, but it has become even more important in addressing major political issues, such the limits of free speech, the boundaries of church-state relations, and reproductive rights. The Court can choose which cases it wishes to hear, and that means the justices can have an even deeper influence on the particular issues they do address, such as the rights of criminal defendants. And even when the justices refuse to hear a case they shape public policy by leaving the law to stand as it was. The broadened use of the writ of certiorari has permitted the Court to emerge as a tribunal of constitutional and statutory interpretation rather than as a mere forum to resolve disputes among parties making competing claims under the Constitution.

The Court has also further refined the rules that it imposes when considering which cases to decide. The most important of these is justiciability. That term entails an important principle: the justices will hear and decide only those disputes that are subject to being resolved through the judicial process. The Court's actions have political consequences, but the Court itself should not be overtly political. The rule of justiciability is the Court's way of deflecting those cases that seek to use it as a political rather than a legal tool. To be justiciable the dispute must present a real case and controversy, the parties to it must have a direct interest in it (called standing), it must be ready for decision (ripeness), and it must not have already been decided by other actions (mootness). For example, the Supreme Court, although not explicitly prohibited from rendering advisory opinions, early in its history decided that it would not do so. The justices reasoned that their future influence depended on being a court of law rather than a political forum.

The justices have also resisted hearing collusive suits (suits in which the parties conspire to bring a case before the Court) and ones that raise political questions (that is, questions better settled by the elected branches). As the contested role of the Court in the 2000 Presidential election between George W. Bush and Al Gore reminds us, the political questions doctrine has itself become the subject of controversy. In the 2000 election, the Court decided by a narrow margin that Al Gore, although he had won the popular vote nationally, could not have officials in Florida perform a recount of the ballots there to see whether he had captured that state's electoral votes. The Court's per curiam opinion made Bush the President of the United States.

"Equal Justice under Law" proclaims the inscription beneath the frieze at the entrance of the Supreme Court Building. The sculpted figures represent liberty, order, and authority. Based on the classical Greek style of architecture and incorporating symbols of law and justice both inside and out, the grand building became the permanent home of the Supreme Court in 1935.

Critics charged that the Court was never intended to resolve such weighty political matters as who should be President and that the justices should never have agreed to hear the case in the first place.

These rules underscore that the Supreme Court is first and foremost a legal institution. Cases have to come to it; it cannot go looking for parties to plead cases of interest to the justices. Those who do appear must argue through the conventional processes of the law, including the use of the important concept stare decisis (literally, "let the decision stand"), or precedent. This idea holds that the justices should extend respect to previous decisions made by the Court as a way of promoting constitutional stability and certainty.

Controversy and constitutional change, however, have gone hand in hand on the Court. The Court is a place where advocates for conflicting political, social, economic, and cultural demands seek the blessing of the justices. Once again, Tocqueville had a critical insight. "Scarcely any political question arises in the United States that is not resolved, sooner or later," he observed, "into a judicial question." Americans generally and their political leaders especially have willingly transformed divisive political disputes—whether over slavery, the hours of work of men and women, the practice of segregation by race, or abortion—into constitutional conflicts. The Court's constitutional decisions, then, reflect the society it serves. Justice Oliver Wendell Holmes Jr. summed up matters nicely when he described the law as a "magic mirror" that reflected the assumptions, attitudes, and priorities of each generation. In that light, the Court can be thought of as the hand holding and turning that mirror. For example, through the nineteenth century, issues involving speech, press, church-state relations, and civil rights drew little attention from the justices. In the twentieth century, on the other hand, just such concerns have framed central conflicts in American society and dominated the Court's docket.

The Court's history has moved through clear phases or epochs. The first of these ran from the English founding in 1607 through the Constitutional Convention in 1787. Though neither the Court nor the Constitution existed, these years were nevertheless critical to establishing broad constitutional principles that endure to this day and to which the Court often turns. These included the value of a written constitution, the doctrine of limited government, the concept of federalism, and the idea of separation of powers.

From the nation's founding in 1787 through the end of Reconstruction in 1877, the most crucial constitutional issues were framed as conflicts between the states and the nation. These included disputes about the power of the federal courts in relation to their counterparts in the states, the power of the national government to regulate commerce, the right of property holders to remain free of regulation by either state or federal governments, and the expansion of slavery into the new territories and states. The struggle over state versus federal authority culminated in the secession movement, the Civil War, and Reconstruction. The constitutional legacy of the era appeared dramatically in the Thirteenth, Fourteenth, and Fifteenth Amendments to the Constitution. Of these, the Fourteenth, through its due process, equal protection, and state action clauses, reframed the work of the high court for the following century and a quarter in the areas of civil liberties and civil rights.

Among the most pressing issues in America from 1877 to 1937 were industrialization and immigration. Industrialization raised new questions about the role of government in regulating the conditions of labor, the rights of laborers to organize, the rights of corporations to control and use their capital, and the appropriateness of government intervention in the marketplace. The First World War brought a direct challenge to the civil liberties of Americans and the first sustained debate in the Court about the scope of freedom of speech and press. Equally important, a wave of immigration and a newly freed black population raised questions about the authority of government to regulate social change. The justices were forced to fit a document crafted in the eighteenth century to the realities of the industrial market economy of the late nineteenth and early twentieth centuries.

Initially, the justices gave preference to the rights of property holders, raised strong objections to government involvement in the marketplace, and viewed corporations more favorably than unions in the struggle between capital and labor. The Great Depression, however, placed increasing pressure on government to take an active role in the economy. The Court raised constitutional objections to many of President Franklin D. Roosevelt's solutions to the massive economic dislocation caused by the depression. In the face of FDR's proposal to pack the Court, the justices in 1937 retreated from their strong objections to government involvement in the economy and signaled their support for both state and federal initiatives designed to bolster the well-being of Americans.

After 1937 the Court again shifted gears, this time placing an emphasis on equality and such human rights as freedom of conscience, expression, and privacy. The emergence of the nation onto the world stage also posed new questions about the scope of Presidential power. The Second World War and then the Cold War, along with conflicts from Korea, to Vietnam, to Iraq, were accompanied by increasingly bold assertions about the authority of the chief executive in time of war. Moreover, the emergence of a national civil rights movement for African Americans, Native Americans, and Latinos, along with the emergence of feminism, tested the boundaries of long-accepted discriminatory practices in housing, employment, schooling, jury service, the right to hold and seek office, and the administration of the death penalty. It also produced a powerful counterreaction from groups that believed the state should not engage in programs such as affirmative action that were designed to favor one group over another as a way of ameliorating the consequences of past discrimination.

These eras of the Court remind us of how the Court has mirrored the times while trying to administer the rule of law. That makes any determination about the most important cases in the history of the Court a challenge. Lawyers interested in serving the immediate needs of their clients might find the most important cases to be those that address a current point of constitutional law. Historians, on the other hand, may search for the impact of the Court over time, attempting to explain how crucial decisions have shaped and been shaped by conflicts in American society. Throughout these various epochs of its history, the Court has developed routine processes by which to dispatch its business.

The modern Court has settled on an established routine for its operations. The justices begin their term the first Monday in October and continue through the third week of June. They meet twice a week, typically on Wednesday afternoon, to hear cases argued on the previous Monday, and on Friday to hear cases argued on Tuesday and Wednesday. At these conferences they screen petitions, deliberate on cases that have been argued, and transact miscellaneous business. They do so in a paneled conference room to which they are summoned by a buzzer. Tradition requires that the justices exchange handshakes and then take preassigned seats around a long table with the chief justice at one end and the senior associate justice at the other end. Once the door closes the conference begins and no other person may enter.

The chief justice presides over the conference, making him first among equals and providing an important opportunity to exercise leadership. The chief directs the justices to consider the certiorari petitions that at least one of the justices considers worthy. Indeed, one of the chief's duties is to indicate to his colleagues why a particular petition should be considered on its merits. If four of the justices conclude that a case on this "discuss list" is sufficiently important, it will be added to the Court's docket for full briefing and oral argument. After the chief speaks, the other eight justices comment in order of seniority.

The chief is responsible for leading the discussion of cases that have been argued. He will start with a review of the facts in the case, its history, and the relevant legal precedent. In descending order of seniority, the other justices then present their views. The justices typically signal how they will likely vote on the case and on that basis the chief justice tallies the vote. If the chief justice is in the majority he will assign responsibility for preparing an opinion; if he is not, then the senior justice in the majority assumes that role. The greatest of the chief justices have used their power to assign opinions to shape the overall direction of the Court.

The conference is a critical stage in the development of the Court's work, but it is not the end of the process. The justice assigned to prepare an opinion will often work through several drafts, sharing her or his work with colleagues and invariably revising and refining the opinion in response to their comments. An important part of the Court's work is the informal interaction among the justices as they develop an opinion. A justice's opinion may well change through the process, and in especially difficult cases maintaining a majority can be challenging. The deliberations that began with the conference continue until the Court announces its decision, a process that can take months.

When the Court convenes in public, the justices sit according to seniority. The chief justice is in the center and the associate justices are on alternating sides, with the most senior associate justice on the chief justice's immediate right. The most junior member of the Court is seated on the left farthest from the chief justice.

To assist them through this process the justices have law clerks. The practice of hiring law clerks began in 1882 when Justice Horace Gray hired a Harvard Law School graduate to assist him with his work on the Court. Today, a justice may have as many as seven clerks, who come from a pool of about 350 applicants to each justice, who has total control over whom is selected. Most of these clerks are graduates of prestigious law schools with extraordinary academic records who have usually clerked for a lower fed-

eral court judge. Their duties include reading, analyzing, and preparing memoranda for the justices and assisting in preparing opinions. Thirty-three clerks have gone on to become justices. They are today the most important of the Court's support staff, without whom the justices could not conduct their business.

Over the course of more than two centuries the justices have issued thousands of opinions. Culling from this long list the handful of decisions that represent pivotal moments in the Court's impact on American life is more an art than a science. With that consideration in mind, we have applied several general criteria. First, the Court's decision had to be a response to a pivotal public issue, which had a deep and abiding impact on the course of U.S. history. The Dred Scott case, for example, represents dead law. No lawyer today would attempt to defend a client based on the Court's actions. Still, the decision was a milestone in the history of the nation with regard to slavery. Second, a case must have overturned a significant precedent and thereby acted as a catalyst for political and social change. The benchmark case of *Brown* v. *Board of Education* (1954, 1955) signaled an end to segregation by race and opened a new chapter in the history of civil rights. Third, the Court's decision must include memorable and edifying statements of enduring American constitutional principles expressed in opinions of justices either for the Court or in dissent. The opinion of Chief Justice John Marshall in *McCulloch* v. *Maryland* (1819), for example, continues to resonate today because of Marshall's approach to the question of the powers of Congress and the Court and the memorable words with which he framed his opinion (for example, "the power to tax, is the power to destroy"). We likewise turn to Justice John Marshall Harlan's dissent in *Plessey* v. *Ferguson* (1896) precisely because it so forcefully rejected the majority's view that race relations could never change.

Fourth, the Court's decision must have been a definitive or illuminating response to an issue about a core principle of American constitutionalism, such as federalism, separation of powers, checks and balances, civil liberties, or civil rights. The justices' decision in *United States* v. *Nixon* (1974) dealt with the fundamental idea that the President is not above the law and the belief that the Court has a duty to establish the outer boundaries of executive privilege. Fifth, the Court's decision in some way must be included in the content standards or curricular frameworks of state departments of education, an indicator of the case's importance in cultivating standards of civic education.

A formal portrait of the Supreme Court after the confirmation of Samuel Alito in 2006. From left to right: Anthony M. Kennedy, Stephen G. Breyer, John Paul Stevens, Clarence Thomas, John G. Roberts Jr., Ruth Bader Ginsburg, Antonin Scalia, Samuel Alito, and David H. Souter.

Sixth, and finally, we have selected cases that tell compelling stories about the personal courage required to bring and sustain a case before the high court, whether on the winning or the losing side.

We also settled on this list of cases because individually and collectively each of them contributed to the dramatic rise in the high court's powers. Not all Americans have agreed with the Court's decisions; indeed, not all Americans agree that the Court should have the final word in saying what the Constitution means. The debates about the justices' powers today stand in sharp relief from the promise made by Alexander Hamilton in *The Federalist No. 78* that the Court would be the "least dangerous branch" to the liberties of Americans. What has emerged is a powerful national institution that has through its history staked out the right to review the constitutionality of the actions of the other branches of federal government and of state governments. This power of judicial review, nowhere explicitly specified in the Constitution, has been a flashpoint for controversy. That power, however, could not have been exercised had the justices not also achieved independence from direct popular and political pressure. But, most important, the Court has fostered successfully the concept of judicial sovereignty. This idea holds, in simple terms, that what the Court says the Constitution means is what it means; its power to interpret the Constitution is final, unless and until it is amended by the people.

No matter how one feels about the current power exercised by the justices, there is no disputing that historically they have played and continue to play an extraordinary role in American life. The United States has had only one national constitutional convention, in part because the Supreme Court has emerged as a kind of continuing constitutional convention, adjusting and modifying the ruling document to suit changing demands. Each case in this volume reminds us of how central the development of judicial review, judicial independence, and judicial sovereignty have been not only to the fate of the Court but to our entire constitutional experiment. As Justice Holmes might have noted, the Supreme Court has been a mirror of America.

The Rise of Judicial Review

Marbury v. *Madison* (1803)

Marbury v. Madison

- 5 U.S. 137 [1 Cr. 137] (1803)

- Decided: February 24, 1803

- Vote: 4–0

- Opinion of the Court: John Marshall

- Not participating: William Cushing and Alfred Moore

Like many Supreme Court cases, the great case of *Marbury* v. *Madison* began simply. William Marbury and three other people did not receive appointments as justices of the peace for the District of Columbia. Their claim before the Court was the result of a general effort by the outgoing administration of President John Adams to place its Federalist supporters in newly created judicial positions. The Federalist-controlled Congress, for example, passed the Judiciary Act of 1801 in the waning days of the Adams's administration, after Thomas Jefferson had been elected the new President. The law was a combination of well-intended judicial reform and political expediency on the part of the outgoing Federalist Party. It reduced the size of the Supreme Court from six to five justices, an action designed to deprive Jefferson's incoming administration of the opportunity to appoint a high court judge quickly.

The act also created sixteen new federal circuit court judgeships, and two weeks later a separate measure established forty-two justices of the peace in Washington, D.C., where the federal Congress had full control. President Adams appointed the new judges and signed the commissions just before he left office, and so the appointees became known as "midnight judges." For reasons that remain historically murky, however, John Marshall, who was both secretary of state and chief justice of the United States for a brief period, failed to have the commissions delivered to the justices of the peace.

Marbury was one of those "midnight judges" who did not receive a commission. When the new secretary of state, James Madison, took office he refused to deliver the commissions to Marbury and the others. Madison knew that President Jefferson and his stalwarts in Congress intended to repeal the Judiciary Act of 1801, which they did a year later, and that the judges and justices of the peace would soon be out of a job. Marbury and the others, however, decided to protest Madison's action. They brought their case under the Supreme Court's original rather than appellate jurisdiction. The Court can have cases presented to it in two ways. First, and most significantly, the justices hear cases on appeal, after another court, state or federal, has heard the dispute. Alternatively, as with *Marbury*, the justices can hear a small number of cases under the Court's original jurisdiction, which means it holds a trial or similar proceedings in order to determine the facts in the dispute and then settles the case by applying the law. This original jurisdiction, however, is narrowly tailored; the justices can hear only those cases involving ambassadors, public ministers, and consuls and suits involving states as parties. The Congress had also, in Section 13 of the Judiciary Act of 1789 that organized the American federal courts and legal system, provided that the Supreme Court could issue writs of mandamus. A writ is simply an order by a court. A writ of mandamus (which in Latin means "we command") is one that directs an individual to do something; in this instance, Marbury asked the court to tell James Madison to deliver the signed commissions to Marbury and his colleagues.

Chief Justice Marshall was in a compromised position because he had been the secretary of state who had failed to deliver the commissions in the first place. Despite this apparent conflict of interest, and in stark contrast to the judicial ethics of today, Marshall not only participated in the case but played an active, defining role, and ultimately wrote the opinion for the Court.

In December 1801 Marshall asked the Jefferson administration to respond to Marbury, but Madison ignored the request. The Jeffersonian Republican Congress also sent a direct, although controversial, message to the justices. It ordered that the Court would not meet for the 1801 term. Article III, section 2 provided that "the supreme Court shall have appellate Jurisdiction, both as to Law and Face, with such Exceptions, and under such Regulations as the Congress shall make." Despite the clear wording of the Constitution, Federalists complained that such an action was unconstitutional because it denied citizens access to the Court, but the Republicans, now in control and determined to press their advantage, were unmoved. As a result, Marbury's case did not reach the Court until 1803, two years after it had been brought. In the meantime, the Jeffersonian Congress repealed the Judiciary Act of 1801 and dismissed the judges appointed under its provisions. Jefferson and his followers believed that the Federalists, having lost at the polls, were determined to use the courts to frustrate the Republicans' legislative program. Moreover, the Republicans in Congress were threatening to impeach Federalist judges who could not be removed simply by repealing the 1801 act. It was in this highly charged political atmosphere that Chief Justice Marshall had to settle Marbury's case.

The case raised two distinct issues. The first was whether the justices could exercise the power of judicial review. This term means the power of a court, in this instance the Supreme Court, to review and potentially strike down an act of Congress as unconstitutional and invalid. Marbury's case presented the justices with an opportunity to expand their authority but also raised the possibility that Congress would react by stripping them of some of their powers if they did so.

The second issue was how extensively the justices should become embroiled in political battles. In many ways the question of whether a commission had been delivered was a political, not a legal one. If the justices tried to settle that question they would leave themselves open to charges that they were interfering in matters over which they had no authority.

The Jefferson administration assumed that the Court did not have the authority to address the question of the commission. It refused to give Marbury his commission and it also refused to appear in Court the day the case was argued. Marbury's counsel did appear, however, and managed to demonstrate to the justices through testimony that the commissions had been signed but had disappeared, to where no one knew.

This portrait of the prosperous Maryland banker William Marbury shows no sign of the disappointment that this ardent Federalist felt at not getting his commission to be a justice of the peace in the District of Columbia. Marbury is the only disappointed office seeker whose picture hangs in the Supreme Court building, alongside that of James Madison, against whom he lodged his unsuccessful suit.

In 1815 Chief Justice John Marshall was at the height of his powers. Marshall seized the opportunity in Marbury v. Madison *(1803) to formulate the concept of judicial review, a power that the Court has used effectively as the basis for its authority.*

Marshall's opinion for the Court held that Marbury was entitled to his commission and that Madison had wrongfully withheld it from him. But Marshall understood that directly attacking the Jefferson administration by giving Marbury what he wanted would potentially threaten the autonomy of the Court. Marshall sidestepped the critical questions while establishing the right of the justices to settle such matters conclusively—to exercise judicial review—and to remain free of political entanglements. As Marshall's opinion made clear, the power of the Court derived from its role as a legal, not political, institution. In fact, Marshall noted in his opinion that asking the justices to decide such questions was "peculiarly irksome, as well as delicate; and excites some hesitation with respect to the propriety of entering into such investigation." What is genuinely impressive about Marshall's opinion was that he managed to weave through the political maze in such a way that he not only affirmed but enhanced the power of the Court he led.

Marshall held that a writ of mandamus was the appropriate remedy. The important question, Marshall concluded, was whether such a mandamus was available under the grant of original jurisdiction to the Supreme Court in Article 3 of the Constitution. Cleverly, Marshall decided the question by comparing the text of Article 3 with Section 13 of the Judiciary Act of 1789, the section giving the Court the power to issue a writ of mandamus in the first place. Marshall found that Congress could not provide for the Court to use a writ of mandamus because no such power was granted to it in the Constitution.

Marshall used this finding to reach an even more important conclusion. When a statute conflicted with the federal Constitution, Marshall explained, it was "the essence of judicial duty" to follow the Constitution. Marshall went on to explain that "the particular phraseology of the Constitution of the United States confirms and strengthens the principle, supposed to be essential to all written constitutions, that a law repugnant to the constitution is void; and that *courts,* as well as other departments, are bound by that instrument." Marshall gave a ringing declaration to Marbury's legal rights. "The government of the United States," he continued, "has been emphatically termed a government of laws, not of men. It will certainly cease to deserve this high appellation, if the laws furnish no remedy for the violation of vested legal right."

Through these words Marshall established two enduring principles of American law: that courts determine what the law means and that they can overturn those laws that fail to conform with the Constitution. In this instance, Marshall affirmed that Marbury was due his commission, but he also concluded that because the justices could not issue a writ of mandamus since Section 13 of the 1789 Judiciary Act was unconstitutional, there was no means by which Marbury could receive his commission. Marshall's decision made it clear that Marbury had lost an important property right when the commission was not delivered to him, but that the Court could do nothing to help him. "The authority," Marshall explained, "given to the Supreme Court by the act establishing the judicial courts of the United States, to issue writs of mandamus to public officers appears not to be warranted by the constitution."

Marshall managed in one opinion to underscore his respect for those property rights and to establish that the judiciary could be, under the right circumstances, a powerful instrument to protect individual rights against legislative action. But because the Jefferson administration was not asked to do anything and Marbury was not going to receive his commission, there was no immediate reason or way for it to strike back and limit the Court's power. Marshall affirmed an enduring principle: what the Court said the Constitution meant was final. Congress can act only within the confines of the Constitution.

Marshall's opinion was an iron fist wrapped in a velvet glove. He asserted unequivocally the Court's power to rule on the constitutionality of congressional laws, but he kept the justices free from direct political conflict by concluding that the Court was powerless to help Marbury secure his commission. Marshall had managed in a highly charged political environment to build the authority of the Court without producing a political backlash that might have diminished it.

The Jeffersonian Republicans were openly frustrated by Marshall's constitutional dexterity, but in the end they could do little more than complain. Judge Spencer Roane, who like Jefferson and Marshall was from Virginia, attacked the *Marbury* decision in newspaper articles. Roane was a staunch advocate of limited federal judicial power. Two decades later, Judge John Bannister Gibson of the Pennsylvania Supreme Court asserted in the case of *Eakin* v. *Raub* (1825) that the decision in *Marbury* was nothing more than judicial usurpation. Roane and Gibson both insisted that an unelected federal judiciary serving terms during good behavior was too remote from the people to decide the validity of a legislative act. Once the people had spoken through their elected representatives, the courts were powerless to reverse the actions of these representatives.

During the summer of 1803 the Jeffersonian Republicans also launched a direct political attack on sitting federal judges appointed by the Federalists. The first victim was a district court judge, John Pickering of New Hampshire. Pickering was both insane and alcoholic, and in 1804 he became the first federal judge to be impeached, convicted, and removed from office. A year later, the Republicans turned their eye on an associate justice of the Supreme Court, Samuel Chase, who had helped Marshall prepare important parts of the *Marbury* opinion.

Chase was a nakedly partisan Federalist who enjoyed taunting his Republican detractors. He earned their special anger as a result of a charge, or instruction, he gave to a grand jury in Baltimore in which he denounced the repeal of the Judiciary Act of 1801, characterized President Jefferson as immoral, and suggested that the Republicans in Congress were seeking to instigate mob rule. Jefferson personally disliked Marshall. He noted later in life that Marshall's judicial method was "very irregular and very censurable." And Marshall returned the disdain. Even after Jefferson's death, Marshall scornfully wrote that "I have never thought him a particularly wise, sound, and practical statesman." Jefferson also disliked Chase intensely. He personally asked his party's leaders in the House of Representatives to impeach Chase, whom he detested even more than Marshall.

In 1805, the House of Representatives did just that, but the Senate failed to muster the two-thirds majority needed to convict him. When Chase's trial began in the United States Senate, the Republicans were in control of the government and certain that they would convict the partisan justice. Many of the senators

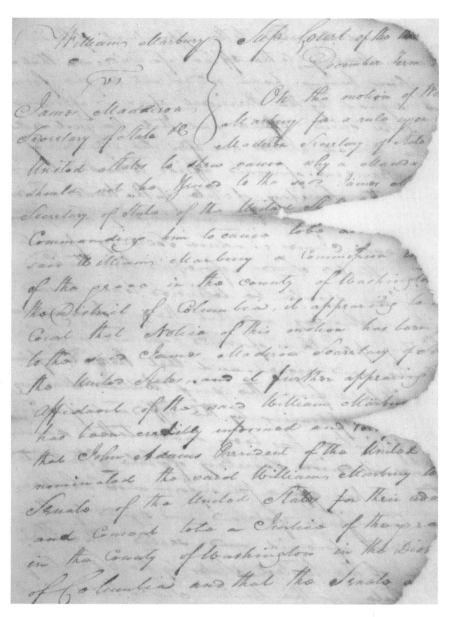

A fragment from the handwritten order that Chief Justice John Marshall gave to Secretary of State James Madison requiring him to show why William Marbury's commission to serve as a justice of the peace in the District of Columbia should not be delivered to him. Marshall's decision to do so suggested that he was not afraid to confront President Thomas Jefferson.

treated the trial as something of a kangaroo court, but the presiding officer, Vice President Aaron Burr, conducted the proceedings with great fairness. Chase's lawyer, Luther Martin, had the opportunity to present a complete defense for his client and, in the end, the Senate acquitted Chase. The verdict discouraged further attempts to impeach justices simply because of their political views. Chase's impeachment, however, sent another message: members of the judiciary were expected to avoid partisan politics. Throughout American history, justices have found themselves in trouble when they have been perceived to be involved in ordinary politics.

Ironically, Vice President Burr himself was wanted for killing Alexander Hamilton in a duel in New Jersey. He was, however, immune from prosecution in Washington, D.C. Two years later, Burr was tried for treason in a case over which Marshall presided and Luther Martin served as Burr's attorney.

Judicial review had certainly been used by other courts before *Marbury*. Both state and lower federal court judges had refused to uphold particular laws because they considered them to be contrary to a state constitution or the federal constitution. Marshall's opinion was important not because it was first but because it was the first statement of the doctrine of judicial review by the nation's highest court. In making his statement Marshall drew his authority from the colonial Massachusetts lawyer James Otis, who had brilliantly argued in the *Writs of Assistance Case* (1761) that judges were prohibited from enforcing laws that were patently unconstitutional. That idea had deep roots in English legal history, stretching at least back to *Dr. Bonham's Case* in 1610. In that instance, Sir Edward Coke, one of the greatest lawyers of English history, articulated the principle that parliamentary statutes contrary to custom and right reason must be held invalid.

Alexander Hamilton drove this same idea home when he argued for the adoption of the Constitution in *The Federalist No. 78* (1788). According to Hamilton, limited government required that courts of justice be empowered to "declare all acts contrary to the manifest tenor of the Constitution void." Marshall's opinion in *Marbury* reflected Hamilton's reasoning and stressed the duty of judges to apply the law to cases before them. Thus, judicial review was a necessary constitutional check on legislative discretion that might rob an individual or his or her life, property, or liberty.

Marbury stated the principle of what is called "coordinate branch" judicial review, in which the Supreme Court limits the power of one of the two other—coordinate—branches of the federal government. The act of judicial review is also important in striking down state laws and judicial decisions that are contrary to the Constitution. The justices have found that when such state measures violate the supremacy clause of Article 6, which says that the Constitution is "the supreme Law of the Land," they cannot pass federal constitutional muster. It was the exercise of this power, the Supreme Court's striking down of state acts, that stirred the greatest outcry in the nineteenth century. The justices did not attempt to void another act of Congress until 1857, when in the Dred Scott case it held invalid the 1820 Missouri Compromise, which involved the regulation of slavery in the western territories. In actuality, the Court's action was little more than a gesture, as Congress had already repealed the compromise when it passed the Kansas-Nebraska Act in 1854.

The significance of *Marbury* has grown over time. When the decision was issued, even its harshest critics, such as Roane, did not appreciate the central role that it would come to play in the American constitutional system and the nation's history generally. Marshall's decision, by establishing the practice of judicial review, granted to future generations of justices one of their central powers. It also underscored that because the justices exercise this power in an often heated political environment they must do so with great care. Today, no other decision by the Court is more frequently cited for its role in American government than *Marbury*.

The Constitution Is the Supreme Law of the Land

Marbury was not the first case in which courts invoked the power of judicial review, but it was the first time that the Supreme Court had done so to invalidate an act of Congress. In his 1803 opinion, Marshall addressed both judicial review and the doctrine of "political questions." He also asserted a fundamental principle that the Constitution is law and that judges are therefore uniquely positioned to interpret its meaning. Marshall made clear to future generations that the justices had an extraordinary role in making sure that the Constitution functioned properly.

The peculiar delicacy of this case, the novelty of some of its circumstances, and the real difficulty attending the points which occur in it, require a complete exposition of the principles on which the opinion to be given by the court is founded.

These principles have been, on the side of the applicant, very ably argued at the bar. In rendering the opinion of the court, there will be some departure in form, though not in substance, from the points stated in that argument....

The first object of inquiry is,

1. Has the applicant a right to the commission he demands?...

Mr. Marbury, then, since his commission was signed by the president and sealed by the secretary of state, was appointed; and as the law creating the office gave the officer a right to hold for five years independent of the executive, the appointment was not revocable; but vested in the officer legal rights which are protected by the laws of his country.

To withhold the commission, therefore, is an act deemed by the court not warranted by law, but violative of a vested legal right.

This brings us to the second inquiry; which is,

2. If he has a right, and that right has been violated, do the laws of his country afford him a remedy? The very essence of civil liberty certainly consists in the right of every individual to claim the protection of the laws, whenever he receives an injury. One of the first duties of government is to afford that protection....

The government of the United States has been emphatically termed a government of laws, and not of men. It will certainly cease to deserve this high appellation, if the laws furnish no remedy for the violation of a vested legal right....

It follows then that the question, whether the legality of an act of the head of a department be examinable in a court of justice or not, must always depend on the nature of that act....

By the constitution of the United States, the president is invested with certain important political powers, in the exercise of which he is to use his own discretion, and is accountable only to his country in his political character, and to his own conscience. To aid him in the performance of these duties, he is authorized to appoint certain officers, who act by his authority and in conformity with his orders....

The conclusion from this reasoning is, that where the heads of departments are the political or confidential agents of the executive, merely to execute the will of the president, or rather to act in cases in which the executive possesses a constitutional or legal discretion, nothing can be more perfectly clear than that their acts are only politically examinable. But where a specific duty is assigned by law, and individual rights depend upon the performance of that duty, it seems equally clear that the individual who considers himself injured has a right to resort to the laws of his country for a remedy....

It is then the opinion of the court,

1. That by signing the commission of Mr. Marbury, the president of the United States appointed him a justice of peace for the county of Washington in the district of Columbia; and that the seal of the United States, affixed thereto by the secretary of state, is conclusive testimony of the verity of the signature, and of the completion of the appointment; and that the

appointment conferred on him a legal right to the office for the space of five years.

2. That, having this legal title to the office, he has a consequent right to the commission; a refusal to deliver which is a plain violation of that right, for which the laws of his country afford him a remedy.

It remains to be inquired whether,

3. He is entitled to the remedy for which he applies. This depends on,

1. The nature of the writ applied for. And,

2. The power of this court.

1. The nature of the writ. . . .

To render the mandamus a proper remedy, the officer to whom it is to be directed, must be one to whom, on legal principles, such writ may be directed; and the person applying for it must be without any other specific and legal remedy. . . .

This, then, is a plain case of a mandamus, either to deliver the commission, or a copy of it from the record; and it only remains to be inquired,

Whether it can issue from this court.

The act to establish the judicial courts of the United States authorizes the supreme court "to issue writs of mandamus, in cases warranted by the principles and usages of law, to any courts appointed, or persons holding office, under the authority of the United States."

The secretary of state, being a person, holding an office under the authority of the United States, is precisely within the letter of the description; and if this court is not authorized to issue a writ of mandamus to such an officer, it must be because the law is unconstitutional, and therefore absolutely incapable of conferring the authority, and assigning the duties which its words purport to confer and assign.

The constitution vests the whole judicial power of the United States in one supreme court, and such inferior courts as congress shall, from time to time, ordain and establish. This power is expressly extended to all cases arising under the laws of the United States; and consequently, in some form, may be exercised over the present case; because the right claimed is given by a law of the United States.

In the distribution of this power it is declared that "the supreme court shall have original jurisdiction in all cases affecting ambassadors, other public ministers and consuls, and those in which a state shall be a party. In all other cases, the supreme court shall have appellate jurisdiction."

It has been insisted at the bar, that as the original grant of jurisdiction to the supreme and inferior courts is general, and the clause, assigning original jurisdiction to the supreme court, contains no negative or restrictive words; the power remains to the legislature to assign original jurisdiction to that court in other cases than those specified in the article which has been recited; provided those cases belong to the judicial power of the United States.

If it had been intended to leave it in the discretion of the legislature to apportion the judicial power between the supreme and inferior courts according to the will of that body, it would certainly have been useless to have proceeded further than to have defined the judicial power, and the tribunals in which it should be vested. The subsequent part of the section is mere surplusage, is entirely without meaning, if such is to be the construction. If congress remains at liberty to give this court appellate jurisdiction, where the constitution has declared their jurisdiction shall be original; and original jurisdiction where the constitution has declared it shall be appellate; the distribution of jurisdiction made in the constitution, is form without substance.

Affirmative words are often, in their operation, negative of other objects than those affirmed; and in this case, a negative or exclusive sense must be given to them or they have no operation at all. . . .

To enable this court then to issue a mandamus, it must be shown to be an exercise of appellate jurisdiction, or to be necessary to enable them to exercise appellate jurisdiction.

It has been stated at the bar that the appellate jurisdiction may be exercised in a variety of forms, and that if it be the will of the legislature that a mandamus should be used for that purpose, that will must be obeyed. This is true; yet the jurisdiction must be appellate, not original.

It is the essential criterion of appellate jurisdiction, that it revises and corrects the proceedings in a cause already instituted, and does not create that case. Although, therefore, a mandamus may be directed to courts, yet to issue such a writ to an officer for the delivery of a paper, is in effect the same as to sustain an original action for that paper, and therefore seems not to belong to appellate, but to original jurisdiction. Neither is it necessary in such a case as this, to enable the court to exercise its appellate jurisdiction.

The authority, therefore, given to the supreme court, by the act establishing the judicial courts of the United States, to issue writs of mandamus to public officers, appears not to be warranted by the constitution; and it becomes necessary to inquire whether a jurisdiction, so conferred, can be exercised.

The question, whether an act, repugnant to the constitution, can become the law of the land, is a question deeply interesting to the United States; but, happily, not of an intricacy proportioned to its interest. It seems only necessary to recognise certain principles, supposed to have been long and well established, to decide it.

That the people have an original right to establish, for their future government, such principles as, in their opinion, shall most conduce to their own happiness, is the basis on which the whole American fabric has been erected. The exercise of this original right is a very great exertion; nor can it nor ought it to be frequently repeated. The principles, therefore, so established are deemed fundamental. And as the authority, from which they proceed, is supreme, and can seldom act, they are designed to be permanent.

This original and supreme will organizes the government, and assigns to different departments their respective powers. It may either stop here; or establish certain limits not to be transcended by those departments.

The government of the United States is of the latter description. The powers of the legislature are defined and limited; and that those limits may not be mistaken or forgotten, the constitution is written. To what purpose are powers limited, and to what purpose is that limitation committed to writing; if these limits may, at any time, be passed by those intended to be restrained? The distinction between a government with limited and unlimited powers is abolished, if those limits do not confine the persons on whom they are imposed, and if acts prohibited and acts allowed are of equal obligation. It is a proposition too

plain to be contested, that the constitution controls any legislative act repugnant to it; or, that the legislature may alter the constitution by an ordinary act.

Between these alternatives there is no middle ground. The constitution is either a superior, paramount law, unchangeable by ordinary means, or it is on a level with ordinary legislative acts, and like other acts, is alterable when the legislature shall please to alter it.

If the former part of the alternative be true, then a legislative act contrary to the constitution is not law: if the latter part be true, then written constitutions are absurd attempts, on the part of the people, to limit a power in its own nature illimitable.

Certainly all those who have framed written constitutions contemplate them as forming the fundamental and paramount law of the nation, and consequently the theory of every such government must be, that an act of the legislature repugnant to the constitution is void.

This theory is essentially attached to a written constitution, and is consequently to be considered by this court as one of the fundamental principles of our society. It is not therefore to be lost sight of in the further consideration of this subject.

If an act of the legislature, repugnant to the constitution, is void, does it, notwithstanding its invalidity, bind the courts and oblige them to give it effect? Or, in other words, though it be not law, does it constitute a rule as operative as if it was a law? This would be to overthrow in fact what was established in theory; and would seem, at first view, an absurdity too gross to be insisted on. It shall, however, receive a more attentive consideration.

It is emphatically the province and duty of the judicial department to say what the law is. Those who apply the rule to particular cases, must of necessity expound and interpret that rule. If two laws conflict with each other, the courts must decide on the operation of each. So if a law be in opposition to the constitution: if both the law and the constitution apply to a particular case, so that the court must either decide that case conformably to the law, disregarding the constitution; or conformably to the constitution, disregarding the law: the court must determine which of these conflicting rules governs the case. This is of the very essence of judicial duty.

If then the courts are to regard the constitution; and the constitution is superior to any ordinary act of the legislature; the constitution, and not such ordinary act, must govern the case to which they both apply.

Those then who controvert the principle that the constitution is to be considered, in court, as a paramount law, are reduced to the necessity of maintaining that courts must close their eyes on the constitution, and see only the law.

This doctrine would subvert the very foundation of all written constitutions. It would declare that an act, which, according to the principles and theory of our government, is entirely void, is yet, in practice, completely obligatory. It would declare, that if the legislature shall do what is expressly forbidden, such act, notwithstanding the express prohibition, is in reality effectual. It would be giving to the legislature a practical and real omnipotence with the same breath which professes to restrict their powers within narrow limits. It is prescribing limits, and declaring that those limits may be passed at pleasure.

That it thus reduces to nothing what we have deemed the greatest improvement on political institutions—a written constitution, would of itself be sufficient, in America where written constitutions have been viewed with so much reverence, for rejecting the construction. But the peculiar expressions of the constitution of the United States furnish additional arguments in favour of its rejection.

The judicial power of the United States is extended to all cases arising under the constitution. Could it be the intention of those who gave this power, to say that, in using it, the constitution should not be looked into? That a case arising under the constitution should be decided without examining the instrument under which it arises?

This is too extravagant to be maintained.

In some cases then, the constitution must be looked into by the judges. And if they can open it at all, what part of it are they forbidden to read, or to obey?

There are many other parts of the constitution which serve to illustrate this subject.

It is declared that "no tax or duty shall be laid on articles exported from any state." Suppose a duty on the export of cotton, of tobacco, or of flour; and a suit instituted to recover it. Ought judgment to be rendered in such a case? Ought the judges to close their eyes on the constitution, and only see the law? . . .

From these and many other selections which might be made, it is apparent, that the framers of the constitution contemplated that instrument as a rule for the government of courts, as well as of the legislature.

Why otherwise does it direct the judges to take an oath to support it? This oath certainly applies, in an especial manner, to their conduct in their official character. How immoral to impose it on them, if they were to be used as the instruments, and the knowing instruments, for violating what they swear to support!

The oath of office, too, imposed by the legislature, is completely demonstrative of the legislative opinion on this subject. It is in these words: "I do solemnly swear that I will administer justice without respect to persons, and do equal right to the poor and to the rich; and that I will faithfully and impartially discharge all the duties incumbent on me as according to the best of my abilities and understanding, agreeably to the constitution and laws of the United States."

Why does a judge swear to discharge his duties agreeably to the constitution of the United States, if that constitution forms no rule for his government? If it is closed upon him and cannot be inspected by him?

If such be the real state of things, this is worse than solemn mockery. To prescribe, or to take this oath, becomes equally a crime.

It is also not entirely unworthy of observation, that in declaring what shall be the supreme law of the land, the constitution itself is first mentioned; and not the laws of the United States generally, but those only which shall be made in pursuance of the constitution, have that rank.

Thus, the particular phraseology of the constitution of the United States confirms and strengthens the principle, supposed to be essential to all written constitutions, that a law repugnant to the constitution is void, and that courts, as well as other departments, are bound by that instrument.

The rule must be discharged.

"An Act of Suicide"

The Supreme Court decided Marbury *during President Thomas Jefferson's first term in office. He objected to the practice of judicial review because he believed that it violated the principle of separation of powers and threatened the very survival of the nation. In its place, he proposed that each branch or department of government decide constitutional questions for itself, with the ultimate responsibility resting with the people. Letters Jefferson wrote between 1804 and 1823 outline his views on judicial review and his "departmental" theory of constitutional review.*

Nothing in the Constitution has given [the judges] a right to decide for the Executive, more than to the Executive to decide for them. Both magistrates are equally independent in the sphere of action assigned to them. The Constitution...meant that its coordinate branches should be checks on each other. But the opinion which gives to the judges the right to decide what laws are constitutional and what not, not only for themselves in their own sphere of action but for the Legislature and Executive also in their spheres, would make the Judiciary a despotic branch.
—Thomas Jefferson to Abigail Adams, 1804

The question whether the judges are invested with exclusive authority to decide on the constitutionality of a law has been heretofore a subject of consideration with me in the exercise of official duties. Certainly there is not a word in the Constitution which has given that power to them more than to the Executive or Legislative branches.
—Thomas Jefferson to W. H. Torrance, 1815

There is another opinion entertained by some men of such judgment and information as to lessen my confidence in my own. That is, that the Legislature alone is the exclusive expounder of the sense of the Constitution in every part of it whatever. And they allege in its support that this branch has authority to impeach and punish a member of either of the others acting contrary to its declaration of the sense of the Constitution. It may, indeed, be answered that an act may still be valid although the party is punished for it, right or wrong. However, this opinion which ascribes exclusive exposition to the Legislature merits respect for its safety, there being in the body of the nation a control over them which, if expressed by rejection on the subsequent exercise of their elective franchise, enlists public opinion against their exposition and encourages a judge or executive on a future occasion to adhere to their former opinion. Between these two doctrines, every one has a right to choose, and I know of no third meriting any respect.
—Thomas Jefferson to W. H. Torrance, 1815

In denying the right [the Supreme Court usurps] of exclusively explaining the Constitution, I go further than [others] do, if I understand rightly [this] quotation from the *Federalist* of an opinion that "the judiciary is the last resort in relation *to the other departments* of the government, but not in relation to the rights of the parties to the compact under which the judiciary is derived." If this opinion be sound, then indeed is our Constitution a complete *felo de se* [act of suicide]. For intending to establish three departments, coordinate and independent, that they might check and balance one another, it has given, according to this opinion, to one of them alone the right to prescribe rules for the government of the others, and to that one, too, which is unelected by and independent of the nation. For experience has already shown that the impeachment it has provided is not even a scarecrow....The Constitution on this hypothesis is a mere thing of wax in the hands of the judiciary, which they may twist and shape into any form they please.
—Thomas Jefferson to Spencer Roane, 1819

2

The National Bank and Federalism

McCulloch v. *Maryland* (1819)

D uring the early years of the nineteenth century, many Americans were primarily loyal to their state rather than to the United States of America. Luther Martin of Maryland, for example, often spoke of Maryland as "my country." In 1787, Martin had represented Maryland at the convention in Philadelphia that framed the United States Constitution, but he refused to sign the document because, in his opinion, it granted too much power to the national government at the expense of the states. Martin later campaigned against ratification of the Constitution, but reconciled himself to it after Maryland and other states approved it. However, he remained wary of the national government and any attempts it might make to encroach against the rights and powers of his state.

Luther Martin was serving as Maryland's attorney general in 1819 when the moment came for him to defend his state against the federal government at the U.S. Supreme Court. A bitterly contested case, *McCulloch* v. *Maryland,* raised critical questions about the nature of federalism in the U.S. Constitution.

McCulloch v. Maryland
• 17 U.S. 316 [4 Wheat. 316] (1819)
• Decided: March 6, 1819
• Vote: 7–0
• Opinion of the Court: John Marshall

The impressive building that housed the First Bank of the United States was constructed in Philadelphia in 1797. Branches of the national bank were located in every state, and it was the Baltimore, Maryland, office that was involved in McCulloch v. Maryland *(1819), during the period of the Second National Bank.*

What exactly was the division of powers between the national government and the particular states within the federal union? Did the Constitution grant Congress the power to create a national bank that could significantly affect the operations of banks chartered by Maryland and other states? And did the state of Maryland, or any other state within the federal union, have the power to excessively tax a branch of the national bank within its territory in order to drive it out of business?

The constitutional issues raised in *McCulloch* v. *Maryland* were not new. They arose initially in 1791, during the first term of President George Washington, when Congress enacted legislation to establish the First Bank of the United States. The President was uncertain about how to respond. After all, the Constitution did not explicitly grant Congress the power to establish a national bank. So before deciding whether to sign or veto the bill, President Washington asked the advice of Secretary of the Treasury Alexander Hamilton and Secretary of State Thomas Jefferson. Hamilton and Jefferson's conflicting responses framed the issue not only for President Washington in 1791 but also for the adversaries and decision makers in *McCulloch* v. *Maryland* in 1819.

In a paper written to the President, Jefferson argued that the Congress did not have power under the Constitution to pass the national bank bill. He could not find any statement about a national bank in Article 1, Section 8, which includes the list of Congress's enumerated powers. Thus, according to Jefferson, Congress could not assume a power not explicitly granted to it by the Constitution. Next, he turned to Clause 18 of Article 1, Section 8 of the Constitution, which granted Congress the power "To make all Laws which shall be necessary and proper for carrying into Execution the foregoing Powers, and all other powers vested by this Constitution in the Government of the United States, or in any Department or Officer thereof." Jefferson claimed that this "necessary and proper" clause could not be interpreted so expansively as to permit the federal government to establish a national bank. In line with his strict construction, or narrow interpretation, of the Constitution, Jefferson advised the President to veto the national bank bill.

Hamilton, by contrast, counseled Washington to sign the bill into law. He pointed out that the Constitution did not prohibit the establishment of the national bank. Thus, he argued, Congress could exercise a power not denied to it by the supreme law of the land if that action was for the good of the country. In a paper written to President Washington, Hamilton said,

> That every power vested in a government is in its nature sovereign, and includes...a right to employ all the means requisite and fairly applicable to the attainment of the ends of such power, and which are not precluded by restrictions and exceptions specified in the Constitution, or not immoral, or not contrary to the essential ends of political society.

Furthermore, Hamilton, unlike Jefferson, loosely interpreted the "necessary and proper" clause of Article 1, Section 8 of the Constitution to permit Congress to enact legislation for a national bank. According to his loose construction, or broad interpretation, of the Constitution, it was "necessary and proper" for Congress to pass the national bank bill in order to adequately carry out such explicitly stated powers as coining and regulating the value of money, borrowing money, and levying taxes. Therefore, according to Hamilton, the Constitution implicitly provided the federal government with the power to establish a national bank.

President Washington followed Hamilton's advice. He signed the national bank bill to make it a federal statute, and the First Bank of the United States was chartered for twenty years. Strong public controversy about the constitutionality and desirability of the First Bank of the United States continued, and Congress decided not to renew the bank's charter in 1811. However, in 1816 a majority in Congress enacted legislation to establish the Second Bank of the United States, which President James Madison signed into law.

Like its predecessor, the second national bank attracted many critics and opponents dedicated to destroying an institution they believed to be an unconstitutional manifestation of federal government power. Unlike the First Bank of the United States, however, the second national bank was poorly managed, and rumors circulated about corruption at the highest levels of the bank's management. Several states responded to growing public opposition to the national bank with legislation directed against it. The state government of Maryland, for example, enacted a law that levied an extremely high tax on any bank operating in the state without a state charter. At that time, the Second Bank of the United States was the only bank in Maryland that was not chartered by the state. James McCulloch, the head cashier of the national bank's Baltimore branch, refused to pay the tax. Maryland successfully sued McCulloch in the Baltimore County Court. The Maryland Court of Appeals upheld the lower court's judgment, and this decision was appealed to the U.S. Supreme Court.

The case attracted national attention because it posed issues about federalism, the extent and limits of states' rights and national government power, which had aroused controversy since the framing of the U. S. Constitution in 1787. Now these controversies had come to a head in the highest court in the land. This case was considered so important that the Court waived its rule limiting each side to two lawyers entitled to present oral arguments before the Court. As a result, three lawyers of national prominence argued for the federal government and the Bank of the United States: Daniel Webster, William Pinkney, and William Wirt, attorney general of the United States. Three lawyers of equal prominence represented the state of Maryland: Joseph Hopkinson, Walter Jones, and Luther Martin, attorney general of Maryland.

The oral arguments were presented before the Supreme Court from February 22 until March 3, 1819. During every day of the proceedings, spectators filled the small courtroom in the basement of the Capitol building, the first long-term home of the Supreme Court. They listened intently as the lawyers presented their cases and responded to questions from the Court.

The advocates for Maryland stressed that the U.S. Constitution did not expressly give Congress the power to charter a national bank. Counsel for the federal government countered by noting the Constitution's Article 1, Section 8, Clause 18, which did grant Congress the power to "make all laws which shall be necessary and proper for carrying into Execution the foregoing Powers." Did the "necessary and proper" clause give Congress adequate power only to do those few things indispensable for carrying out its listed, or enumerated, pow-

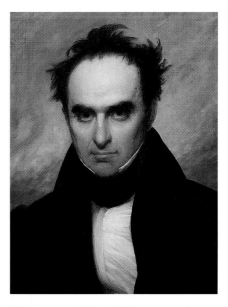

This portrait of Daniel Webster, painted some sixteen years after his argument in the McCulloch *case, hangs in the Hood Museum of Art at Dartmouth College, Webster's alma mater. Webster used his vast knowledge, extraordinary oratorical skills, and the imposing demeanor evident in this painting to prevail in most of his courtroom contests. He appeared before the Supreme Court in 168 cases.*

ers? Maryland's lawyers believed it did because they supported a narrow and restrictive interpretation of the U. S. Constitution in general and the "necessary and proper" clause in particular. The federal government's lawyers argued for a broadly constructed Constitution and a loosely interpreted "necessary and proper" clause to justify the incorporation of a national bank by Congress.

The contending lawyers also addressed the question of a state government's power to tax an institution chartered by the federal government. Maryland's lawyers, of course, defended their state's right to tax a branch of the national bank located within its borders. The federal government's lawyers held this to be an unconstitutional state government action in defiance of the U.S. Constitution, which according to its Article 6 is "the supreme Law of the Land."

Only three days after the oral arguments ended, Chief Justice John Marshall presented the Court's unanimous opinion, declaring Maryland's tax on the national bank to be unconstitutional. Marshall's opinion for the Court, the greatest one in his long and illustrious career as chief justice, was a strong refutation of the states' rights arguments of Maryland's lawyers.

Marshall began by considering this question: does Congress have the power to incorporate a national bank? His affirmative response emphasized a nationalist interpretation of the federal union's origin. The chief justice wrote, "The government of the Union . . . is, emphatically and truly, a government of the people. In form and in substance, it emanates from them. Its powers are granted by them, and are to be exercised directly on them, and for their benefit." Marshall emphasized "that the government of the Union, though limited in its powers [by the Constitution] is supreme within its sphere of action." He noted that Article 6 declared the Constitution and laws of the United States to be "the supreme law of the land" that must prevail against conflicting actions by a state government.

Like Alexander Hamilton many years earlier, the chief justice held that Congress could constitutionally establish a national bank even though this power was not explicitly mentioned in the U.S. Constitution. So long as the Constitution did not prohibit Congress from chartering a bank, it could do so under the power granted to it through the "necessary and proper" clause. Marshall argued that the framers of the Constitution included the "necessary and proper" clause among the powers of Congress to provide for the enlargement of these powers, not their strict limitation. Drawing upon the ideas of Alexander Hamilton in the twenty-third paper of *The Federalist*, written in 1787 to explain the Constitution and promote its ratification, and his 1791 paper addressed to President Washington, the chief justice exclaimed, "Let the end be legitimate, let it be within the scope of the constitution, and all means which are appropriate, which are plainly adapted to that end, which are not prohibited, but consist with the letter and spirit of the constitution, are constitutional."

Marshall noted that the Constitution is not a legal code that specifically describes every power to be exercised by Congress. Rather, it is a general framework of the federal government's structure and powers in which only the most important "objects" are set forth and the rest of its powers may "be deduced from the nature of the objects themselves." He emphasized that in considering the powers of Congress and the latitude of the "necessary and proper" clause "we must never forget that it is a Constitution we are expounding." Thus, a broad interpretation of congressional powers is warranted.

The chief justice foresaw long-term benefits in a flexible use of Congress's powers in the Constitution. He memorably wrote,

> It must have been the intention of those who gave these powers to insure... their beneficial execution.... This provision is made in a Constitution intended to endure for ages to come, and consequently to be adapted to the various crises of human affairs. To have prescribed the means by which Government should, in all future time, execute its powers would have been to change entirely the character of the instrument and give it the properties of a legal code. It would have been an unwise attempt to provide by immutable rules for exigencies which, if foreseen at all, must have been seen dimly, and which can be best provided for as they occur.

Marshall next turned to the question of whether Maryland could tax the branch of the national bank within its borders without violating the U.S. Constitution. He responded for the Court "that the law passed by the Legislature of Maryland, imposing a tax on the Bank of the United States is unconstitutional and void." He argued that allowing a state government to tax any part of the national government would violate the supremacy clause of the Constitution's Article 6. Marshall observed "that the power to tax involves the power to destroy." In conclusion, he denounced the state of Maryland's attempt to burden and destroy the national bank, which Congress had created constitutionally, by enacting an unconstitutional tax against this federal institution. "This was not intended by the American people," wrote Marshall. "They did not design to make their [federal] Government dependent upon the states."

GENERAL JACKSON SLAYING THE MANY HEADED MONSTER.

In this 1832 political cartoon, President Andrew Jackson (far left) and Vice President Martin Van Buren (center), who, like many Americans, disagreed with the Court's decision in McCulloch v. Maryland, *attack the bank, a monster whose multiple heads represent Nicholas Biddle, the bank's president, and the directors of the several branch banks in the states. Congress passed a bill to renew the national bank's charter, but President Jackson vetoed it, and the Second Bank of the United States passed away in 1836.*

The Supreme Court's ruling in *McCulloch* v. *Maryland* established two enduring constitutional principles. The first, the implied powers doctrine, assumes that the "necessary and proper" clause of the Constitution can be interpreted broadly so that Congress may choose the means it wishes to carry out powers granted to it in the Constitution. The second principle forbids the state governments to obstruct the constitutionally permitted operations of the federal government. It affirms the supremacy of the Constitution and federal laws over state laws that conflict with them.

Over the long term, the *McCulloch* ruling has supported a loose construction of the Constitution that enables the federal government to apply its constitutionally granted powers flexibly in order to meet the new problems of changing times. This landmark decision also strengthened the Court's power of judicial review over acts of state government. It thus infuriated supporters of states' powers and rights, such as Luther Martin, the attorney general of Maryland, who unsuccessfully argued his state's position in *McCulloch* v. *Maryland*.

Despite its long-term significance in American constitutional history, the Court's decision in *McCulloch* was very unpopular in the short term. Anger against Chief Justice Marshall and the Supreme Court was especially strong not only in Maryland but also in Virginia and Ohio. In February 1819, while *McCulloch* v. *Maryland* was before the U.S. Supreme Court, the state government of Ohio enacted a law to levy very high taxes on the branches of the national bank in Cincinnati and Chillicothe. In defiance of the Supreme Court's decision against Maryland in the *McCulloch* case, Ohio enforced its tax laws against the national bank branches within the state. However the national bank's officers obtained a federal court order that obligated the Ohio tax collectors to immediately return the money they had taken from the bank.

The controversy simmered until 1824, when the case of *Osborn* v. *The Bank of the United States* went to the U.S. Supreme Court. The issues and arguments before the Court were practically the same as those of the 1819 *McCulloch* case, and the Court's unanimous decision in *Osborn* reaffirmed the decision in *McCulloch*. However, public opinion in Ohio and many other parts of the United States generally remained hostile to the national bank and the Marshall Court's decisions about it. Nonetheless, during John Marshall's lifetime the Supreme Court's decisions in the national bank cases weighed heavily in the ongoing struggle between the national and state governments over the balance of power within the federal system. Only long after his death in 1835, however, was Chief Justice Marshall's opinion for the Court in *McCulloch* v. *Maryland* fully vindicated through its strong impact on the development and meaning of federalism in the United States.

From the post–Civil War era to the present, the balance of power in the federal system has shifted steadily away from the states and toward the federal government. During the twentieth century, the Court's decision in *McCulloch* v. *Maryland* buttresessed the federal government's extensive exercise of power to establish social welfare programs and regulate the economy. John Marshall's loose construction of the Constitution continues to influence the decisions of the Supreme Court in the twenty-first century.

84)

Henry Aston

53

vs

Bazaleel Wells & the
heirs and Representatives of
Arnold H. Dohrman decd.

This cause came on to be heard on
the transcript of the Record and was
argued by Counsel on consideration whereof— It is Decreed and
ordered, that the Decree of the Circuit
Court for the District of Ohio in this
case be and the same is hereby
affirmed with Costs— March 6th

James W. McCulloch

66

vs

The State of Maryland &
John James, as well for the
State as for himself

This cause came on to be heard on
the transcript of the Record of the
Court of Appeals of the State of
Maryland, and was argued by Counsel,
on consideration whereof, It is the
opinion of this Court, that the act of the Legislature of Maryland
entitled "An act to impose a tax on all Banks or Branches thereof
in the State of Maryland not chartered by the Legislature" is
contrary to the Constitution of the United States and void, and
therefore that the said Court of Appeals of the State of Maryland
erred in affirming the Judgment of the Baltimore County Court
in which Judgment was rendered against James W. McCulloch
but that the said Court of Appeals of Maryland ought to have
reversed the said Judgment of the said Baltimore County Court
and to have given Judgment for the said appellant McCulloch—
It is therefore adjudged and ordered, that the said Judgment of the
said Court of Appeals of the State of Maryland in this case be
and the same is hereby reversed and annulled— and this Court
proceeding to render such Judgment as the said Court of Appeals
should have rendered; It is further adjudged and ordered, that
the judgment of the said Baltimore County Court be reversed
and annulled, and that Judgment be entered in the said Baltimore County Court for the said James W. McCulloch.—
                                        March 6th

The Court's decision in McCulloch v. Maryland *was recorded in the handwritten minutes of
the Supreme Court.*

Chief Justice John Marshall Defends
the *McCulloch* Decision in the Popular Press

John Marshall is the only chief justice in American history to write newspaper articles in support of an opinion he wrote for the Supreme Court. Why did he do it?

Negative opinion pieces published in the newspapers of Virginia about the chief justice and the Court, in the wake of the McCulloch v. Maryland *decision, prompted him to wield his pen in defense of his own reputation and that of the Court. Marshall was especially sensitive about sharply critical articles against him in his hometown newspaper, the* Richmond Enquirer. *The articles were signed with the pen names Amphictyon and Hampden, and the newspaper's editor, Thomas Ritchie, introduced them with comments that Marshall found offensive.*

Ritchie's preface to a series of articles by Hampden, reputed to be the pen name of Spencer Roane, chief justice of the Virginia Court of Appeals and a lifelong nemesis of Marshall, infuriated Marshall almost as much as did Hampden's essays. Ritchie wrote,

> *We solemnly believe the opinion of the supreme court in the case of the bank to be fraught with alarming consequences, the federal constitution to be misinterpreted, and the rights of the states and the people to be threatened with danger. We solemnly believe that Hampden has refuted the opinion of the supreme court, and placed it in its proper light before the public.*

Marshall answered Thomas Ritchie and Hampden in a series of nine articles published in the Alexandria Gazette *between June 30 and July 15, 1819. To hide his identity, Marshall used the pen name "A Friend of the Constitution."*

In his third number Hampden states those specific objections to the opinion of the supreme court, which are to justify the virulent invectives he has so unsparingly bestowed on the judicial department

Before noticing these objections, I must be allowed to observe that, in recapitulating what he supposes himself to have established in his preceding numbers, he entirely misrepresents what he has himself attempted to prove....

I now proceed to the errors ascribed by Hampden, to the opinion of the supreme court.

The first is that the court has agreed in favor of an enlarged construction of the clause authorizing congress "to make all laws necessary and proper for carrying into execution" the powers vested in the government....

I will advert to the particular instances of this error, which he has selected in support of his charge.

The first is that the supreme court has said that this clause "is placed among the powers of the government, and not among the limitations on those powers."

That it is so placed, is acknowledged. But the court is supposed to be highly culpable for stating the truth, because it was stated for a purpose which this writer [Hampden] condemns.

To demonstrate that this argument was not used for the purpose, or in the manner alleged by Hampden, it is only necessary to advert to the opinion itself.

The court has laid down the proposition that "the government which has a right to do an act, and has imposed upon it the duty of performing that act must according to the dictates of reason, have a right to select the means." Having reasoned on this proposition, the court adds: "But the constitution of the United States has not left the right of congress to employ the necessary means for the execution of the powers conferred on the government to general reasoning. To its enumeration of powers is added that of making 'all laws which shall be necessary and proper.'"

The meaning of the court cannot be mistaken. It is that this clause expresses what the preceding reasoning showed must be implied.

The court then proceeds, "The counsel for the state of Maryland have urged various arguments to prove that this clause, tho' in terms a grant of power, is not so in effect; but is really restrictive of the general right, which might otherwise be implied, of selecting means for executing the enumerated powers."

The court then proceeds to combat these arguments of counsel—and combats them so successfully as to draw from Hampden himself the acknowledgment that "the words prohibit nothing to the general government." "It is only contended," he says, "that they create no enlargement of the powers previously given." Yet after explicitly yielding the point which was really in contest, he attempts to turn this total defeat into a victory, by contending that those arguments which were urged to prove that this clause did not restrain the powers of congress were brought forward to prove that it enlarges them, and fails of doing so.

No man, I think, who will even glance at the opinion, will fall into the error into which Hampden would lead him.... "This clause," the court adds, "as construed by the state of Maryland, would abridge, and almost annihilate this useful and necessary right

of the legislature to select its means. That this could not be intended, is, we should think, had it not been already controverted, too apparent for controversy. We think so for the following reasons: The clause is placed among the powers of congress, and not among the limitations on those powers."

The court proceeds to state several other reasons, to show that the clause could not have been intended by the convention to abridge those powers which congress would otherwise have possessed, and concludes with expressing the entire conviction that it could not be construed "to impair the right of the legislature to exercise its best judgment in the selection of measures to carry into execution the constitutional powers of the government." Hampden himself refers to that part of this conclusion which assigns to the clause the office of removing all doubt respecting the right "to legislate on that vast mass of incidental powers, which must be involved in the constitution," and approves it. Yet he has mentioned this argument, "that the clause is placed among the powers of congress, and not among the limitations on those powers," as his first objection to the opinion of the court; and he objects to it, not because the statement is untrue, but because the court urged it to establish an enlarged construction, an "extension" of the powers of congress.

I appeal to any man of the most ordinary understanding, when I ask if Hampden can possibly have misunderstood the opinion of the supreme court on this point? If he has not, why has he misrepresented it?...

July 3, 1819
A FRIEND OF THE CONSTITUTION

3

Steamboats, States' Rights, and the Powers of Congress

Gibbons v. *Ogden* (1824)

Gibbons v. Ogden

- 22 U.S. 1 [9 Wheat. 1] (1824)
- Decided: March 2, 1824
- Vote: 6–0
- Opinion of the Court: John Marshall
- Concurring opinion: William Johnson
- Not participating: Smith Thompson

During the summer of 1787, Philadelphia was the site of two notable events, one more obviously significant than the other, but both more important to the future of the United States than contemporary observers could possibly have realized. First, at the Pennsylvania State House (now known as Independence Hall) in the center of the city, a convention of political leaders produced the United States Constitution. This document became a workable framework for federal union among thirteen American states and a sturdy platform from which to expand the number of states and to regulate the interactions among them. Meanwhile, from the bank of the Delaware River flowing out of Philadelphia to the Atlantic Ocean, John Fitch launched a new kind of ship, a steamboat. Fitch's crude but innovative vessel was later refined and used commercially, generating economic prosperity and constitutional controversies.

Thirty-seven years later, in 1824, there was a momentous intersection of the powers granted to Congress in the Constitution and the development of businesses based on steamboats. A dispute between two New York steamboat owners, Thomas Gibbons and Aaron Ogden, raised questions about the powers of Congress to regulate commercial activity within the states and among the different states of the union. Thus, the U.S. Supreme Court was called upon in *Gibbons* v. *Ogden* (1824) to settle for the first time a controversy about the meaning of the commerce clause in Article 1, Section 8 of the Constitution. This clause provides Congress with power "To regulate Commerce with foreign Nations, and among the several States, and with the Indian Tribes."

Aaron Ogden and Thomas Gibbons had been partners in a steamboat business. Gibbons joined Ogden in managing a franchise purchased in 1815 from a steamboat company formed several years earlier by Robert Livingston and Robert Fulton, after they had successfully launched an improved steam-powered ship on New York's Hudson River in 1807. The New York State government in 1808 had granted Livingston and Fulton or their heirs a thirty-year monopoly to operate steamboats on the waterways of the state and on contiguous coastal waters of the Hudson River, which divides the states of New York and New Jersey. Ten years earlier, John Fitch had died after failing to build a better steam-driven ship, and Robert Fulton had become the preeminent American steamboat developer.

By 1815, both Livingston and Fulton were dead, and the inheritors of the Livingston-Fulton Company controlled their potential and actual rivals, such as Aaron Ogden and Thomas Gibbons, by selling rights to them, under the terms of their monopoly grant, to operate steamboats between specified points within New York and New Jersey. Ogden and Gibbons became partners, and their business acquired a license to be the sole steamboat transporter of passengers from Elizabethtown, New Jersey, to New York City via the Hudson River.

Simmering personal antagonisms destroyed the Ogden-Gibbons partnership in 1818, and the former business associates became bitter rivals in competition for passengers on the same waterway their boats had once traveled in concert. The ruthless tactics of Gibbons's tough teenaged assistant, Cornelius Vanderbilt, especially miffed Ogden, who lost passengers and profits to him. Later, as an adult, Vanderbilt used similar bold actions, on a larger scale, to develop railroads and related enterprises throughout the United States.

Robert Fulton launched his steamboat the Clermont *on the Hudson River on August 17, 1807, and the 150-foot paddlewheel vessel made a roundtrip voyage from New York City to Albany. This event marked the beginning of commercial steamboat navigation.*

Ogden struck back at Gibbons through the state courts of New York. He claimed to be the rightful holder of the franchise granted by the Livingston and Fulton monopoly. So Ogden charged Gibbons with unlawfully operating an unlicensed steamboat, and in 1819 he successfully sued in the New York courts for an injunction to prevent Gibbons from competing with him. In 1820 the highest New York State court decided this case on appeal and granted a permanent injunction against Gibbons. Ogden seemed to have won. However, young Cornelius Vanderbilt, acting with approval from his boss, brazenly disregarded the injunction and continued to take steamboat business from Ogden. And Gibbons retaliated against Ogden through the federal judiciary with an appeal to the U.S. Supreme Court, which agreed to hear arguments on this case in 1824.

Gibbons based his appeal on a license he had acquired in 1818 under a federal statute, the Coasting Act of 1793. He claimed this federal law provided him the right to navigate his steamboats on the waterways of any state in the nation, and that it superseded any conflicting state statute, such as the New York laws establishing the monopoly that granted Ogden rights to operate on the Hudson. Further, Gibbons maintained that the commerce clause of the Constitution's Article 1, Section 8 gave the U.S. Congress exclusive authority to regulate interstate commerce, as it had done through the federal Coasting Act, which made lawful his transportation of steamboat passengers from points on the Hudson River between New Jersey and New York.

An overflow audience gathered in the cramped courtroom of the Supreme Court to observe the start of oral arguments in *Gibbons* v. *Ogden* on February 4, 1824. Lively discussions about the issues of this case had been circulating throughout Washington, D.C., among newspaper reporters, members of Congress, and political leaders. They realized that more was at stake than the obvious issues of the steamboat monopoly case. Advocates of states' rights in

Before his legal conflict with Thomas Gibbons, Aaron Ogden had been an officer in the American army during the War of Independence, a U.S. senator from New Jersey, and governor of New Jersey. After the Supreme Court decided against him in 1824, he withdrew from his steamboat navigation business and served as a customs inspector for the state of New Jersey until his death in 1839.

the South feared that a decision in favor of Gibbons would strengthen the commerce power of Congress such that it could be used to halt the internal slave trade or even to abolish the institution of slavery throughout the nation. In addition, members of the nationally dominant Democratic-Republican Party in all sections of the country, including those who opposed slavery, feared that the Court might once again interpret the Constitution broadly to the general detriment of state powers within the federal system. From its origin in the 1790s, the Democratic-Republican Party had supported states' rights and powers within the federal system and had criticized previous decisions of the Supreme Court that supported the federal government's powers relative to those of the states.

By contrast with the states' rights supporters, many business owners yearned for a Supreme Court decision that would support the power of Congress to overturn state-protected monopolies controlled by a few rich individuals and to encourage free enterprise, productivity, and the accumulation of wealth among more and more people. Many also hoped that a decision based on an expansion of the federal government's power would encourage Congress to enact laws in support of public works, such as federally funded highways, bridges, and canals, which would contribute to the development of business and industry throughout the country. Thus, they hoped, both individuals and communities nationwide could benefit from a freer and more prosperous economy.

In addition to the high-stakes issues of *Gibbons* v. *Ogden*, the nationally renowned lawyer Daniel Webster, representing Gibbons, attracted extraordinary public attention to the oral arguments. The physically imposing Webster, a flamboyant orator, had performed impressively in other cases before the Court and was a rising star in Congress as a representative from Massachusetts. Members of Congress do not typically represent clients in Supreme Court cases, but Webster was an exceptional lawyer. He readily accepted opportunities to promote his interpretation of the Constitution.

Webster argued that the commerce power of Congress was broad and exclusive; it was not a power shared equally by Congress and the state governments; and it could be used to regulate transportation on all the navigable waters of the country. Thus, Congress could legislate against state-granted monopolies or regulate other aspects of commerce among the states, if it wished to do so. If not, then its silence was sufficient to leave the matter for the states to resolve. But if so, the acts of Congress within this sphere of its authority would override conflicting state statutes.

Webster recognized that every state government had enacted various regulations regarding health, safety, and other public matters that pertained to both intrastate and interstate commerce. Webster, however, classified these regulations as traditional and valid uses of the state's police power within the federal system, and not directly or exclusively connected to interstate and foreign commerce. This domain of the state's police power, said Webster, was constitutionally protected against control by Congress and did not conflict with Congress's constitutional grant of power over interstate commerce.

Finally, Webster argued for the supremacy of congressional power relative to state statutes that directly contradicted an act of Congress to regulate interstate commerce, such as the federal Coasting Act of 1793. Gibbons's license under this federal law, said Webster, superseded any New York State–mandated monopoly granted to Ogden or anyone else, and gave his client the right to "navigate freely the waters of the United States."

On March 2, 1824, Chief Justice John Marshall presented the unanimous decision of the participating justices in favor of Thomas Gibbons. (Associate Justice Smith Thompson did not participate because of the recent death of his daughter.) Marshall's written opinion for the Court reflected the influence of Daniel Webster's advocacy for Gibbons. Later, the cocky Webster bragged that Marshall had imbibed his arguments before the Court "as a baby takes in his mother's milk." This overstatement overlooked the eloquence of Marshall's written opinion, in which he agreed with most of Webster's ideas, but refined them into a durable decision that eventually became the sturdy foundation of constitutional law on the commerce power.

The first issue Marshall addressed was the meaning and scope of Congress's commerce power. What is it? And what does it include? Marshall responded with a broad and flexible definition. He said, "Commerce undoubtedly, is traffic, but it is something more; it is intercourse. It describes the commercial intercourse between nations, and parts of nations, in all its branches, and is regulated by prescribing rules for carrying on that intercourse."

According to the chief justice, the commerce power of Congress encompassed the regulation of steamboat navigation on the nation's waterways. Marshall also argued that the power "to regulate Commerce...among the several States" implies the extension of federal power across the boundaries of states if the object of regulation pertains to more than one state. He wrote, "A thing which is among others, is intermingled with them. Commerce among the states, cannot stop at the external boundary line of each state, but may be introduced into the interior."

The commerce power of Congress, Marshall explained, "is the power to regulate, that is, to prescribe the rule by which commerce is to be governed. This power, like all others vested in Congress, is complete in itself, may be exercised to its utmost extent, and acknowledges no limitations other than are prescribed in the Constitution." Marshall said that "the sovereignty of Congress" in regard to its enumerated powers had always been "limited to specific objects," but it was and is "plenary [or complete] as to those objects." Thus, Congress's commerce power includes "navigation, within the limits of every State in the Union, so far as that navigation may be in any manner connected with commerce with foreign Nations, or among the several States, or with the Indian Tribes." In this part of his opinion for the Court, Chief Justice Marshall emphasized Congress's power to fully regulate commerce within a state as long as it could be connected to commerce between the states, with one or more foreign countries, or with the tribes of native peoples. Further, Marshall held Congress's commerce power to be supreme relative to the state governments as long as it is exercised within the limitations set forth within the Constitution.

Next, Marshall raised the issue of whether the federal government's commerce power is exclusive, or whether the states also possess some power to regulate interstate commerce within their borders. In response to these questions, Marshall tempered his broad interpretation of the commerce power in recogni-

Robert Livingston was a highly respected lawyer and judge who represented New York in the Continental Congress and participated in the committee that helped Thomas Jefferson draft the Declaration of Independence. Livingston used his wealth and influence to finance Robert Fulton's development of a practical steamboat and to secure for their company a monopoly on steamboat navigation on New York's waterways.

tion of the rights of states in the federal union. And he unambiguously recognized the state governments' control over intrastate commerce:

> The genius and character of the whole government seem to be that its action is to be applied to all the external concerns of the nation, and to those internal concerns which affect the state generally; but not to those which are completely within a particular state, which do not affect other states, and with which it is not necessary to interfere for the purpose of executing some of the general powers of the government. The completely internal commerce of a state, then, may be considered as reserved for the state itself.

Marshall accepted Webster's argument against Ogden's lawyers' claim that the federal and state governments could equally share commerce power. However, the chief justice partially accommodated the concerns of states' rights supporters when he accepted Daniel Webster's classification of certain kinds of traditional state government regulations affecting interstate commerce as police powers. For example, when a state government enacted laws to protect the safety or security of travelers and goods involved in either interstate or intrastate commerce, the state exercised police powers reserved to it under the U.S. Constitution's principle of federalism. Although these regulations may affect interstate commerce they do not conflict with Congress's commerce power, because they are exercised by the states to maintain law, order, and the public good within their borders.

Marshall suggested, in line with Webster's presentation, which he called the "silence of Congress argument," that the states were free to exercise commerce powers in regard to any subjects not addressed by congressional laws. However, he did not rule conclusively on this matter. Thus the Court left open the possibility that the states might have partial power to regulate some aspects of interstate commerce within their borders. In addition, the Court did not rule exactly about the extent to which the states could regulate commerce that Congress was also regulating. As a result, important issues remained unresolved, leaving them open to fresh judicial interpretation in the future. These issues were addressed variously by decisions of the Court throughout the nineteenth and twentieth centuries.

The final issue of this case, and the one most important to Gibbons and Ogden, was settled exactly. Marshall stated directly that state statutes in conflict with a validly enacted federal law regarding commerce could not be sustained under the supremacy clause of the U.S. Constitution's Article 6. Thus, because the New York State laws granting monopoly rights to steamboat companies such as Ogden's conflicted with the federal Coasting Act of 1793, they were unconstitutional. Gibbons and his associates were licensed through this federal law to navigate freely the waterways of New York and New Jersey without state government interference.

Some states' rights proponents blasted Marshall's opinion for the Court, fearing that it could be used to strike against the interstate slave trade. Thomas Jefferson and his followers also saw the decision as one more instance, among many others, of Marshall's excessive nationalism, disregard of powers reserved to the states, and wrongful exercise of federal judicial powers.

Despite criticism from states' rights boosters and disappointed benefactors of steamboat monopolies, Marshall's decision in *Gibbons* v. *Ogden* was one of his most popular opinions, and it won general public praise. Business owners and passengers alike generally hated the steamboat monopolies in New York and other states for their obstruction of free-flowing commerce and economic opportunity. A burst of entrepreneurial steamboat navigation in the wake of the *Gibbons* decision boosted industrial development and economic growth throughout the country.

In the short term, the federal government made slight use, beyond regulation of steamboat enterprises, of the expanded commerce powers provided by Marshall's opinion in the *Gibbons* case. But the decision opened the way for a broad use of federal government regulation of commerce in the twentieth century. From the mid-1930s to the 1990s, *Gibbons* v. *Ogden* was the precedent that justified an expansive use of the commerce clause that enabled Congress to regulate manufacturing, child labor, workplace safety, farm production, mass media of communication, wages and hours of work, the activities of labor unions, protection of civil rights, buying and selling at marketplaces, and various other activities. Any activity affecting interstate commerce in some way seemed to be subject to federal government regulation.

During much of the twentieth century, Congress's use of its commerce power brought a relative decline in the regulatory power of state governments relative to that of the federal government. However, during the 1990s the Court did strike down a few federal statutes as unconstitutional extensions of Congress' commerce power. For example, *United States* v. *Lopez* (1995) struck down a federal law banning individuals from carrying a gun near a school. Nonetheless, on balance, the commerce power of Congress, based on the Court's ruling in *Gibbons* v. *Ogden*, remains a strong instrument for federal government regulation within and among the states.

The Court's decision in Gibbons v. Ogden *prohibited state governments from interfering with the power of Congress, granted in Article 1, Section 8 of the U.S. Constitution, to regulate commerce among the separate states.*

"Congress Shall Have Power to Regulate Commerce"

———◆———

Justice William Johnson was the only member of the Marshall Court who did not sign on to the chief justice's opinion in Gibbons v. Ogden. *Although he agreed with the Court's decision for Thomas Gibbons, Johnson wrote his own concurring opinion that presented reasons at variance with those of Marshall.*

Johnson, who had been an associate justice since 1804, was President Jefferson's first appointment to the Supreme Court. Although Johnson was a member of the Democratic-Republican Party, founded by Jefferson, he was an independent thinker whose decisions often disappointed Jefferson. He also was the associate justice most likely to disagree with Chief Justice Marshall, who usually influenced the Court's other members to go along with him.

Johnson's main difference from Marshall in this case was his stronger assertion of Congress's commerce power. Johnson argued that Marshall could have struck down the New York steamboat monopoly law without reference to its contradiction of the federal Coasting Act of 1793. He claimed that Congress had complete power over interstate commerce, and a state government could neither challenge nor share in this power.

The chief justice, however, prudently tempered his expression of federal power so the Court's other members would join him. Furthermore, Marshall, very aware that the Court had no power to enforce its decisions, realized that even a slight acknowledgment of states' rights in his opinion would contribute greatly to public approval of the Court's decision, thereby making it easier to enforce. Johnson's concurring opinion dismayed states' rights supporters such as Thomas Jefferson because of its strong nationalistic tone. Despite the contemporary controversy about Johnson's concurring opinion, many future leaders, both in Congress and the Supreme Court, hailed his strong expression of federal regulatory power. In contrast with Marshall's opinion, Johnson's concurrence was clear and specific about the exclusive powers granted in the commerce clause.

———◆———

The Judgment entered by the Court in this cause, has my entire approbation, but, having adopted my conclusions on views of the subject materially different from those of my brethren, I feel it incumbent on me to exhibit those views. I have also another inducement: in questions of great importance and great delicacy, I feel my duty to the public best discharged by an effort to maintain my opinion in my own way. . . .

The words of the Constitution are, "Congress shall have power to regulate commerce with foreign nations, and among the several States, and with the Indian Tribes." . . .

My opinion is founded on the application of the words of the grant to the subject of it.

. . . The power of a sovereign state over commerce . . . amounts to nothing more than a power to limit and restrain it at pleasure. And since the power to prescribe the limits to its freedom necessarily implies the power to determine what shall remain unrestrained, it follows that the power must be exclusive; it can reside but in one potentate, and hence the grant of this power carries with it the whole subject, leaving nothing for the State to act upon. . . .

Power to regulate foreign commerce is given in the same words, and in the same breath, as it were, with that over the commerce of the States and with the Indian tribes. But the power to regulate foreign commerce is necessarily exclusive. The States are unknown to foreign nations, their sovereignty exists only with relation to each other and the General Government. Whatever regulations foreign commerce should be subjected to in the ports of the Union, the General Government would be held responsible for them, and all other regulations but those which Congress had imposed would be regarded by foreign nations as trespasses and violations of national faith and comity.

But the language which grants the power as to one description of commerce grants it as to all, and in fact, if ever the exercise of a right or acquiescence in a construction could be inferred from contemporaneous and continued assent, it is that of the exclusive effect of this grant [of power to Congress to regulate commerce]....

A right over the subject has never been pretended in any instance except as incidental to the exercise of some other unquestionable power.

The present [case in New York] is an instance of the assertion of that kind, as incidental to a municipal [police] power; that of superintending the internal concerns of a State, and particularly of extending protection and patronage, in the shape of a monopoly, to genius and enterprise [the Livingston-Fulton steamboat company and its heirs].

The grant to Livingston and Fulton [by the New York State government] interferes with the freedom of intercourse, and on this principle, its constitutionality is contested.

When speaking of the power of Congress over navigation, I do not regard it as a power incidental to that of regulating commerce; I consider it as the thing itself, inseparable from it as vital motion is from vital existence.

Commerce, in its simplest significance, means an exchange of goods, but in the advancement of society, labour, transportation, intelligence, care, and various mediums of exchange become commodities, and enter into commerce, the subject, the vehicle, the agent, and their various operations become the objects of commercial regulation. Shipbuilding, the carrying trade, and propagation of seamen are such vital agents of commercial prosperity that the nation which could not legislate over these subjects would not possess power to regulate commerce.

...[T]he decree of the court of New York..., which perpetually enjoins the said Thomas Gibbons, the appellant, from navigating the waters of the state of New York with the steamboats the *Stoudinger* and the *Bellona* by steam or fire, is erroneous, and ought to be reversed, and the same is hereby reversed and annulled, and this Court doth further DIRECT, ORDER, and DECREE that the bill of the said Aaron Ogden be dismissed, and the same is hereby dismissed accordingly.

4

Denying an Appeal for Freedom

Scott v. *Sandford* (1857)

Scott v. Sandford

- 60 U.S. 393 [19 How. 393] (1857)

- Decided: March 6, 1857

- Vote: 7–2

- Opinion of the Court: Roger B. Taney

- Concurring opinions: James M. Wayne, Samuel Nelson, Robert C. Grier, Peter V. Daniel, John A. Campbell, and John Catron

- Dissenting opinions: John McClean and Benjamin R. Curtis

In 1857 the Supreme Court refused to grant Dred Scott's petition for freedom from slavery. In the 1830s, Dred Scott had moved from St. Louis with his owner, Dr. Emerson, to the free state of Illinois. After Emerson's death, Scott returned to St. Louis with the doctor's widow. Scott sued for his freedom in a Missouri state court based on the fact that he had resided in a state where slavery was illegal, but he failed to win his case. The Supreme Court accepted Scott's appeal, but ultimately decided against Scott in 1857. Chief Justice Roger B. Taney's opinion in this case, *Scott* v. *Sandford*, immediately prompted intense controversy. For example, Frederick Douglass, a prominent antislavery leader, called Taney's opinion for the Court an "infamous decision." Nonetheless, its historical significance has been huge.

The seeds that yielded the Court's infamous decision in the Dred Scott case were planted long before 1857, during the country's colonial period, when European traders brought slaves from Africa to America. This seedbed was cultivated anew during the founding of the United States of America, when slavery became a hot issue at the 1787 Constitutional Convention in Philadelphia. Some delegates owned slaves, and many others did not; but most were worried that controversy about slavery could disrupt and destroy the convention and ultimately the United States. Most delegates opposed the importation of slaves into their country, and a few wanted to abolish slavery throughout the nation, but others resisted any constitutional prohibition of slavery or the slave trade. Delegates of such slave states as South Carolina and Georgia even threatened to withdraw from the convention if a clause to ban slavery or the slave trade was put into the Constitution.

In response to these threats, the delegates compromised about the bitterly contested slavery issue. For example, the Constitution permitted the importation of slaves, but only until 1808, when a congressional act could end the slave trade. The Constitution also allowed slavery to exist within the new nation, but the government of each state in the federal union could decide independently whether to abolish or protect it. However, a fugitive slave clause was included (Article 4, Section 2); it provided for the return to slavery of anyone who had escaped to a free state or territory.

Clashing opinions about slavery continued to divide the nation following the ratification and implementation of the U.S. Constitution. This nefarious institution was never solidly established in most states of the northeastern section of the country, and it eventually was abolished there. Slavery was abolished in Massachusetts before 1787; it was undergoing gradual abolition in Pennsylvania based on a 1782 law; it was practically gone from New Hampshire and Rhode Island by 1790; and the Vermont Constitution prohibited it. In 1787 the Northwest Ordinance, an act of Congress, prohibited slavery in the federal territories north and west of the Ohio River. New states formed in the Northwest Territory were therefore bound to enter the federal union free of slavery. The federal government did not ban slavery in its southwestern territories, which at that time extended to the Mississippi River, and states carved out of this region entered the federal union as slave states.

The territory of the United States expanded far beyond the west bank of the Mississippi River in 1803, when President Thomas Jefferson authorized the purchase of Louisiana from France, which raised, once again, political arguments about whether slavery should be permitted in U.S. territories. Congress resolved this dispute, at least for a while, with the Missouri Compromise of 1820. This federal legislation established a boundary extending to the western edge of the country; territory south of this line, including Missouri, was open to slavery, but territory north of it was not. Thus, the United States continued to be divided along north-south lines by the presence or absence of slavery, a condition that had persisted in one way or another from its earliest years until *Scott* v. *Sandford* came before the Court in 1857.

The originator of this case, Dred Scott, was brought to Missouri from Virginia by way of Alabama by his owner Peter Blow. In 1832, the Blow family sold Scott to Dr. John Emerson. Dred Scott traveled with Emerson to Rock Island, a town in the free state of Illinois. Later, Scott went with his owner to Fort Snelling in the Territory of Wisconsin (an area now part of the state of Minnesota). Both the 1787 Northwest Ordinance and the 1820 Missouri Compromise had forbidden slavery in this territory. After Dr. Emerson's death in 1843, Scott and his family (a wife and two children) became the property of Mrs. Emerson, and they returned to St. Louis. In 1846, Dred Scott sued Eliza Irene Emerson in a Missouri state court to gain his freedom from bondage.

The sons of the late Peter Blow, who had been Dred Scott's original owner, financially supported Scott's claim for freedom, which was based on his period of residence north of the Missouri Compromise line, where slavery was outlawed. Scott appeared to have a strong case because Missouri law recognized claims for emancipation by slaves who had resided in states or territories where slavery was illegal. After winning at trial, Scott's case was mired in legal complexities and not settled until 1852, when the Missouri Supreme Court overturned the lower court decision that had favored Scott. The court rejected Scott's claim of freedom based on residence in a free territory and held instead that the current law of Missouri prevailed, despite precedents to the contrary.

The Dred Scott case, which had been decided by the U.S. Supreme Court on March 6, 1857, was the cover story of the June 27, 1857, issue of Frank Leslie's Illustrated Newspaper. *Pictures of Dred Scott and his wife, Harriet, appear at the bottom of the page, and their children, Eliza and Lizzie, are depicted above. They had been freed from slavery on May 26, 1857, by Taylor Blow, who had purchased the Scotts from John Sanford in order to free them.*

The state court's decision seemed to be the final word on Dred Scott's quest for freedom. Scott's lawyers, however, found a way to bring the issue to the federal judicial system, where they might seek a favorable outcome for their client. Their strategy was made possible by the remarriage of Mrs. Emerson, who subsequently transferred her ownership of Scott and his family to her brother, John F. A. Sanford. Scott's new owner carried out business in St. Louis, Missouri, but his primary residence was in New York. Scott, who claimed to be a citizen of Missouri, had the legal right to sue a citizen of another state in a federal court, because Article 3 of the U.S. Constitution gave jurisdiction in such cases to the federal courts. The Blow family continued to support Scott's case by hiring lawyers and paying the legal expenses.

A federal judge validated Scott's claim to citizenship, which enabled his case to proceed in the federal district court in Missouri. The judge, however, instructed the jury that their decision should be based on the prevailing law of Missouri and not on Scott's claims to freedom based on his residence in a slavery-free state or territory of the United States. Thus, the jury quickly returned a verdict against Scott

Scott's lawyers appealed to the U.S. Supreme Court on the claim of a writ of error, charging that the presiding federal judge had improperly instructed the jury and, therefore, biased its decision. The U.S. Supreme Court accepted the appeal and conducted hearings on *Scott* v. *Sandford* in 1856. The clerk of the U.S. Supreme Court misspelled the last name of John F. A. Sanford by adding a "d" to it, and the misspelled name remains in the official record of this case.

The Supreme Court conducted hearings on the Dred Scott case in February 1856, and Sanford's lawyers raised a new issue. They claimed that the Missouri Compromise was unconstitutional. If so, then Scott's residence in northern federal territory could not make him free. Many observers believed that Congress's

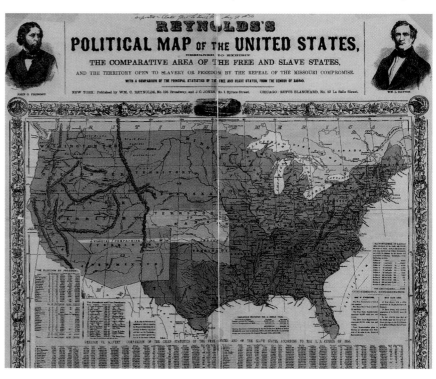

Portraits of the antislavery Republican Party candidates for the 1856 Presidential election are displayed at the top of this map, which compares the area of the free states and territories (in pink) to that of the states and territories permitting slavery (in gray). At the left is John C. Fremont, the party's Presidential candidate, and at the right is his running mate, William L. Dayton.

Kansas-Nebraska Act of 1854 had superseded the Missouri Compromise by authorizing the residents of Kansas and Nebraska to decide by majority vote whether to permit slavery. However, Sanford's lawyers believed that this federal statute applied only to Kansas and Nebraska, and they wanted to ensure that the popular sovereignty principle of the Kansas-Nebraska Act would be extended to all the western territories by influencing the Supreme Court to declare the Missouri Compromise unconstitutional.

Congressional and Presidential election campaigns were going on in 1856, and heated arguments about slavery consumed the attention of political candidates and voters. The justices thought it prudent not to decide the Dred Scott case in such a contentious climate, and they chose to hold oral arguments again in December, when the elections were over.

The Court's decision to conduct a second round of oral arguments heightened public interest in a case fraught with momentous political consequences in the bitter debate over slavery. The Washington, D.C., newspaper reporters and members of Congress paid close attention when the hearings on the Dred Scott case began on December 15, 1856. The oral arguments continued for twelve hours spread across four days.

Counsel for Scott argued that residency on free soil justified his claim to be a free man. Even if Missouri did not recognize the antislavery laws of Illinois, where Scott had resided, the "supremacy clause" in Article 6 of the U.S. Constitution required all states to obey federal laws, such as the Missouri Compromise, which justified Scott's claim to freedom from slavery. They also claimed that Scott could bring suit in a federal court because his right to citizenship had been sufficiently recognized by the judge who permitted his case to proceed in a federal district court.

Sanford's lawyers contended that Dred Scott was not a citizen and therefore could not bring suit in a federal court. Furthermore, they asserted that Congress had no power to regulate slavery in the territories of the United States and consequently the Missouri Compromise was unconstitutional.

The Supreme Court ruled against Scott on March 6, 1857. Although Chief Justice Taney wrote officially for the Court, every other justice authored an opinion, and only Justice James M. Wayne agreed with Taney on every particular of his opinion. Despite the bulk, variety, and opacity of the opinions, it was clear that the Court's majority had rejected Scott's claim to freedom and had accepted the chief justice's argument that black Americans were excluded from citizenship in the United States.

Writing for the Court, Chief Justice Roger B. Taney addressed three separate issues. First, could a person such as Dred Scott claim to be a citizen of the United States and thereby bring suit in a federal court? If not, then the Supreme Court had no jurisdiction in this case. Second, did Congress have power under the U.S. Constitution to ban slavery in the nation's western territories? Third, did the federal statute authorizing the Missouri Compromise of 1820 violate property rights protected under the Fifth Amendment of the Constitution?

Chief Justice Taney first argued that Scott could not sue in a federal court because he was not a citizen of the United States. He claimed that no black person, slave or free, could be a citizen. The chief justice wrote,

The question is simply this: Can a negro, whose ancestors were imported into the country, and sold as slaves, become a member of the political community formed and brought into existence by the Constitution of the United States, and as such become entitled to all the rights, and privileges and immunities guaranteed by that instrument to the citizen?"

Taney answered, "We think they are not...included, and were not intended to be included, under the word 'citizen' in the Constitution." Rather, the chief justice asserted that at the time the Constitution was written black persons were "considered as a subordinate and inferior class or beings, who had been subjugated by the dominant race, and whether emancipated or not . . . had no rights or privileges but such as those who held the power and the Government might choose to grant them." Taney concluded that Dred Scott "could not be a citizen of the State of Missouri, within the meaning of the Constitution of the United States, and consequently, was not entitled to sue in its courts."

Having decided that Scott had no right to sue in a federal court, Taney might have stopped. After all, he had concluded that the Court had no jurisdiction in this case. However, the issue of slavery in the federal territories was an important political question, and Taney wanted to let the nation know where the Court stood on it. He may even have thought that the Court could positively influence a resolution of the contentious issue and restore harmony to the divided country; but Taney's superfluous slurs against African Americans were inflammatory. For example, he claimed that African Americans were regarded as "so far inferior, that they had no rights which the white man was bound to respect."

Taney easily disposed of Scott's claim to freedom based on the antislavery laws of Illinois, where he had temporarily resided. The chief justice held that when Scott left Illinois, he lost whatever claim to freedom he had while residing there, and no law or precedent obligated Missouri, where slavery was legal, to enforce Illinois's antislavery laws.

Scott's claim based on the Missouri Compromise was also dismissed by the chief justice, who declared this act of Congress to be unconstitutional. Taney recognized that Article 4, Section 3 of the Constitution gives Congress "Power to dispose of and make all needful Rules and Regulations respecting the Territory or other Property belonging to the United States." Congress had used this power to govern the federal territories through enactments such as the Northwest Ordinance, the Missouri Compromise, and the Kansas-Nebraska Act. However, the chief justice interpreted the "territories clause" of Article 4 in a novel and implausible way to support his judgment that the Missouri Compromise was unconstitutional. Taney wrote that the clause was

confined, and was intended to be confined, to the territory which at that time [1787] belonged to, or was claimed by, the United States...and can have no influence upon a territory afterwards acquired from a foreign Government. It was a special provision for a known and particular territory, and to meet a present emergency, and nothing more.

According to Taney, Congress could enact laws to regulate the territory north and west of the Ohio River, as it did in the Northwest Ordinance of 1787. But it had no constitutional authority to regulate the vast territories

This portrait of Chief Justice Roger Brooke Taney was painted in 1858, the year following his infamous opinion for the Court in Scott v. Sandford. *A member of a prominent Maryland family, Taney freed his inherited slaves when he was a young adult, but his personal actions did not preserve his reputation from ruin following his reviled opinion in the* Scott *case.*

gained by the Louisiana Purchase in 1803, as it did by enacting the Missouri Compromise. The chief justice could present neither historical evidence nor judicial precedent to support this bizarre interpretation of the Article 4 clause about the governance of federal territories.

An additional argument by Taney against the constitutional validity of the Missouri Compromise was based on the Constitution's Fifth Amendment, which guaranteed that a person could not be deprived of his property without "due process of law" and "just compensation." The Missouri Compromise, he argued, deprived persons, such as Dred Scott's owner, of their property in slaves simply for entering federal territories. Thus, Taney held that the Missouri Compromise was an unconstitutional violation of the Fifth Amendment.

This was only the second time that the Supreme Court had used its power of judicial review to strike down an act of Congress. Judicial review against a coordinate branch of the federal government had first been used by the Court in *Marbury* v. *Madison* (1803).

Two justices, John McLean and Benjamin R. Curtis, wrote strong dissenting opinions. Both McLean and Curtis disputed and demolished the historical accuracy and legal reasoning of the chief justice's opinion for the Court. McLean, for example, argued that the U.S. Constitution did not protect slavery, which existed in particular states only because of laws protecting it within these slave states. Further, he stressed that Dred Scott's sojourn in Illinois and the Wisconsin Territory justified his claim to freedom.

Justice Curtis wrote an elaborate dissent that cogently refuted Chief Justice Taney's opinion for the Court on every one of its main points. In particular, Curtis compiled evidence to demonstrate that many black Americans were citizens in several states when the U.S. Constitution was written and ratified. He pointed to historical records documenting that free black males had the right to vote during the 1780s and 1790s in Massachusetts, New Hampshire, New Jersey, New York, and North Carolina.

Thus, Curtis argued, free blacks had always been citizens in the nation, and if Scott was free the Court had jurisdiction to hear and decide his case. Curtis wrote,

> I can find nothing in the Constitution which, *proprio vigore* [by its own force], deprives of their citizenship any class of persons who were citizens of the United States at the time of its adoption . . . nor any power enabling Congress to disfranchise persons born on the soil of any State, and entitled to citizenship of such State by its Constitution and laws. And my opinion is, that, under the Constitution of the United States, every free person born on the soil of a State, who is a citizen of that State, by force of its Constitution or laws, is also a citizen of the United States.

Curtis also argued for the constitutionality of the Missouri Compromise, which he noted had existed as accepted law for more than three decades. During this time, it mitigated regional controversy that had threatened to disrupt and destroy the federal union. Curtis correctly noted that Congress was justified in enacting the Missouri Compromise by Article 4, Section 3 of the U.S. Constitution, which granted Congress the power to enact laws regulating

*This newspaper advertisement for a pamphlet
containing the Supreme Court's decision in
the* Scott *case presents a positive view of the
Court's decision, and is directed to a proslavery
and antiabolitionist audience.*

the federal territories. Under the terms of the Missouri Compromise, Dred Scott was a free man due to his residence on free soil. Thus, he certainly had the right to bring suit in a federal court.

Finally, Justice Curtis used historical evidence to contradict Chief Justice Taney's argument that a claim to freedom from slavery based on the Missouri Compromise violated the due process and just compensation clauses of the Constitution's Fifth Amendment. He pointed out that Article 1, Section 9 of the U.S. Constitution gave Congress power to enact legislation prohibiting the importation of slaves after 1808. Congress acted according to this provision of the Constitution to enact legislation banning the external slave trade. Curtis then used this hypothetical example based on Article 1, Section 9:

> A citizen of the United States owns slaves in Cuba, and brings them to the United States, where they are set free by the legislation of Congress. Does this legislation deprive him of his property without due process of law? If so, what becomes of the laws prohibiting the slave trade? If not, how can a similar regulation respecting a Territory [the Missouri Compromise] violate the fifth amendment of the Constitution?

Newspaper editorials throughout the northern states hailed Justice Benjamin Curtis's dissent, and denounced the Supreme Court's opinion in the Dred Scott case. In contrast, public opinion throughout the southern states praised Chief Justice Taney's opinion for the Court, and reviled the dissenting opinions of Justices Curtis and McClean. The Dred Scott case was a pivotal topic in the 1858 debates between Stephen A. Douglas and Abraham Lincoln in their campaign for election to the U.S. Senate from Illinois.

Chief Justice Taney had imagined that his opinion in *Scott* v. *Sandford* would settle the issue of slavery in the federal territories and mitigate the acute tensions that had disrupted relationships of the northern and southern states. Instead, the Court's decision became a hotly disputed issue. After 1857, sectional conflict became so enflamed that civil war ensued in 1861. When this bloody conflict between the North and South ended in 1865, the Thirteenth Amendment to the Constitution, abolishing slavery throughout the United States, was enacted. The Fourteenth Amendment, which guaranteed the citizenship of black Americans, was enacted in 1868. Thus, by amending their Constitution, the people of the United States overturned the Supreme Court's decision in *Scott* v. *Sandford*.

Although the Supreme Court denied Dred Scott's claim to freedom, he gained it through the beneficence of his lifelong friends, the sons of his deceased first owner, Peter Blow. They purchased Dred Scott, his wife Harriet Scott, and their two children from John F. A. Sanford. Then the Blow brothers freed Dred Scott and his family. Nine months later, on February 17, 1858, tuberculosis ended Dred Scott's life, but he died a free man. John F. A. Sanford died in an insane asylum only two months after the conclusion of the Dred Scott case.

Frederick Douglass Responds to the *Scott* v. *Sandford* Decision

————◆————

The Supreme Court's opinion in the Dred Scott case prompted an outpouring of public commentary. Among the public figures who responded negatively to the decision was Frederick Douglass, the most prominent black American during the years just before the Civil War. Douglass was born a slave in Maryland in 1817. He escaped to the free state of Massachusetts in 1838. At first he worked as a laborer in the shipyards. A short time later, he joined the movement to abolish slavery led by William Lloyd Garrison and quickly became an outstanding orator and writer for the abolitionist cause.

By the time of the Supreme Court's decision in Scott v. Sandford, *Douglass was the acclaimed editor of his own abolitionist newspaper,* The North Star, *and a very popular public speaker. Douglass was invited by the American Anti-Slavery Society to make a speech in response to the Supreme Court's decision in the Dred Scott case. His speech, presented to a large audience in New York City on May 11, 1857, was later published and distributed widely in the northern states.*

————◆————

This infamous decision of the Slaveholding wing of the Supreme Court maintains that slaves are, within the contemplation of the Constitution of the United States, property; that slaves are property in the same sense that horses, sheep, and swine are property; that the old doctrine that slavery is a creature of local law is false; that the right of the slaveholder to his slave does not depend on the local law, but is secured wherever the Constitution of the United States extends; that Congress has no right to prohibit slavery anywhere; that slavery may go in safety anywhere under the star-spangled banner; that colored persons of African descent have no rights that white men are bound to respect; that colored men of African descent are not and cannot be citizens of the United States.

I have no fear that the National Conscience will be put to sleep by such an open, glaring, and scandalous tissue of lies as that decision is, and has been, over and over, shown to be.

The Supreme Court of the United States is not the only power in this world. It is very great, but the Supreme Court of the Almighty is greater. Judge Taney can do many things, but he cannot perform impossibilities. He cannot bale [*sic*] out the ocean, annihilate this firm old earth, or pluck the silvery star of liberty from our Northern sky. He may decide, and decide again; but he cannot reverse the decision of the Most High. He cannot change the essential nature of things—making evil good, and good, evil.

Happily for the whole human family, their rights have been defined, declared, and decided in a court higher than the Supreme Court....

Your fathers have said that man's right to liberty is self-evident. There is no need of argument to make it clear. The voices of nature, of conscience, of reason, and of revelation, proclaim it as the right of all rights, the foundation of all trust, and of all responsibility. Man was born with it.... To decide against this right in the person of Dred Scott, or the humblest and most whip-scarred bondman in the land, is to decide against God....

Such a decision cannot stand.... All that is merciful and just, on earth and in Heaven, will execrate and despise the edict of Taney....

I base my sense of the certain overthrow of slavery, in part, upon the nature of the American Government, the Constitution, the tendencies of the age, and the character of the American people; and this, notwithstanding the important decision of Judge Taney....

The argument [of Taney] here is, that the Constitution comes down to us from a slaveholding period and a slaveholding people; and that, therefore, we are bound to suppose that the Constitution recognizes colored persons of African descent, the victims of slavery at that time, as debarred forever from all participation in the benefit of the Constitution and the Declaration of Independence, although the plain reading of both includes them in their beneficent range.

As a man, an American, a citizen, a colored man of both Anglo-Saxon and African descent, I denounce this representation as a most scandalous and devilish perversion of the Constitution, and a brazen misstatement of the facts of history....

It may be said that it is quite true that the Constitution was designed to secure the blessings of liberty and justice to the people who made it, and to the posterity of the people who made it, but was never designed to do any such thing for the colored people of African descent.

This is Judge Taney's argument...but it is not the argument of the Constitution. The Constitution imposes no such mean and satanic limitations upon its own beneficent operation. And, if the Constitu-

tion makes none, I beg to know what right has anybody, outside of the Constitution, for the special accommodation of slaveholding villainy, to impose such a construction upon the Constitution?

The Constitution knows all the human inhabitants of this country as "the people." It makes, as I have said before, no discrimination in favor of, or against, any class of the people, but is fitted to protect and preserve the rights of all, without reference to color, size, or any physical peculiarities. Besides, it has been shown...that in eleven of the old thirteen States, colored men were legal voters at the time of the adoption of the Constitution.

In conclusion, let me say, all I ask of the American people is, that they live up to the Constitution, adopt its principles, imbibe its spirit and enforce its provisions.

When this is done, the wounds of my bleeding people will be healed, the chain will no longer rust on their ankles, their backs will no longer be torn by the bloody lash, and liberty, the glorious birthright of our common humanity, will become the inheritance of all the inhabitants of this highly favored country.

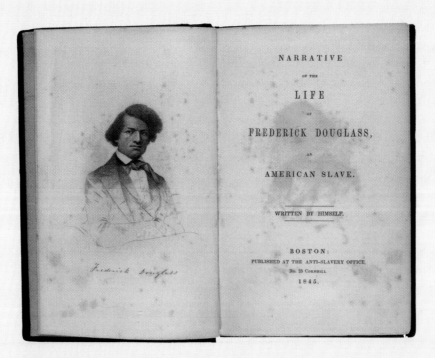

Frederick Douglass described life as a slave and his escape from the South in his autobiography, published in 1845. As an abolitionist and a former slave, Douglass lashed out at the claim, presented in the Dred Scott decision, that slaves are property.

5

Civil Liberties and the Civil War

Ex parte Milligan (1866)

The security of the nation and the protection of civil liberties are essential goals of government in the United States. The Preamble to the U.S. Constitution proclaims the intent to "insure domestic Tranquility, provide for the common defence... and Secure the Blessings of Liberty." However, during a national crisis, such as the Civil War, there is inevitably severe tension between these two imperatives of constitutional government: maintaining both the security of the nation and the security of civil liberties for every individual within the nation. Shortly after the outbreak of war, President Abraham Lincoln made a speech to Congress in which he expressed his concern about whether the government, in order to maintain national security and safety, "must be too strong for the liberties of its own people" or, in order to respect constitutional guarantees of rights to liberty, must be "too weak to maintain its own existence."

More than three years later, on December 28, 1864, Lambdin P. Milligan was convinced that the U.S. government had acted too strongly against his constitutional rights to liberty. A federal military commission had convicted Milligan of treason against the United States and sentenced him to be hanged on May 19, 1865. Milligan was an alleged participant in a plot to release Confederate prisoners from jail and provide them with arms so they could join a Rebel invasion of Indiana. From his prison cell in Indianapolis, Milligan wrote a letter to Edwin M. Stanton, Lincoln's secretary of war. Milligan claimed that he had been wrongly imprisoned and convicted and asked the help of his "old acquaintance and friend."

More than nineteen years before his imprisonment, Lambdin Milligan and Edwin Stanton had taken the bar exam together in order to practice law in Ohio. Milligan hoped that Stanton might remember him favorably and ask the President to pardon him or at least overturn his death sentence in favor of a lesser punishment. There is no evidence that Stanton replied to Milligan.

Lambdin Milligan's predicament was a product of President Lincoln's strong response to the outbreak of the Civil War that followed the secession of several southern states from the federal union in 1861 and their founding of the Confederate States of America. Lincoln quickly imposed extraordinary limitations on civil liberties in order to defend the United States against unusual threats posed by war between the United States and the Confederacy. He suspended the privilege of the writ of habeas corpus first in Maryland, where

> ## Ex parte Milligan
>
> - 71 U.S. 2 [4 Wall. 2] (1866)
> - Decided: April 3, 1866
> - Vote: 9–0
> - Opinion of the Court: David Davis
> - Concurring opinion: Salmon P. Chase (James M. Wayne, Noah Swayne, and Samuel F. Miller)

Lambdin P. Milligan (left, center) and these four other men were arrested in 1864 and charged with the crime of conspiracy against the United States in support of the Confederate States. All five men appealed their convictions in a military court, and their case went to the U.S. Supreme Court under the name of Ex parte Milligan. *Following the Court's decision all of them were freed.*

many Confederate sympathizers posed a threat to the U.S. government in nearby Washington, D.C., and later in other parts of the country in order to permit the military to take punitive action against anyone who threatened the safety or security of the United States.

A writ of *habeas corpus* (in Latin, "you shall have the body") requires officials to bring a person whom they have arrested and held in custody before a judge in a court of law, where they must convince the judge that there are lawful reasons for holding the prisoner. If the judge finds the reasons unwarranted, then the judge frees the prisoner. Thus, the writ of habeas corpus is a strong protection for individuals against government officials who might want to jail them because they belong to unpopular groups or express criticism of the government. Article 1, Section 9 of the Constitution says, "The privilege of the Writ of Habeas Corpus shall not be suspended, unless when in Cases of Rebellion or Invasion of the public Safety may require it."

On May 27, 1861, President Lincoln's suspension of the writ of habeas corpus was challenged by John Merryman, who had been arrested for allegedly burning bridges in order to stop federal troops from passing through Maryland on their way to defend Washington, D.C., against an imminent attack by Confederate forces. Merryman was confined in a military prison. He sought relief in a federal court, which resulted in the case of *Ex parte Merryman*; Chief Justice Roger Taney presided, sitting in this instance as a circuit court judge. (When the Latin phrase *ex parte*, meaning "from the part of," is used in the title of a case it signifies that the action was taken on behalf of the person named in the title of the case. It does not require the notification of or participation by an opposing party.)

Chief Justice Taney rebuked President Lincoln by ruling that only Congress had the authority to suspend the writ of habeas corpus, as the constitutional provision for suspending the writ appears in Article 1 of the Constitution, which pertains to the powers and duties of Congress. Taney also pointed to the rights of a person accused of crimes listed in the Fifth and Sixth Amendments of the Constitution, which, in his opinion, precluded the trial of Merryman in a military tribunal instead of a civilian court. The chief justice ordered John Merryman released from prison.

President Lincoln ignored Chief Justice Taney's decision in the *Merryman* case. A few weeks later, in his message to a special session of Congress on July 4, 1861, the President justified his suspension of the writ of habeas corpus and other limitations on civil liberties as necessary to defend the United States in the national emergency created by the Civil War. Congress voted for a resolution to endorse the President's restrictions on civil liberties and gave public notice that the Constitution provides for the suspension of the writ "when in

Cases of Rebellion or Invasion the public safety may require it." John Merryman, however, was never brought to trial.

Bolstered by the support from Congress, President Lincoln expanded his national security policy. The President issued an executive order to ban the U.S. Postal Office from distributing any "disloyal" publications. He extended suspension of the writ of habeas corpus beyond Maryland to other regions of the United States critically threatened by its enemies, such as the border states of Kentucky and Missouri, and Northern states with many Confederate sympathizers, such as Indiana. Consequently, thousands of civilians were arrested and held without trial.

On September 24, 1862, President Lincoln issued the following executive order:

> Now, therefore, be it ordered, first, that during the existing insurrection and as a necessary measure for suppressing the same, all Rebels and insurgents, their aiders and abettors within the United States, and all persons discouraging volunteer enlistments, resisting militia drafts, or guilty of any disloyal practice, affording aid and comfort to Rebels against the authority of the United States, shall be subject to and liable to trial and punishment by Courts Martial or Military Commission: the Writ of Habeas Corpus is suspended in respect to all persons arrested, or who now, or hereafter during the rebellion shall be, imprisoned in any fort, camp, or arsenal, military prison, or other place of confinement by any military authority or by the sentence of any Court Martial or Military Commission.

Congress not only endorsed this executive order, but a few months later, in March of 1863, reinforced the order by enacting legislation to provide that "any order of the president, or under his authority, made at any time during the existence of the present rebellion, shall be a defense in all courts to any action or prosecution . . . for any search, seizure, arrest, or imprisonment."

Following these national security measures taken by the President and Congress, people suspected of aiding the wartime enemy, such as Lambdin Milligan, were detained in military prisons and tried by military tribunals. Military authorities had gathered evidence of Milligan's participation in a conspiracy to release and arm Rebel prisoners. Milligan certainly was an outspoken Confederate sympathizer, but it was not necessarily clear that he had committed treason by conspiring against his country in time of war.

Milligan was tried in a military court even though civilian courts were open and operating in Indiana throughout the Civil War. Although Confederate raiders had occasionally entered Indiana from Kentucky for short periods, Indiana was not an ongoing theater of military operations during the Civil War, and it seemed safe and secure from any military threat at the time of Milligan's arrest. In a civil court, there would have been full recognition of his right to a fair trial under the Constitution, but in a military tribunal the rights of an accused person were quite constricted.

The military court convicted Milligan of conspiracy against the United States and sentenced him to death. Milligan applied to a U.S. circuit court in Indiana for a writ of habeas corpus. He claimed that his trial and conviction were unconstitutional and asked for his constitutional right to a trial by jury in a civil court.

On December 28, 1864, writing from his prison cell in Indianapolis, Lambdin Milligan sent this desperate plea to his former acquaintance Edwin Stanton, who had become secretary of war under President Abraham Lincoln. Milligan asked Stanton for help in overturning his conviction and death sentence for conspiring against the United States. There is no evidence that Stanton replied to Milligan or acted on his behalf.

While Milligan's appeal was pending, an assassin killed President Lincoln. His successor, President Andrew Johnson, ordered a stay of Milligan's execution until June and then commuted the sentence to life in prison. The case finally went to the U.S. Supreme Court as "a petition for discharge from unlawful imprisonment." The justification for this petition on behalf of Milligan was that he had been unlawfully incarcerated, tried, and convicted by a military commission when the appropriate venue for his case was a civil court within Indiana. Oral arguments before the Court began on March 6, 1866, nearly a year after the end of the Civil War. Attorney General James Speed led the lawyers representing the federal government. Prominent among the counsel for the petition on behalf of Milligan was James A. Garfield of Ohio, who later became the twentieth President of the United States. The issue before the Court did not involve the question of Milligan's guilt or innocence. Rather, it pertained to whether the government in wartime could suspend the constitutional rights of citizens under the Fifth and Sixth Amendments and set up military courts in areas that were free from invasion or rebellion and in which the civilian courts were open and operating.

The government's lawyers argued for the primacy of martial law and military authority in this case and claimed that civil liberties were "peace provisions of the Constitution, and like all other conventional and legislative laws and enactments are silent amidst arms, and when the safety of the people becomes the supreme law."

Counsel for the petitioner disagreed vehemently with the government's argument that civil liberties could be suspended during a war that threatened the very existence of the nation. James A. Garfield said,

> Such a doctrine...is too monstrous to be tolerated for a moment; and I trust and believe that...it will receive its just and final condemnation. Your decision will...establish forever this truth, of inestimable value to us and to mankind, that a republic can wield the vast enginery of war without breaking down the safeguards of liberty; can suppress insurrection, and put down rebellion, however formidable, without destroying the bulwarks of law; can, by the might of its armed millions, preserve and defend both nationality and liberty.

The Court unanimously decided for the petition on behalf of Milligan. Justice David Davis presented the opinion of the Court, in which four justices joined him. Chief Justice Salmon Chase presented a concurring opinion, which was joined by three justices.

The Court ruled that suspending the writ of habeas corpus and trying civilians in a military court when there were civilian courts open and operating violated the Constitution. Because Indiana had been far removed from the battle zone, the Court argued, the military tribunal had no jurisdiction to try Milligan; neither the President nor Congress could legally deny his rights to a civilian trial by jury and due process of law as guaranteed by the Fifth and

Sixth Amendments. Justice David Davis memorably wrote in support of constitutionally guaranteed rights to civil liberty in wartime,

> The Constitution of the United States is a law for rulers and people, equally in war and in peace, and covers with the shield of its protection all classes of men, at all times, and under all circumstances. No doctrine, involving more pernicious consequences, was ever invented by the wit of man than that any of its provisions can be suspended during any of the great exigencies of government. Such a doctrine leads directly to anarchism or despotism, but the theory of necessity on which it is based is false; for the government, within the Constitution, has all the powers granted to it, which are necessary to preserve its existence; as has been happily proved by the result of the great effort to throw off its just authority.

Further, Justice Davis wrote for the Court's majority against the contention by the government's lawyers that a military commission had jurisdiction in this case under the "laws and usages of war." Davis said,

> This court has judicial knowledge that in Indiana the Federal authority was always unopposed, and its courts always open to hear criminal accusations and redress grievances; and no usage of war could sanction a military trial there for any offence whatever of a citizen in civil life, in no wise connected with the military service. Congress could grant no such power.... One of the plainest constitutional provisions was, therefore, infringed when Milligan was tried by a court not ordained and established by Congress, and not composed of judges appointed during good behavior.

The Court's majority acknowledged that the privilege of the writ of habeas corpus could be suspended under the terms of the Constitution's Article 1, Section 9. However, suspension of the writ, said Davis, allows only the detention of suspects by the government, not their trial by a military tribunal when the civil courts are open. Davis wrote, "Martial law cannot arise from a threatened invasion. The necessity must be actual and present; the invasion real, such as effectually closes the courts and deposes the civil administration." Davis noted that this was not the situation in Indiana.

In his concurring opinion, Chief Justice Salmon Chase agreed with the Court's majority that there were no legal grounds for keeping Milligan in custody and that he should be released. However, the chief justice disagreed with the part of Justice Davis's opinion that held the federal government could never authorize military trials of civilians when the civil courts were open. Rather, Chase argued that under its war powers Congress could make laws needed to successfully conduct a war. Thus, if Congress concluded that the civil courts were not capable of punishing treason, it could enact legislation providing for military courts to try suspects. Chief Justice Chase wrote,

> Congress has the power... to provide by law for carrying on war. This power necessarily extends to all legislation essential to the prosecution of war with vigor and success....
>
> In Indiana... the state was a military district, was the theater of military operations, had been actually invaded, and was constantly threatened with invasion. It appears, also, that a powerful secret association, composed of citizens and others, existed within the state, under military organization, conspiring against the draft, and plotting insurrection, the liberation of the prisoners of war at various depots, the seizure of the state and national

A detainee is escorted to his cell at the prison in Guantánamo Bay, Cuba, a military facility used to detain persons accused of terrorist actions against the United States. The U.S. Supreme Court decided in Hamdan v. Rumsfeld *(2006) that the trial of Guantánamo detainees by military commissions violated federal and international laws and could not proceed as planned.*

arsenals, armed cooperation with the enemy, and war against the national government.

We cannot doubt that, in such a time of public danger, Congress had power, under the Constitution, to provide for the organization of a military commission, and for trial by that commission of persons engaged in this conspiracy. The fact that the Federal courts were open was regarded by Congress as sufficient reason for not exercising the power; but that fact could not deprive Congress of the right to exercise it. Those courts might be open and undisturbed in the execution of their functions, and yet wholly incompetent to avert threatened danger, or to punish, with adequate promptitude and certainty, the guilty conspirators.

In Indiana, the judges and officers of the court were loyal to the government. But it might have been otherwise.

The Court's decision in *Ex parte Milligan* brought a mixed public response. Civil libertarians hailed it. However, many loyal citizens who had sacrificed and suffered for the Union's cause in the Civil War resented Milligan's release from prison because evidence in his case suggested that he may have been a traitor and certainly had been a Confederate sympathizer. Many Republican Party leaders in Congress not only detested such disloyal citizens as Milligan, but also feared that the Court's ruling could unduly restrict their plans for "reconstruction" of the former Confederate states. For example, the 1867 Reconstruction Act passed by Congress authorized military tribunals to maintain public safety in southern states where black persons had been targets of violence. Congressional leaders feared that the *Milligan* ruling could be used to disallow this use of martial law to protect black people, whose rights might be at risk under the authority of local civilian courts, in which judges and juries might be unfairly prejudiced against them.

In the long run, legal experts have hailed the Court's *Milligan* decision as a bulwark of liberty in times of war or internal turmoil, and the Court has never repudiated it. But the Supreme Court has not always strictly followed its own ruling. During World War II, when the Court permitted the internment of U.S. citizens of Japanese ancestry, it ignored limits on the government's war powers implied by the *Milligan* decision. And criticism of parts of Justice Davis's opinion for the Court in *Ex parte Milligan* has continued, from Chief Justice Chase's concurring opinion to supporters of the federal government's policy in the twenty-first-century "War on Terror." These critics have expressed concern that the Court's categorical ban of martial law whenever and wherever civilian courts are open could disable the government from acting quickly and decisively in a crisis for the protection of national security.

President Lincoln's Message to Congress
in Special Session

Shortly after the start of the Civil War in mid–April 1861, President Abraham Lincoln called a special session of Congress to convene on July 4, Independence Day. The President intended to present his plans for conducting a war to maintain the integrity of the United States against the rebellion of several of its southern states. In his speech to this special session of Congress, President Lincoln explained his goals in the Civil War and presented his plans for conducting and winning this war. In particular, he offered reasons for restricting civil liberties under certain conditions in order to maintain the nation during an unparalleled national crisis.

Fellow-citizens of the Senate and House of Representatives:

Having been convened on an extraordinary occasion, as authorized by the Constitution, your attention is not called to any ordinary subject of legislation.

At the beginning of the present Presidential term, four months ago, the functions of the Federal Government were found to be generally suspended within the several States of South Carolina, Georgia, Alabama, Mississippi, Louisiana, and Florida. . . .

Finding this condition of things, and believing it to be an imperative duty upon the incoming Executive, to prevent, if possible, the consummation of such attempt to destroy the Federal Union, a choice of means to that end became indispensable. . . .

And this issue embraces more than the fate of these United States. It presents to the whole family of man the question, whether a constitutional republic, or a democracy—a government of the people, by the same people—can, or cannot, maintain its territorial integrity, against its own domestic foes. It presents the question, whether discontented individuals, too few in numbers to control administration, according to organic law, in any case, can always, upon the pretences made in this case, or on any other pretences, or arbitrarily, without any pretence, break up their Government, and thus practically put an end to free government upon the earth. It forces us to ask: Is there, in all republics, this inherent and fatal weakness? Must the government, of necessity, be too strong for the liberties of its own people, or too weak to maintain its own existence?

So viewing the issue, no choice was left but to call out the war power of the government; and so to resist force, employed for its destruction, by force, for its preservation. . . .

Soon after the first call for militia, it was considered a duty to authorize the Commanding General, in proper cases, according to his discretion, to suspend the privilege of the writ of habeas corpus; or, in other words, to arrest, and detain, without resort to the ordinary processes and forms of law, such individuals as he might deem dangerous to the public safety. This authority has purposely been exercised but very sparingly. Nevertheless, the legality and propriety of what has been done under it, are questioned; and the attention of the country has been called to the proposition that one who is sworn to "take care that the laws be faithfully executed" should not himself violate them. . . . The whole of the laws which were required to be faithfully executed, were being resisted, and failing of execution, in nearly one-third of the States. Must they be allowed to finally fail of execution, even had it been perfectly clear, that by the use of the means necessary to their execution, some single law, made in such extreme tenderness of the citizen's liberty, that practically, it relieves more of the guilty, than of the innocent, should to a very limited extent, be violated?

A photograph by Matthew Brady captures Abraham Lincoln's somber and determined manner at the start of the Civil War. When he suspended the writ of habeas corpus, a right guaranteed by the Constitution, Lincoln claimed extraordinary emergency powers.

To state the question more directly, are all the laws, but one, to go unexecuted, and the government itself go to pieces, lest that one be violated? Even in such a case, would not the official oath be broken, if the government should be overthrown, when it was believed that disregarding the single law would tend to preserve it? But it was not believed that this question was presented. It was not believed that any law was vio- lated. The provision of the Constitution [about the privilege of the writ of habeas corpus in Article 1, Section 9]...is a provision that such privilege may be suspended when, in cases of rebellion, or invasion, the public safety does require it. It was decided that we have a case of rebellion, and that the public safety does require the qualified suspension of the privilege of the writ which was authorized to be made. Now it is insisted that Congress, and not the Executive, is vested with this power. But the Constitution itself, is silent as to which, or who, is to exercise the power; and as the provision was plainly made for a dangerous emergency, it cannot be believed the framers of the instrument intended, that in every case, the danger should run its course, until Congress could be called together; the very assembling of which might be prevented, as was intended in this case, by the rebellion....

It was with the deepest regret that the Executive found the duty of employing the war-power, in defence of the government, forced upon him. He could not but perform this duty, or surrender the existence of the government....You will now, according to your own judgment, perform yours. He sincerely hopes that your views, and your action, may so accord with his, as to assure all faithful citizens, who have been disturbed in their rights, of a certain, and speedy restoration to them, under the Constitution, and the laws. And having thus chosen our course, without guile, and with pure purpose, let us renew our trust in God, and go forward without fear, and with manly hearts.

ABRAHAM LINCOLN
July 4, 1861

6

Separate but Not Equal

Plessy v. *Ferguson* (1896)

On June 7, 1892, Homer Plessy waited at the Press Street railroad depot in New Orleans. He had a first-class ticket for a thirty-mile trip to Covington, Louisiana. The train arrived on time at 4:15 in the afternoon, and the nicely dressed, well-groomed young man entered the first-class carriage, took a seat, gave his ticket to the conductor, and boldly spoke words that led to his arrest and trial in a court of law. Although he looked white, Homer Plessy announced that he was a "colored man." According to Louisiana law, he was an "octoroon"—a person whose ancestry is one-eighth black. The conductor ordered Plessy to sit in a separate car reserved for non-white passengers. When he refused, the conductor summoned a policeman, who arrested the disobedient passenger for breaking a state law.

Because it was against the law in Louisiana for a "colored" person to sit with whites in a railroad car, Homer Plessy had become a criminal. So on this fateful day he did not travel to the town of Covington, the destination printed on his railway ticket. In fact, Plessy had never intended to go there. Instead, he started a journey to seek justice through the Louisiana courts, and if necessary at the U.S. Supreme Court.

Plessy's trip was part of a carefully made plan to use the highest law of his country, the U.S. Constitution, to overturn a racist law of his home state, Louisiana. Plessy reached his final destination in 1896, when the U.S. Supreme Court agreed to decide his case.

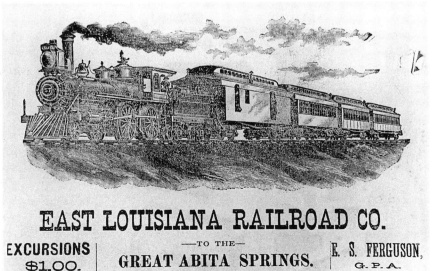

The East Louisiana Railroad Company placed this advertisement in a New Orleans paper for excursions to the Louisiana resort town of Great Abita Springs. Homer Plessy was arrested for sitting in the "whites only" carriage of one of the company's trains that was heading to Covington, Louisiana.

In 1890, the Louisiana General Assembly had enacted the Separate Car Law. According to this statute "all railway companies carrying passengers in their coaches in this State, shall provide equal but separate accommodations, for the white, and colored races.... No person or persons, shall be permitted to occupy seats in coaches, other than the ones assigned to them on account of the race to which they belong." This law empowered the train conductors "to assign each passenger to the coach or compartment used for the race in which such passenger belongs." If any passengers refused to sit in their assigned places, they were liable to a fine or imprisonment. There was one exception: "Nothing in this act shall be construed as applying to nurses attending children of the other race."

On September 31, 1891, a group of prominent Creole men in New Orleans formed the Citizens' Committee to Test the Constitutionality of the Separate Car Law. The Creoles, people of mixed French, Spanish, and African heritage, belonged to a community that had originated and thrived in Louisiana long before the United States purchased that territory from France in 1803. Many of the older Creoles were well-educated, highly respected members of New Orleans society, and had not been slaves before the Civil War.

These Creoles and their children had experienced a large measure of toleration in their dealings with white residents of New Orleans after the Civil War. Thus they particularly resented the Separate Car Law, claiming that it violated the Thirteenth and Fourteenth Amendments of the Constitution, and they vowed to overturn it through legal action in the state or federal courts.

The Thirteenth and Fourteenth Amendments were enacted after the Civil War to ensure that black Americans had rights equal to those enjoyed by whites. The Thirteenth Amendment abolished "slavery or involuntary servitude" for everyone but convicted criminals. The Fourteenth Amendment provided that "persons born or naturalized in the United States...are citizens of the United States and of the State wherein they reside." Further, state governments were prohibited from violating "the privileges and immunities of citizens of the United States," and no state could "deprive any person of life, liberty, or property, without due process of law; nor deny to any person within its jurisdiction the equal protection of the laws." The Creole leaders of New Orleans did not believe that Louisiana's Separate Car Law was compatible with the literal meaning of the Thirteenth and Fourteenth Amendments.

Homer Plessy's case was not the first one planned by the Citizens' Committee to test the constitutional validity of the Separate Car Law. Rather, Daniel Desdunes, a young Creole man whose ancestry was one-eighth African and seven-eighths European, was the voluntary protagonist in the first case contrived by the committee. On February 24, 1892, Desdunes boarded a train in New Orleans bound for Mobile, Alabama. He took a seat in the white coach, announced his identity as a colored man, and was arrested for violating the state law. His case was dismissed when the Louisiana Supreme Court ruled that the Separate Car Law could not constitutionally be enforced against passengers traveling across state boundaries, because only the Congress had power under the Constitution's commerce power (Article 1, Section 8) to regulate interstate transportation. Plessy, however, had been an intrastate passenger when he was arrested, and his case went forward.

The Citizens' Committee invited Albion Tourgée, a New York State resident and a nationally recognized advocate for the rights of black Americans, to join local attorney James C. Walker as counsel for Daniel Desdunes in the first case to test the Separate Car Law. Tourgée and Walker also represented Plessy.

The issue in Plessy's case was straightforward. Did the Louisiana Separate Car Law violate the rights guaranteed to Plessy by the Thirteenth and Fourteenth Amendments? Judge John Howard Ferguson presided at the state district court that originally heard Plessy's case and ruled against him. Plessy appealed to the Louisiana Supreme Court, which ruled that the state government had the power to regulate transportation strictly within the state's borders and that "separate but equal" accommodations for persons of different races did not violate the U.S. Constitution. The U.S. Supreme Court accepted Plessy's appeal of the state's decision, and the federal case of *Plessy* v. *Ferguson* was decided nearly four years later, because Plessy's lawyer, Albion Tourgée, acted very slowly to move the case forward.

At first, Tourgée thought the Court's delay in hearing arguments on Plessy's case would be a tactical advantage. He hoped to use the time to influence public sentiment in support of his client. But this strategy did not succeed because the tide of public opinion was turning strongly against him. The Louisiana law mandating racial segregation in railroad cars was only one of many instances of legalized racial discrimination against black Americans in southern states that were enacted after the federal government abandoned its post–Civil War policies to protect formerly enslaved persons. Most pronounced in the South, this anti–African American trend was also visible in other sections of the country. For example, there were unchallenged laws segregating blacks and whites on public conveyances not only in Florida and Alabama, but also in Pennsylvania, among other places throughout the country. And racial segregation in public schools, which had long existed under the authority of Congress in the District of Columbia, was increasingly practiced not only in the South but in other regions, too. Thus, the social context within which the Court would make its decision seemed quite unfavorable to Plessy's cause.

Despite the long odds against him, Albion Tourgée was determined to demonstrate the validity of his client's case. So on April 13, 1896, Tourgée joined Samuel F. Phillips, an old friend and prominent Washington, D.C., lawyer, to present oral arguments for Plessy to the Supreme Court.

Lawyers for Louisiana had maintained that the Separate Car Law was a constitutional exercise of the state's power to maintain public health and safety reserved to it by the U.S. Constitution's Tenth Amendment. They claimed that indiscriminant mingling of blacks and whites in public conveyances was a potential threat to the public good that the state was obligated and authorized to maintain. Furthermore, they insisted, their state's law was consistent with the Fourteenth Amendment's equal protection clause because the separate accommodations for blacks and whites were equal. As "separate but equal" was the foundation of the state's argument, the case became known by this phrase.

Tourgée and Phillips countered their adversaries' argument by stressing the incompatibility of the Louisiana Separate Car Law with the Thirteenth and Fourteenth Amendments. The state statute, Tourgée claimed, violated the

Albion W. Tourgée, a lawyer from upstate New York, was the chief counsel for Homer Plessy in his legal fight against racial segregation laws, which culminated in the 1896 Supreme Court case of Plessy v. Ferguson. *A strong advocate for public education and political and civil rights for all citizens, Tourgée inscribed this photograph with the phrase "Ignorance and neglect are the mainsprings of misrule."*

Thirteenth Amendment because it was "designed to discriminate against the colored citizens" and thereby "reduce them to a dependent and servile condition." Racial segregation, argued Tourgée, was "coincident with the institution of slavery" because "slavery was a caste, a legal condition of subjection to the dominant class." He said the Separate Car Law established a new type of "bondage quite separable from the incident of ownership."

Tourgée scorned the Louisiana law's claim of "equal but separate accommodations" for the segregated passengers and asserted that any legally enforced form of racial separation violated the equal protection clause of the Fourteenth Amendment. The intention of the Louisiana law, argued Tourgée, was not to promote public health and safety, as the statute's advocates claimed, but to promote a sense of superiority among whites at the expense of blacks. He exclaimed, "Justice is pictured as blind and her daughter, the law, ought at least to be color-blind." Thus, Tourgée claimed, laws requiring racial discrimination are inherently unjust and unconstitutional.

To the dismay of Albion Tourgée, Homer Plessy, and the New Orleans Citizens' Committee, the Supreme Court ruled against them. In his opinion for the Court's majority, Justice Henry B. Brown first of all narrowly interpreted the Thirteenth Amendment by holding that it prohibited only the institution of slavery and was not relevant to other race-based distinctions. Brown said that a law "which implies merely a legal distinction between the white and colored races...has no tendency to...re-establish a state of involuntary servitude." Thus, according to Brown, the Separate Car Law did not violate the Thirteenth Amendment.

Next, Justice Brown rejected the claim that Louisiana had violated the Fourteenth Amendment's requirement for "equal protection of the laws." He acknowledged that the purpose of the amendment was "to enforce the absolute equality of the two races before the law." But, he added, "it could not have been intended to abolish distinctions based upon color, or to enforce social, as distinguished from political equality, or a commingling of the two races upon terms unsatisfactory to either." Thus, Brown made a sharp distinction between social and political equality and argued that a state law providing "separate but equal" facilities for blacks and whites did not violate political equality, or the equal status of citizens, and therefore was compatible with the Fourteenth Amendment.

He noted, "the establishment of separate schools for white and colored children [in several southern and northern states], which has been held to be a valid exercise of the legislative power even by courts of States [such as Massachusetts] where the political rights of the colored race have been longest and most earnestly enforced." By this standard, argued Brown, "we cannot say that a law which authorizes or even requires the separation of the two races in public conveyances is unreasonable."

According to Justice Brown, it was a reasonable policy for the public good to provide "separate but equal" facilities for persons of different races. After all, both whites and blacks were equally prohibited from sitting in the railway cars assigned to the other race. And the different carriages, though separate, equally accommodated the needs of each racial group. He emphatically rejected the claim that racially segregated facilities implied inferiority or superiority of one race relative to the other. Justice Brown wrote,

> We consider the underlying fallacy of the plaintiff's argument to consist in the assumption that the enforced separation of the two races stamps the colored race with a badge of inferiority. If this be so, it is not by reason of anything found in the act, but solely because the colored race chooses to put that construction upon it....
>
> Laws permitting, and even requiring their separation in places where they are liable to be brought into contact, do not necessarily imply the inferiority of either race to the other, and have been generally, if not universally, recognized as within the competency of the state legislatures in the exercise of their police power.

Justice Brown maintained that the Fourteenth Amendment was not intended to enforce social equality or to abolish distinctions based on race. He wrote, "If the two races are to meet upon terms of social equality, it must be the result of natural affinities, a mutual appreciation of each other's merits and a voluntary consent of individuals." In conclusion, he justified his interpretation of the Fourteenth Amendment with this statement: "If the civil and political rights of both races be equal one cannot be inferior to the other civilly or politically. If one race be inferior to the other socially, the Constitution of the United States cannot put them upon the same plane."

The lone dissenter in this case, Justice John Marshall Harlan, strongly criticized the opinion of the Court. Although he had been a slaveholder in Kentucky before and during the Civil War, Harlan subsequently developed an unyielding commitment to the equal rights of blacks and whites, which were guaranteed by the Constitution.

Taking a cue from Tourgée's presentation to the Court, Justice Harlan wrote, "Our Constitution is color-blind, and neither knows nor tolerates classes among citizens." He insisted that the "separate but equal" doctrine established by the Court in the *Plessy* case was not compatible with the Fourteenth Amendment's

The members of the U.S. Supreme Court in the year they decided the 1896 case of Plessy v. Ferguson, *in a rare courtroom photograph. From left to right are Edward D. White, Henry B. Brown, Horace Gray, Stephen J. Field, Chief Justice Melville W. Fuller, John Marshall Harlan, David J. Brewer, George Shiras Jr., and Rufus W. Peckham.*

Racially segregated facilities, such as this "white ladies only" lavatory in Durham, North Carolina, became commonplace as a result of the "separate but equal" doctrine fashioned by the Supreme Court in Plessy. *The separate facilities for black Americans, however, were rarely equal to those provided for whites.*

guarantees of personal liberty and equal legal protection. Finally, he criticized Justice Brown's attempt to justify the Separate Car Law as reasonable. Harlan said it is the responsibility of the political branches of government to determine whether a public policy is reasonable. By contrast, it is the Court's duty to determine the constitutionality of statutes, not their reasonableness, and the state law at issue, he held, was manifestly at odds with the words of the U.S. Constitution.

Justice Harlan presciently declared that the *Plessy* decision would become a precedent in support of racial segregation. For the next fifty-eight years, the "separate but equal" doctrine established by the Court in *Plessy* v. *Ferguson* was "settled law," that is, it was a well-established precedent that guided subsequent decisions of the Court. Consequently, the precedent set by *Plessy* bolstered pervasive state-ordered racial segregation throughout the South and in some other parts of the country as well.

It seems incredible to us today to recall that state laws required black persons to use separate toilets, water fountains, streetcars, and waiting rooms. They had to attend separate schools and were segregated from whites in prisons, hospitals, hotels, restaurants, parks, theaters, cemeteries, and other public facilities. "Separate but equal" was the law, but the reality of racial segregation usually was very unequal facilities for black Americans, which handicapped them severely in all facets of life, irrespective of the Constitution's lofty guarantees of equal rights to liberty and justice for all. Legal challenges to racial segregation were defeated in the courts, where the *Plessy* precedent prevailed until it was overturned unanimously by the U.S. Supreme Court in the 1954 case of *Brown* v. *Board of Education*.

Homer Plessy, although he courageously resisted an unjust law, failed to achieve justice in his own time. And John Marshall Harlan, strong and brave in his sharp dissent against a popular Supreme Court opinion, endured public contempt and repudiation. In the long term, however, they inspired others to fulfill their common quest for equal justice under the Constitution; and today Plessy and Harlan, not their adversaries, have an honored place in our history.

"Our Constitution Is Color-Blind"

Justice John Marshall Harlan wrote one of the greatest dissenting opinions in the history of the Supreme Court in response to the majority's decision in Plessy v. Ferguson. *This former slave-holder from Kentucky fervently defended the constitutional rights of black Americans, many of whom had once been slaves. A product of his times, Harlan harbored racially biased opinions, as certain sentences in this dissenting opinion indicate. But his commitment to constitutional principles and values, the very idea of equal rights under the law, superseded any reservations he may have held about the capabilities or character of nonwhite Americans. Most of all, he rejected the very idea of a color-conscious interpretation of the U.S. Constitution. Rather, he believed that racial identity was not relevant to constitutional guarantees of civil rights and liberties.*

Justice Harlan predicted accurately the deplorable consequences of the Court's decision in the Plessy *case, foreseeing that this decision one day would be viewed almost as negatively as the Court's 1857 ruling in* Scott v. Sandford. *Harlan also was well aware that the majority of Americans in his time disagreed with him on issues of race relations, but he looked beyond the responses of his contemporaries. His dissent was an appeal to Americans of the future, who might be sufficiently inspired and instructed by his words to correct the mistakes of the past and achieve durable justice in the relationships of black and white Americans.*

In respect of civil rights, common to all citizens, the Constitution of the United States does not, I think, permit any public authority to know the race of those entitled to be protected in the enjoyment of such rights. Every true man has pride of race, and under appropriate circumstances when the rights of others, his equals before the law, are not to be affected, it is his privilege to express such pride and to take such action based upon it as to him seems proper. But I deny that any legislative body or judicial tribunal may have regard to the race of citizens when the civil rights of those citizens are involved. Indeed, such legislation as that here in question, is inconsistent not only with that equality of rights which pertains to citizenship, National and State, but with the personal liberty enjoyed by every one within the United States....

It was said in argument that the statute of Louisiana does not discriminate against either race, but prescribes a rule applicable alike to white and colored citizens. But this argument does not meet the difficulty. Every one knows that the statute in questions had its origin in the purpose not so much to exclude white persons from railroad cars occupied by blacks, as to exclude colored people from coaches occupied by or assigned to white persons.... The fundamental objection, therefore, to the statute is that it interferes with the personal freedom of citizens....

If a State can prescribe, as a rule of civil conduct, that whites and blacks shall not travel as passengers in the same railroad coach, why may it not so regulate the use of the streets of its cities and towns as to compel white citizens to keep on one side of a street and black citizens to keep on the other? Why may it not, upon like grounds, punish whites and blacks who ride together in street cars or in open vehicles on a public road or street? Why may it not require sheriffs to assign whites to one side of a court-room and blacks to the other? And why may it not also prohibit the commingling of the two races in the galleries of legislative halls or in public assemblages convened for the consideration of the political questions of the day? Further, if this statute of Louisiana is consistent with the personal liberty of citizens, why may not the State require the separation in railroad coaches of native and naturalized citizens of the United States, or of Protestants and Roman Catholics?...

John Marshall Harlan's dissent in Plessy *was vindicated in 1954 when the Court, in* Brown v. Board of Education, *declared the "separate but equal" doctrine unconstitutional. Although Harlan was born into a prominent Kentucky family and had owned slaves, he fought against segregating the nation by race.*

The white race deems itself to be the dominant race in this country. And so it is, in prestige, in achievements, in education, in wealth and in power.... But in view of the Constitution, in the eye of the law, there is in this country no superior, dominant, ruling class or citizens. There is no caste here. Our Constitution is color-blind, and neither knows nor tolerates classes among citizens. In respect of civil rights, all citizens are equal before the law. The humblest is the peer of the most powerful. The law regards man as man, and takes no account of his surroundings or of his color when his civil rights as guaranteed by the supreme law of the land are involved. It is, therefore, to be regretted that this high tribunal, the final expositor of the fundamental law of the land, has reached the conclusion that it is competent for a State to regulate the enjoyment by citizens of their civil rights solely upon the basis of race.

In my opinion, the judgment this day rendered will, in time, prove to be quite as pernicious as the decision made by this tribunal in the Dred Scott case.... The recent amendments of the Constitution [Thirteenth, Fourteenth, and Fifteenth], it was supposed, had eradicated these principles [of the *Dred Scott* decision] from our institutions. But it seems that we have yet, in some of the States, a dominant race— a superior class of citizens, which assumes to regulate the enjoyment of civil rights, common to all citizens, upon the basis of race. The present decision...will not only stimulate aggressions, more or less brutal and irritating, upon the admitted rights of colored citizens, but will encourage the belief that it is possible, by means of state enactments to defeat the beneficent purposes which the people of the United States had in view when they adopted the recent amendments of the Constitution....The destinies of the two races, in this country, are indissolubly linked together, and the interests of both require that the common government of all shall not permit the seeds of race hate to be planted under the sanction of law....

The arbitrary separation of citizens on the basis of race, while they are on a public highway, is a badge of servitude wholly inconsistent with the civil freedom and the equality before the law established by the Constitution. It cannot be justified upon any legal grounds.

...We boast of the freedom enjoyed by our people above all other peoples. But it is difficult to reconcile that boast with a state of the law which, practically, puts the brand of servitude and degradation upon a large class of our fellow citizens, our equals before the law. The thin disguise of "equal" accommodations for passengers in railroad coaches will not mislead any one, nor atone for the wrong this day done....

I am of opinion that the statue of Louisiana is inconsistent with the personal liberty of citizens, white and black, in that State, and hostile to both the spirit and letter of the Constitution of the United States. If laws of like character should be enacted in the several States of the Union, the effect would be in the highest degree mischievous....

For the reasons stated, I am constrained to withhold my assent from the opinion and judgment of the majority.

The Rights of Labor and the Rights of Women

Lochner v. *New York* (1905)

Muller v. *Oregon* (1908)

*L*ochner v. *New York* (1905) and *Muller* v. *Oregon* (1908) addressed the important question of how far state governments could go in regulating the impact of the late-nineteenth-century industrial revolution on labor and women. Writing in 1787, the framers of the Constitution reserved to the states broad powers to deal with matters of health, safety, morals, and welfare. Taken together they were called the police powers, and the states exercised them to intervene in the day-to-day lives of people in the interest of the public good. The states' regulatory efforts—addressing such issues as sanitation and the hours and conditions of work—however, sparked criticism among the owners of small and medium-size businesses who believed that the laws threatened their ability to manage their workers. They turned first to state and then federal courts for protection.

Lochner and *Muller* were two attempts to curb state regulation of business. In *Lochner*, the Court overturned a New York State law meant to regulate the hours that bakers could work, but three years later, in *Muller*, the justices upheld an Oregon regulation limiting the hours that women could work. In the end, it turned out, the gender of the workers made a difference in the ability of the state to exercise its police powers. Gender was the deciding factor because the roles of women and men, not just in the labor force but in society as a

Lochner v. New York

- 198 U.S. 45 (1905)
- Decided: April 17, 1905
- Vote: 5–4
- Opinion of the Court: Rufus Peckham
- Dissenting opinions: John Marshall Harlan (Edward D. White and William R. Day) and Oliver Wendell Holmes Jr.

Muller v. Oregon

- 208 U.S. 412 (1908)
- Decided: February 24, 1908
- Vote: 9–0
- Opinion of the Court: David J. Brewer

Joseph Lochner's flour-strewn, factory-like bakery in Utica, New York, was typical of the facilities that spurred the New York State legislature to pass the Bakeshop Act of 1895. Lochner retained Henry Weismann, who had originally supported the law, as his legal counsel before the Supreme Court, where he successfully argued that the act be declared unconstitutional.

whole, were seen as fundamentally different. In both cases, however, the justices posed the question of how reasonable the regulations were.

The constitutional underpinnings of both cases involved the general issue of the due process clause of the Fourteenth Amendment and the specific issue of a new constitutional concept the justices developed to evaluate state attempts to regulate the economy through the police powers; this tool was substantive due process of law. The justices had developed the concept over the previous twenty years, although its roots stretched back before the Civil War, surfacing, for example, in the 1857 Dred Scott case.

Historically, due process had meant that the Constitution guaranteed only that individuals would be treated fairly by the judicial process. If the procedure was fair, then the law would stand, regardless of its content. But the courts began to think not just about whether the right procedures were followed but about the practical impact of doing so. That is, the justices worried about the *substance* or results of legislative actions. So the Court invented a new concept—substantive due process of law, an approach more concerned with the ends than the means of legislation.

Under the new theory of substantive due process, courts assumed the power to examine the content of legislation—its substance—notably its economic implications. The Supreme Court began in the late 1880s to invoke the doctrine to overrule state attempts at regulating railroads. From there the doctrine expanded as the justices used it increasingly to invalidate economic legislation enacted by states that they determined to be in conflict with key rights protected by the Constitution. The new doctrine, which the justices themselves had largely created, clothed them with additional authority to protect individual rights but at the same time turn aside the popular wishes of the people as expressed through state legislative enactments. Initially, substantive due process was applied to state legislative efforts to regulate the economy, but over the next century the justices extended it to other areas, notably to state limitations on birth control and abortion. Substantive due process meant that certain rights, not just economic rights, were so fundamental that the state could take them away only under the most extraordinary of circumstances.

Lochner and *Muller* were important moments in the development of judicial power and attempts by the high court to address the demands of the new industrial era. They also mirrored the underlying and often contradictory values of that era. Americans wanted economic growth, but they were conflicted about how to distribute the benefits of that growth. Should corporations and businesses be free to do as they wished in order to produce the greatest wealth? Or was it better to regulate these activities, especially as workers and owners were often not equal in their bargaining power?

In 1895 the New York legislature passed the Bakeshop Law, which regulated sanitary conditions in bakeries and limited the hours that bakers could work to ten per day and sixty per week. The law was a startling change for a business in which journeymen bakers often worked more than one hundred hours per week. There was a mix of motives behind passage of the law. Some legislators were genuinely concerned for the health of the workers. Bakers were exposed to flour dust, which produced a condition known as white lung disease, a type of emphysema with symptoms such as shortness of breath. The long hours also took a toll, particularly in cities, where bakeries were often located in the cramped, damp cellars of tenement houses. There was also a concern that consumers would suffer from unsafe and low-quality baked goods.

Also, the baking business itself was changing. Small operators were being replaced by large corporate bakeries that often provided better working conditions and shorter hours. The bakers' union was eager, therefore, to make sure that small and medium-sized bakeries became safe places to work. The new bakeshop laws had their fullest impact on small and medium-sized bakeries, not large operations whose scale permitted them to distribute the costs over many more productive workers. Union leaders actually found support for regulatory legislation from large bakeries because these large operators believed that the costs associated with the legislation would drive more and more smaller bakers out of business. The owners of the smaller bakeries, however, resisted regulation because they knew that their profits depended on their ability to control the terms under which they employed their bakers. If they could have fewer bakers working longer hours, they believed, they would be better able to compete with the large baking factories.

The owners of small and medium-sized bakeries blasted the 1895 act known as the Bakeshop Law as an unwarranted governmental invasion of individual bakers' rights to reach the best agreement they could with their employers. If these workers wished to work long hours and earn more money, then the state should not stop them, especially as baking was not an unusually hazardous occupation. The case brought together an unusual cast of characters. Henry Weismann, the leader of the New York Journeymen Bakers' Union, was a native of Germany who had helped to organize bakers in California before moving to New York City. There he joined with Edward Marshall, a muckraking reporter, to urge passage of the Bakeshop Law. Joseph Lochner, a so-called boss baker in Utica, New York, owned several small shops, the success of which depended on five or fewer assistant bakers. Like other boss bakers, Lochner worked on thin profit margins, which he maintained by regulating the hours that his assistants worked. In 1902 he was fined fifty dollars for allowing an employee to work more than sixty hours in one week. Lochner appealed his conviction to the appellate division of the New York Supreme Court, where he lost by a vote of 3 to 2. He then appealed to the New York Court of Appeals, where he lost again, in a 4-to-3 ruling.

In one of the great ironies of Supreme Court and American constitutional history, the person who came to Lochner's aid was none other than former labor leader Henry Weismann. After a falling out with the bakers' union, Weismann had opened two bakeshops and became, like Lochner, an active member of the Master Bakers' Association. He also studied law, although he never gained formal admission to the bar of

These women sewing by hand around a table in a New York City sweatshop in 1908 were part of the influx of immigrant and rural women who flocked to major American cities at the end of the nineteenth and beginning of the twentieth century. Women became an important part of the labor market, but employers often exploited them through long hours and low pay.

the Supreme Court of the United States. Weismann is one of the few lawyers in the history of the Court to have argued and won a case before it without ever having been formally admitted to practice before the justices. He was granted "special permission" to appear before the Court.

Arguments before the Court lasted for two days. With the help of attorney Frank Harvey Field, Weismann argued on Lochner's behalf that the Bakeshop Law substantively violated the Fourteenth Amendment by depriving his client of life, liberty, or property without due process of law. The New York State law, he insisted, singled out bakers for regulation without any real justification for doing so. Weismann reminded the justices that homemakers, who also baked, were not covered by the law. He agreed that the state retained its historical police powers, but the New York State legislature did not have the right to invoke them in such a way that interfered with the "freedom to exercise a trade or calling." If the Court had any doubt on the matter, Weismann continued, then it should err on the side of protecting individual liberty. Because baking was not a dangerous occupation, the state had no legitimate interest in attempting to regulate it, the way it might do, for example, with mining. Most important, Weismann insisted that the New York act was actually not a "labor law"; instead it was a piece of discriminatory social engineering that was inappropriate under the state's police powers.

New York's attorney general, Julius M. Mayer, argued the case for the state. Mayer insisted that at trial Lochner had not raised any constitutional issues and he had in any case been found guilty, not once but twice, of violating the law. The act was a reasonable exercise of New York's broad police powers, which should be viewed as "necessarily elastic" in order to address the new and changing conditions of industrial life. On the question of where to draw the line on the use of the police power, Mayer insisted that such a determination should be left to the legislative branch and not to the courts. To prove that the state had an interest in having a healthy work force, Mayer reminded the justices that bakers might be called to defend the state in a time of crisis.

The justices decided the case by a vote of five to four. Following two days of argument, the Court in conference initially gave the task of writing the opinion to Justice John Marshall Harlan, but he was unable to keep a majority when either Justices Henry Billings Brown or Joseph McKenna switched sides. Justice Peckham then emerged as the author of the majority opinion. Justice Rufus Peckham's opinion for the Court held that in order for a law to pass constitutional muster, the legislature had to demonstrate that it was invoking the police power in a legitimate, fair, and reasonable way. Peckham rejected Mayer's arguments about internal security and national defense, as he found that these criteria were so broad they could be used to justify almost any kind of state interference. Peckham also insisted that the Court had a duty to decide not only whether the legislature had the power to pass a law but whether the law itself was reasonable. According to Peckham the only reason to pass such regulatory legislation was to protect the health of the worker or the consumer, a tie that the justice concluded in this instance was "too shadowy and thin" to sustain the law. Baking might be unhealthful in some ways, he admitted, but it was not a dangerous occupation, and, in any case, the issue was not protection of the bakers but rather the health of the public as a whole. "[W]holesome bread," Peckham wrote in one of the most memorable phrases of American constitutional history, "does not depend upon whether the baker works but ten hours per day or only sixty hours a week." By asserting a standard of reasonableness in measuring a legislative act the justices were effectively becoming the final umpire of what was rational. And what was reasonable was to be measured by the results of the legislation, not whether it was passed according to established procedures.

Peckham denounced the New York law as an infringement of the individual liberty of the bakers. The due process clause of the Fourteenth Amendment provided full protection to the bakers by clothing them and their workers with "liberty to contract." Simply stated, this concept meant that both labor and management should be free of the interference of the state to negotiate the best possible arrangement among themselves. If the bakers and the workers found the terms acceptable, then the state was in no position to question their agreement. Peckham went even further. He concluded that the law was nothing more than "class legislation," a measure designed to help one class—workers—at the expense of the other—owners. What was supposed to be a health regulation was actually a piece of social engineering, an activity that legislators should avoid at all costs.

Justice Harlan, joined by Justices Edward D. White and William R. Day, authored one of two powerful dissents. Harlan claimed that employees did not stand on an equal footing with employers, so the state had a legitimate role in helping to restore the balance between them. Moreover, based on medical evidence, the legislature had a reasonable ground upon which to conclude that its police powers should be used to protect the bakers. As long as the legislature had such a reasonable basis to act, the Court should not interfere. "Unless they are plainly and palpably beyond all question in violation of the fundamental law of the Constitution," Harlan explained, legislative enactments should be enforced.

Justice Oliver Wendell Holmes Jr. added his own dissent and even more strongly articulated the idea that judges should defer to the wishes of legislators. He concluded that the statute did not infringe upon any fundamental liberties and that Peckham was simply dead wrong. Holmes echoed Harlan on the use of judicial power, asserting that the majority of justices had substituted their views of what was reasonable for those of the New York legislature. Holmes also accused the majority of invoking a constitutional theory with which a majority of Americans and New York State citizens disagreed. A constitution, according to Holmes, was not meant to embody a particular economic theory, and the justices were bound to respect the will of the majority, even if they did not share its views. Holmes believed that the justices should defer to popular will instead of imposing their own views. "The Fourteenth Amendment had not enacted," Holmes wrote in a now-famous phrase, "Mr. Herbert Spencer's Social Statics." Spencer was a British philosopher and sociologist who insisted that the human race progressed most effectively through a process of natural selection in which the rich and powerful dominated the poor and weak. According to his view of "social statics," or the interactions among the classes, differences between the working and upper classes were not only inevitable but good, and he insisted that law should promote these differences.

Lochner was the high point in the Court's application of substantive due process of law against economic regulation. What made the case so controversial was that the justices took exception to a well-intentioned state effort to address the social and economic consequences of industrialization through a bold, almost breathtaking, use of judicial review. The majority of the Court made clear that they were prepared not just to weigh the constitutionality of a particular law but also to match their beliefs about how reasonable a law was against those of a legislative majority. Critics complained that the justices had become directly involved in formulating policy rather than interpreting the law. As Holmes pointed out, *Lochner* embraced one theory of the function of government at the expense of all others. Justice Peckham's theory held that government should not engage in social engineering, but instead leave the marketplace to decide economic winners and losers. The responsibility of courts was to make sure that government did not intervene unreasonably. The opposing theory, articulated by Holmes, held that government had a duty to ensure a level economic playing field on which workers and management could bargain equally. The justices, therefore, were to give broad scope to legislative action because it represented the will of the people. For these reasons the case stands as a symbol of unrestrained judicial activism, in which the justices substituted their views for those of the legislature.

In subsequent years, both state and federal courts did uphold many state regulations, but the justices invalidated others, including minimum wage laws, child labor laws, and regulations of the banking, insurance, and transportation industries. The courts found enough reform statutes unconstitutional that the history of constitutional law during the first third of the twentieth century came to be known as the *Lochner* era.

In the more immediate term, the decision in *Lochner* generated rumors of a threatened national strike, but it never happened. The high court came under sharp attack for its decision in *Lochner* from reform groups, who charged that the justices were too eager to place the interests of management above those of labor. The *Lochner* ruling was widely interpreted as a blow to state regulation of hours in any nonhazardous occupation. Peckham's opinion and Harlan's dissent did agree in one area: if a connection could be made between the legitimate use of a state's police power and a particular law, it would stand constitutional muster. The two justices simply disagreed on whether the facts in *Lochner* made such a connection.

This notion was tested three years later in *Muller* v. *Oregon* (1908). In this case, in stark contrast to *Lochner,* the justices unanimously accepted an Oregon law that limited the hours that women could work, leaving men as the only group clothed by the "protection" of liberty to contract that was established in *Lochner.* In 1903, Oregon set a maximum of ten hours of work a day for women employed in factories and laundries. The rationale behind the legislation was simple: women were the weaker sex and therefore required protection from the ravages of industrialization. But on September 4, 1905, Joe Haselbock, a foreman in the Grand Laundry run by Curt Muller in Portland, Oregon, ordered one of his female employees to work more than ten hours a day. The employee took Muller to court; two weeks later the owner was convicted of violating the

Kurt Muller (center) employed mostly female workers at the Lace House Laundry in Portland, Oregon. Although women might seem ideal workers for such a business, as they supposedly had domestic skills, in practice laundries were unhealthful and dangerous places. The Court concluded in Muller v. Oregon *(1908) that as a sex they were so physically weak that the state could impose limits on the maximum number of hours they were permitted to work.*

ten-hour law and fined ten dollars. Muller then appealed to the Oregon Supreme Court, which upheld his conviction. Bolstered by the decision in *Lochner,* Muller appealed to the U.S. Supreme Court.

The result was entirely different from what Muller expected. Louis D. Brandeis, who argued the case for the state of Oregon, was the force that drove the reversal in the Court's opinion.. The National Consumers' League, a group devoted to social reform measures, persuaded Oregon's attorney general to hire Brandeis, one of the nation's most accomplished lawyers and a progressive advocate of social change through the law. Brandeis, with the assistance of Florence Kelley and his sister-in-law Josephine Goldmark, who were officials of the league, constructed a novel brief in support of the Oregon law. Instead of focusing directly on the law in question and on the precedents set by the Court in previous rulings, Brandeis instead amassed evidence that demonstrated that women's health problems and long hours of work were directly connected to one another. The two women exhaustively compiled for Brandeis every medical and governmental report dealing with the relationship of working conditions and women's health, not just in the United States but around the world.

Brandeis then translated this material into more than one hundred pages of the most pointed and poignant excerpts from these reports, while giving only two pages to the legal precedents. The brief made clear that Oregon was not alone in it approach to the dangers posed by long hours of work to women's health; other states and nations had used government power to preserve women's well-being. Brandeis did the same in his oral argument, reminding the justices that the majority in *Lochner* had agreed that if it could be demonstrated that there was a rational state interest in regulation it would survive judicial scrutiny. What, Brandeis essentially asked, could be more important that preserving the health of women?

The Court answered unanimously: nothing. Justice David J. Brewer upheld the law and praised Brandeis for his brief and oral presentation. Thereafter, a new form of brief, or written argument, known as the Brandeis brief, emerged before the Court, as lawyers turned increasingly to social science data to complement their legal arguments.

The importance of the new reasonableness test became immediately clear. What the justices thought was reasonable now became the law. Justice Brewer's opinion found that the state of Oregon acted rationally in passing the legislation, even though this seemed to contradict the finding only three years earlier in *Lochner*. Why was the law reasonable? Because women were different from men. The Court acknowledged that a "woman's physical structure and the performance of maternal functions place her at a disadvantage in the struggle for subsistence." Women were not only the weaker sex and therefore in need of greater state protection than men, but they also had a special role in society as mothers that government was obligated to foster. Long hours of labor would take a toll on women. "And as healthy mothers are essential to vigorous offspring, the physical well-being of women becomes an object of public interest and care," Brewer concluded.

The decision underscored the paternalism men directed toward women and the latter's second-class citizenship. Because men were "tougher" they could enjoy a greater level of "liberty to contract"; women, on the other hand, because of their supposed inherent physical weakness, were granted a lower degree of constitutional protection of their rights and accorded a higher level of state interference to protect their well-being. The conflict with the earlier *Lochner* decision was clear. And Justice Brewer went out of his way to note that the decision in *Muller* did not "in any respect" weaken either the doctrine of substantive due process or the importance of the holding in *Lochner*.

Despite Brewer's assurances, the application of substantive due process to matters of economic regulation shifted over the next two decades from unsettled to uncertain to unsupportable. The Court in *Bunting* v. *Oregon* (1917) accepted another Oregon law that limited the hours of all factory workers, but it invoked the doctrine of liberty to contract, and with it substantive due process of law, in *Adkins* v. *Children's Hospital* (1923). The justices in *Adkins* prohibited Congress from authorizing a commission to establish minimum wages in the District of Columbia. The Great Depression of the 1930s demonstrated that the economic assumption behind the *Lochner* decision, that each worker should be left to make the best possible contract for his work, was untenable given the uneven balance of power between labor and business.

While the application of substantive due process to economic regulation waned, the doctrine itself retained considerable vitality. A new generation of justices beginning in the 1960s resurrected it as a means of reaching behind the text of the Constitution to address whether other noneconomic regulations were reasonable. They often concluded that they were not. The justices identified a host of new fundamental rights, including such hot-button matters as privacy, birth control, and abortion, that are nowhere mentioned in the Constitution, as well as less controversial issues including the rights of women, the disabled, and immigrants. The shadow of *Lochner* continues to fall over these and other areas of contemporary American law as its underlying doctrine of substantive due process grants the justices a controversial ability to adapt constitutional law to changing social practices.

The Dangers of Long Hours

Louis D. Brandeis was known in the early twentieth century as the People's Attorney because of his prominent role in advocating public-interest causes. Brandeis pressed his social agenda through legal briefs laden with sociological evidence rather than legal precedent. These "Brandeis briefs" recognized that when courts considered the reasonableness of legislation, evidence of the social circumstances and the impact of constitutional doctrines might persuade judges and justices. The 1908 Muller v. Oregon *case was noteworthy because both Brandeis's brief (below) and the Court's ruling dovetailed with the prevailing societal view that because of their physical limitations, women had to be treated differently than men when it came to hours and conditions of work.*

THE WORLD'S EXPERIENCE UPON WHICH THE LEGISLATION LIMITING THE HOURS OF LABOR FOR WOMEN IS BASED

I. The Dangers of Long Hours

A. Causes

(1) Physical Differences Between Men and Women

Report of Select Committee on Shops Early Closing Bill, British House of Commons, 1895.

Dr. Percy Kidd, physician in Brompton and London Hospitals:

The most common effect I have noticed of the long hours is general deterioration of health; very general symptoms which we medically attribute to over-action, and debility of the nervous system; that includes a great deal more than what is called nervous disease, such as indigestion, constipation, a general slackness, and a great many other indefinite symptoms.

Are those symptoms more marked in women than in men?

I think they are much more marked in women. I should say one sees a great many more women of this class than men; but I have seen precisely the same symptoms in men, I should not say in the same proportion, because one has not been able to make anything like a statistical inquiry. There are other symptoms, but I mention those as being the most common. Another symptom especially among women is anemia, bloodlessness or pallor, that I have no doubt is connected with long hours indoors.

Report of the Massachusetts Bureau of Labor Statistics, 1875.

A "lady operator," many years in the business, informed us: "I have had hundreds of lady compositors in my employ, and they all exhibited, in a marked manner, both in the way they performed their work and in its results, the difference in physical ability between themselves and men. They cannot endure the prolonged close attention and confinement which is a great part of type-setting. I have few girls with me more than two or three years at a time; they must have vacations, and they break down in health rapidly. I know no reason why a girl could not set as much type as a man, if she were as strong to endure the demand on mind and body." Report of the Nebraska Bureau of Labor and Industrial Statistics, 1901B1902.

They (women) are unable, by reason of their physical limitations, to endure the same hours of exhaustive labor as may be endured by men without injury to their health [which] would wreck the constitution and destroy the health of women, and render them incapable of bearing their share of the burdens of the family and the home. The State must be accorded the right to guard and protect women as a class against such a condition, and the law in question to that extent conserves the public health and welfare.

In strength as well as in rapidity and precision of movement women are inferior to men. This is not a conclusion that has ever been contested. It is in harmony with all the practical experience of life. It is perhaps also in harmony with the results of those investigators who have found that, as in the blood of women, so also in their muscles, there is more water than in those of men. To a very great extent it is a certainty, a matter of difference in exercise and environment. It is probably, also, partly a matter of organic constitution.

The motor superiority of men, and to some extent of males generally, is, it can scarcely be doubted, a deep-lying fact. It is related to what is most fundamental in men and in women, and to their whole psychic organization.

There appears to be a general agreement that women are more docile and amenable to discipline; that they can do light work equally well; that they are steadier in some respects; but that, on the other hand, they are often absent on account of slight indisposition, and they break down sooner under strain....

It has been estimated that out of every one hundred days women are in a semi-pathological state of health for from fourteen to sixteen days. The natural congestion of the pelvic organs during menstruation is augmented and favored by work on sewing machines and other industrial occupations necessitating the constant use of the lower part of the body. Work during these periods tends to induce chronic congestion of the uterus and appendages, and dysmenorrhea and flexion of the uterus are well known affections of working girls....

D. Bad Effect upon Morals

Report of British Chief Inspector of Factories and Workshops, 1900.

One of the most unsatisfactory results of the present system of lack of working hours in laundries is the unfortunate moral effect on the women and girls. Women who are employed at arduous work till far into the night are not likely to be early risers nor given to punctual attendance in the mornings, and workers who on one or two days in the week are dismissed to idleness or to other occupations, while on the remaining days they are expected to work for

Louis D. Brandeis sat for this portrait in 1916, when President Woodrow Wilson nominated him to the Supreme Court. Brandeis was the first Jew to serve on the high court, and his confirmation sparked a four-month battle in the Senate, in part because of his use of the so-called Brandeis brief, in which he emphasized the social and economic effects of law rather than legal precedents in order to advocate social justice.

abnormally long hours, are not rendered methodical, industrious, or dependable workers by such an unsatisfactory training. The self-control and good habits engendered by a regular and definite period of moderate daily employment, which affords an excellent training for the young worker in all organized industries, is sadly lacking, and, instead, one finds periods of violent over-work alternating with hours of exhaustion. The result is the establishment of a kind of "vicious circle"; bad habits among workers make compliance by their employers with any regulation as to hours very difficult while a lack of loyal adherence to reasonable hours of employment by many laundry occupiers increases the difficulty for those who make the attempt in real earnestness.

8

The Latitude and Limits of Free Speech

Schenck v. *United States* (1919)

Abrams v. *United States* (1919)

The First Amendment to the U.S. Constitution says, "Congress shall make no law...abridging the freedom of speech." It expresses an absolute prohibition of legislation that would deny this freedom. Constitutional protection of this fundamental civil liberty, however, has not been absolute. Congress has enacted laws limiting freedom of speech under certain conditions, and the federal courts, in certain cases, have endorsed these restrictive acts.

It took a very long time, more than 125 years after ratification of the First Amendment in 1791, for the first cases about federal laws limiting free speech to arrive at the U.S. Supreme Court. During the years that America participated in World War I, from April 6, 1917, until November 11, 1918, Congress enacted laws limiting freedom of speech in order to protect national security against spies, saboteurs, and obstructers of the national war effort.

Government leaders and many in the general public also believed that the Communist Party that came to power in Russia during the 1917 Russian Revolution, one year before the end of World War I, posed a threat to America. Russia's Communist rulers advocated subversion and the overthrow of noncommunist governments throughout the world, which led many Americans to suspect that Socialists and Communists in the United States would collaborate with the international communist movement against the interests of the United States. Thus, laws enacted to protect national security during World War I were also used during and after the war to curtail activities of American supporters of communism and socialism.

In June 1917, barely two months after the nation's entry into World War I, Congress passed the Espionage Act, which enabled the federal government to punish certain kinds of dissent against its wartime policies. The Espionage Act provided that

> whoever...shall willfully make or convey reports or false statements with intent to interfere with the operation or success of the military or naval forces of the United States or to promote the success of its enemies and whoever...shall willfully cause or attempt to cause insubordination, disloyalty, mutiny, or refusal of duty, in the military or naval forces of the United States...shall be punished by a fine of not more than $10,000 or imprisonment for not more than 20 years or both."

Schenck v. United States

- 249 U.S. 47 (1919)
- Decided: March 3, 1919
- Vote: 9–0
- Opinion of the Court: Oliver Wendell Holmes Jr.

Abrams v. United States

- 250 U.S. 616 (1919)
- Decided: November 10, 1919
- Vote: 7–2
- Opinion of the Court: John H. Clarke
- Dissenting opinion: Oliver Wendell Holmes Jr. (Louis D. Brandeis)

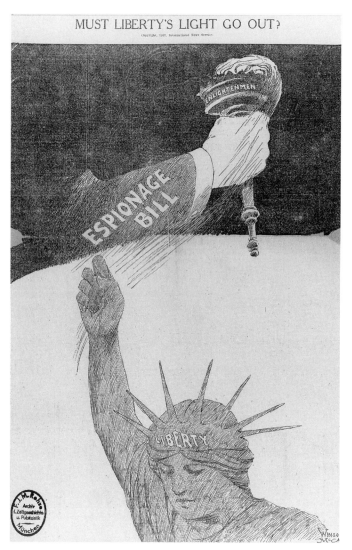

MUST LIBERTY'S LIGHT GO OUT?

Copyright, 1917, International News Service.

In this political cartoon, the Espionage Bill takes the torch of enlightenment from the Statue of Liberty. Despite such expressions of opposition to the limits the federal government imposed on free speech during World War I, the Supreme Court upheld the Espionage Act in Schenck v. United States *(1919).*

In May 1918, Congress passed the Sedition Act, which augmented the already strong powers provided in the Espionage Act of 1917, by outlawing any speech or writing that in any way might impugn and undermine the U.S. government, flag, military forces, or Constitution or intend to promote resistance against federal government policies, such as the drafting of able-bodied men into the armed forces.

Many Americans believed the Espionage and Sedition Acts violated the Constitution's First Amendment guarantees of free speech and press. But from June 1917 until the middle of 1921, more than two thousand people were prosecuted for violating these restrictive federal laws, and more than one thousand were convicted. Among the several convictions appealed to the U.S. Supreme Court, those of Charles Schenck and Jacob Abrams became significant cases in the development of the Court's doctrine on the latitude and limits of free speech. Schenck's case originated with his August 1917 arrest for violating the Espionage Act. Abrams's case began one year later, in August 1918, when police arrested and jailed him and his associates for breaking the law under the Espionage and Sedition Acts.

Charles Schenck, general secretary of the Socialist Party in the United States, was an outspoken critic of America's participation in World War I. To express opposition to the war, Schenck and his Socialist Party associates printed and mailed about 1,500 leaflets to men eligible for the draft. The leaflets denounced the draft as involuntary servitude and therefore a violation of the Thirteenth Amendment to the Constitution. The pamphlet also argued that participation in World War I did not serve the best interests of the American people. It claimed that conscripting men into the armed forces to fight in the war was a "monstrous wrong against humanity in the interest of Wall Street's chosen few."

Schenck was arrested and convicted of violating the Espionage Act. At his trial, Schenck claimed that his First Amendment right to free speech had been violated. For the first time, the U.S. Supreme Court directly faced the question of whether the federal government might limit speech under special circumstances.

The Court unanimously decided against Schenck, upholding his conviction and ruling that the Espionage Act did not unconstitutionally limit his First Amendment rights of free speech and press. Writing for the Court, Justice Oliver Wendell Holmes Jr. presented a novel test to determine when and how the government might limit free speech. When spoken or written words "create a clear and present danger" of bringing about evils that Congress has the authority to prevent, said Holmes, then the government has an obligation to stop them. Holmes argued that Schenck's actions had created the kind of circumstance that the federal government could constitutionally prevent through the Espionage Act.

Holmes next provided one of the most memorable examples ever used in a Supreme Court opinion to clarify an argument. "The most stringent protection of free speech would not protect a man in falsely shouting fire in a theatre and causing a panic." Thus, Holmes linked the latitude or limits of political speech to the "circumstances in which it is done."

Holmes argued that Schenck and his associates intended to influence others from compliance with the federal draft law. If enough men had responded favorably to Schenck's message, then the federal government would have been prevented from carrying out the will of the people, endorsed by their representatives in Congress, who had voted overwhelmingly to participate in the war in order to defend critical national interests. Schenck's attempt to severely obstruct the war effort was certainly among "the kind of substantive evils that Congress had a right to prevent," wrote Holmes.

Under different circumstances, such as those in peacetime, Schenck's ideas would have been protected by the Constitution's First Amendment, said Holmes. But urging men to resist the draft during a time of war presents a "clear and present danger" to the nation. Thus Holmes declared, "When a nation is at war, many things that might be said in time of peace are such a hindrance to its efforts that their utterance will not be protected by any constitutional right."

Before the *Schenck* case, both state and federal courts had relied only upon a doctrine called "the bad tendency" test to adjudicate freedom of speech cases. If speech tended to have bad effects, then it might be constitutionally restricted. For example, speech that threatened public order, subverted established standards of morality, or obstructed national defense in wartime could be legislatively restricted. Further, there was a presumption of constitutionality for laws limiting speech according to the "bad tendency" test, if the restrictive legislation clearly reflected traditional community standards.

In two cases decided only a few days after *Schenck,* Court watchers were surprised by Justice Holmes' opinions. In *Frohwerk* v. *United States* (1919) and *Debs* v. *United States* (1919), Holmes based the Court's decisions only on the conventional "bad tendency" test and did not mention the "clear and present danger" doctrine.

The Court unanimously upheld the conviction of Jacob Frohwerk, who had written articles for a German-language newspaper that urged resistance to the military draft. Holmes said that Frohwerk's words violated the Espionage Act, because they might "be enough to kindle a flame of resistance." Indeed, this was a "bad tendency" but Holmes did not make a causal connection to a particular circumstance, as his "clear and present danger" test made necessary.

The Court also unanimously upheld the conviction of Eugene Debs, the leader of the American Socialist Party. Debs had delivered a speech filled with socialist ideology in Canton, Ohio. He criticized the very idea of war and advocated resistance to the government's World War I policies. Debs said, "I would oppose war if I stood alone." Further, he argued that the war benefited wealthy capitalists while harming everyone else. Holmes concluded that Debs's words "had as their natural tendency and reasonable probable effect to obstruct the [military] recruitment service." But Holmes did not seem to care that no direct causal connection could be made between Debs' theoretical expressions of socialist ideology and behavior that might practically obstruct the government's military operations. Because the "bad tendency" test did not require evidence of a direct link between particular speech and unlawful behavior, prosecutors and judges used it to facilely and unsubstantially impose rather strict limitations on First Amendment freedoms.

Leading legal scholars and commentators who had praised Holmes for his promising new "clear and present danger" doctrine in *Schenck* criticized him and the Supreme Court for eschewing it in the *Frohwerk* and *Debs* decisions. For example, Harvard professor Zechariah Chafee wrote in the June 1919 issue of the *Harvard Law Review* that Holmes's "clear and present danger" doctrine had the potential through application and refinement in future cases to make "the punishment of words for their bad tendency impossible." Chafee was disappointed that Holmes and the Court relied only on the "bad tendency" test in *Frohwerk* and *Debs*.

Ernst Freund, a law professor at the University of Chicago, wrote an article for *The New Republic* to emphatically express disappointment in the Court's *Debs* opinion. Freund criticized Holmes's opinion for the Court because it upheld Debs's conviction merely on an assumption, but without hard evidence, that his speech was somehow connected to the "bad tendency" of obstructing the draft. Freund charged there was "nothing to show actual obstruction or an attempt to interfere with any of the recruitment process." Thus, those who had used the "bad tendency" test against Debs had decided against him by merely "guessing" about "the tendency and possible effect" of Debs's speech. This manner of decision making offered flimsy and whimsical protection, instead of solid security, for the individual's First Amendment rights. Freund urged the Court to return to the "clear and present danger" doctrine so that it might be improved and developed into a just test for determining the breadth and limits of free speech.

Holmes heeded the critical responses of scholars to the Court's March 1919 free speech decisions. For example, he read carefully what Zechariah Chafee and Ernst Freund wrote in the *Harvard Law Review* and *The New Republic,* and he met with Professor Chafee and other legal experts and scholars to discuss free speech issues during the summer of 1919. In particular, Holmes paid close attention to Chafee's advice about developing the "clear and present danger" doctrine to establish more clearly the line between speech that is protected by the First Amendment and that which is not. Chafee also urged Holmes to emphasize the social and political importance of a broader scope for freedom of speech. Thus, in November 1919, when the Supreme Court considered its next free speech case, *Abrams* v. *United States,* Justice Holmes was prepared to think and write anew about constitutional issues of freedom of speech.

The case of Jacob Abrams began with his arrest in New York City on August 23, 1918. Abrams and several friends had written, printed, and distributed copies of leaflets that severely criticized President Woodrow Wilson and the U.S. government. The leaflets opposed Wilson's decision to send a small American military force to Russia during the civil war there, which followed the communist revolution of 1917. The Communists, led by Vladimir Lenin, were fighting against anticommunist Russians and various foreign military forces to retain control of the government. Abrams's leaflets urged American workers to walk off their jobs in protest against President Wilson and the U.S. government and in support of the new communist government in Russia.

Abrams and his friends were arrested and convicted for violating the Espionage Act of 1917 and the Sedition Act of 1918. They claimed, however, that their First Amendment rights had been violated because both the Espionage and Sedition Acts were unconstitutional infringements of free speech. By a vote of 7–2, the Court upheld the conviction of Abrams and his friends.

Writing for the Court, Justice John H. Clarke cited the *Schenck* decision as precedent and invoked the "bad tendency" test to support the ruling against Abrams. Justice Clarke wrote that "men must be held to have intended and to be accountable for the effects which their acts were likely to produce." In particular, Clarke used the "bad tendency" test to argue that if workers had followed the call of Abrams's leaflets to walk away from their jobs in a general strike, then the production of munitions would have been interrupted, thereby impairing the U.S. government's ability to defend the country in wartime. Clarke's opinion ignored the fact that Abrams's message did not influence workers, and there was no strike in protest of American government policies. The mere possibility of such a bad effect was sufficient, according to Justice Clarke, to justify strict limitation of a person's constitutional right to free speech.

Justice Holmes, joined by Justice Louis D. Brandeis, wrote a strong dissent, in which he developed his "clear and present danger" doctrine as Zechariah Chafee and others had urged him to do. He completely repudiated the "bad tendency" test and refined his "clear and present danger" doctrine to require an immediate or "imminent" harmful effect as the only justification for restricting the content of speech.

Holmes recognized that the government had the right to protect itself against speech that immediately and directly threatened the security and safety of the country and its people. He argued that the First Amendment protects the expression of all opinions "unless they so imminently threaten immediate interference with the lawful and pressing purposes of the law that an immediate check is required to save the country." Holmes emphasized that a "clear and present danger" sufficient to restrict free speech could not exist unless there was an impending lawless action connected directly to the words of a speaker or writer. Holmes concluded that Abrams's actions and intentions were not an imminent danger sufficient to justify limitation of his constitutional right to free speech.

Justice Holmes concluded his dissent with a compelling theory of free speech in a constitutional democracy. Arguing for a "free trade in ideas,"

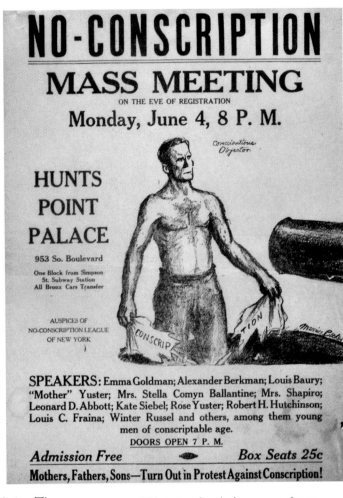

This poster advertised a mass meeting to protest military conscription featuring such radical speakers as Emma Goldman and Alexander Berkman. The Espionage Act of 1917 made any actions that impeded conscription, including organizing or attending such a meeting, criminal offenses.

Holmes said: "[T]he best test of truth is the power of the thought to get itself accepted in the competition of the market.... That at any rate is the theory of our Constitution. It is an experiment, as all life is an experiment."

The Court's opinion in *Abrams* prevailed in the short run, but Holmes's dissent eventually influenced the Court. Today, it is recognized as the foundation for contemporary constitutional doctrine on the individual's right to free speech.

The fate of those victimized by the Espionage and Sedition Acts varied. Most served their sentences, but Eugene Debs, a national celebrity of sorts, was pardoned by President Warren G. Harding in 1921. Jacob Abrams and his associates were less fortunate. Upon completion of their prison sentences, they were deported, at their own expense, to Soviet Russia. However, the land they had imagined as a "paradise for workers" turned out to be more like hell for them. They had little latitude for freedom of expression or any other kind of civil liberty under the totalitarian regime of the Soviet Union, which also eventually deported them.

From 1919 until his retirement from the Court in 1932, Justice Holmes continued to argue for the refined version of the "clear and present danger" doctrine expressed in his *Abrams* dissent. However, the Court did not use this doctrine to uphold a freedom of speech claim until 1937, in *Herndon* v. *Lowry*, when by a narrow vote of 5–4 the free speech rights of an American Communist Party member were protected. In the 1969 case *Brandenburg* v. *Ohio,* the Court again applied the ideas about free speech first expressed by Holmes in the 1919 *Abrams* case. The Court unanimously upheld the free speech rights of a Ku Klux Klan leader and struck down a state of Ohio law restricting speech that had a tendency to cause public harm. Free speech rights had become broad enough to protect even a despicable racist message, which was constitutionally permissible unless it could be demonstrably and immediately linked to lawless behavior.

Based on everything we know about Holmes, it is certain that he would have rejected the contemptible racist speech of a Ku Klux Klan leader, but he would have hailed the latitude for civil liberty afforded even such a person. Holmes, at the peak of his legal career, came to believe that the best way to fight a flawed message was to refute it with superior ideas in a constitutionally protected public arena of free-flowing opinion. And it seems beyond doubt that Holmes would have been pleased that his dissent in the 1919 *Abrams* case was the foundation of the Court's 1969 opinion in *Brandenburg.* Today's constitutional law broadly protecting free speech can be linked to the fertile mind of Justice Oliver Wendell Holmes Jr.

"Free Trade in Ideas"

Oliver Wendell Holmes Jr. is among the most remarkable people ever to serve on the Supreme Court. A heroic medal-winning soldier in the U.S. Army, three times wounded during the Civil War, he served as a highly respected associate justice of the Supreme Court from 1902 until his retirement in 1932. Born in 1841 in Boston, Massachusetts, Holmes died in 1935 in Washington, D.C., and was buried with other military veterans in the national cemetery at Arlington, Virginia.

Holmes was an avid reader of books about literature and philosophy and had a keen intellect and a memorable style of speaking and writing. Many of his Supreme Court opinions, both for the Court and in dissent, are exemplars of a literary style that both informs and inspires the reader. In his later years on the Court, Holmes became known as a champion of the constitutional right to free speech, and he wrote many quotable phrases about it in dissents against the Court's majority, such as this one in United States v. Schwimmer *(1929): "If there is any principle of the Constitution that more imperatively calls for attachment than any other, it is the principle of free thought—not free thought for those who agree with us but freedom for the thought that we hate."*

Many experts in constitutional law consider Holmes's dissent, below, in Abrams v. United States *to be the best legal defense of free speech ever written by an American. A sterling example of profound constitutional thought and eloquent literary style, Holmes's dissent in* Abrams *set a constitutional standard that eventually won enduring endorsement from the Supreme Court.*

I never have seen any reason to doubt that the questions of law that alone were before this Court in the cases of *Schenck, Froherk* and *Debs*... were rightly decided. I do not doubt for a moment that by the same reasoning that would justify punishing persuasion to murder, the United States constitutionally may punish speech that produces or is intended to produce a clear and imminent danger that it will bring about forthwith certain substantive evils that the United States constitutionally may seek to prevent. The power undoubtedly is greater in time of war than in time of peace because war opens dangers that do not exist at other times.

But as against dangers peculiar to war, as against others, the principle of the right to free speech is always the same. It is only the present danger of immediate evil or an intent to bring it about that warrants Congress in setting a limit to the expression of opinion where private rights are not concerned. Congress certainly cannot forbid all effort to change the mind of the country. Now nobody can suppose that the surreptitious publishing of a silly leaflet by an unknown man, without more, would present any immediate danger that its opinions would hinder the success of the government arms or have any appreciable tendency to do so. Publishing those opinions for the very purpose of obstructing however, might indicate a greater danger and at any rate would have the quality of an attempt.... But it seems pretty clear to me that nothing less than that would bring these papers within the scope of the law....

I do not see how anyone can find the intent required by the statute in any of the defendants' words....

Persecution for the expression of opinions seems to me perfectly logical. If you have no doubt of your premises or your power and want a certain result with all your heart you naturally express your wishes in law and sweep away all opposition. To allow opposition by speech seems to indicate that you think the speech impotent. As when a man says that he has squared the circle, or that you do not care whole-heartedly for the result, or that you doubt either your power or your premises. But when men have realized that time has upset many fighting faiths, they may come to believe even more than they believe the very foundations of their own conduct that the ultimate good desired is better reached by free trade in ideas—that the best test of truth is the power of the thought to get itself accepted in the competition of the market, and that truth is the only ground upon which their wishes safely can be carried out. That at any rate is the theory of our Constitution. It is an experiment, as all life is an experiment. Every year if not every day we have to wager our salvation upon some prophecy based upon imperfect knowledge. While that experiment is part of our system I think that we should be eternally vigilant against attempts to check the expression or opinions that we loathe and believe to be fraught with death, unless they so imminently threaten immediate interference with the lawful and pressing purposes of the law that an immediate check is required to save the country.... Only the emergency that makes it immediately dangerous to leave the correction of evil counsels to time warrants making any exception to the sweeping command, "Congress shall make no law... abridging the freedom of speech." Of course I am speaking only of expressions of opinion and exhor-

Oliver Wendell Holmes wrote 873 opinions, more than any other justice, during his years on the Supreme Court. Both his arguments and his eloquence created classic opinions that have continued to influence the Court and resonate with the American public.

tations, which were all that were uttered here, but I regret that I cannot put into more impressive words my belief that in their conviction upon this indictment the defendants were deprived of their rights under the Constitution of the United States.

Mr. Justice Brandeis concurs with the foregoing opinion.

9

Affirming the New Deal

West Coast Hotel v. *Parrish* (1937)

The Great Depression that followed the Wall Street panic of November 1929 was an economic scourge of mammoth proportions. Its effects lingered for a decade and spread around the world. Unemployment soared to almost one-quarter of the American labor force in 1933, a twentieth-century high. Between 1929 and 1932 more than five thousand banks closed their doors and the life savings of millions of Americans evaporated.

In 1932 the Democratic Presidential candidate Franklin D. Roosevelt swept to victory over the Republican incumbent, Herbert Hoover. FDR offered a middle-of-the-road approach to the depression through what he called a "New Deal for America." This program embraced certain social-welfare assumptions, including the idea that government had a positive duty to provide a minimum floor for the well-being of its citizens. FDR enjoyed broad support from the Democratic Congress as well as from the business community, which realized that something had to be done to restore economic confidence. In an effort to do so, FDR created an alphabet soup of agencies. The President successfully urged Congress to pass legislation to create the Securities and Exchange Commission (SEC) to oversee Wall Street and the Tennessee Valley Authority (TVA) to promote economic development in the poverty-stricken Tennessee River Valley. He pushed Congress to pass the Glass-Steagall Act to guarantee bank deposits and the Agricultural Adjustment Act (AAA) to subsidize farmers and prop up commodity prices. The New Deal put people to work on public projects through the Works Progress Administration (WPA) and then provided unemployment insurance and old-age pensions through the Social Security Act (1935).

The most controversial New Deal measure was the National Industrial Recovery Act (NIRA). The act was intended to regulate vast areas of business and labor that had previously been left untouched. The NIRA not only broke down many of the traditional lines blocking government involvement in the economy, but it also shifted significant authority from Congress to the President and through him to a new administrative agency, the National Recovery Administration (NRA).

The New Dealers were pragmatic and determined to end the depression, but they were often impatient with prevailing constitutional rules. FDR, for example, ordered the committee charged with writing the NIRA to complete its work in one week. That impatience proved costly, as critics turned to the Supreme Court for assistance. The justices raised questions about it and other legislation that involved the scope of Presidential emergency powers, the dele-

---

West Coast Hotel v. Parrish

- 300 U.S. 379 (1937)
- Decided: March 29, 1937
- Vote: 5–4
- Opinion of the Court: Charles Evans Hughes
- Dissenting opinion: George Sutherland (Willis Van Devanter, James C. McReynolds, and Pierce Butler)

In 1932, the year that Franklin Roosevelt was first elected President, hundreds of people stand in line to receive food in New York City. FDR's New Deal was designed to relieve such distress, but it encountered strong opposition from the Supreme Court until the decisions in West Coast Hotel v. Parrish *and* NLRB v. Jones & Laughlin Steel Corporation *(both 1937) signaled its willingness to permit the government to actively regulate the economy.*

gation by Congress of its authority to administrative agencies, the breadth of the commerce clause, and the intervention by the national government in matters previously the domain of the states. The result was a collision between the Court—a majority of whose justices saw their responsibility as remaining faithful to the principle that government should have only a limited role in the economy—and the administration, which trumpeted constitutional innovation as the best way to address the plight of millions of Americans.

The make-up of the Court ensured a collision. Its conservative wing was composed of the Four Horsemen, sarcastically named by their New Deal critics after the Four Horsemen of the Apocalypse—war, famine, pestilence, and death—identified in chapter 6 of the Bible's Book of Revelation. Justices Willis Van Devanter, James McReynolds, George Sutherland, and Pierce Butler consistently voted as a bloc against the New Deal. On the other wing were three generally liberal justices: Benjamin N. Cardozo, Louis D. Brandeis, and Harlan Fiske Stone, who supported the New Deal and also believed that judges should defer to the legislative branch. Between these two blocs were the swing votes of Chief Justice Charles Evans Hughes and Justice Owen J. Roberts.

So-called Little New Deals—legislation at the state level intended to offer economic relief—came before the Court for review. In *New State Ice Company* v. *Liebman* (1932), for example, they struck down an Oklahoma law that made the manufacture and sale of ice a public business susceptible to regulation by the state. The justices condemned the law as a state-sanctioned monopoly that interfered with the opportunity for new ice producers to enter the market. Four years later the justices, in a 5–4 decision, rejected a model New York state minimum wage law in *Morehead* v. *New York ex rel. Tipaldo* (1936). The phrase "ex rel." is Latin for "on behalf of." In this instance, the state of New York was acting on behalf of Tipaldo, a private citizen.

Even the liberal members of the Court were skeptical about the constitutional basis of the early New Deal measures. On so-called Black Monday, May 27, 1935, a unanimous Court struck down several key provisions of the New Deal recovery plan: *Louisville Bank* v. *Radford* threw out a mortgage relief act for farmers; *Humphrey's Executor* v. *United States* limited the President's powers to replace members of independent boards; and *Schechter Poultry Company* v. *United States* declared the NRA unconstitutional. The AAA was rejected, as well.

Roosevelt won a landslide victory in 1936 over his Republican opponent, Alfred Landon, with a campaign in which he regularly attacked the Court. He began his second term by directly confronting the justices. Roosevelt was especially frustrated because during his first term no vacancies had occurred on the high bench. FDR's supporters complained that the justices were too old and too out of touch with the times. The newspaper columnists Drew Pearson and

Robert S. Allen in 1936 wrote an exposé of the Court, and the public fastened its title, *The Nine Old Men,* on the justices. The description was far from accurate; the oldest member of the Court, Louis D. Brandeis, was in fact a member of the Court's liberal wing.

With his election triumph only months old, FDR on March 9, 1937, laid out his plans for the Court in one of his nationwide "Fireside Chats" on the radio. This talk was designed to garner public support for his Judiciary Reorganization Bill. FDR proposed to appoint one additional justice to the Court for every sitting justice over the age of seventy, up to a limit of six new justices. There were five justices over seventy and that meant the Court would grow immediately to fourteen. The plan also called for a significant increase in the number of federal circuit and district court judges.

The proposal ignited a storm of protest, even from commentators angry with the Court's hostility to the New Deal. The President seemed to many Americans to place politics above the rule of law. Critics charged FDR with an ill-advised attack on a bedrock American institution, the Supreme Court, and dubbed the plan "court-packing," a title that stuck to FDR's proposal. The plan was entirely legal, as Congress has constitutional authority to change the size of the high court. Nonetheless, it focused intense scrutiny on the Court, appeared to be a direct threat to the independence of the justices, and raised the specter of a President seeking to usurp constitutional power. The measure also divided congressional Democrats, in part because FDR failed to reach out to them before announcing his plan.

Roosevelt cloaked his court-packing scheme in the rhetoric of judicial reform. More judges were required to clear the dockets of the lower federal courts, he explained. The argument met a cold response from the justices. The dockets of these courts had expanded dramatically in the twentieth century, but Chief Justice Charles Evans Hughes reminded Congress that putting more justices on the Court would only slow its work. In the final analysis, the President attempted to pull every possible lever to make his blatantly political proposal work. For example, Roosevelt and his attorney general, Homer Cummings, sought support from the labor unions by stressing that Democratic appointees to the lower courts would curtail the practice of federal judges issuing injunctions against workers engaged in strikes and lockouts.

The Judiciary Reorganization Bill, while probably doomed from the outset, suffered from some bad luck. Senator Joseph T. Robinson, of Arkansas, the Senate floor manager for the bill and a strong ally of the President, died during the summer while the measure was being debated. The Court itself also seemingly influenced the outcome; at least some historians believe that a few of the justices read and understood the 1936 election returns—FDR had the support of the American public.

It was in the context of this most aggressive attack on the Court in its history that the justices heard the case of *West Coast Hotel* v. *Parrish* (1937). Their decision in the case marked the beginning of the end of the era of economic substantive due process law. Scholars of the Court have described it as a "A Switch in Time That Saved Nine." That is, the two swing votes on the Court, Hughes and Roberts, aligned themselves with the liberal wing to give a constitutional green light to the next generation of New Deal legislation. The most important "switch" was Roberts, who had voted with the majority in *Morehead* to strike down the New York State minimum wage law.

Elsie Parrish was a chambermaid at the Cascadian Hotel in Wenatchee, Washington, where she was paid twelve dollars for a forty-eight-hour week. Under a 1913 state minimum wage law she should have received $14.50. She sued the hotel in state court and won, but the hotel appealed. The case was argued two months before President Roosevelt announced his court-packing program and decided two weeks afterward.

By 1937, the Court had more than thirty years of experience with laws protecting women in industry. In 1908, in *Muller* v. *Oregon,* the Court upheld a ten-hour workday law for women workers while simultaneously affirming the precedent of liberty to contract for men established in *Lochner* v. *New York* (1903). In 1917, in *Bunting* v. *Oregon,* the justices approved a ten-hour law for both men and women without ever mentioning *Lochner.* In 1923, in *Adkins* v. *Children's Hospital,* however, the Court resurrected the precedent set in *Lochner* and struck down a federal minimum wage law for women working in the District of Columbia. The majority in this 5–3 case (Brandeis recused himself because his daughter worked for the District's minimum wage board) insisted that workers should be free to find the best employment terms. In 1936, the Court relied on the *Adkins* precedent to overturn the New York State minimum wage law in *Morehead.* In the words of Justice Pierce Butler, one of the Four Horsemen, the "State is without power by any form of legislation to prohibit, change, or nullify contracts between employers and adult women workers as to the amount of wages to be paid."

The decision in *Morehead,* with its strident and uncompromising tone in the midst of the Great Depression, was one of the Court's biggest mistakes. The building of a majority, however, depended especially on the vote of Justice Roberts. In this instance Roberts sided with his conservative colleagues, providing the fifth vote to reject the minimum wage legislation. Speculation was that he would do the same in *West Coast Hotel.* As it turned out, he did not.

The underlying constitutional issues in the case cut to the core of the New Deal: the power of legislators to pass measures designed to cushion the blow delivered by the depression. The legal counsel for the hotel company believed he and his client were on safe ground in attacking Washington State's 1913 minimum wage law. First, it had been passed well before the depression even began and therefore could not be justified as "emergency" legislation designed to deal with a broken economy. Second, the controlling precedent was *Adkins* v. *Children's Hospital* (1923), in which the justices had struck down a 1918 minimum wage law for women working in the District of Columbia. The Washington State statute was unconstitutional, counsel argued, because it set up one standard—that wages must be sufficient to provide for adult women workers' needs—but it

Elsie Parrish worked as a chambermaid at the ten-story Cascadian Hotel in Wenatchee, Washington, which was owned by the West Coast Hotel Company. Parrish won her suit to be paid the minimum state wage, but because the minimum wage for women rested on the idea that women were inferior to men, feminists opposed the decision on the grounds that it was an impediment to employment opportunities for women.

did not require that the wage have any reasonable relationship to the value of the worker's services.

Counsel for Parrish argued that the timing of the passage of the law was irrelevant. If it was important in 1913, then surely it was even more important in the midst of the depression. The only issue was whether the 1913 act was a reasonable exercise of the state's police powers over health, safety, morals, and welfare. The Constitution did not prohibit any state from regulating such matters. The Court, Parrish's counsel noted, had previously upheld similar legislation in *Nebbia* v. *New York* (1934) by a vote of 5–4. In that case, Justice Roberts had voted with the majority and proclaimed that legislators could act as long as they did so with the goal of promoting the public welfare. Parrish's counsel drew on Roberts's arguments to remind the other justices that they should defer to legislators, as they and not judges were best positioned to determine what matters of public welfare required attention. In passing the minimum wage law, the Washington legislature had considered appropriately the needs of the people of the state.

Parrish's counsel also suggested that the Court's long-standing commitment to the rule of reason should be set aside in this case. That rule provided that the justices could overturn legislative acts that interfered with economic activity as unwise or unreasonable, highly subjective standards and ones that gave the justices broad powers to second-guess legislative actions. What was reasonable was largely in the minds of the justices. Parrish's counsel argued against these subjective standards of judicial oversight and for recognition of two obvious realities. First, the Constitution granted the state of Washington the power to enact minimum wage laws through the police powers. And, second, the law had received the approval of the state's highest court. The justices of the U.S. Supreme Court should defer to the decisions of state court judges, especially as they had never reversed any state supreme court decision that upheld a local minimum wage regulation.

Chief Justice Charles Evans Hughes wrote the majority opinion for a badly divided Court. It was said that no one ever slapped Charles Evans Hughes on his back and called him "Charlie." He was stern, hardworking, religious, and noted more for his intelligence than his conviviality. He had a photographic memory that intimidated his colleagues. Yet he was generous, kind, and forbearing in an institution in which egos typically came in only one size: extra large.

The key support for Hughes's 5 to 4 majority came from Justice Roberts, who shifted to the liberal side, as he had done in *Nebbia*. The Court upheld the Washington State law and overturned *Adkins* v. *Children's Hospital*. Hughes's opinion affirmed the principle that the Constitution forbade deprivation of liberty to contract if done without due process of law, but confirmed that the legislature has broad scope to restrain or regulate this liberty. Legislation such as the law passed in Washington was constitutional when it was adopted for the protection of the community. In dealing with the relationship of employer and employee, the legislature had to have wide discretion, including responsibility to insure that conditions of work were wholesome and free from oppression. The state, Hughes concluded, had a special interest in protecting women against employment contracts that through poor working conditions, long hours, or scant wages could undermine their health. Because the health of women was tied closely to preserving "the strength and vigor of the race," the state had to protect women from being exploited by unscrupulous employers. The Washington minimum wage law was not an act of arbitrary discrimination because it did not extend to men; instead, as had been true in *Muller* v. *Oregon* (1908), it was a realistic response to the vulnerable condition of women. Hughes also observed that the unparalleled demands for relief that arose during the Great Depression remained and that the states had, through their police powers, the authority to address its consequences.

Justice George Sutherland wrote for the dissenting Four Horsemen. Sutherland was born in England but raised in Utah, where he practiced law and achieved a measure of Republican political prominence. He offered his vote and voice in support of substantive due process, liberty to contract, and continuing judicial barriers to state government regulation and control. From Sutherland's perspective, Washington State had unreasonably violated the holding in *Adkins*. Women and men, he insisted, were equals, and legislation should not treat them differently. The setting of a minimum wage for women was an arbitrary form of discrimination prohibited by the due process clause of the Fourteenth Amendment.

West Coast Hotel heralded greater Supreme Court deference to state economic regulation. It also forged a strange ideological partnership; the Four Horsemen and feminists formed an awkward alliance. Because the minimum wage for women rested on a theory of women's inequality, and because labor restrictions based on gender interfered with women's employment opportunities, many feminists denounced Hughes's opinion and opposed minimum wage laws for women in general.

The decision helped close the door on FDR's court-packing plan because a majority of the justices signaled that they were moving toward supporting New Deal economic measures. That signal became even more clear two weeks later when the justices, in *NLRB* v. *Jones & Laughlin Steel Corporation*, upheld one of the most important and radical pieces of New Deal legislation, the National Labor Relations Act, also known as the Wagner Act. That measure, passed in 1935, guaranteed workers' right to organize unions and prohibited employers from dismissing them for doing so. Once again the justices split 5 to 4, with the Four Horsemen in the minority. By

This 1937 leaflet urges hotel maids to attend a union organizing meeting to demand minimum wage protection. The decisions in West Coast Hotel *and* Jones & Laughlin *stimulated union efforts to secure additional benefits for their members.*

Hotel Maids!

NOW IS THE TIME TO ACT!

By joining your union you can get these benefits now enjoyed by those hotel maids already organized:

1. Limited number of rooms
2. Increase in wages
3. Time off for lunch
4. Vacations with pay
5. Job security

UNORGANIZED
You're underpaid and tired, have no job security

Every day you delay joining the union means a day's delay in obtaining these benefits.

The law protects your job when you carry on organization work

THE LAW

known as the New York State Labor Relations Act says it is illegal for your employer to discriminate against you because of union activities or to intimidate you in your efforts to join a labor union.

●

HOTEL DIVISION

Hotel, Restaurant and Cafeteria Employees Organization Committee
Affiliated with the American Federation of Labor
711 — 8th Avenue New York City

ORGANIZED
You smile because you win better conditions

upholding the legislation, the Court made it clear that it would no longer block congressional efforts to regulate the national economy.

The Court proceeded to affirm other key elements of FDR's program. On May 24, 1937, in *Steward Machine Company* v. *Davis*, the justices upheld the Social Security Act, a landmark law that established mechanisms to provide for unemployment compensation and old-age benefits. The unemployment provision meant that workers thrown out of their jobs would receive a basic level of support until they could find new work. The old-age benefit meant that for the first time, the national government would provide a limited financial safety net through pensions to workers beyond a certain age. The *West Coast Hotel* and *Jones & Laughlin* decisions also provided legal support for another piece of New Deal legislation, the Fair Labor Standards Act of 1938, which the Court upheld in *United States* v. *Darby Lumber Company*. This law provided for the setting of federal minimum wages and maximum hours for all employees in industries whose products were shipped through interstate commerce.

Although the justices did not formally abandon substantive due process in economic regulatory cases, there was no doubt that they had retreated from the business of trying to regulate business. Between 1937 and 1980, the Supreme Court cited *West Coast Hotel* and *Jones & Laughlin* some forty-one times, a fair indication of the importance of the cases in affirming the new administrative and social welfare state wrought by the New Deal.

The impact of the Court's decisions in *West Coast Hotel* and *Jones & Laughlin* was far reaching. With these new precedents in place, the Court upheld virtually every federal and state regulation of business for the next half century. By indicating that they would no longer use liberty to contract and substantive due process as a basis to interfere with economic legislation, the justices were able to turn their attention to civil liberties and civil rights, issues that dominated the post–World War II Court. In the conservative glow of the 1990s the Court did begin to question whether Congress was too actively engaged in regulating the economy, but the New Deal precedents retain great importance.

In the end, the Court emerged from FDR's attack stronger than ever. The American people concluded that law and politics should be separated, and that while the justices might not be above politics, they served the nation best when they acted as if they were.

"Packing the Court"

President Franklin D. Roosevelt understood the necessity of reassuring the average American and also asserting his Presidential authority during the Great Depression and World War II. He also realized that the new technology of radio could help him in doing so. FDR broadcast his fireside chats from the White House between 1934 and 1944, delivering his remarks in a confident voice that held much of the nation spellbound. This particular fireside chat was delivered on March 9, 1937, shortly after his landslide reelection.

Tonight, sitting at my desk in the White House, I make my first radio report to the people in my second term of office.

In 1933 you and I knew that we must never let our economic system get completely out of joint again—that we could not afford to take the risk of another great depression.

We also become convinced that the only way to avoid a repetition of those dark days was to have a government with power to prevent and to cure the abuses and the inequalities which had thrown that system out of joint.

The American people have learned from the depression. For in the last three national elections an overwhelming majority of them voted a mandate that the Congress and the President begin the task of providing that protection—not after long years of debate, but now.

The Courts, however, have cast doubts on the ability of the elected Congress to protect us against catastrophe by meeting squarely our modern social and economic conditions.

We are at a crisis, a crisis in our ability to proceed with that protection.

I want to talk with you very simply tonight about the need for present action in this crisis—the need to meet the unanswered challenge of one-third of a Nation ill-nourished, ill-clad, ill-housed.

Last Thursday I described the American form of Government as a three-horse team provided by the Constitution to the American people so that their field might be plowed. The three horses are, of course, the Congress, the Executive and the Courts. Two of the horses, the Congress and the Executive, are pulling in unison today; the third is not. Those who have intimated that the President of the United States is trying to drive that team, overlook the simple fact that the President, as Chief Executive, is himself one of the horses.

It is the American people themselves who are in the driver's seat. It is the American people themselves who want the furrow plowed.

It is the American people themselves who expect the third horse to pull in unison with the other two.

I hope that you have re-read the Constitution of the United States in these past few weeks. Like the Bible, it ought to be read again and again.

It is an easy document to understand when you remember that it was called into being because the Articles of Confederation under which the original thirteen States tried to operate after the Revolution showed the need of a National Government with power enough to handle national problems. In its Preamble, the Constitution states that it was intended to form a more perfect Union and promote the general welfare; and the powers given to the Congress to carry out those purposes can best be described by saying that they were all the powers needed to meet each and every problem which then had a national character and which could not be met by merely local action.

But the framers went further. Having in mind that in succeeding generations many other problems then undreamed of would become national problems, they gave to the Congress the ample broad powers "to levy taxes and provide for the common defense and general welfare of the United States."

That, my friends, is what I honestly believe to have been the clear and underlying purpose of the patriots who wrote a Federal Constitution to create a National Government with national power, intended as they said, "to form a more perfect union for ourselves and our posterity."...

Then in 1803...the Court claimed the power to declare [a federal law] unconstitutional and did so declare it. But a little later the Court itself admitted that it was an extraordinary power to exercise and through Mr. Justice Washington laid down this limitation upon it. He said: "It is but a decent respect due to the wisdom, the integrity and the patriotism of the Legislative body, by which any law is passed, to presume in favor of its validity until its violation of the Constitution is proved beyond all reasonable doubt."

But since the rise of the modern movement for social and economic progress through legislation, the Court has more and more often and more and more boldly asserted a power to veto laws passed by the Congress and by State Legislatures in complete disregard of this original limitation, which I have just read.

In the last four years the sound rule of giving statutes the benefit of all reasonable doubt has been cast aside. The Court has been acting not as a judicial body, but as a policy-making body.

The Court, in addition to the proper use of its judicial functions, has improperly set itself up as a third House of the Congress—a super-legislature, as one of the Justices has called it—reading into the Constitution words and implications which are not there, and which were never intended to be there.

We have, therefore, reached the point as a Nation where we must take action to save the Constitution from the Court, and the Court from itself. We must

Franklin D. Roosevelt, surrounded by microphones from the three major radio networks, delivers one of his thirty fireside chats to the nation. The President used this medium on March 9, 1937, in a failed effort to have Congress adopt legislation that would permit him to "pack" the Supreme Court with supporters of his New Deal legislation.

find a way to take an appeal from the Supreme Court to the Constitution itself. We want a Supreme Court which will do justice under the Constitution—not over it. In our Courts we want a government of laws and not of men.

I want—as all Americans want—an independent judiciary as proposed by the framers of the Constitution. That means a Supreme Court that will enforce the Constitution as written—that will refuse to amend the Constitution by the arbitrary exercise of judicial power—amendment, in other words, by judicial say-so. It does not mean a judiciary so independent that it can deny the existence of facts which are universally recognized.

What is my proposal? It is simply this: Whenever a Judge or Justice of any Federal Court has reached the age of seventy and does not avail himself of the opportunity to retire on a pension, a new member shall be appointed by the President then in office, with the approval, as required by the Constitution, of the Senate of the United States.

That plan has two chief purposes. By bringing into the Judicial system a steady and continuing stream of new and younger blood, I hope, first, to make the administration of all Federal justice, from the bottom to the top, speedier and, therefore, less costly; secondly, to bring to the decision of social and economic problems younger men who have had personal experience and contact with modern facts and circumstances under which average men have to live and work. This plan will save our national Constitution from hardening of the judicial arteries....

Those opposing this plan have sought to arouse prejudice and fear by crying that I am seeking to "pack" the Supreme Court and that a baneful precedent will be established.

What do they mean by the words "packing the Supreme Court"?

Let me answer this question with a bluntness that will end all honest misunderstanding of my purposes.

If by that phrase "packing the Court" it is charged that I wish to place on the bench spineless puppets who would disregard the law and would decide specific cases as I wished them to be decided, I make this answer—that no President fit for this office would appoint, and no Senate of honorable men fit for their office would confirm, that kind of appointees to the Supreme Court.

But if by that phrase the charge is made that I would appoint and the Senate would confirm Justices worthy to sit beside present members of the Court who understand modern conditions—that I will appoint Justices who will not undertake to override the judgment of the Congress on legislative policy—that I will appoint Justices who will act as Justices and not as legislators—if the appointment of such Justices can be called "packing the Court," then I say that I, and with me the vast majority of the American people, favor doing just that thing—now....

So, I now propose that we establish by law an assurance against any ill-balanced Court in the future. I propose that hereafter, when a Judge reaches the age of seventy, a new and younger Judge shall be added to the Court automatically. In this way I propose to enforce a sound public policy by law instead of leaving the composition of our Federal Courts, including the highest, to be determined by chance or the personal decision of individuals....

Like all lawyers, like all Americans, I regret the necessity of this controversy. But the welfare of the United States, and indeed of the Constitution itself, is what we all must think about first. Our difficulty with the Court today rises not from the Court as an institution but from human beings within it. We cannot yield our constitutional destiny to the personal judgment of a few men who, being fearful of the future, would deny us the necessary means of dealing with the present.

This plan of mine is no attack on the Court; it seeks to restore the Court to its rightful and historic place in our system of Constitutional Government and to have it resume its high task of building anew on the Constitution "a system of living law." The Court itself can best undo what the Court has done.

10

The Flag-Salute Cases

Minersville School District v. *Gobitis* (1940)
West Virginia State Board of Education v. *Barnette* (1943)

In a constitutional democracy such as the United States, there inevitably is tension between majority rule and the rights of individuals in the minority. Citizens and their government continually confront two challenging questions. At what point, and under what circumstances, should the will of the majority be limited in order to protect the rights of individuals in the minority? And, conversely, what limits must be placed on the rights of dissenting individuals in order to maintain the authority of majority rule? These questions are never answered definitively, because the justifiable placement of limitations will inevitably vary according to the circumstances of particular cases. Further, a conclusive response in favor of one principle over the other—majority rule over minority rights or vice versa—would deeply disturb a delicate balance necessary to maintain justice in a constitutional democracy.

During the early 1940s, the U.S. Supreme Court confronted two cases in which majority rule came into conflict with minority rights. Both cases involved clashes between the authority of majorities in state or local governments to mandate patriotic rituals in public schools and the rights of individuals in the minority not to comply. In the first case, *Minersville School District* v. *Gobitis,* the Court decided in 1940 to uphold a local school board requirement that all students must recite the Pledge of Allegiance while saluting the flag of the United States in a classroom ceremony. Only three years later, the Supreme Court faced essentially the same issue in *West Virginia State Board of Education* v. *Barnette* and struck down a state school board mandate that public school students must participate daily in the same kind of patriotic ritual upheld by the 1940 *Gobitis* decision.

The Court's decision in the *Barnette* case to overturn a decision made only three years earlier in *Gobitis* was most unusual. Ordinarily the Court follows its rule of stare decisis, a Latin phrase meaning, "let the decision stand." According to stare decisis, judges should maintain consistency and stability in the law by following precedents of earlier decisions in similar cases. The rule of stare decisis is binding upon judges in federal district courts and circuit courts of appeals. By contrast, Supreme Court justices, while reluctant to tamper with precedents, have more latitude to modify or overturn them. This is not done often and hardly ever within a three-year period, as the Court did in the *Barnette* decision in 1943. The flag-salute cases, as they came to be called, are instructive examples of how and why the Court may overturn a precedent.

The central issues of the *Gobitis* and *Barnette* cases arose in 1936, when twelve-year-old Lillian Gobitas and her ten-year-old brother William came

---

Minersville School District v. Gobitis

- 310 U.S. 586 (1940)
- Decided: June 3, 1940
- Vote: 8–1
- Opinion of the Court: Felix Frankfurter
- Dissenting opinion: Harlan Fiske Stone

West Virginia State Board of Education v. Barnette

- 319 U.S. 624 (1943)
- Decided: June 14, 1943
- Vote: 6–3
- Opinion of the Court: Robert H. Jackson
- Concurring opinions: Hugo L. Black (William O. Douglas) and Frank Murphy
- Dissenting opinion: Felix Frankfurter
- Dissenting without opinion: Stanley F. Reed and Owen J. Roberts

home from school with news that disturbed their parents. (The family's name is correctly spelled "Gobitas," but a court clerk misspelled it "Gobitis" and the case involving this family is officially known by the misspelled name.) The Gobitas children had been expelled from their Minersville, Pennsylvania, school for refusing to salute the American flag during the morning patriotic exercises. The Gobitas family belonged to the Jehovah's Witnesses, a religion that prohibits any act, including saluting the flag, that is like worshipping a graven image or idol, which is an offense against God.

Lillian and William's father, Walter Gobitas, appealed to the Minersville School Board to excuse his children from the flag-salute requirement. The board refused, and Gobitas withdrew his children from the public school and placed them in a private school, where the patriotic exercises were not required. Then he sued in the federal district court at Philadelphia to stop the school board from requiring children in public schools to salute the flag. He claimed that his children's rights to religious liberty under the First and Fourteenth Amendments to the U.S. Constitution had been violated.

Lawyers for the Minersville School Board argued that the flag-salute requirement was a reasonable way to teach good citizenship to students. They claimed that it was strictly a "secular regulation" that had nothing to do with religion and everything to do with patriotic education. Furthermore, they argued that permitting some students to opt out of the ceremony would interfere with the school's duty to promote national loyalty and unity. They concluded by claiming that the school's expulsion of children who dissented against the flag-salute ceremony did not violate their constitutional rights.

Public school students in Southington, Connecticut, participate in a patriotic ceremony in May 1942. Such ceremonies involving the Pledge of Allegiance and the national flag were commonly conducted across the United States to express popular support for American military forces during World War II.

Judges of the federal district court and later the U.S. Court of Appeals for the Third Circuit decided against the Minersville School District. The local school board responded with an appeal to the U.S. Supreme Court, which heard the case in 1940.

Three times previously, the Court had let stand flag-salute requirements in terse, unsigned per curiam (by the court) opinions that deferred to lower court decisions and the rights and powers of state governments to deal with this issue. Only one year earlier, for example, the Court had unanimously denied an appeal of a California Supreme Court decision that had ruled in favor of a local flag-salute law. However, the *Gobitis* case was different because this time the lower courts had ruled against a flag-salute requirement on the grounds that it denied the plaintiff's constitutional right to religious liberty. The context had also changed; patriotic sentiment was rising throughout the United States in response to national security threats posed by the eruption of World War II in Europe and Asia.

Big-time legal talent came forward to argue against the flag-salute requirement of the Minersville School District. George Gardner of the Harvard Law School faculty was the leading advocate, and lawyers representing the American Civil Liberties Union and the Bill of Rights Committee of the American Bar Association filed supporting briefs. Zechariah Chafee, another professor at Harvard Law School and the primary author of the Bill of Rights Committee's brief, wrote that "there is no such public need for the compulsory flag salute as to justify the overriding of the religious scruples of the children."

The weighty arguments of the lawyers were to no avail. The Court voted 8–1 to reverse the two lower federal court decisions and thereby to uphold the school district's requirement that students participate in the daily flag-salute ceremony.

Justice Felix Frankfurter wrote the opinion of the Court. He maintained that the individual's right to religious liberty in this case must give way to state authority, as long as the state neither directly promoted nor restricted religion. The school board's flag-salute requirement was constitutional because it met this requirement.

Frankfurter reasoned that the students' right to religious liberty in this case had to be balanced against the school board's right to exercise authority in regard to a patriotic ceremony. The Court's challenge was to "reconcile two rights to prevent either from destroying the other." He assumed that national unity is the basis for national security, which must be promoted for the common good. Thus, if a local school board believed that a compulsory flag salute promoted national unity, especially in a time of crisis, then the Court should not prevent that school board from requiring such a patriotic ceremony.

Frankfurter concluded that in cases such as this one the Court should not use judicial review to thwart majority rule. Instead, it should defer to the will of the people and their democratically elected representatives in government. At this time, when World War II had begun and America seemed threatened, public opinion strongly favored patriotic and civic obligations, which undoubtedly influenced the Court's *Gobitis* decision.

Justice Frankfurter had hoped for a unanimous decision, but he could not dissuade Justice Harlan Fiske Stone from writing a strong dissent. Stone argued that when the government attempts to force individuals to express a belief they do not genuinely hold, it violates their First and Fourteenth Amendment rights. Furthermore, he pointed to other ways in which patriotism could be instilled in students without recourse to coercion or punishment.

Within three years, the majority of the Court came to agree with Stone's dissent, and the precedent set by *Gobitis* was overturned. Two factors appear to account for this reversal. First, there was an outburst of negative responses to the *Gobitis* decision in newspaper editorials and magazine articles. More than 170 newspapers throughout the country opposed the Court's decision. For example, the *St. Louis Post-Dispatch* repudiated the *Gobitis* ruling with this abrupt statement: "We think this decision of the United States Supreme Court is dead wrong." Most professors at the leading law schools were also very critical of the *Gobitis* decision, which certainly caught the attention of the justices.

Second, the *Gobitis* decision aroused a nationwide rash of violence by misguided "super-patriots" against members of the unpopular Jehovah's Witnesses, which likely prompted reconsideration among some of the justices about their ruling. For example, a mob in Kennebunk, Maine, burned a Jehovah's Witnesses meeting hall. In Connersville, Indiana, an unruly crowd assaulted a lawyer who was trying to help besieged Jehovah's Witnesses and drove him out of town. In Odessa, Texas, townspeople rounded up Jehovah's Witnesses and told them to salute their nation's flag; when the Witnesses refused this command, the mob threw stones at them. These are three examples of the violence that typified the harsh treatment of Jehovah's Witnesses in all regions of the United States. This flagrant persecution of a vulnerable minority certainly aroused concern among the justices and among many in the general public. Such a blatant violation of human rights in America seemed especially appalling at a time when the Nazis were persecuting and killing Jews and other targeted minorities in Europe.

Two years after the *Gobitis* decision, three justices publicly reported that they had changed their minds about compulsory flag-salute ceremonies in schools. Hugo L. Black, William O. Douglas, and Frank Murphy, who had joined Justice Frankfurter in the *Gobitis* decision, dissented from the Court's majority opinion in a 1942 case, *Jones* v. *Opelika,* about free exercise of religion by Jehovah's Witnesses. In their dissent, they declared, "Since we joined in the opinion of the *Gobitis* case, we think this is an appropriate occasion to state that we now believe that it was also wrongly decided."

Another factor accounting for the Court's reversal of opinion about the *Gobitis* decision was a change in its membership and leadership. Two new members, Robert H. Jackson and Wiley B. Rutledge, who joined the Court after the *Gobitis* decision, were known for their strong support of civil liberties, and both seemed likely to oppose coerced participation in patriotic rituals. And Harlan Fiske Stone, the lone dissenter against the *Gobitis* decision, had replaced Charles Evans Hughes as chief justice. A new point of view regarding compulsory flag-salute ceremonies seemed to be emerging within the Court.

An opportunity for the Supreme Court to reverse the *Gobitis* decision came in 1943 with the case of *West Virginia State Board of Education* v. *Barnette.* At issue was a state board of education resolution that required all schools to make the flag-salute ceremony a regular part of the daily schedule. The resolution ominously declared that noncompliance would be "regarded as an act of insubordination and shall be dealt with accordingly"; noncomplying students would be expelled from school. Schools could not readmit them until they agreed to perform the salute, and the state would consider them "unlawfully absent." Recalcitrant students could be punished by confinement in a state reformatory for juvenile offenders, and their parents could be fined fifty dollars and sentenced to thirty days in jail.

Walter Gobitas supports his children, William and Lillian, after they were expelled from school for refusing to salute the American flag. More than fifty years later, Lillian expressed satisfaction in the stand for civil liberties she had made as a twelve-year-old. "I would do it again in a second," she said.

Soon after proclaiming the flag-salute resolution in January 1942, public school officials in Charleston, West Virginia, expelled several Jehovah's Witnesses, including the children of Walter Barnette, for refusing to participate with their classmates in the required patriotic ceremony. Barnette, joined by other Jehovah's Witnesses, asked the federal district court for an injunction to stop enforcement of the flag-salute requirements, and this request was granted by a three-judge panel. The lower federal courts usually followed precedent, but the three-judge panel in this instance chose to break away from the *Gobitis* precedent.

Judge John J. Parker acknowledged that the lower federal court typically would "feel constrained to follow an unreversed decision of the Supreme Court of the United States, whether we agreed with it or not." But he doubted that *Gobitis* was still binding because the strong dissents of three justices in the *Opelika* case appeared to have undermined the decision's authority. Furthermore, Parker explained that the three-judge panel considered the West Virginia flag-salute requirement to be "violative of religious liberty when required of persons holding the religious views of the plaintiffs." He concluded that it would be a dereliction of judicial duty to "deny protection to rights which we regard as among the most sacred of those protected by constitutional guarantees."

West Virginia school officials reluctantly obeyed the federal court's order. No more Jehovah's Witnesses were expelled from schools for noncompliance with the flag-salute resolution, and those previously punished were permitted to return to their classes.

The issue seemed to be settled until the West Virginia State Board of Education decided to appeal the case directly to the U.S. Supreme Court, which readily accepted this opportunity to settle the status of constitutional law on this hot issue. Once again the American Civil Liberties Union and the American Bar Association's Committee on the Bill of Rights rallied to support the constitutional rights of an unpopular minority group, and they submitted briefs to the Court in support of Barnette.

By a 6–3 vote, the Supreme Court upheld the lower federal court's ruling and reversed the precedent that had been established in the *Gobitis* decision.

On November 5, 1935, Billy Gobitas wrote this letter to the public school directors of Minersville, Pennsylvania, to explain why he refused to participate in a mandated classroom flag-salute ceremony. He quotes the biblical passage that prohibits the worship of any graven image to demonstrate that it would violate his religious beliefs to salute the flag of the United States.

> Minersville, Pa.
> Nov. 5, 1935
>
> Our School Directors
> Dear Sirs
>
> I do not salute the flag because I have promised to do the will of God. That means that I must not worship anything out of harmony with God's law. In the twentieth chapter of Exodus it is stated, "Thou shall not make unto thee any graven image, nor bow down to them nor serve them for I the Lord thy God am a jealous God visiting the iniquity of the fathers upon the children

Voting with the Court's majority were Chief Justice Stone and Justices Black, Douglas, Murphy, Jackson, and Rutledge. Justice Robert Jackson wrote the opinion of the Court. Felix Frankfurter, who had written for the Court in *Gobitis,* was now in the minority, and he wrote a dissenting opinion.

In his opinion for the Court in *Barnette,* Justice Jackson did not focus narrowly on the abridgment of the individual's First Amendment right to free exercise of religion, as others had done in cases of this kind. Instead, he based his opinion broadly on several individual freedoms in the Bill of Rights, especially freedom of speech, which he linked to free exercise of religion. Jackson thought the basic issue in *Gobitis* and *Barnette* was whether the government has authority under the Constitution to compel participation in any kind of public ceremony, regardless of the person's religious beliefs. He held that the government had no such authority to infringe upon the individual's constitutionally protected rights to freedom of expression.

Deeply embedded in Justice Jackson's opinion is a fundamental principle of constitutional democracy in the United States regarding majority rule and minority rights. There is majority rule by representatives of the people, who are elected by voters in free, fair, and competitive elections, but the First Amendment rights to freedom of speech, press, religion, assembly, and petition cannot be overridden by the opinions or the votes of a majority. Rather, these rights, the inviolable possession of each individual, are guaranteed by the rule of law in the Constitution, and they will continue to be protected as long as this document is the supreme law of the land.

Justice Felix Frankfurter opened his dissenting opinion with a memorable statement that evoked pathos, especially in view of Nazi atrocities against Jews during the world war that was raging at the time of the *Barnette* decision. Frankfurter, a Jewish immigrant to America from Austria, wrote,

> One who belongs to the most vilified and persecuted minority in history is not likely to be insensible to the freedoms guaranteed by our Constitution. Were my purely personal attitude relevant, I should wholeheartedly associate myself with the general libertarian views in the Court's opinion, representing, as they do, the thought and action of a lifetime. But, as judges, we are neither Jew nor Gentile, neither Catholic nor agnostic. We owe equal attachment to the Constitution, and are equally bound by our judicial obligation whether we derive our citizenship from the earliest or the latest immigrants to these shores.

Having revealed his deep and abiding sentiments, Justice Frankfurter expressed his sense of judicial duty, which was, in his opinion, to observe stare decisis and respect the precedent of the Court's *Gobitis* decision, and thereby to support the constitutional authority of the state school board in requiring public school students to salute the U.S. flag. He argued that the Court had overstepped its bounds by imposing its judgments on the people in place of decisions by their democratically elected representatives in government. In a democracy, argued Frankfurter, public policy is properly made by the political branches of government, and the judiciary, exercising restraint, should not readily overturn these decisions.

Frankfurter especially objected to Jackson's argument that questions associated with the Bill of Rights, especially the First Amendment, should be beyond the reach of local officials and legislatures, who presumably represented the majority opinion of the people. Frankfurter believed judges had a duty to respect and defer to the discretion of democratically elected legislatures and the laws they enacted.

Justice Frankfurter's opinions in *Gobitis* and *Barnette* have passed away, while Justice Jackson's opinion in *Barnette* has not only persisted as a precedent, but has been hailed as one of the greatest statements on civil liberties ever written. Because of the *Barnette* ruling, students today may choose not to participate in patriotic ceremonies conducted in their schools.

An Inspirational Defense of
First Amendment Rights

—◆—

Justice Robert Jackson's opinion for the Court in West Virginia State Board of Education *v.*
Barnette, *presented on Flag Day, June 14, 1943, is a masterpiece. He explained brilliantly
and memorably the relationships among limited government, the rule of law, and security for
the rights of individuals against the ever-present threat of majority tyranny in a democracy.
And Justice Jackson took a strong stand for the immutable First and Fourteenth Amendment
rights of unpopular individuals against the majority's representatives in government, who
might abuse their power to abridge those rights.*

Justice Jackson's opinion overturned the short-term precedent set by the Court in its Gobitis
decision. He replaced it with the enduring precedent of the Barnette *decision. And he did it
with words that remind us of a foundational principle of constitutional democracy: majority
rule must be limited by the rule of law in the people's Constitution in order to equally protect
the rights of everyone, including disliked minorities.*

—◆—

There is no doubt that, in connection with the pledges, the flag salute is a form of utterance. Symbolism is a primitive but effective way of communicating ideas. The use of an emblem or flag to symbolize some system, idea, institution, or personality, is a short cut from mind to mind. Causes and nations, political parties, lodges, and ecclesiastical groups seek to knit the loyalty of their followers to a flag or banner, a color or design....

It is also to be noted that the compulsory flag salute and pledge requires affirmation of a belief and an attitude of mind.... To sustain the compulsory flag salute we are required to say that a Bill of Rights, which guards the individual's right to speak his own mind, left it open to public authorities to compel him to utter what is not in his mind....

The very purpose of a Bill of Rights was to withdraw certain subjects from the vicissitudes of political controversy, to place them beyond the reach of majorities and officials and to establish them as legal principles to be applied by the courts. One's right to life, liberty, and property, to free speech, a free press, freedom of worship and assembly, and other fundamental rights may not be submitted to vote; they depend on the outcome of no election.

In weighing arguments of the parties it is important to distinguish between the due process clause of the Fourteenth Amendment as an instrument for transmitting the principles of the First Amendment and those cases in which it is applied for its own sake.

The test of legislation which collides with the Fourteenth Amendment, because it also collides with the principles of the First, is much more definite than the test when only the Fourteenth is involved. Much of the vagueness of the due process clause disappears when the specific prohibitions of the First become its standard.... It is important to note that while it is the Fourteenth Amendment which bears directly upon the State it is the more specific limiting principles of the First Amendment that finally govern this case....

National unity as an end which officials may foster by persuasion and example is not in question. The problem is whether under our Constitution compulsion as here employed is a permissible means for its achievement....

Those who begin coercive elimination of dissent soon find themselves exterminating dissenters. Compulsory unification of opinions achieves only the unanimity of the graveyard.

A staunch defender of minority rights, Justice Robert Jackson also recognized the need for public order and safety. Eight years after the Barnette *case, he voted with the majority of the Court in* Dennis v. United States *to uphold the convictions of Communist party leaders who advocated overthrowing the U.S. government.*

It seems trite but necessary to say that the First Amendment to our Constitution was designed to avoid these ends by avoiding these beginnings. There is no mysticism in the American concept of the State or of the nature or origin of its authority. We set up government by consent of the governed, and the Bill of Rights denies those in power any legal opportunity to coerce that consent. Authority here is to be controlled by public opinion, not public opinion by authority.

The case is made difficult not because the principles of its decision are obscure but because the flag involved is our own. Nevertheless, we apply the limitations of the Constitution with no fear that freedom to be intellectually and spiritually diverse or even contrary will disintegrate the social organization. To believe that patriotism will not flourish if patriotic ceremonies are voluntary and spontaneous instead of a compulsory routine is to make an unflattering estimate of the appeal of our institutions to free minds. We can have intellectual individualism and the rich cultural diversities that we owe to exceptional minds only at the price of occasional eccentricity and abnormal attitudes. When they are so harmless to others or the State as those we deal with here, the price is not too great. But freedom to differ is not limited to things that do not matter much. That would be a mere shadow of freedom. The test of its substance is the right to differ as to things that touch the heart of the existing order.

If there is any fixed star in our constitutional constellation, it is that no official, high or petty, can prescribe what shall be orthodox in politics, nationalism, religion, or other matters of opinion or force citizens to confess by word or act their faith therein. If there are any circumstances which permit an exception, they do not now occur to me.

We think the action of the local authorities in compelling the flag salute and pledge transcends constitutional limitations on their power and invades the sphere of intellect and spirit which it is the purpose of the First Amendment to our Constitution to reserve from all official control.

The decision of the Court in *Minersville School District* v. *Gobitis* and the holdings of those few *per curiam* decisions which preceded and foreshadowed it are overruled, and the judgment enjoining enforcement of the West Virginia Regulation is Affirmed.

11

Internment of Japanese Americans during World War II

Hirabayashi v. *United States* (1943)
Korematsu v. *United States* (1944)

Hirabayashi v. United States

- 320 U.S. 81 (1943)

- Decided: June 21, 1943

- Vote: 9–0

- Opinion of the Court: Harlan Fiske Stone

- Concurring opinions: William O. Douglas, Frank Murphy, and Wiley Rutledge

Korematsu v. United States

- 323 U.S. 214 (1944)

- Decided: December 18, 1944

- Vote: 6–3

- Opinion of the Court: Hugo L. Black

- Concurring opinion: Felix Frankfurter

- Dissenting opinions: Owen J. Roberts, Frank Murphy, and Robert H. Jackson

A nation at war with a formidable enemy is a nation at risk. National security becomes a paramount concern of the government, which may, under certain conditions, decide to subordinate the constitutional rights of some individuals to the collective safety of the people. But in the United States, a primary purpose of the government has always been to provide equal protection for the constitutional rights of all the nation's people. So, during a wartime crisis, critical questions about individual liberty and collective security are inevitable.

Can strong war powers, which the national government may need to defeat a fearsome foreign enemy, be reconciled with the immutable constitutional rights of individuals? Or must the liberty of some persons be sacrificed temporarily to the exigencies of national survival? These questions were raised in the United States after an attack by Japanese aircraft against Pearl Harbor, Hawaii, on December 7, 1941. And they were associated with two cases brought to the U.S. Supreme Court within the context of World War II: *Hirabayashi* v. *United States* and *Korematsu* v. *United States*.

The Japanese attack on Pearl Harbor was a disaster for the United States. The American naval forces on Hawaii, stunned and surprised, suffered a devastating defeat. The Japanese disabled or destroyed five American battleships and three cruisers, and they killed 2,355 military personnel and wounded 1,178. President Franklin D. Roosevelt, speaking by radio to a shocked and scared nationwide audience, said that the American people would remember this "date which will live in infamy" and exact revenge for Japan's "sneak attack" against the United States. Congress declared war against Japan. Germany and Italy, military allies of Japan, then declared war on the United States. Thus, the United States entered World War II.

Within three months, Japanese forces invaded and occupied nearly all of Southeast Asia and had taken the U.S. territories of Guam and the Philippines. Americans feared a Japanese invasion of the Hawaiian Islands and the states along their country's Pacific coast, California, Oregon, and Washington.

General J. L. DeWitt, who was responsible for defending the Pacific coastal region, felt threatened by the more than 112,000 people of Japanese ancestry who lived on the West Coast. More than two-thirds were U.S. citizens, and most others were long-settled resident aliens. General DeWitt wanted to relocate all of them to the interior of the country, where they could be prevented from having contact with the enemy.

Members of President Roosevelt's cabinet debated General DeWitt's national security recommendations, which were supported strongly by top political leaders in California, including the state's attorney general, Earl Warren, a future chief justice of the United States. However, U.S. Attorney General Francis Biddle urged caution; he believed that forcible relocation of the Japanese Americans would violate their due process rights under the Fifth Amendment to the Constitution. Other Presidential advisers stressed that military necessity and national survival were the paramount concerns of this moment, and President Franklin D. Roosevelt agreed with them.

On February 22, 1942, President Roosevelt issued Executive Order 9066, providing authority for military commanders to establish special zones from which civilians might be excluded for reasons of national defense. The President based his order on the Espionage Act of 1918 and statutes enacted by Congress in 1940 and 1941 to enhance the chief executive's wartime powers. On March 18, President Roosevelt issued Executive Order 9102 to establish the War Relocation Authority. This executive agency was empowered to relocate the people identified by military commanders under the provisions of the previously issued Executive Order 9066.

On March 21, the President signed a law, enacted unanimously by Congress, that supported the previously issued executive orders pertaining to national security. The way was cleared for military commanders to remove Japanese Americans from the Pacific Coast to regions within the interior of the United States.

On March 24, General DeWitt announced a daily curfew. From 8:00 p.m. until 6:00 a.m., all persons of Japanese ancestry living within Military Area 1, which comprised the entire Pacific coastal region, were required to stay indoors. This command was a prelude to the exclusion order that came on May 9, when General DeWitt directed the removal of all persons of Japanese ancestry from Military Area 1. They had to check in at "civilian control centers" from where they were sent to internment camps in the interior of the country.

The internment camps were forbidding places of confinement, ringed by barbed-wire fences and guarded by armed soldiers. The internees came to their sparsely furnished dwellings with few possessions, having been forced to sell or leave behind most of what they had owned. Homes, farms, and places of business were mostly sold on short notice for a small percentage of their true value.

Most of the relocated people were citizens of the United States, who had been born and raised in America and were thoroughly American in their

An American of Japanese ancestry owned this store at Thirteenth and Franklin Streets in Oakland, California. On December 8, 1941, the day after Japan's attack on Pearl Harbor, Hawaii, the store owner placed the sign reading "I AM AN AMERICAN" on his front window to proclaim his loyalty to the United States. Federal government evacuation orders forced him to close the store, which later was sold, and report to a relocation center. He lived in an internment camp until the end of World War II.

beliefs and behavior. They considered themselves to be loyal citizens of their country, , with little or no allegiance to Japan, which most of them had never visited. They were incarcerated because some government officials and military commanders suspected them of sympathy with a wartime enemy, even though no hard evidence was ever produced that any of them had acted disloyally against the United States.

During 1942, the Office of Naval Intelligence commissioned an investigation on the loyalty of Japanese Americans. An official report based on this study, written by Navy Commander Kenneth Ringle, concluded that fewer than 3 percent of Japanese Americans could be considered possible threats to national security. Further, most of those suspected of disloyalty had already been arrested. Thus, the Ringle Report strongly advised against any kind of mass relocation and internment of Japanese Americans as unnecessary and most likely unconstitutional. Unfortunately the policy makers who mandated the internment and the federal judges who allowed the legislation to stand disregarded this report.

The internment of the Japanese Americans certainly raised serious issues about constitutional rights. For example, the Constitution's Fifth Amendment says, "No person shall be . . . deprived of life, liberty, or property, without due process of law." Had the federal government deprived the interned Japanese Americans of their Fifth Amendment rights? Or did the wartime emergency justify the federal government's placement of extraordinary limitations on the constitutional rights of a particular group of Americans? Federal courts soon confronted these critical issues about the government's use of war powers and the constitutional rights of Japanese Americans.

The first Japanese American internment case to come before the U.S. Supreme Court concerned Gordon Hirabayashi, a U.S. citizen born and raised in Seattle, Washington. Prior to his problems with the federal government, he was a highly regarded student at the University of Washington in Seattle.

In 1942, Japanese Americans register for work at the War Relocation Authority center at Manzanar, California, after being evacuated from their homes by order of the federal government. More than 10,000 Japanese Americans were imprisoned at Manzanar during World War II.

Hirabayashi had been arrested and convicted for violating General DeWitt's curfew order and for refusing to register at a control station in preparation for transportation to an internment camp. His noncompliance with federal regulations was based strongly on principle. Hirabayashi believed that the President's executive orders, and the federal laws enacted in support of them, were racially discriminatory violations of the U.S. Constitution. He later said: "I must maintain the democratic standards for which this nation lives....I am objecting to the principle of this order which denies the rights of human beings, including citizens."

The Court unanimously upheld the curfew law for Japanese Americans living in Military Area 1 and ruled that the federal government had appropriately used its war powers under the Constitution. It did not directly confront the issue of whether the exclusion and internment order violated Hirabayashi's Fifth Amendment rights, as the Court focused on the constitutional justifications for the curfew law during a wartime crisis, a law that Hirabayashi clearly had violated.

Writing for the Court, Chief Justice Harlan Fiske Stone recognized that discrimination based upon race was "odious to a free people whose institutions are founded upon the doctrine of equality." In this case, however, Stone ruled that the need to protect national security in time of war compelled consideration of race and ancestry as reasons for confinement of a certain group of people. The chief justice wrote, "We cannot close our eyes to the fact...that in time of war residents having ethnic affiliations with an invading enemy may be a greater source of danger than those of a different ancestry."

Although the Court's decision in Hirabayashi was unanimous, Justice Frank Murphy did not wholeheartedly endorse it, and he wrote a concurring opinion that verged on dissent. In fact, Murphy had at first decided to write a dissenting opinion, but Chief Justice Stone, with help from Justice Felix Frankfurter, talked him out of it. Frankfurter argued that in a socially sensitive case like this one, it was important for the Court to present an appearance of unity. Nonetheless, Murphy's concurrence was sprinkled with sharply stated reservations about the Court's opinion. For example, Murphy expressed great concern that "we have sustained a substantial restriction of the personal liberty of citizens of the United States based on the accident of race or ancestry....In my opinion, this goes to the very brink of constitutional power."

The tenuous unity of the Hirabayashi opinion was broken in the next Japanese American internment case to reach the Supreme Court, *Korematsu v. United States.*

Born and raised in Oakland, California, Fred Korematsu was, like Gordon Hirabayashi, a U.S. citizen of Japanese ancestry who was thoroughly American in culture and loyalty to the United States. In June 1941, more than five months before the United States entered World War II, Korematsu volunteered to join the U.S. Navy. Although actively seeking enlistments, the Navy recruitment officials rejected Korematsu's application for reasons of poor health. He then found employment as a welder at a shipyard in northern California, a job related to national defense.

On the day he was ordered to report at an assembly area for his likely relocation and internment, Korematsu refused to go, and for good reasons. He

In 1942, Gordon Hirabayashi, a twenty-three-year-old student at the University of Washington in Seattle, disobeyed a federal government curfew law directed against Japanese Americans as a principled act of civil disobedience.

wanted to marry his girlfriend and move to Nevada. She was not a Japanese American and thereby not affected by the removal order. Furthermore, Korematsu could not imagine that he in any way threatened the security of the United States. Federal government officials thought otherwise. They arrested and convicted him of violating the law requiring him to report to the assembly center and sentenced him to five years in prison. Then the court paroled Korematsu, who was taken to an internment camp in Utah. From there, he appealed directly to the U.S. Supreme Court, which decided his case on December 18, 1944.

The Supreme Court upheld the federal law requiring Japanese Americans in the Pacific coastal region to report to an assembly center for likely relocation and internment in another part of the country. The war powers of the federal government, provided by the Constitution, were the Court's justification for upholding the federal law under which Korematsu had been arrested and convicted.

In his opinion for the Court, Justice Hugo Black began by noting "that all legal restrictions which curtail the civil rights of a single racial group are immediately suspect. That is not to say that all such restrictions are unconstitutional. It is to say that courts must subject them to the most rigid scrutiny. Pressing public necessity may sometimes justify the existence of such restrictions, racial antagonism never can." Thus, Justice Black recognized that the type of intentional racial classification applied against Japanese Americans in this case would normally be ruled unconstitutional. It was justified in this instance, according to Black's opinion for the Court, only by the compelling interest of the federal government to protect the nation during a wartime emergency.

Justice Black recognized that Japanese American citizens of the United States, such as Korematsu, had endured severe hardships because of the federal order at issue in this case. "But hardships are a part of war," wrote Black, "and war is an aggregation of hardships." Justice Black said the federal government's orders at issue had not been directed against Japanese Americans because of race or ancestry, but for reasons of national security and military necessity.

The Court's ruling did not directly address the constitutionality of the federal law authorizing the internment of Japanese Americana. It sidestepped that sensitive question, emphasizing the national crisis caused by the war as justification for the extraordinary actions of the federal government. Further, Justice Black's opinion separated the law requiring Japanese Americans to report to an assembly center from the law forcing them to be excluded from the Pacific coastal region and relocated to an internment camp. As Korematsu had been convicted only for not reporting to an assembly center, the Court did not directly consider the constitutionality of the orders forcing Japanese Americans into the internment camps.

Black concluded:

> Korematsu was not excluded from the Military Area because of hostility to him or his race. He was excluded because we are at war with the Japanese Empire, because the properly constituted military authorities feared an invasion of our West Coast and felt constrained to take proper security measures, because they decided that the military urgency of the situation demanded that all citizens of Japanese ancestry be segregated from the

West Coast temporarily, and finally, because Congress, reposing its confidence in this time of war in our military leaders—as inevitably it must—determined that they should have the power to do just this.

Three justices—Owen Roberts, Frank Murphy, and Robert Jackson—strongly dissented from the Court's decision. Roberts thought it a plain "case of convicting a citizen as punishment for not submitting to imprisonment in a concentration camp solely because of his ancestry."

Murphy claimed that the exclusion orders violated the right of citizens to due process of law and were a "legalization of racism." He wrote, "Racial discrimination in any form and in any degree has no justifiable part whatever in our democratic way of life." Murphy admitted that the Court majority's argument citing military necessity carried weight, but he insisted that such a claim must "subject itself to the judicial process" to determine "whether the deprivation is reasonably related to a public danger that is so immediate, imminent, and impending." Finally, Murphy concluded that "individuals must not be left impoverished in their constitutional rights on a plea of military necessity that has neither substance nor support."

Jackson expressed grave concern about the future uses of the precedent set in this case. He wrote:

> A military order, however unconstitutional, is not apt to last longer than the military emergency. . . . But once a judicial opinion rationalizes such an order to show that it conforms to the Constitution . . . the Court for all time has validated the principle of racial discrimination in criminal procedures and of transplanting American citizens. The principle then lies about like a loaded weapon, ready for the hand of any authority that can bring forward a plausible claim of an urgent need.

On December 18, 1944, the very day of its *Korematsu* decision, the Court also reported its ruling in *Ex parte Endo,* a related case. A writ of habeas corpus had been filed on behalf of Mitsuye Endo, an American of Japanese ancestry, who had been sent in May 1942 from her home in California to an internment camp by order of the War Relocation Authority. Unlike Korematsu, Endo had obeyed the relocation order and so had not violated a federal law. Like Korematsu, she was a loyal American citizen. The Court unanimously agreed that Endo "should be given her liberty" because there was no evidence that she had done anything to justify her detention.

The gates of the internment camps were opened in January 1945, less than one month after the *Endo* decision. Major General Henry C. Pratt, commander of Military Area 1 at that time, suspended the exclusion orders, and more than fifty thousand Japanese Americans were set free. The war against Japan was in its final phase, and there no longer was any threat to the U.S. mainland from Japanese military forces. More than thirty thousand internees, however, continued in their confinement until the end of World War II, because military authorities remained skeptical of their loyalty to the United States.

Among those returning to civilian life after the war were more than 1,200 members of a U.S. Army brigade comprised entirely of Japanese American volunteers who were Nisei, or second-generation Japanese Americans. This Nisei Brigade fought heroically against the German military occupiers of Italy during

In March 1942, Fred Korematsu was struggling to earn enough money to marry his Italian American fiancée. Korematsu, who had undergone plastic surgery on his eyes and nose to disguise his Japanese heritage, did not join his parents and three brothers on May 9, 1942, when they reported to the Assembly Center at Tanforan, California. He was arrested three weeks later for violating the federal government's exclusion order.

the U.S. Army's invasion in 1943. Soldiers of the Nisei Brigade won more medals for bravery in action than any other military unit in American history.

Shortly after the end of World War II, Japanese Americans who had been relocated to internment camps filed grievances with the federal government to seek compensation for unjust treatment. In 1948, Congress responded by enacting the Japanese American Evacuation Claims Act, which provided compensation to internees who had evidence to prove the amount of their property losses. However, no more than $37 million was paid in compensation, despite estimates that Japanese Americans had suffered property losses totaling more than $400 million. Furthermore, compensation was not provided for losses of income or profits that they would have earned during the period of detention in the relocation centers.

In 1980, Congress established the Commission on Wartime Relocation and Internment of Civilians to investigate the treatment of Japanese Americans during World War II and to make recommendations about financial compensation to the victims. After careful examination of the evidence, including testimony from 750 witnesses, the commission issued a report on February 25, 1983. The commission found no evidence of espionage or sabotage by any of the Japanese Americans. In addition, it noted that officials of both the Federal Bureau of Investigation and the Office of Naval Intelligence had opposed the exclusion and internment orders because they believed the Japanese Americans collectively posed no threat to the country's security. The report concluded: "A grave injustice was done to American citizens and resident aliens of Japanese ancestry who, without individual review or any probative evidence against them, were excluded, removed, and detained by the United States during World War II."

In January 1983, Gordon Hirabayashi and Fred Korematsu petitioned the federal judiciary to vacate and overturn their criminal convictions. They claimed procedural errors and faulty use of information had influenced the judicial decisions against them. First Korematsu and later Hirabayashi achieved reversal of their convictions, which were erased from federal court records.

In 1988, on the basis of the 1983 report by the federal government commission, Congress officially recognized the wrongs done to Americans of Japanese ancestry by the exclusion and relocation policies. It enacted legislation to provide twenty thousand dollars in compensation to each person still living who had been detained in a relocation center or to the heirs of deceased victims. More than forty-six years after the fateful executive orders that had victimized them were issued, the Japanese American community received a belated token of compensatory justice.

On August 10, 1988, President Ronald Reagan signs the reparations bill enacted by Congress to compensate Japanese Americans for their unjust internment during World War II. The President said, "Yes, the nation was then at war, struggling for its survival—and it's not for us to pass judgment upon those who may have made mistakes while engaged in that great struggle. Yet we must recognize that the internment of Japanese Americans was just that—a mistake. For throughout the war, Japanese Americans in the tens of thousands remained utterly loyal to the United States."

Gordon Hirabayashi Remembers
His Conviction and Its Reversal

*From the beginning of his ordeal, Gordon Hirabayashi protested the injustice of the federal reg-
ulations forcing the exclusion and removal of Americans of Japanese ancestry from the Pacific
Coast, and he refused on principle to comply with them. Consequently, Gordon spent more than
three years in county jails and federal prisons; but he never accepted the legitimacy of the judgments against him and resolved to overturn them.*

*Following World War II and his release from federal custody, Hirabayashi completed work
for his undergraduate degree at the University of Washington, and continued on at the university to earn his Ph.D. in sociology in 1952. He later worked as a professor at the University of
Alberta in Canada, until he retired in 1983.*

*Two years before his retirement, Professor Peter Irons of the University of California at San
Diego contacted Hirabayashi and advised him to reopen his case. While doing research for a book
on the Japanese American internment cases, Irons discovered information that could be used to
help Hirabayashi achieve justice. Irons became Hirabayashi's legal adviser and assisted him in
filing a petition in a federal district court seeking a reversal of his long-ago conviction on
grounds of an erroneous and invalid use of evidence by the prosecutors in this case.*

*Hirabayashi won complete vindication in 1987, when the federal Court of Appeals for the
Ninth Circuit ruled in his favor. His convictions for violating both the curfew and exclusion
orders were overturned. In the course of his research, Irons interviewed Hirabayashi about his
case, and Hirabayahsi recounted his courageous effort to achieve justice.*

After the Curfew order was announced, we knew there would be further orders to remove all persons of Japanese ancestry from the West coast. When the exclusion orders specifying the deadline for forced removal from various districts of Seattle were posted on telephone poles, I was confronted with a dilemma. Do I stay out of trouble and succumb to the status of second-class citizen, or do I continue to live like other Americans and thus disobey the law?

When the curfew was imposed I obeyed for about a week.... I think if the order said *all* civilians must obey the curfew, if it was just a nonessential restrictive move, I might not have objected. But I felt it was unfair, just to be referred to as a "non-alien"—they never referred to me as a citizen. This was so point-edly, so obviously a violation of what the Constitution stood for, what citizenship meant....

After that, I just ignored the curfew. But nothing happened. And it became a kind of expression of free-dom for me to make sure that I was out after eight....

When the exclusion order came, which was very close to that time, I was expecting to go along. I had dropped out of school at the end of the winter quarter, which was the end of March. I knew I wasn't going to be around very long, so I just didn't register for spring quarter...

Eventually, I wrote out a statement explaining the reasons I was refusing evacuation, and I planned to give it to the FBI when I turned myself in....

The day after the University district deadline for evacuation, Art [Gordon's lawyer] took me to the FBI office to turn myself in. At first, I was only charged with violating the exclusion order. They threw in the curfew count afterward....

My trial in October lasted just one day. It started in the morning and they took a noon recess and continued in the afternoon until my conviction. . . .

Two days after I was sentenced, we appealed, and I continued to remain in jail because the judge and I couldn't agree on bail conditions. He said that if my backers put up the bail he would release me to one of the barbed-wire interment camps. And I said, If my backers put up the bail, I should be released out the front door like anybody else. He said, There's a law that says you're not allowed out in the streets, so I can't do that. . . .

When the Supreme Court decision in my case came down in June 1943, I expected I would have to serve my sentence. . . .

When I came out of prison, the war had just finished, and so I was released to Seattle. . . .

After the Supreme Court decided my case in 1943, there was always a continuous hope and interest on my part that the case could be reviewed at some point. Not being a lawyer, I didn't know exactly what my options were. . . .

It wasn't until Peter Irons called me from Boston in 1981, saying that he had discovered some documents that might present an opportunity under a rarely used legal device to petition for a rehearing, that I felt there was a chance. I said to him, I've been waiting for over forty years for this kind of phone call. So he arranged to fly to Edmonton, and eventually we got a legal team organized that filed a petition in the federal court in Seattle to vacate my conviction.

My petition was filed in January 1983 and we had a two-week evidentiary hearing in June 1985. Judge Donald Voorhees, who presided over the case, impressed me as a very fair judge. He was obviously interested in the case and well-informed about the evidence. Naturally, I was delighted that he ruled that my exclusion order conviction had been tainted by government misconduct. But I was disappointed that he upheld the curfew conviction, and we appealed that. The government also appealed on the exclusion order. We had arguments before the appellate judges in March 1987, and they handed down a unanimous opinion in September, upholding Judge Voorhees on the exclusion order and also striking down the curfew conviction. So I finally got the vindication that I had wanted for forty years, although I'm a little disappointed that the Supreme Court didn't have a chance to overrule the decision they made in 1943.

When my case was before the Supreme Court in 1943, I fully expected that as a citizen the Constitution would protect me. Surprisingly, even though I lost, I did not abandon my beliefs and values. And I never look at my case as just my own, or just as a Japanese American case. It is an American case, with principles that affect the fundamental human rights of all Americans.

12

A Decision to Limit Presidential Power

Youngstown Sheet & Tube Co. v. *Sawyer* (1952)

Separation of powers among three branches of government is a central principle in the U.S. Constitution. According to Articles 1, 2, and 3, the Congress makes laws, the President as chief executive enforces them, and the federal judges interpret them in specific cases. The separation of powers is neither rigid nor comprehensive, because the Constitution includes a system of checks and balances that provides each branch of government with ways to limit the powers of the others. Further, the Constitution requires each branch to cooperate with the others to carry out certain duties. The system of separated powers with checks and balances prevents one branch from accumulating so much power that it can dominate the others and rule tyrannically.

In designing the nation's new government, James Madison emphasized the separation of powers as a fundamental characteristic of a limited and free government. In the forty-seventh paper of *The Federalist*, he wrote, "The accumulation of all powers, legislative, executive, and judiciary, in the same hands, whether of one, a few, or many, and whether hereditary, self-appointed, or elective, may justly be pronounced the very definition of tyranny."

At times, federal government leaders and other citizens have clashed about whether a particular action by Congress or the President so exceeds the proper limits set in the Constitution that it tilts the powers in government toward tyranny. For example, President Harry S. Truman tested the limits of Presidential power when he ordered the federal government to take control of the nation's steel mills during a wartime crisis in 1952. Was President Truman's use of executive power constitutional? Did it threaten to upset the balance of powers among the three branches of government as established by the Constitution? Was it an assault on the very idea of a constitutionally limited and free government? Or was it a necessary exercise of executive power on behalf of national security during wartime? As usual, when political conflicts in American government raise basic constitutional issues, the judiciary becomes the arbiter. So it happened in regard to Truman's extraordinary exercise of Presidential power, which raised issues settled by the U.S. Supreme Court in *Youngstown Sheet & Tube Co.* v. *Sawyer*.

This issue about the latitude or limits of Presidential power arose within the context of the Korean War, which started in the summer of 1950 when military forces of North Korea invaded South Korea. The United Nations condemned the invasion and called upon its members to assist South Korea. President

> **Youngstown Sheet & Tube Co. v. Sawyer**
>
> - 343 U.S. 579 (1952)
> - Decided: June 2, 1952
> - Vote: 6–3
> - Opinion of the Court: Hugo L. Black
> - Concurring opinions: Felix Frankfurter, William O. Douglas, Robert H. Jackson, Harold H. Burton, and Tom Clark
> - Dissenting opinion: Fred M. Vinson (Stanley F. Reed and Sherman Minton)

The Campbell Works was one of three plants operated by the Youngstown Sheet & Tube Company in Mahoning County, Ohio, a region that produced 11 percent of the nation's steel in 1950. The company also had two factories in the Chicago area, the second largest center for steel production in the country.

Truman responded by committing American forces to the conflict without seeking a formal declaration of war by Congress. The North Koreans received military supplies and encouragement from the communist governments of China and the Soviet Union, and near the end of 1950, the Chinese Army entered the war against the United States and its allies.

During the spring of 1952, President Truman encountered a problem on the home front that endangered the American military engagement in Korea. Steelworkers throughout the United States were on the verge of a strike against their employers, owners of the big steel mills, whose products were critical to the military campaign in Korea. President Truman feared that a long work stoppage would deprive front-line soldiers of weapons and ammunition needed for victory in Korea.

On April 8, 1952, a few hours before the strike was slated to begin, the President issued Executive Order 10340, which directed Secretary of Commerce Charles Sawyer to temporarily take control of the nation's steel mills on behalf of the federal government and keep them operational. President Truman officially informed Congress of his action, but he received no response.

Secretary Sawyer told the steel mill managers that they would report to him during this period of national emergency, and he ordered them to maintain normal production schedules. The steel company owners reluctantly accepted President Truman's executive order, but they filed suit in a federal district court to halt the federal government's seizure and management of their property.

Taking temporary control of the steel mills was not the only alternative available to President Truman. He had another way to deal with the strike but chose not to use it.

In 1947, Congress had enacted a labor-management relations statute, the Taft-Hartley Act, which provided the President with authority to obtain a court order to delay a strike for eighty days. Had the President invoked this "cooling off" period, the steelworkers' union and the mill owners would have had ample time to negotiate and attempt to settle their differences. However, Truman had publicly pledged never to use the Taft-Hartley Act, because he thought it provided unfair advantages to employers in their dealings with labor unions. The President had vetoed this law, but Congress had overridden his veto. He was determined not to use legislation that he despised to settle the dispute between steelworkers and steel mill owners.

The President's sympathies in this labor-management conflict were entirely with the steelworkers' union. In his opinion, the blame for the strike lay entirely with the employers. He pointed out that the union had already postponed the strike four times in an effort to reach a settlement. Government arbitrators had recommended a compromise, which the union had accepted. The steel company owners, however, had rejected these recommendations, which included significant increases in the workers' wages, even though in 1951 the companies had earned their greatest profits in more than thirty years. The President believed the steel company owners were using the national crisis of the Korean War to force the steelworkers to accept lower wages than they deserved.

President Truman decided to seize the steel mills to prevent the workers from walking away from their jobs in a strike against the owners, because he strongly believed the owners were to blame for this problem. The President did not base his action on statutory authority provided by Congress. Rather, he claimed inherent constitutional powers of the President as justification for his Executive Order 10340. The steel company owners, however, believed the President's action against them violated the Constitution's separation of powers principle and quickly sought relief in the federal district court of Washington, D.C. On April 29, Judge David A. Pine issued an injunction against the federal government and ordered the return of the steel mills to the owners. Secretary Sawyer countered with a plea to the court of appeals, which stayed, or stopped, Judge Pine's injunction. Then the steel companies appealed directly to the Supreme Court, which very quickly accepted the case in order to settle a critical issue in a time of national crisis.

The issues in the case pertained directly to the separation of powers among three branches of government, and the lawyers for both sides framed their arguments around this essential principle of the Constitution. During oral arguments before the Court, lawyers for the steel companies emphasized that Congress had not authorized President Truman's executive order. No law had been enacted to empower the President to seize and operate the steel mills. Thus, the President was, in effect, making law—a power reserved to Congress by Article 1 of the Constitution which says, "All Legistaltive Powers herein granted shall be vested in a Congress of the United States." Furthermore, they argued that there was no inherent constitutional power that authorized the President's action in response to a national emergency.

In 1947, the Greater New York Industrial Union Council organized this massive rally of labor union supporters at Madison Square Garden in New York City. Participants met to protest the Taft-Hartley Act, claiming that this federal law was detrimental to the interests of labor unions and urging Congress to repeal it.

They recognized the existence of a wartime crisis but argued that the wrong branch of government had stepped forward in response. According to the Constitution, they argued, only Congress could authorize the kind of action taken by the President in this case. In the absence of congressional endorsement, the President had overstepped the constitutional limits of his power.

Counsel for the federal government argued that the President's inherent power under Article 2 of the Constitution gave him authority to maintain production of steel needed for military purposes in the Korean War. Article 2 says "The executive power should be vested in a President of the United States of America," which requires action necessary to defend the nation against domestic and foreign enemies. Furthermore, they said that the President's power as commander in chief allowed him to take actions necessary to protect the lives of American troops. This executive power included ensuring a steady flow of steel to produce weapons and ammunition for the war effort.

President Truman lost the argument at the Supreme Court, which by a 6–3 vote ruled against him. The Court's majority decided that the President's executive order authorizing seizure of the steel mills was an unconstitutional exercise of power. Writing for the Court, Justice Hugo Black said, "The President's power, if any, to issue the order must stem either from an act of Congress or from the Constitution itself. There is no statute that expressly authorizes the President to take possession of property as he did here. Nor is there any act of Congress to which our attention has been directed from which such a powers can fairly be implied." Further, Black argued that the President's order could not be justified by any grant of power in the Constitution. He held that the President did not have inherent power, derived from Article 2 of the Constitution, to seize private property, even temporarily during a national emergency.

Justice Black noted that in writing the 1947 Taft-Hartley Act, Congress had rejected the idea that a President could seize a private business in order to forestall a strike by unionized employees. Thus, by his executive order the President had attempted to make a law, which the Constitution does not permit him to do. "The Founders of this Nation entrusted the lawmaking power to the Congress alone in both good and bad times," wrote Black. "It would do no good to recall the historical events, the fears of power and the hopes for freedom that lay behind their choice. Such a review would but confirm our holding that this seizure order cannot stand." Thus, the Court affirmed the decision of the federal district court to stop the President's takeover of the steel mills.

Concurring opinions by Justices Felix Frankfurter, William O. Douglas, Robert H. Jackson, and Harold H. Burton all stressed that only Congress could constitutionally authorize a seizure of the steel mills during a national crisis through its power to legislate. Justice Douglas said he was shocked by the "legislative nature of the action taken by the President." Justice Jackson's concurring opinion emphasized the connection of executive power to congressional approval in all matters where there is no explicit grant of power to the President from the Constitution. Jackson said that the executive's power is greatest when the President acts with the authorization of Congress. When the President acts against the explicit will of Congress, however, his authority is least likely to be sustained. Justice Jackson explained the fundamental importance of the separation of powers principle as a bulwark against despotism: "With all its defects, delays and inconveniences, men have discovered no technique for long preserving free government except that the Executive be under the law, and the law be made by parliamentary deliberations."

Justice Tom Clark concurred in the Court's decision to declare unconstitutional the President's seizure of the steel mills. However, he disagreed with Justice Black's opinion in support of the Court's decision because it seemed to deny any extraordinary power for the President in a national emergency. Clark wrote that "such a grant may well be necessary to the very existence of the Constitution."

Three justices, all appointed to the Court by President Truman, dissented. The dissenting opinion was written by Chief Justice Fred Vinson and joined by Justices Stanley Reed and Sherman Minton. Vinson argued that during a grave national crisis, such as the Korean War, the Constitution allowed the President to exercise unusual powers. The Chief Justice wrote, "Those who suggest that this is a case involving extraordinary powers should be mindful that these are extraordinary times." He added that Truman's actions followed the tradition of taking bold actions during a time of crisis established by other Presidents: Abraham Lincoln during the Civil War, Woodrow Wilson during World War I, and Franklin Roosevelt during World War II.

President Truman promptly returned control of the steel mills to their owners, in compliance with the Supreme Court's decision. But he continued to strongly disagree with it and to praise Chief Justice Vinson's dissent. Later, in his *Memoirs,* Truman wrote, "I would, of course, never conceal the fact that the Supreme Court's decision, announced on June 2 [1952] was a deep disappointment to me. I think Chief Justice Vinson's dissenting opinion hit the nail right on the head, and I am sure that someday his view will come to be recognized as the correct one."

The President's immediate distress about the Court's opinion in the "steel seizure" case was somewhat eased by Justice Hugo Black's display of gracious hospitality at his home. Sensing Truman's severe disappointment at his opinion for the Court in the "steel seizure" decision, Justice Black invited the President and his fellow justices to a party. Black's purpose was to reduce tensions arising from a decision that Truman considered a personal rebuke. In his autobiography, Justice William O. Douglas remembered, "Truman was gracious though a bit testy at the beginning of the evening. But after the bourbon and canapés were passed, he turned to Hugo [Black] and said, 'Hugo, I don't much care for your law but, by golly, this bourbon is good.'"

The President did not at all like the immediate effect of the Court's decision upon the steel industry and its production of goods needed for the war in Korea. The steelworkers' union called a strike against the steel mills. When it ended, after fifty-three days, the steel companies agreed to a contract within one cent of the settlement that had been recommended by the government arbitrators. True to his pledge, President Truman never used the Taft-Hartley Act to intervene in the negotiations between the union and the companies. But the President did insist that the strike caused shortages of ammunition for the soldiers fighting against their country's enemies in Korea.

The Court's decision in the *Youngstown* case clearly and enduringly established limits on the powers a President can derive from the Constitution during a national emergency. It demonstrated how the Supreme Court can act decisively to preserve the separation of powers principle in the Constitution, which defines the American political system. Finally, the "steel seizure' decision became an important precedent in the Court's subsequent decisions about the limits of Presidential power, such as its rulings in response to the Watergate crisis that led to the resignation of President Richard Nixon in 1974.

In this political cartoon a massive hand labeled "Presidential seizure" breaks through the Constitution to grasp private property in the form of a factory. The cartoonist depicts the President's action as an unconstitutional use of executive power that violated the private property rights of steel mill owners.

Separation of Powers and
Where to Draw the Line

On May 16, 1952, the justices met privately in the conference room of the Supreme Court to discuss the issues in the Youngstown *case. Like all Supreme Court conferences, no official record of the meeting was kept, and no formal report of the proceedings was issued. However, justices usually make notes for themselves to keep track of main points and important details of the discussions, which they often leave to a public repository, such as the Library of Congress or the National Archives, after their retirement or death. The notes that the participating justices made in the conference for the* Youngstown *case provide a sense of how they worked together to resolve a troubling issue about separation of powers under the Constitution. The bracketed comment in one instance is a note written by Justice Burton that pertains to the comment made by Justice Frankfurter. In the second instance, it is a note written by Justice Douglas about the comments of Justice Minton.*

Chief Justice Fred Vinson: To take either position—that the president has either unlimited power or no power—is untenable. It runs in the face of the history of our government. At the one end, it is said that the president's power is unlimited. But unlimited power is not urged here, and it could not be. On the other end, it is urged that the executive has no power of his own and that he must rely on an act of Congress. I don't agree with that....

The president was called upon to seize. If he had not seized, the howls would have been greater than the howls we hear now. It was his duty, and he would have been derelict if he had not seized....

Hugo Black: The issue is whether the president can make laws. Here we have a labor dispute and law-making concerning it. That power, under the constitution, is in the Congress.... [W]e do not, even in war, turn over legislative power to the president. We depend on the legislative branch as supreme in declaring the relations of citizens to property, and so forth....

I am afraid of any use of an "emergency" system. This is not a case of the president tearing down the house in order to stop a fire. The conditions are not that serious.... This will take power from Congress. I affirm [the judgment of the federal district court that issued an injunction against the president's order].

Stanley Reed: I am starting where Hugo concluded....I agree as to separation of powers. The question is *where to draw the line.* The lines between the powers of the three branches of government are not clear....

The president does not have unlimited power—*only in an emergency.* When is it a sufficient "emergency"? That is the issue....

There plainly is an emergency here. Steel is very important.... *I would leave the President in control....*

Felix Frankfurter: I agree with Vinson that there is no unlimited power of the president, or of Congress. The doctrine of separation of powers is wound into this case.

[Harold H. Burton: Frankfurter refers to a long piece on separation of powers he wrote twenty-five years ago.] I agree with Black on this.

...President Truman cannot lump all of his powers together and thereby get authority....

The 1787 constitution was not meant for efficiency, but to preclude arbitrary power....I affirm.

William O. Douglas: Much has been said, but I am inclined to agree with Hugo. This is a legislative function. . . . [T]he President was not authorized to do that [seize the steel mills]. There should be no temporary seizure pending Congressional action—I would not agree with Felix on that. If Congress were to act, it would make the case moot. As of now, I affirm.

Robert H. Jackson: . . . This Court should not review whether there is an emergency! Stanley Reed might involve us in that. *If the president declares an emergency, I will take the president's judgment. The question of how the president deals with an emergency is different.* . . . The president is in an untenable situation. (1) *The government does claim* inherent powers here! (2) The president can throw the Constitution overboard—but we can't. . . . Whatever emergency is claimed does not support such drastic action [as seizing the steel mills]. I would affirm. . . .

Harold H. Burton: The remedy at law is not adequate. The validity of the seizure should be passed on, and there is no reason to postpone a decision on the merits. This is a decision that requires policy-making and therefore it is for Congress to decide. Congress has the power to provide a remedy. . . . I affirm.

Tom Clark: In any event, we should limit our decision to this case. I am unwilling to say that the President has no power to act. It is a useful power. Here, we have a situation that could have been averted by two statutory methods not involving seizure. . . .

Sherman Minton: . . . I cannot believe that this government was constructed without a power of self-defense. There are not dark spots or power vacuums, where no one can act when the nation's safety is imperiled.

The power of self-defense resides in Congress, and in the president, and in everyone in public life. We have an acute emergency hanging over the world. The president seized the mills in self-defense of the nation. . . . Truman seized the plants because the defense of the country required it. *That is not a legislative power—it is a defensive seizure.* [William O. Douglas: Minton is very excited about this and pounds on the table.]

. . . The president gets his inherent power from the power to defend the nation in a day of peril. I reverse.

13

Public School Desegregation

Brown v. *Board of Education of Topeka, Kansas* (1954, 1955)

*B*rown v. *Board of Education* was the Court's greatest twentieth-century decision, a pivotal case that separated one era from another and that permanently reshaped the debate about race and American society. *Time* magazine declared that, with the exception of *Scott* v. *Sandford,* no other decision in the Court's history was more significant. The Dred Scott case was universally acknowledged as a "wrong" decision and often considered the worst decision in Supreme Court history, whereas *Brown* was seen, outside the South, as a great moral victory. Thurgood Marshall, who argued the case for the National Association for the Advancement of Colored People (NAACP) and was later appointed to the high court, was especially pleased. He recalled that when he heard about the result, "I was so happy I was numb."

The decision was actually two decisions, both unanimous and both authored by Chief Justice Earl Warren. The first, issued in 1954, is known as *Brown* I. In a nontechnical, direct, and unanimous opinion, the Court ended the practice of legal racial segregation in public schools. Warren explained that even if racially segregated schools had equal facilities and teachers, they would nevertheless always be unconstitutional under the equal protection clause of the Fourteenth Amendment. That clause provides that "No State shall make or enforce any law which shall…deny to any person within its jurisdiction the equal protection of the laws." In the 1896 case of *Plessy* v. *Ferguson* the Court had previously interpreted equal protection to mean that a state could divide people along racial lines as long as it provided equal facilities for them; this doctrine became known as "separate but equal." In the context of schools, for example, the *Plessy* ruling meant that black students could be sent to one school and white students to another as long as the facilities and teachers were of equal quality. The concept was something of a sham, because all-white legislatures and school boards seldom showered equal resources on white and black schools. In 1954, however, the Court rejected the position established in *Plessy.*

A year later the justices issued a second decision, known as *Brown* II. The Court knew that ending racial segregation and setting aside the "separate but equal" doctrine would be controversial. At the time of the *Brown* decision, segregation existed throughout the United States, but the Court's ruling would have particular significance in the South. In most of the country, segregation was de facto, meaning that it existed not by force of law but by social custom

Brown v. Board of Education of Topeka, Kansas
• 347 U.S. 483 (1954)
• Decided: May 17, 1954
• Vote: 9–0
• Opinion of the Court: Earl Warren

Brown v. Board of Education of Topeka, Kansas
• 349 U.S. 294 (1955)
• Decided: May 31, 1955
• Vote: 9–0
• Opinion of the Court: Earl Warren

In 1954, Linda Brown (foreground) attended the third grade at the all-black Monroe School in Topeka, Kansas. Linda's father, Oliver Brown, sued the school board to permit his daughter to attend the all-white school that was blocks from her home rather than walking a mile through a railroad switchyard in order to catch a bus to Monroe.

and practice. In the South, however, it was de jure, meaning that it was established by law, and that put it in conflict with the Fourteenth Amendment's equal protection clause. The justices in *Brown* II, therefore, called for an end to de jure segregation with "all deliberate speed."

What we today call the *Brown* decisions were actually composed of five different cases, four from southern and border states (South Carolina, Virginia, Delaware, and Kansas) and one from the District of Columbia. In each instance, Thurgood Marshall played a critical role.

In *Briggs* v. *Elliott,* Harry Briggs and more than sixty other black parents sued the Clarendon County, South Carolina, schools district to demand equal facilities. In Clarendon, white children rode buses to modern schools while black children walked as far as five miles to dilapidated buildings. The political leaders of South Carolina attempted to undercut the litigation by pouring money into black schools in an effort to make them materially equal to white schools, to fulfill the *Plessy* definition of "separate but equal." Marshall, however, insisted that the impact of segregation was felt most fully and most tragically by black children. To support his position he hired the black social psychologist Kenneth Clark, who used experiments with black and white dolls to test black children's self-image. When asked which doll was "nice" or which they liked best, black children repeatedly chose the white doll.

Three other state cases raised similar issues but in different ways. In *Davis* v. *County School Board of Prince Edward County, Va.*, the plaintiffs, ninth grader Dorothy Davis and 106 other students, complained about the poor facilities of all-black Moton High School in Farmville, Virginia. In *Gebhart* v. *Belton,* Ethel Belton and seven other black parents in Wilmington, Delaware, angry that their children had to travel downtown to attend an all-black high school that was inferior to a nearby all-white school, sued so their children would be able to attend the closer school. Finally, in *Brown* v. *Board of Education of Topeka, Kansas,* Oliver Brown had tried to enroll his daughter Linda in the Sumner School, a few blocks from their home. School authorities denied his request and directed Linda to attend the all-black Monroe School. To do so, Linda had to walk a mile through a railroad switchyard to catch a school bus. After the schools turned down his request, Brown went to the NAACP, which filed suit.

The fifth case, *Bolling* v. *Sharpe,* which involved the District of Columbia, was argued at the same time, although separately from the four other state cases. A representative for twelve-year-old Spotswood Bolling Jr. charged that racially segregated schools in the District were woefully deficient. Although the problem was the same as in the states, the fact that Congress controlled the District meant that Bolling's counsel could not base his case on the Fourteenth Amendment, which applied to the states. In this instance, the argument was that de jure segregation by race violated the due process clause of the Fifth Amendment, which applied to the federal government.

The power of the *Plessy* precedent was obvious when the cases were argued in the lower federal courts. In each instance, except for Delaware, the blacks seeking desegregation lost. The cases made their way to the high court separately but were consolidated by the justices in order to expedite hearing them and addressing the broad issues they raised. As Brown was first alphabetically, it became the case name with which we associate the litigation.

Revolutionary though they were, the two *Brown* decisions and that in *Bolling* stemmed from nearly sixty years of litigation designed by the NAACP to bring an end to what was known as Jim Crow. The term originated in the 1830s when a white performer blackened his face with charcoal and danced a jig while singing the song "Jump Jim Crow." By the 1850s the Jim Crow character had become a standard of American minstrel shows that depicted stereotypical images of black inferiority. The term *Jim Crow* became a racial slur synonymous with black, colored, or Negro in the vocabulary of many whites; and by the end of the century acts of racial discrimination toward blacks were often referred to as Jim Crow laws and practices.

Beginning in the 1880s, states in the American South imposed so-called Jim Crow laws that segregated the races in public accommodations, schools, and transportation. In 1896 the high court in *Plessy* v. *Ferguson* gave constitutional validity to these laws. By a vote of 7 to 1, the justices held that state-imposed racial segregation was constitutionally acceptable under the equal protection clause of the Fourteenth Amendment as long as the facilities and personnel were equal. The author of the majority opinion, Justice Henry Billings Brown, observed that no law could overcome the prejudice that whites held against blacks. Under these circumstances, Brown concluded, segregation by race was "reasonable." The lone dissenter in the case, Justice John Marshall Harlan, a former Kentucky slaveholder, reached exactly the opposite conclusion. Harlan explained, "Our Constitution is color-blind, and neither knows nor tolerates classes among citizens. In respect of civil rights, all citizens are equal before the law." In *Brown* the justices made Harlan's dissent the law of the land.

By the 1930s the increasingly aggressive NAACP had developed what it hoped would be a successful strategy to force the Court to abandon *Plessy*. The organization's legal arm, the Legal Defense and Education Fund, and students and faculty at the Howard University Law School in Washington, D.C., led the charge. The NAACP, founded in 1909, took as its mission the expansion of rights for African Americans. The association struggled, however, to develop a coordinated legal strategy. In 1922, Charles Garland, a white Boston millionaire, established the Garland Fund for the purpose of providing legal defense to African Americans. The NAACP drew on its funds to finance the legal campaign to end segregation. In 1934 the NAACP appointed Charles Hamilton Houston, dean of the Howard Law School and the first black member of the *Harvard Law Review,* its first full-time counsel. Houston brought strong administrative leadership and excellent legal judgment to the task of resolving issues of discrimination, violence, and segregation. He also transformed the Howard Law School into a laboratory for civil rights litigation and trained two generations of African American lawyers.

Among Howard's graduates was Thurgood Marshall, who would later become the first African American appointed to the U.S. Supreme Court. Marshall graduated first in his class in 1933 and then joined Houston on the front lines of the civil rights struggle. Marshall worked full time for the NAACP, first as a counsel and then as the director of the Legal Defense and

This NAACP recruiting poster from 1946 illustrates its goals of ensuring voting rights, quality education, and employment opportunities for African Americans. The NAACP sought to influence the Supreme Court through both direct political action and a successful legal strategy that began by attacking segregation in higher education and then moved to public schools.

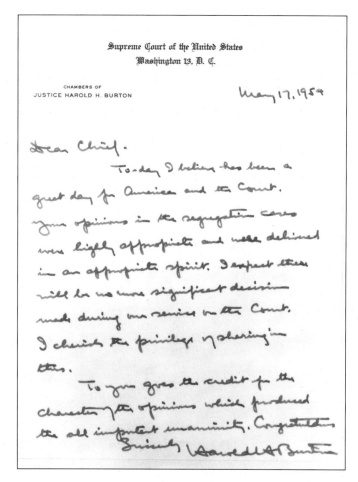

May 17, 1954

Dear Chief,

To-day I believe has been a great day for America and the Court. Your opinions in the segregation cases were highly appropriate and well delivered in an appropriate spirit. I expect there will be no more significant decision made during our service in the Court. I cherish the privilege of sharing in them.

To you goes the credit for the character of the opinions which produced the all important unanimity. Congratulations.

Sincerely, Harold H. Burton

Justice Harold Burton sent this handwritten congratulatory note to Chief Justice Earl Warren on May 17, 1954, the day the Court handed down its decision in Brown v. Board of Education, *making racial segregation in public education illegal. Burton was Warren's ally in many such cases involving civil liberties and civil rights.*

Education Fund. The purpose of the fund, which was established in 1939 and had its roots in Garland's earlier contribution, was to "give the Southern Negro his constitutional rights." Marshall achieved twenty-nine Supreme Court victories, including *Brown*.

Marshall and Houston realized that they could not directly confront *Plessy*. They knew that *Plessy* was a powerful precedent and that white southern parents were opposed to having their children mix with blacks in elementary and secondary schools. Instead, they strategically whittled away at the precedent by attacking segregation in professional and graduate education. Their first breakthrough came in *Missouri ex rel. Gaines* v. *Canada* (1938). The University of Missouri School of Law denied Lloyd Gaines admission solely because of his race. The state offered to pay his tuition at a public law school in an adjacent state, but Gaines refused. He argued that he had a constitutional right to pursue a legal education in the state where he lived. Chief Justice Charles Evans Hughes wrote the majority opinion that invalidated Missouri's out-of-state tuition program for African American law students and required the state to provide appropriate facilities. After winning his victory, however, Gaines disappeared. Rumors circulated that he had been a victim of the Ku Klux Klan or other vigilantes opposed to racial equality, but no one has ever discovered his fate.

The litigation campaign reached another milestone in 1948 with *Shelley* v. *Kraemer*. In this case, for the first time, the attorney general of the United States submitted an amicus curiae (friend of the court) brief.. The action not only signaled the positive support of the federal government for the NAACP's strategy, but also placed the government on the winning side. The justices held that restrictive covenants, agreements placed in real estate contracts to block the sale of property to a black person, were unenforceable.

Two years later the Legal Defense and Education Fund scored another victory when the Court, ruling in *McLaurin* v. *Oklahoma State Board of Regents* and *Sweatt* v. *Painter*, invalidated segregation first in graduate and then in legal education. Jim Crow, the justices held, could not be supported merely by claiming that facilities were equal; instead, the Court indicated that there were other intangible consequences to segregation by race. Among these was the isolation that blacks suffered from being unable to interact with white classmates.

Racial exclusion in other areas was also unraveling. For example, in *Smith* v. *Allwright* (1944) the Court began to strike down state laws that made it difficult if not impossible for blacks to vote in the southern states. With this string of successes, in the early 1950s the NAACP decided to move directly against segregation in elementary and secondary schools.

Chief Justice Fred Vinson, a Kentuckian and the author of the Court's opinions in *Sweatt* and *McLaurin*, was reluctant to hear the five cases that led to the *Brown* decision. So, too, were other members of the Court. They recognized how fully issues of race had become insinuated into American life. Any action by the Court would provoke a backlash from a southern white population secure in the precedent established by *Plessy*. The justices also understood that de facto desegregation had become a common feature of life in the North, but their attention was drawn most fully to the separation of race that was created in the South by law. That concern, and not the fate of blacks in segregated schools of the North, drew their almost exclusive attention. They recognized that any decision on segregation would affect millions of schoolchildren, their parents, and dozens of states where it was formal state policy.

Despite these concerns, the justices heard the *Brown* cases and the *Bolling* case in 1952. The result was a sharp division. Most of the justices accepted that legal segregation was wrong, but they disagreed sharply over the questions of how and how quickly to provide relief. The 1952 term ended with no decision.

Then fate intervened. Chief Justice Vinson, who was deeply worried about the impact that eliminating segregation would have on his native South, died. His replacement was Earl Warren, former attorney general and governor of California and aspirant for the Republican Presidential nomination in 1952. That nomination went instead to Dwight D. Eisenhower, who gained the Californian's support at the Republic National Convention by promising him the first vacancy on the high bench. In retrospect, Eisenhower considered his selection of Warren to be his biggest political mistake. The new chief justice quickly moved to redefine much of the nation's fundamental law, usually in ways with which President Eisenhower disagreed. Warren's opinion in *Brown* was merely the first of what proved to be flood of landmark rulings.

Warren knew above all else that the Court had to speak with a unanimous voice on such a controversial matter as segregation. He persuaded his fellow justices that the best course of action was to order the cases to be reargued. The Court also asked the solicitor general of the United States to file an amicus curiae brief. (The solicitor is the government lawyer who argues its positions before the justices.) The new Eisenhower administration was reluctant to do so, in part because the issue was so divisive, in part because Eisenhower believed that the states should be left to handle racial issues, and in part because the President wanted to keep the support of the four southern states he had won. The Republicans also had captured the House and Senate, and they were reluctant to hurt their chances of building additional strength in the South. However, the administration reluctantly filed in support of desegregation, fearing that if Eisenhower failed to do so he would run the risk of alienating northern moderates in his party.

While the government was putting together its brief in the summer of 1953, Marshall and the NAACP organized an extensive research effort that drew on the work of historians and social scientists to establish the intent of the framers of the Fourteenth Amendment. The post–Civil War Congress had passed the amendment as one of several ways of making the states more responsible to the national government on matters of civil rights. The amendment was composed of five sections, of which the first and the fifth were the most important. The first provided, among other things, that

No State shall make or enforce any law which shall abridge the privileges or immunities of citizens of the United States; nor shall any state deprive any person of life, liberty, or property, without due process of law; nor deny to any person within its jurisdiction the equal protection of the laws.

This powerful language meant that certain forms of state action, such as establishing access to schools, hotels, and trains based on race, might well be subject to scrutiny in the federal courts. The Supreme Court had examined these actions in *Plessy*, but it had found that separate but equal facilities were in fact constitutional.

The fifth section of the amendment provided that "The Congress shall have power to enforce, by appropriate legislation, the provisions of this article." These words wrote a revolution in the relationship between the states and the federal government, but how broad a revolution was open to speculation. Did the framers of that amendment contemplate that it would encompass desegregation of public facilities in general and schools in particular? The NAACP's research proved inconclusive on the specific question of their intent, but it did affirm that the framers were pointing toward a broad, egalitarian future, a finding at odds with *Plessy*.

The reargument of *Brown* and *Bolling* occurred in December of 1953. Marshall contended that, contrary to *Plessy*, racial segregation was an unreasonable action because it was based on an arbitrary and capricious use of race and color. Marshall, drawing on the precedents he had fashioned over the previous two decades, reminded the justices that they had already found racial distinctions in violation of the equal protection clause in cases involving higher education. The same principle, he insisted, should be extended to public education and all public facilities. In an appendix to his brief Marshall also invoked Kenneth Clark's research using black and white dolls to show that segregation had negatively affected black children. Not only did black children suffer from low self-esteem, but they were unable to live, work, and cooperate with the children of the majority population.

In a Maryland courtroom, Thurgood Marshall (standing) and another attorney, Charles Hamilton Houston, argue that their client, Donald Gaines Murray, should be admitted to the University of Maryland Law School. Marshall was the lead attorney for the NAACP's Legal Defense and Education Fund, created in 1939, and later became the first black appointed to the Supreme Court.

On the other side was John W. Davis, a legal powerhouse. He had argued more than 250 cases before the Supreme Court, more than any other lawyer in the twentieth century. At the time of *Brown*, Davis was a corporate lawyer with a lucrative practice in New York City. During an unsuccessful campaign for President, Davis had denounced the Ku Klux Klan. However, many considered Davis to be a "gentleman racist," a passionate conservative who dismissed federal woman suffrage and antilynching bills as egalitarian meddling in the rights of states to regulate their own social policies.

Davis's argument was a straightforward mix of established law and pragmatism. *Plessy* remained binding precedent, he argued, which the justices would set aside at their own peril. Moreover, Kansas had a history of segregation and it had produced little criticism from either blacks or whites. That state's legislature, not the courts, should be the deciding body on such a matter because it knew best what the local conditions were. Laws, Davis reminded the Court in words that echoed Henry Billings Brown's opinion in *Plessy*, never had and never could destroy prejudice. When facilities were materially equal or when the states were working hard to make them equal, there could be no violation of the equal protection clause. Davis also reminded the justices that, historically, social and political equality had been treated as entirely different matters under the Fourteenth Amendment, the purpose of which was merely to provide for the latter. Finally, Davis argued, segregation was fading and would soon be gone. Patience would be a virtue for the Court and the nation, since overturning *Plessy* would only produce social turmoil. The law of *Plessy* was clear: the principle of "separate but equal" was constitutional.

Warren had inherited a Court divided. The split among the justices reflected their differing beliefs about the social costs that would accompany the desegregation of thousands of schools with millions of students. Some justices believed that the Court should not intervene in matters that were best left to the states to handle as they saw fit. A majority agreed, however, that legally based segregation by race was socially and constitutionally wrong and that the Court had to do something to set the record right.

Warren's leadership was critical in two ways. First, he persuaded his colleagues to decide the merits of segregation in one opinion and to leave the question of relief to a second one following yet another reargument. Second, Warren used every persuasive power he could command to achieve unanimity. His two greatest challenges were Robert H. Jackson, who threatened to issue a concurring opinion, and Stanley F. Reed, a Kentuckian who planned to dissent. Jackson's law clerk, the future Supreme Court justice William H. Rehnquist, provided a memorandum that urged Jackson to accept the constitutionality of *Plessy*, a position that he ultimately resisted. Reed, fearing that his dissent would become fuel for racists and segregationists and with Warren's urging, decided to join the rest of the Court.

There is little doubt about Warren's sentiments. Although he had supported the relocation and internment of Japanese Americans during World War II, he understood clearly the social and human costs associated with segregation. For example, shortly before the Supreme Court announced its decision, Warren decided to visit a few of the Civil War battlefields in Virginia. He cut his trip short after his black chauffeur was unable to find lodging in the racially segregated region. Greatly upset by the incident, Warren viewed this experience as evidence of the need to overturn segregation.

Warren devised a strategy designed to foster harmony among the justices, convening three separate conferences to discuss the case. In the first conference he presented the issue in a moral perspective. The underlying proposition in *Plessy* was that blacks were in fact inferior to whites. Warren reminded his colleagues that to uphold *Plessy*, the Court would have to agree with such a presumption. At the second conference, Warren appeased his southern colleagues by assuring them that a decision in favor of desegregation would be flexible on the matter of a remedy, which would be addressed in a separate opinion. Warren announced as well that he would take on the task of preparing the opinion of the Court. At the third conference, he presented the broad outline of his opinion.

Brown I held unanimously that segregation in public schools was unconstitutional under the equal protection clause of the Fourteenth Amendment. The chief justice used a short, nontechnical, and nonaccusatory opinion to make this basic point. "We come then to the question presented," Warren wrote. "Does segregation of children in public schools solely on the basis of race, even though the physical facilities and other 'tangible' factors may be equal, deprive the children of the minority group of equal educational opportunities? We believe that it does," he concluded in words that no one could ignore. Segregation, regardless of circumstances, had deprived minority children of equal educational opportunities and probably generated feelings of inferiority among them. While *Plessy* may have been good law at one time, it was no longer supported by what Warren called "modern authority" and current psychological knowledge. In public education, separate facilities were inherently unequal even if materially the same.

Warren's opinion was unusual in that it drew upon few legal authorities and offered no immediate remedy. Instead, Warren stated what he and his colleagues believed to the right, correct, and just thing to be done—children should not be categorized by race when it came to attending a public school. Warren avoided the use of extensive legal citations because doing so offered the best way of getting his somewhat divided colleagues to reach a decision in favor of desegregation. As important, legal precedent did not weigh fully on Warren's side and, as a result, he knew that invoking it would only confuse those who would read his opinion. The absence of legal authority, however, left the Chief Justice and the Court open to charges that they were substituting their own views for those of the elected representatives from the states where legal segregation by race was to end. Warren also avoided entangling the broad principle that he stated with a specific course of action, which meant that the elimination of racial segregation in public schools could be addressed fully as a moral matter rather than be framed as a specific set of difficult steps to bring about its end. The Court, therefore, requested that the parties provide further argument about how to remedy segregation, which would be addressed in a later opinion.

In a separate opinion in the *Bolling* case, Warren found for a unanimous court that segregation by race in the District of Columbia was unconstitutional. As the equal protection clause of the Fourteenth Amendment did not apply to the federal government, Warren turned instead to the due process clause of the Fifth Amendment. He concluded that it implicitly forbade most racial segregation by the federal government. If the states were constitutionally prohibited from segregating in public schools, then it would be "unthinkable . . . to impose a lesser duty" in the District of Columbia. Because the Fifth Amendment did apply to the federal government, which governed the District, then it followed that the amendment's due process clause forbade racial discrimination.

Warren also wrote for the Court in *Brown* II. The chief justice reiterated that racial discrimination and segregation in the public schools were unconstitutional and that state school authorities had the primary burden of enforcing this principle. He made the federal district courts in the affected states responsible for legal oversight of the school authorities. The defendants, under the supervision of district court judges, were required to admit children of color to the public schools on a nondiscriminatory basis "with all deliberate speed." These words were meant to assure both sides that action would be taken but not in a hasty way. As it turned out, the impact of the decision was more deliberate than speedy.

The two *Brown* opinions and that in *Bolling* mixed moral symbolism with pragmatic expediency. The Court proclaimed an end to legal segregation based on race but then stopped short of demanding an immediate solution. No matter the immorality of segregation, it could only be eliminated gradually. The result was almost two decades of waffling and tardy implementation. Nevertheless, the *Brown* decision continued the venture of seeking democratic equality through the judicial system. Although Marshall and his colleagues were elated at first, they quickly realized that *Brown* was just the beginning.

Many southern officials labeled the day of the announcement of the *Brown* I decision as Black Monday, and most southern members of Congress signed a Southern manifesto, which denounced the decision and the justices. In 1957, Governor Orval Faubus of Arkansas ordered the state's National Guard to physically prevent black students from attending Central High School in Little Rock. In response to a federal court order, Faubus removed the National Guard, and violence followed. A mob outside the school beat several black reporters, who were there to cover the event. Mothers yelled to their children, "Come out! Don't stay with those niggers!" Inside the school, white students spat on the black students, who were forced to escape through a rear door. The editor of the *Arkansas Gazette* summed up the situation this way, "The police have been routed, the mob is in the streets and we're close to a reign of terror." President Eisenhower took control of the situation by placing the guard under his control and ordering U.S. Army troops to restore order and escort black students to their classes.

Following the events at Central High School, the Little Rock School District suspended desegregation efforts for two and a half years. The NAACP challenged this decision, and in the 1958 case of *Cooper* v. *Aaron,* the Court handed down an angry 9–0 opinion criticizing local officials' resistance to *Brown.* Following the lead of Governor Faubus, the Arkansas legislature amended the state's constitution to outlaw desegregation. William G. Cooper, President of the Little Rock School District, sued to have the desegregation program ended, claiming that the opposition of state government and public hostility created an intolerable situation. In effect, Arkansas and the Little Rock School District were thumbing their noses at the Supreme Court and its decision in *Brown.* In an unusual action, all nine justices signed the Court's opinion, underscoring not just their unanimity but their decisiveness on the issue of a state attempting to subvert one of their decisions. "No state legislator or executive or judicial officer," the Court explained, "can war against the

Constitution without violating his undertaking to support it." The justices were emphatic: they alone could interpret conclusively the meaning of the Constitution and no state authority had any power to intervene.

Issues of white flight from southern cities to the suburbs and de facto residential segregation in northern school districts further complicated the implementation of *Brown*. After resisting further direct involvement with the issue, the justices in 1970 accepted a new and controversial solution: bussing of children from one part of town to another to achieve integration, the active pursuit of racial diversity in the schools, not merely desegregation, and the ending of legally enforced racial separation. In the landmark case of *Swann* v. *Charlotte-Mecklenburg Board of Education* (1971) the Court permitted lower federal court judges to impose busing to achieve desegregation of school districts.

In the mid-1990s, however, after several rulings from a more conservative Supreme Court, federal judges abandoned the issue of integration. They asserted that local officials had made a good faith effort to desegregate and that was all that could be required.

The impact of *Brown* extended beyond school desegregation. Shortly after the decision, federal courts at all levels were citing *Brown* in cases challenging different forms of segregation. These included segregated beaches in Baltimore, golf courses in Atlanta, and public housing in Michigan and Missouri. In this way, *Brown* helped to break down the system that had made blacks the nation's official pariahs. For example, by the early 1980s, at least according to public opinion surveys, the color line was close to disappearing completely. Ninety-four percent of Americans, both black and white, subscribed to the principle that black and white children should go to the same schools.

Today, save for extraordinarily few holdouts, racism and the color line that went with it are deemed unacceptable, and racial diversity is viewed as a public good. That said, there is still substantial disagreement about how to achieve diversity and how to use the state's power to allot some of society's most important rewards and benefits, such as access to a college education. We live, today, in a nation where African Americans make up more than 50 percent of the prison population, even though they make up just 12 percent of the general population. Black males between ages eighteen and twenty-four are almost ten times more likely than white males of the same age to be the victims of homicide. Black children are far more likely than white children to live in poverty; their parents are far more likely to be unemployed or to earn low incomes.

We are also in the middle of a national trend toward school resegregation. That process has pushed more and more African American and Latino students into those schools with 75 percent or more minority children. Gary Orfield, codirector of Harvard University's Civil Rights Project, released a major research report in 2001 that documented the emergence of a substantial group of American schools that are virtually nonwhite. Many school systems outside the South are more racially segregated today than they were in 1954. And in the South the picture is mixed. Take, for example, Clarendon County, South Carolina, where one of the *Brown* desegregation cases began. The public schools there are 98 percent black; the private schools established following court orders that compelled integration are 98 percent white.

By using drawings and dolls, psychologists Kenneth and Mamie Clark conducted groundbreaking studies of the effects of segregation on schoolchildren. They discovered that black children preferred white dolls and drawings and that they often colored figures of themselves a lighter shade than their own skin color. They concluded, "It is clear that the Negro child, by the age of five is aware of the fact that to be colored in contemporary American society is a mark of inferior status." Their research was submitted as evidence in the case of Brown v. Board of Education.

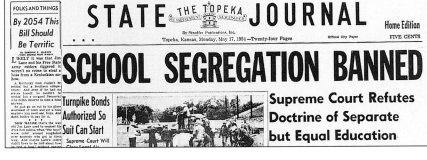

The front page of the Topeka State Journal *reported on May 17, 1954, that the Court reached its unanimous decision but was vague about how and when school segregation would end. More than a decade passed before the next important development on this front: the passage of the Civil Rights Act of 1964.*

Both the U.S. military and major corporations have concluded that having well-educated minority students is essential to providing leaders for the nation's increasingly diverse population. By the beginning of the twenty-first century, persons from minority backgrounds occupied posts of major national trust, including the secretary of state, national security advisor to the President, secretary of education, chairman of the joint chiefs of staff, and attorney general. Since 1968 there has been an African American on the high court.

These developments were, in 1954, beyond comprehension, and they signal a profound change in American life. Did *Brown* make these developments possible? The answer is clearly yes, although it does not follow that *Brown* alone made them possible.

During the period in which the high court considered *Brown,* the members of the Court viewed the changes taking place among blacks as astounding. Justice Robert Jackson noted privately that the advances made by blacks since the Civil War were among the most impressive in human history. Justice Felix Frankfurter agreed, and he even made the point to his colleagues as they deliberated *Brown* that, in the end, it was these changes that should prompt the Court to support desegregation.

Finally, *Brown* stirred a massive backlash, one that is hard for Americans who did not live through the decades of the 1950s and 1960s to appreciate. The decision, for example, inspired action from the South's white supremacists. It profoundly radicalized southern politics and made such figures as arch-segregationist governor George C. Wallace of Alabama temporarily legitimate. In his 1963 inauguration speech Wallace intoned the words, "segregation today... segregation tomorrow... segregation forever." Such words stirred violence against peaceful civil rights demonstrators, but they also mobilized national political support for civil rights and voting rights legislation that struck at the heart of segregation.

In 2004, the fiftieth anniversary of the Court's decision in *Brown,* critics were out in force, arguing that the justices' landmark ruling had accomplished little. It would be a mistake, they insisted, to attribute too much to the work of the Court. Yet the appropriate measure of the Court's success is not what it should have done measured against today's standards but instead what it did during the 1950s and 1960s. In that context, the decision was one of the great milestones in the course of human rights and freedom, a conclusion the rest of the world seems to recognize. In international human rights law, *Brown* is one of the most, if not *the* most, respected of American cases.

The Southern Declaration on Integration

Chief Justice Earl Warren's opinions in Brown I *and* Brown II *ignited a storm of protest in the South. An entire generation of segregationists, such as George C. Wallace of Alabama, built their careers by claiming that the decision was unconstitutional. Wallace and other southern political leaders understood what the broader white population wanted: resistance to the Court and, more generally, to federal authorities demanding that they yield their historic race-based social practices. The "Southern Declaration on Integration" was the first step in a program of resistance to* Brown *that stretched over more than two decades. This document was signed by ninety-six southern congressmen—practically the entire southern delegation in the House of Representatives—and published in the* Congressional Record.

We regard the decision of the Supreme Court in the school cases as clear abuse of judicial power. It climaxes a trend in the Federal judiciary undertaking to legislate, in derogation of the authority of Congress, and to encroach upon the reserved rights of the states and the people.

The original Constitution does not mention education. Neither does the Fourteenth Amendment nor any other amendment. The debates preceding the submission of the Fourteenth Amendment clearly show that there was no intent that it should affect the systems of education maintained by the states.

The very Congress which proposed the amendment subsequently provided for segregated schools in the District of Columbia.

When the amendment was adopted in 1868, there were thirty-seven states of the Union. Every one of the twenty-six states that had any substantial racial differences among its people either approved the operation of segregated schools already in existence or subsequently established such schools by action of the same law-making body which considered the Fourteenth Amendment.

As admitted by the Supreme Court in the public school case (*Brown* v. *Board of Education*), the doctrine of separate but equal schools "apparently originated in *Roberts* v. *City of Boston* (1849), upholding school segregation against attack as being violative of a state constitutional guarantee of equality." This constitutional doctrine began in the North—not in the South—and it was followed not only in Massachusetts but in Connecticut, New York, Illinois, Indiana, Michigan, Minnesota, New Jersey, Ohio, Pennsylvania and other northern states until they, exercising their rights as states through the constitutional processes of local self-government, changed their school systems.

In the case of *Plessy* v. *Ferguson* in 1896 the Supreme Court expressly declared that under the Fourteenth Amendment no person was denied any of his rights if the states provided separate but equal public facilities. This decision has been followed in many other cases....

This interpretation, restated time and again, became a part of the life of the people of many of the states and confirmed their habits, customs, traditions, and way of life. It is founded on elemental humanity and common sense, for parents should not be deprived by Government of the right to direct the lives and education of their own children.

Though there has been no constitutional amendment or act of Congress changing this established legal principle almost a century old, the Supreme Court of the United States, with no legal basis for such action, undertook to exercise their naked judicial power and substituted their personal political and social ideas for the established law of the land.

This unwarranted exercise of power by the court, contrary to the Constitution, is creating chaos and confusion in the states principally affected. It is destroying the amicable relations between the white and Negro races that have been created through ninety years of patient effort by the good people of both races. It has planted hatred and suspicion where there has been heretofore friendship and understanding.

Without regard to the consent of the governed, outside agitators are threatening immediate and revolutionary changes in our public school systems. If done, this is certain to destroy the system of public education in some of the states.

With the gravest concern for the explosive and dangerous condition created by this decision and inflamed by outside meddlers:

We reaffirm our reliance on the Constitution as the fundamental law of the land.

We decry the Supreme Court's encroachments on rights reserved to the states and to the people, contrary to established law and to the Constitution.

We commend the motives of those states which have declared the intention to resist forced integration by any lawful means.

We appeal to the states and people who are not directly affected by these decisions to consider the constitutional principles involved against the time when they too, on issues vital to them, may be the victims of judicial encroachment.

Even though we constitute a minority in the present Congress, we have full faith that a majority of the American people believe in the dual system of government which has enabled us to achieve our greatness and will in time demand that the reserved rights of the states and of the people be made secure against judicial usurpation.

We pledge ourselves to use all lawful means to bring about a reversal of this decision which is contrary to the Constitution and to prevent the use of force in its implementation.

In this trying period, as we all seek to right this wrong, we appeal to our people not to be provoked by the agitators and troublemakers invading our states and to scrupulously refrain from disorder and lawless acts.

14

Establishing Equality in Voting and Representation

Baker v. *Carr* (1962)

Reynolds v. *Sims* (1964)

Baker v. Carr

- 369 U.S. 186 (1962)

- Decided: March 26, 1962

- Vote: 6–2

- Opinion of the Court: William J. Brennan

- Concurring opinions: William O. Douglas, Tom Clark, and Potter Stewart

- Dissenting opinions: Felix Frankfurter and John Marshall Harlan II

- Not participating: Charles E. Whittaker

Reynolds v. Sims

- 377 U.S. 533 (1964)

- Decided: June 15, 1964

- Vote: 8–1

- Opinion of the Court: Earl Warren

- Concurring opinions: Tom Clark and Potter Stewart

- Dissenting opinion: John Marshall Harlan II

Representative democracy has deep roots in the United States. It is based on free, fair, competitive, and periodic elections by which citizens vote to choose their representatives in government. These representatives of the people—chosen by a majority, or a plurality, of the voters—serve the interests and needs of their constituents. When the people's representatives make decisions and otherwise carry out their duties in the government, there is an expectation of accountability. If they do not satisfy the citizens they represent, then most voters are likely to cast their ballots for someone else or for another political party in the next election.

Given the centrality of the electoral process in a representative democracy, the right to vote is the citizen's most precious political possession. By using the vote responsibly, citizens can contribute significantly to the achievement of good government.

But what if some votes count more than others? Can there be an authentic representative democracy if equal representation of constituents is not achieved through the electoral process? Can government be fair, if the interests of some groups of voters have more weight than those of less privileged groups in the decisions of their representatives?

Public concern about questions of equality in voting, and in the representation of voters, led to a series of notable cases at the Supreme Court. The first of these cases, *Baker* v. *Carr* in 1962, and the last, *Reynolds* v. *Sims* in 1964, yielded the pivotal decisions that established, once and for all, the fundamental democratic principle of "one person, one vote" also with regard to Congressional elections.

These Supreme Court decisions were made in response to unequal representation in state governments and disparate voting power of citizens residing in different places within the states. When each legislator represents an electoral district with approximately the same number of people, then the voting power of the people in all districts of the state is roughly equal. But this kind of equality in representation and voting power was nonexistent in most parts of the country. This inequity developed during the first half of the twentieth century when the distribution of the nation's population changed.

Representation of voters in state governments throughout the United States became more and more unequal due to mass movements of people from rural to urban residences. During the 1920s, for the first time in American history, more people were living in cities than in rural areas, but in most states, the government had not changed the legislative districts to reflect this dramatic change. The result was disproportionate voting power for people living in underpopulated and overrepresented rural districts.

In 1960 nearly every state had some urban legislative districts with populations that were at least twice as large as those in the state's rural districts. In Alabama, for example, the smallest congressional district had a population of 6,700 and the largest had a population of more than 104,000; nonetheless, each district had one congressional seat. In a representative democracy, people's votes possess equal value only when each member of the legislative body represents approximately the same number of people.

Clearly, the people in more populous urban districts and the people in the less populous rural districts were not represented equally. Consequently, city and suburban problems did not receive appropriate attention in state legislatures that were dominated by representatives from districts with many farms and small towns. The powerful rural representatives refused to redistrict in order to ensure that each member of the legislature would represent roughly the same number of people. Some simply ignored the sections of their state constitutions requiring redistricting every ten years. Others merely redistricted and reapportioned representation in ways that continued to favor rural interests. There was little voters could do to change things through the electoral process, because apportionment of representatives heavily favored the rural areas, which stubbornly resisted reform.

Disgruntled urban leaders turned to the legal process to seek equitable representation in government. Charles Baker, the mayor of Millington, Tennessee, a rapidly growing suburb of Memphis, and the leader of the legislative reapportionment movement in Tennessee, was extremely frustrated by the indifference of state legislators to problems in the rapidly growing cities of Tennessee. The state lawmakers routinely snubbed petitions for assistance from urban leaders such as Baker, because the cities of Tennessee were grossly underrepresented in the legislature. By contrast, the overrepresented rural voters got most of the attention and benefits from the state government, because they were the constituents of the vast majority of the legislators.

Approximately 11 percent of the state's population lived in the rural areas of Tennessee, but more than 60 percent of the representatives in the state legislature were elected by voters residing in the rural areas. Because of this imbalance, the legislature neglected the problems and needs of urban voters. For example, the leader of the Tennessee House of Representatives said, "I believe

"But there must be some way around him."

This political cartoon, which ran in the Alabama newspaper the Birmingham News, *depicts rural politicians' attempt to find "some way around" the Supreme Court's firm stand on reapportionment of electoral districts. This resistance, however, was futile and all fifty states eventually followed the Court's redistricting principle of "one person, one vote."*

In Baker v. Carr, *the Court considered detailed statistical evidence of voter populations to demonstrate that residents of Tennessee's large cities, such as Memphis (Shelby County), had lost voting power over the previous fifty years.*

County	Voting Pop.	Total Rep. Schotland 1901	Prop.	Total Rep. Lewin 1901	Prop.	Total Rep. Combined 1901	Prop.
Lincoln	15,092	2.50	1.60	2.71	1.78	5.21	3.38
Henry	15,465	2.83	2.00	2.75	1.78	5.58	3.72
Lawrence	15,847	2.00	1.60	2.23	1.81	4.43	3.41
Giles	15,935	2.25	1.60	2.23	1.81	4.48	3.41
Tipton	15,944	3.00	1.60	1.68	1.13	4.68	2.72
Robertson	16,456	2.83	1.60	2.63	1.85	5.46	3.44
Wilson	16,459	3.00	1.75	3.02	1.21	6.02	2.96
Carroll	16,472	2.83	1.50	2.89	1.81	5.72	3.31
Hawkins	16,900	3.00	1.75	1.92	1.81	4.92	3.56
Putnam	17,071	1.70	1.48	2.50	1.87	4.20	3.29
Campbell	17,477	.76	2.00	1.41	1.93	2.17	3.93
Roane	17,639	1.75	1.50	1.27	1.27	3.02	2.77
Weakley	18,007	2.33	2.00	2.64	1.84	4.97	3.84
Bradley	18,273	1.25	1.60	1.67	1.93	2.92	3.53
McMinn	18,347	1.75	1.60	1.96	1.93	3.71	3.53
Obion	18,434	2.00	1.75	2.29	1.93	4.29	3.68
Dyer	20,062	2.00	2.00	2.35	2.33	4.35	4.33
Sumner	20,143	2.33	1.85	3.56	2.55	5.88	4.40
Carter	23,303	1.10	3.00	1.50	2.56	2.60	5.56
Greene	23,649	1.99	2.08	2.06	2.67	4.05	4.75
Maury	24,556	2.25	1.93	3.82	2.85	6.07	4.78
Rutherford	25,316	2.00	2.25	3.01	2.39 / 2.40	5.01	4.65
Montgomery	26,284	3.00	1.75	3.73	3.05	6.73	4.82
Gibson	29,832	5.00	2.25	5.00	2.86	10.00	5.11
Blount	30,353	1.60	2.50	2.11	2.18	3.71	4.68
Anderson	33,990	1.25	2.50	1.31	3.63	2.56	6.13
Washington	36,967	1.99	3.00	2.64	3.44	4.63	6.44
Madison	37,245	3.50	2.50	4.85	3.69	8.35	6.19
Sullivan	55,712	3.00	4.00	4.08	5.56	7.08	9.56
Hamilton	131,971	6.00	12.70	6.00	15.10	12.00	27.80
Knox	140,559	7.25	13.50	8.16	15.20	15.41	28.70
Davidson	211,930	12.50	19.25	12.92	21.56	25.42	40.81
Shelby	312,345	15.00	29.60	16.85	31.55	31.85	61.15

in collecting the taxes where the money is—in the cities—and spending it where it's needed—in the country."

As state government officials were unwilling to reform the electoral system, Charles Baker turned to the federal courts for relief. In 1959, he brought suit against Joseph Cordell Carr, the Tennessee secretary of state, to force reapportionment of the legislature. But the federal district court dismissed the suit because of the legal precedent set in *Colegrove v. Green* (1946).

The *Colegrove* case involved reapportionment in Illinois, where population distribution in congressional districts was similar to the situation in Tennessee. However, the U.S. Supreme Court did not respond to this problem. Writing for the Court's majority in *Colegrove*, Justice Felix Frankfurter dismissed the case for lack of jurisdiction, which means that the Court had no authority or legal right to consider this case. Frankfurter held that this case was not justiciable. That is, it was not an appropriate case for the Court to decide, because it posed political questions properly settled by the executive and legislative branches of government, whose leading members are elected by the people. He said, "It is hostile to a democratic system to involve the judiciary in the politics of the people." He concluded with the admonition that the courts "ought not enter this political thicket."

Charles Baker appealed the district court's decision, and in 1962 his case went to the U.S. Supreme Court, which seemed interested in reconsidering the issues first presented to it by *Colegrove* in 1946. Only one of the Court's majority in *Colegrove*, Justice Frankfurter, was still a member of the Court in 1962. But two of the dissenters, Justices Black and Douglas, remained and they influenced Chief Justice Warren and the other justices to side with them in accepting the *Baker v. Carr* case. Charles Rhyne, counsel for Charles Baker, argued that urban voters in Tennessee were denied the equal protection of the laws guaranteed by the Fourteenth Amendment. He requested that the state be ordered to redraw its legislative districts so that each person's vote would be of equal weight. The Court, however, restricted its decision to questions of whether the Court should hear the case; that is to issues about jurisdiction, justiciabililtiy, and standing—a direct interest in the outcome of the case. Thus, the Court decided not to pass judgment on the merits of the complaint brought by the plaintiff about unequal and unfair representation of voters in the state legislature. Nonetheless, the Court's decision in *Baker* overturned the precedent established in the 1946 *Colegrove* case, which was a significant breakthrough for the cause of electoral reform.

Justice William Brennan, writing for the majority, ruled that the Court had jurisdiction or authority to hear this case; he said that "the right [to equal apportionment of representation] is within the reach of judicial protection under the Fourteenth Amendment." Brennan held that Baker and his associates had standing to bring this complaint to the Court; because as registered voters in an underrepresented urban area, they had an undeniable claim to injury based on unequal representation and thus a stake in the outcome of this case.

The most important part of Brennan's ruling was that the issue in this case was not a political question and thus was justiciable, or appropriate for the judiciary to decide. He held that the issue in *Baker* v. *Carr* was not a political question because it had nothing to do with the principle of separation of powers among the three coordinate branches of government: "[W]e have no questions decided, or to be decided, by a political branch of government coequal with the Court." Justice Brennan stressed that the issues in the case did not pertain to Article 4, Section 4 of the Constitution, the guaranty of a republican form of government. Questions involving this part of the Constitution were traditionally understood to be outside the Court's authority. Justice Brennan wrote,

> Of course, the mere fact that the suit seeks protection of a political right does not mean it presents a political question.... Rather, it is argued that the apportionment cases...can involve no federal constitutional right except one resting on the guaranty of a republican form of government [Article 4, Section 4], and the complaints based on that clause have been held to present political questions which are nonjusticiable. We hold that the claim pleaded here neither rests upon nor implicates the guaranty Clause and that its justiciability is therefore not foreclosed by our decisions of cases involving that clause.

Brennan concluded "that the complaint's allegations of a denial of equal protection [under the Fourteenth Amendment] present a justiciable constitutional cause." Thus, Baker was entitled to a trial, and the case was remanded (sent back) to the federal district court, which now had the authority to make a substantive decision in this case. The court decided in favor of Baker.

Two justices, Felix Frankfurter and John Marshall Harlan II, dissented from the Supreme Court's decision in *Baker* v. *Carr*. In his final opinion as an associate justice (a heart attack forced his retirement on August 28, 1962), Frankfurter lamented the overturning of precedent established in *Colegrove* v. *Green*, because he claimed the issue in *Baker*, as in *Colegrove*, was essentially political, and not judicial. Thus, he argued, the issue should be left to the executive and legislative branches to decide. Further, Frankfurter claimed that the *Baker* decision was a "massive repudiation of the experience of our whole past in asserting destructively novel judicial power." He said it departed from a long tradition of judicial restraint that could be traced to the founding of the republic, whereby the exercise of judicial power was curtailed in order to avoid usurping authority belonging to the political branches of government.

Justice Harlan agreed strongly with Frankfurter, and he argued there was nothing in the U.S. Constitution that required state legislatures to be apportioned in order to equally represent each voter. Both dissenters asserted that the Court's decision in this case was a product of unwarranted judicial activism, which intruded wrongly into the democratic political process.

The dissenters' opinions, however, were overwhelmed not only within the Court but throughout the United States. Most major newspapers published favorable editorials about the Court's decision, and public opinion generally seemed to support it. U.S. Attorney General Robert Kennedy spoke for the majority of Americans when he called this decision "a landmark in the development of representative government."

Baker v. *Carr* was the first in a series of cases that led to legislative redistricting throughout the nation. The principle of "one person, one vote"—often associated with *Baker*—was actually expressed one year later by Justice Douglas in his opinion for the Court in *Gray* v. *Sanders* (1963). In this case, the Court ruled against a Georgia law that assigned greater electoral weight to sparsely populated rural counties than to heavily populated urban areas. In his argument against the Georgia electoral system, Douglas wrote, "The conception of political equality from the Declaration of Independence, to Lincoln's Gettysburg Address, to the Fifteenth, Seventeenth, and Nineteenth Amendments can mean only one thing—one person, one vote."

The culminating case on equality in voting and representation was *Reynolds* v. *Sims* (1964), which originated in Alabama. Voters in Jefferson County, the state's most densely populated county, which included the big city of Birmingham, claimed that the unequal representation of citizens in Alabama districts violated the equal protection clause of the Fourteenth Amendment.

The Supreme Court ruled in *Reynolds* that the Fourteenth Amendment requires states to establish equally populated electoral districts for both houses of state legislatures. Writing for the majority, Chief Justice Earl Warren stated that plans for setting up legislative districts could not discriminate against people on the basis of where they live (city versus country in this case) any more than they could discriminate on the basis of a person's race or economic status.

The Court rejected the idea that state legislatures could create electoral districts differently for each of two houses of the state legislature—the representation in one house based on districts roughly equal in population and in the other house based on equal representation of areas regardless of population differences. Instead, Chief Justice Warren argued, the voters of a state must be treated equally by equal representation of electoral districts in both houses of the state legislature. "Legislators represent people, not trees or acres," declared the Chief Justice. Warren pointed out that counties within a state were not the political equivalents of the states within the federal union of the United States. Thus, unlike the states, which have equal representation in the Senate regardless of differences in population, the counties within a state could not have

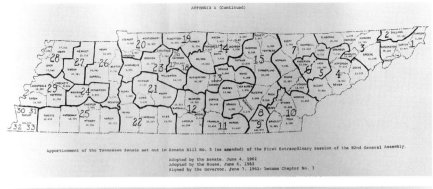

APPENDIX A (Continued)

Apportionment of the Tennessee Senate set out in Senate Bill No. 3 (as amended) of the First Extraordinary Session of the 82nd General Assembly.

Adopted by the Senate, June 4, 1962
Adopted by the House, June 6, 1962
Signed by the Governor, June 7, 1962: became Chapter No. 3

TENNESSEE SENATORIAL DISTRICTS - 1972

Tennessee was one of the states affected by the Supreme Court's reapportionment decisions, and Shelby County, in the lower left corner of the state, represents a microcosm of how the principle of "one man, one vote" changed voting maps across the country. In the 1962 map (top), the county's four representatives, numbered thirty through thirty-three, are distributed evenly through the county. In 1972, several small districts are clustered in the densely populated urban area of Memphis, and the more rural part of the county now has one representative covering a broad territory.

equal representation, regardless of population differences, in either house of a state legislature.

The Court ruled that state legislatures did not have to draw legislative districts with "mathematical exactness or precision." However, such districts did have to be based "substantially" on equal population. The Court thus reinforced a bedrock principle of electoral democracy: "one person, one vote."

As he did in *Baker* v. *Carr,* two years before, Justice John Marshall Harlan II dissented against the Court's ruling, holding firm in his belief that redistricting was an issue best left to the elected representatives of the people in the political branches of state governments. He claimed, as he had in 1962, that this case involved no violation of anyone's constitutional rights.

The Court's *Reynolds* decision was the end of a process initiated by *Baker* v. *Carr* in 1962 that transformed the electoral landscape of America by establishing that rural minorities throughout the United States could no longer control state legislatures. After this 1964 decision, forty-nine state legislatures reapportioned their legislative districts on the basis of equal population. (Oregon had already done so in 1961.) This decision also affected national politics because state legislatures draw the lines for the U.S. Congressional districts. This certainly was a great victory for urban voters throughout America. It was also a triumph for the very idea of democracy, which entails rule by the people based on the votes of the majority.

Reflecting on his illustrious career as chief justice of the United States, Earl Warren said these cases were landmarks "in the development of representative government." Near the end of his life, Warren said the Court's decisions in *Baker* v. *Carr* and *Reynolds* v. *Sims*—forever remembered as the "one person, one vote" cases—were the most important ones decided during his sixteen years as the chief justice, because they strengthened significantly the practice of democracy, government of the people, which is based on equality in voting and representation.

"The Right to Vote Is the Greatest Civil Right"

After the Supreme Court decides to accept a case, a date and time for oral argument is set. Attorneys on both sides of the case speak before the assembled justices in the chamber, or courtroom, of the Supreme Court Building. It is a long-standing tradition for attorneys to begin their formal presentations with the phrase, "May it please the Court." The justices typically interrupt an attorney's presentation with questions or comments. In 1955, Chief Justice Earl Warren launched an oral history project—the audio recording of oral arguments in cases that come before the Supreme Court. Charles Rhyne's oral argument in Baker v. Carr *was recorded on April 19, 1961. Rhyne, representing Charles Baker, challenged the unequally apportioned voting districts in Tennessee and called for equality in voting for representatives in government.*

Warren: Mr. Rhyne?

Rhyne: Chief Justice Warren, and may it please the Court.

This is a voting rights case. It's brought here on appeal by eleven Tennessee voters who seek federal court protection to end flagrant discrimination against their right to vote. These eleven Tennessee voters live in five of the largest cities of Tennessee. They are the intended and actual victims of a statutory scheme which devalues, reduces, their right to vote to about one-twentieth of the value of the vote given to certain rural residents. Since the right to vote is the greatest civil right, the most fundamental civil right under our system of government, this system under the statute of Tennessee is as shocking as it is purposeful and successful....

The way in which these voting rights of the plaintiffs have been effectively denied—so effectively, we say, as to be effectively destroyed—is by a so-called reapportionment statute adopted in 1901. Now, the ultimate thrust of that statute today is that one-third of the qualified voters living in the rural areas of the state of Tennessee elect two-thirds of the state legislature. Now, that 1901 statute...violates the requirement of equality in the Fourteenth Amendment of the Constitution of the United States of America....

The Fourteenth Amendment strikes down discriminations whether they are sophisticated or simpleminded; and we think that, whether you cloak it under the terms of reapportionment or any other cloak,... that this is a discrimination which is clear from the facts in the complaint, and under these facts these voters have a constitutional right that is invaded and have standing to maintain this suit. Because a man's right to vote is personal to him....And when these people have their right to vote invaded, diluted, rendered worthless or practically so by the 1901 act, it's a personal wrong to them to have their vote so affected....

Court [identity of the justice is undetermined]: Do you claim that the Fourteenth Amendment requires that each person's vote in the state be given equal weight?

Rhyne: Reasonable equality, reasonable equality.

Court: As a matter of...

Rhyne: Not mathematical equality.

Court: Not mathematical equality?

Rhyne: But reasonable equality. I think that that is the thrust of the equal protection of the laws requirement of the Fourteenth Amendment....

Frankfurter: Will you... tell us what the remedy is to be here, other than to declare this unconstitutional?...

Rhyne: Number one, there is a clear violation of a constitutional right. Number two, there is no reasonable basis for the voting discrimination which is laid out in the complaint, and the defendants offer no justifications for it, and they cannot offer it on these facts.

And, as I have just said, there is no other remedy. We're at the end of the road. If this is a judicial no-man's land, these people, the two-thirds of the voters of Tennessee, are consigned to be second-class citizens for the rest of their life, because these defendants exalt their position into an untouchable absolute.

15

Freedom of the Press in a Free Society

New York Times Co. v. *Sullivan* (1964)

The First Amendment of the U.S. Constitution protects the rights of individuals to freedom of speech and the press by restricting the powers of the federal government. In a single, pithy phrase, it says: "Congress shall make no law...abridging the freedom of speech, or of the press." The U.S. Supreme Court has applied these First Amendment freedoms against state governments through the due process clause of the Fourteenth Amendment, which says, "No State shall...deprive any person of life, liberty, or property without due process of law...." Since the 1920s, the Court has ruled consistently that First Amendment rights to freedom of speech and press are linked to the individual's general right to liberty guaranteed by the Fourteenth Amendment, which no state government may abridge.

Throughout American history, however, libelous speech had been outside the protection of the First Amendment. Libel is the act of defaming or hurting a person's reputation by saying negative and damaging things about her or him that are untrue or misleading. Libel laws, which exist in every state, provide that a person can be sued for damages by speaking or printing words that defame someone. A government official in the state of Alabama, for example, could sue a citizen of the state for speaking or printing libelous words about her or him. From the ratification of the First Amendment in 1791 until the 1960s, no one had successfully challenged in a court of law the traditional understanding that the state governments could make laws prohibiting and punishing libelous speech. Because cases involving state libel laws did not raise issues under the U.S. Constitution, they were strictly within the jurisdiction of the state courts.

On a fateful Tuesday morning—March 29, 1960—the *New York Times* ran a full-page advertisement that sparked fresh controversy about whether all presumably libelous speech, under all conditions, was outside the protection of the First Amendment. Could a city government official in Montgomery, Alabama, for example, use the libel laws of the state to successfully sue and punish the publisher and managers of a newspaper for printing words he perceived as defamatory? Or could the publisher of a newspaper, such as the *New York Times*, claim its right under the First Amendment to decide what to print and distribute to the public, despite a state government's libel laws? These constitutional issues were raised and settled by the U.S. Supreme Court in *New York Times Co.* v. *Sullivan* (1964).

New York Times Co. v. Sullivan

- 376 U.S. 254 (1964)
- Decided: March 9, 1964
- Vote: 9–0
- Opinion of the Court: William J. Brennan
- Concurring opinions: Hugo L. Black (William O. Douglas) and Arthur Goldberg

The controversial advertisement was placed in the *New York Times* by a group of black civil rights leaders, the Committee to Defend Martin Luther King and the Struggle for Freedom in the South. Then as now, the *Times* often published advertisements written by people who desired to promote not a product but a particular point of view about a current political or social issue. In this case, the civil rights leaders wanted to generate financial support and rally public opinion for their ongoing struggle to change laws in southern states that unjustly discriminated against black Americans, especially laws that unfairly denied black people their constitutional right to vote in public elections.

The headline of the advertisement blared, "Heed Their Rising Voices." It was derived from a *New York Times* editorial of March 19, 1960, which included these words: "The growing movement of peaceful mass demonstrations by Negroes is something new in the South, something understandable.... Let Congress heed their rising voices, for they will be heard."

The opening paragraph of the paid advertisement said:

> As the whole world knows by now, thousands of Southern Negro students are engaged in widespread non-violent demonstrations in positive affirmation of the right to live in human dignity as guaranteed by the U.S. Constitution and the Bill of Rights. In their efforts to uphold these guarantees, they are being met by an unprecedented wave of terror by those who would deny and negate that document which the whole world looks upon as setting the pattern for modern freedom.

In subsequent paragraphs, this advertisement provided examples of the violent tactics police and other public officials had used to stop black people from protesting peacefully against racially biased policies of state and local governments. The ad praised Dr. Martin Luther King Jr. for his heroic leadership of a peaceful civil rights movement. It also stated that the brutal behavior of local government officials had obstructed his efforts, and specifically noted that the policemen of Montgomery, Alabama, had unfairly punished King and his supporters. The concluding paragraphs of the advertisement asked for help from sympathetic citizens throughout the United States:

> We must extend ourselves above and beyond moral support and render the material help so urgently needed by those who are taking the risks, facing jail, and even death in a glorious re-affirmation of the Constitution and its Bill of Rights.
>
> We urge you to join hands with our fellow Americans in the South by supporting with your dollars, this Combined Appeal for all three needs— the defense of Martin Luther King—the support of the embattled students—and the struggle for the right to vote.

The names listed in support of this advertisement were leaders and supporters of the black civil rights movement from all parts of the country, including twenty black ministers of various Christian denominations in the South. This passionate appeal for help was certainly designed to attract attention, rally respondents, and compel change for the common good; and so it did, far beyond the expectation or imagination of the writers and publishers of this full-page piece in the nation's most prominent newspaper, the *New York Times*.

An unanticipated reaction came from an unlikely source, L. B. Sullivan, the police commissioner of Montgomery, Alabama, who was not known to be a reader of the *New York Times*. Actually, few Alabamans before or during the 1960s ever saw the *Times*. In 1960, the daily circulation of this nationally distributed newspaper was approximately 650,000, and, of this total, only 394 copies went to subscribers and newsstands in Alabama. L. B. Sullivan was not among the subscribers. But he read the ad about the black civil rights movement, and he decided to use the libel laws of Alabama to sue the publisher and four of the men whose names were listed in support of the document.

Ray Jenkins, the city editor of the *Alabama Journal* (a daily newspaper published in Montgomery) was, unlike most residents of his city, a regular reader of the *Times,* and he saw the prominently displayed ad. Jenkins surmised that many readers of his newspaper might like to know what the ad said about violence throughout the southern states against black civil rights protesters, especially the charges of brutality against policemen in Montgomery. So Jenkins wrote an article about the contents of the advertisement, which appeared in the April 5, 1960, issue of the *Alabama Journal.*

When Sullivan saw Jenkins's story, he perceived general hostility to southern law enforcement officials and particular animus against the police force of Montgomery, Alabama, which he supervised. Feeling personally maligned by the charges against the police force he supervised, Sullivan could barely restrain his anger, and he resolved to strike back as hard as he could at the perpetrators of this insult to him, his police force, and his city. The third paragraph of the ad was especially troubling to Sullivan. It said:

> In Montgomery, Alabama, after students sang "My Country 'Tis of Thee" on the State Capitol steps, their leaders were expelled from school, and truckloads of police armed with shotguns and tear-gas ringed the Alabama State College Campus. When the entire student body protested to state authorities by refusing to re-register, their dining hall was padlocked in an attempt to starve them into submission.

On April 8, only three days after seeing the ad, Sullivan wrote a letter to the *New York Times.* He claimed that the ad impugned his reputation by wrongly charging him with "grave misconduct" and "improper actions and omissions as an official of the City of Montgomery." He demanded that the *Times* publish "a full and fair retraction of the entire false and defamatory matter." Sullivan also sent identical letters to four black Christian ministers in Alabama whose names had appeared in the advertisement among a long list of supporters. The governor of

The names of numerous celebrities, both black and white, and former first lady Eleanor Roosevelt were listed in support of this full-page advertisement that ran in the New York Times *on March 29, 1960, to protest false accusations against Martin Luther King Jr. and generate support for the civil rights movement. The singer Nat King Cole was the treasurer of the cultural division of the Committee to Defend Martin Luther King and the Struggle for Freedom in the South, which sponsored the ad.*

Alabama, John Patterson, sent similar letters to the New York Times Company and to the four black ministers.

These letters were clear-cut signals of intent to sue for damages under Alabama law in the state's courts. The targeting of the four black ministers was a tactic to keep the suit out of the federal judicial system, which would occur only in cases in which residents of one state sued those of another state. The petitioners understood that their chances for a legal victory were greatest if their case was tried completely within the Alabama legal system. The only other way this case, as constructed by the petitioners, could go to the U.S. Supreme Court was if a constitutional issue was involved. And from the founding of the country until 1960, libel cases arising completely under the jurisdiction of a particular state were considered to be outside the scope of federal constitutional law and strictly the business of the state.

Sullivan claimed that the *New York Times* failed to respond satisfactorily to his demands. Therefore, he sued the publisher and the four black ministers listed as signers of the advertisement. Sullivan's name was not mentioned in the advertisement. Nonetheless, Sullivan claimed to have been maligned because he was the city's commissioner in charge of the police force. Thus, he perceived the negative statements about the police force to be "of and concerning him."

Further, Sullivan charged that the ad was libelous because it contained false statements. For example, the lawyer for Sullivan said that the students mentioned in the ad's third paragraph had sung "The Star Spangled Banner" and not "My County 'Tis of Thee," as the ad claimed. He also noted that the police deployed at Alabama State College to maintain order did not exactly "ring" the campus as claimed in the ad. Furthermore, the college students were suspended not for protesting on the state capitol steps but at a lunch counter at the county courthouse. Finally, by contrast with his list of petty mistakes in the ad, the counsel for Sullivan pointed to one rather significant error: the students had not been locked out of their college's dining hall "to starve them into submission," as claimed in the third paragraph of the ad.

The jury for the local trial court decided in favor of Sullivan and awarded him damages of $500,000 to be paid by the defendants. This award was a large amount of money in 1964, the equivalent of more than $3 million in the early twenty-first century. Counsel for the *New York Times* appealed to the Supreme Court of Alabama, which upheld the decision of the trial court.

The issue seemed to be settled in favor of Sullivan, because there appeared to be no grounds for an appeal to the U.S. Supreme Court. The only possibility was to claim that the Alabama libel laws violated the U.S. Constitution's First Amendment protections of freedom of speech and the press. But the precedents were entirely against such a claim, because prevailing constitutional law held that libel laws of the states could not be overturned through an appeal to First Amendment guarantees. Nonetheless, the U.S. Supreme Court did accept this case on appeal from the New York Times Company because the justices believed that very significant First Amendment issues had been raised.

Lawyers for L. B. Sullivan made the same case for their client to the highest court in the land that they had made to the state courts of Alabama. They particularly stressed that the advertisement in this case was libelous because it contained untrue statements that impugned Sullivan's reputation. Finally, they claimed that the U.S. Constitution does not protect speech that is false or misleading about the actions of a person, and that the state laws on libel were outside the scope of federal constitutional law.

The primary lawyer for the *Times* in the arguments to the U.S. Supreme Court was Columbia University law professor Herbert Wechsler, who was a respected lecturer and author on topics in constitutional law. He had served as the chief technical adviser to the American judges at the Nazi war crimes trial at Nuremberg, Germany, in 1945–46. His written and oral presentations to the Court compellingly claimed that the First Amendment absolutely protects criticism of public officials, such as L. B. Sullivan, no matter what a state's libel laws may say. He drew upon the political ideas of such American founding fathers as James Madison and Thomas Jefferson to argue that genuine representative government, based on consent of the governed, is impossible without very broad constitutional guarantees for freedom of speech and of the press, which protect the individual's right to criticize the government. Wechsler noted James Madison's support for freewheeling criticism of government officials in a democratic republic. In a speech before the House of Representatives in 1794, Madison had declared that in the American system "the censorial power is in the people over the Government and not in the Government over the people." Wechsler concluded by claiming Alabama's legal restrictions in this case, on presumably false speech about public officials, were unconstitutional infringements of First and Fourteenth Amendment freedoms to criticize the government.

Movie star Sidney Poitier (left) and singer Harry Belafonte (center)—the cultural chairmen of the group that placed the "Heed Their Rising Voices" advertisement in the New York Times—*join actor Charlton Heston at the Lincoln Memorial during the 1964 Civil Rights March on Washington, D.C.*

The Court agreed with most of Wechsler's arguments and unanimously reversed the decision of the Alabama Supreme Court. Writing for the Court, Justice William Brennan began with an attention-getting statement that announced a new direction in constitutional law: "We are required in this case to determine for the first time the extent to which the constitutional protections for speech and press limit a State's power to award damages in a libel action brought by a public official against critics of his official conduct."

Brennan next described in detail the facts of the case. Based on what had happened, he concluded:

> We reverse the judgment. We hold that the rule of law applied by the Alabama courts is constitutionally deficient for failure to provide the safeguards for freedom of speech and of the press that are required by the First and Fourteenth Amendments in a libel action brought by a public official against critics of his official conduct.

Brennan wrote extensively about ideas concerning the critical importance of free speech and press in the constitutional democracy of the United States, which had been expressed since the founding era. Brennan's historical commentary set the stage for this dramatic conclusion:

Thus, we consider this case against the background of a profound national commitment to the principle that debate on public issues should be uninhibited, robust, and wide-open, and that it may well include vehement, caustic, and sometimes unpleasantly sharp attacks on government and public officials.... The present advertisement, as an expression of grievance and protest on one of the major public issues of our time, would seem clearly to qualify for... constitutional protection.

Brennan then rejected the claim that errors in the advertisement at issue justified payment of damages to Sullivan. He said that "erroneous statement is inevitable in free debate, and that it must be protected if freedoms of expression are to have the 'breathing space' that they need... to survive." He also rejected the claim that free expression should be restrained to protect the reputation of public officials. "Just as factual error affords no warrant for repressing speech that would otherwise be free, the same is true of injury to official reputation."

If citizens and the media are to be effective critics of their representatives in government, as they should be in a democracy, then restrictions against freedom of expression must be reduced. As a result, public officials may not be awarded damages for defamatory statements about their official conduct merely because the statements are false or damaging to one's reputation. Brennan wrote, "If neither factual error nor defamatory content suffices to remove the constitutional shield from criticism of official conduct, the combination of the two elements is no less inadequate."

Brennan, however, avoided an absolutist position on immunity from libel suits by providing constitutional protection only for false statements made in good faith, without malice or gross indifference to the consequences. He set forth this standard: "The Constitutional guarantees require, we think, a federal rule that prohibits a public official from recovering damages for a defamatory falsehood relating to his official conduct unless he proves that the statement was made with 'actual malice'—that is, with knowledge that it was false or with reckless disregard of whether it was false or not."

Brennan emphasized that the burden is always on the plaintiff to demonstrate "actual malice" and "reckless disregard" in the expression of false and defamatory statements.

Brennan's opinion concluded "that the facts do not support a finding of actual malice" by the *New York Times*. "The judgment of the Supreme Court of Alabama is reversed and the case is remanded to that court for further proceedings not inconsistent with this opinion." Thus Sullivan gained no satisfaction from his claim to damages for libel.

The *New York Times* case can be fully comprehended only in the context of the civil rights movement of the 1960s. In historical perspective, it appears that the infringement of First Amendment freedoms was not the only factor that influenced the Court's decision. The justices also took into account the protests of black Americans against racially biased laws and unfair social conventions, which caused great suffering among them and great embarrassment among all Americans who believed in equal justice under the Constitution. The Supreme Court justices realized that Alabama officials were using the state's libel laws to stifle the voices of those critical of their opposition to civil rights protestors. So the Court's decision in this case strongly supported the role of a free press in a free society, which contributed significantly to the eventual success of the civil rights movement in the South.

The Court's decision in the *New York Times* case has also had significant legal consequences for the press. It has made it very difficult for public officials to bring libel actions against the media. As a result, the ability of the press and the public to discuss freely, and publicly, the actions of government has been greatly expanded. Journalists and broadcasters have been encouraged to play the role of watchdog, with broad, if not unbounded, freedom to investigate questionable or improper actions by public officials, and this freedom has contributed greatly to the maintenance and advancement of liberty and democracy in the United States.

Although generally lauded, *New York Times Co.* v. *Sullivan* also created new problems. It forced the Court to face challenging new issues regarding the meaning of "actual malice" and "reckless disregard," as well as about the distinctions between public figures, with minimal protection from libel, and private persons, who may still sue for libel under the traditional state laws.

In subsequent cases, such as *Gertz* v. *Welch* (1974), the Supreme Court modified and clarified the constitutional law set forth in *New York Times Co.* v. *Sullivan*. Elmer Gertz, a civil liberties lawyer, sued Robert Welch, publisher of *American Opinion,* because an article in that magazine included false and libelous statements about him. The article wrongly stated that Gertz was a communist who advocated violent overthrow of the U.S. government and that he had a criminal record. Gertz had angered Welch, leader of the rabidly anti-communist John Birch Society, by representing a family in their civil suit against a Chicago policeman who had shot and killed their son. Welch charged Gertz with conducting a communist-inspired campaign to undermine the U.S. government by discrediting law enforcement officers.

Gertz won his case at trial by proving that Welch had libeled him. This verdict, however, was overturned in a federal court because it violated the standards set in *New York Times Co.* v. *Sullivan,* which required Gertz to prove "actual malice" and "reckless disregard" rather than mere falsity in order to win payment of damages from Welch. The case went on appeal to the Supreme Court, which reversed the lower federal court's decision and used the occasion to clarify and modify its holdings in cases about freedom of expression and libel.

In his opinion for the Court, Justice Lewis F. Powell began with a strong assertion of the First Amendment guarantees of free expression. "Under the First Amendment, there is no such thing as a false idea. However pernicious an opinion may seem, we depend for its correction not on the conscience of judges and juries but on the competition of other ideas." However, he also held that a balance must be sought in the law between protection for free speech and press and protection of individual reputations at risk from inadequately limited expression in the media.

Powell distinguished public figures, who should have less protection against libel, from private persons, who should have more. He also defined two types of public figures. One is so prominent as to always be a public figure, such as the governor of a state. The other type is a conditional public figure,

On July 23, 1964, policemen in Birmingham, Alabama, used powerful bursts of water from fire hoses to subdue demonstrators participating in a nonviolent public protest for civil rights. *The Supreme Court made its decision in* New York Times Co. v. Sullivan *to protect the freedoms of speech and press within the context of this struggle for equal justice by black Americans.*

someone who holds this status only within a certain context, such as a single issue or event in which the individual has been involved. Justice Powell concluded that Elmer Gertz did not meet the standard for being a public figure and was strictly a private person. Therefore, Gertz did not have to bear the high burdens of proof against Welch set by the *Sullivan* case.

Finally, Justice Powell set forth a rule for plaintiffs such as Elmer Gertz. Although the plaintiff is a private person, said Justice Powell, he must demonstrate more than the expression of libelous falsehoods about himself, because the content of the reports about him were matters of public concern. Someone in a situation like Gertz's, said Justice Powell, must also show that the publisher acted negligently. Thus, a new burden of proof entered the field of libel law, which, if more lenient than the standard of "actual malice" and "reckless disregard" set forth in the *Sullivan* case, was nonetheless in the spirit of that decision. It raised the bar for justifying certain claims of libel and thereby expanded protection for free expression in cases involving private individuals.

The *Gertz* decision exemplifies the Court's case-by-case process of responding to problems raised by *Sullivan*, the need to distinguish public and private figures and their varying claims to protection by state libel laws. This developmental process has yielded the following rules in constitutional law. First, a completely private figure, about whom a publisher spreads lies on a subject of no general public interest, can sue for libel in any way that a state law permits, and the U.S. Constitution is not applicable to the case. Second, a private person libeled about a matter of public concern, such as Elmer Gertz, must meet both the requirements of state libel law and the First Amendment standard of proving negligence on the part of the publisher. Third, a purely public figure, such as L. B. Sullivan of Montgomery, Alabama, who seeks damages for libel, has the heavy burden of proving "actual malice" and "reckless disregard" by the publisher in order to win a favorable decision.

Thus, *New York Times Co.* v. *Sullivan* practically brought an end in the United States to the crime of seditious libel (making defamatory comments against public officials and government). It marked the beginning of a freer and riskier political environment, which has made public officials more accountable to the people they serve. But it also has discouraged some talented persons from putting their reputations at risk by entering a political arena open wide to the unpredictable currents of free expression no longer fettered by state libel laws.

The Rights and Restraints of a Free Press

Newspapers and news magazines throughout the country commented on the decision for broad free speech and press rights the Supreme Court handed down in the New York Times *case. Most of the commentary, such as this* New York Times *editorial of March 10, 1964, "Free Press and Free People," was positive.*

The unanimous decision of the Supreme Court yesterday in a case involving this newspaper is a victory of first importance in the long—and never ending—struggle for the rights of a free press. But it is more than that. It is also a vindication of the right of a free people to have unimpeded access to the news and to fair comment on the news.

What the decision means is that in presenting the news or additional comment on the news, as well as in editorial-type advertisements, the freedom to criticize that is absolutely vital to an unfettered press is protected, subject only to the reasonable limitation that the criticism be made in good faith and not maliciously....

It is an increasingly important function of the press...if the press is to...encourage the free give-and-take of ideas and, above all, to be free to express criticism of public officials and public policies. This is all part of the lifeblood of a democracy. In its landmark decision yesterday, the Supreme Court of the United States has struck a solid blow not only for the freedom of the press but for the prerogatives of a free people.

Some editorials, however, offered criticisms and cautions about the Court's opinion, such as a March 10, 1964, opinion piece in the Evening Star *of Washington, D.C., entitled "New Libel Test."*

For the first time the court has held that the First Amendment's guarantees of free press and free speech confer an immunity from the normal libel or slander suit involving statements made about public officials....

As a practical matter, this means that a public official, except in the most extreme cases, has no legal protection against statements concerning his official conduct, which are false and damaging to his reputation....

This decision came in the case of a libel suit against the *New York Times*...that allegedly libeled an Alabama official. The jury returned a damage award of $500,000 and this was upheld by the Alabama appellate courts. Clearly, this was a punitive...award which bore no relation to any damage...suffered by the plaintiff, who was not even named in the ad.

This, however, was an extreme case which had its roots in racial prejudice. But the sweep of the principle laid down by the court is not limited to such cases. The immunity which is conferred applies to all manner of statements and publications, and consequently, or so it seems to us, imposes the very highest standard of responsibility on the press and on individuals.

It may now be possible, for example, to falsely accuse a public official of stealing public funds, and not be liable to him for damages. This is a freedom which the court holds to be necessary to full and uninhibited discussion and debate of public affairs. But it is also a freedom especially in the case of the press, which must be exercised with much care and restraint.

16

Finding a Right to Privacy

Griswold v. *Connecticut* (1965)

Griswold v. Connecticut

- 381 U.S. 479 (1965)

- Decided: June 7, 1965

- Vote: 7–2

- Opinion of the Court: William O. Douglas

- Concurring opinions: Arthur Goldberg (Earl Warren and William Brennan), John Marshall Harlan II, and Byron White

- Dissenting opinions: Hugo Black and Potter Stewart

Does the U.S. Constitution protect an individual's right to privacy? Many Americans think it does. Others say it does not. The word "privacy" cannot be found in the U.S. Constitution. Yet the U.S. Supreme Court, by a vote of 7 to 2, based its decision in *Griswold* v. *Connecticut* (1965) on the presumption of a constitutionally protected right to privacy. The Court's "discovery" of a right to privacy in the U.S. Constitution was lauded by many Americans and derided by many others, including two justices of the Supreme Court, who wrote sharp dissenting opinions against the Court's majority in the *Griswold* case.

Both before and since the *Griswold* decision in 1965, Americans within and outside of the judicial branch of government have argued about whether the Constitution, correctly construed, includes a right to privacy. Today, although most Americans acknowledge a personal right to privacy, there are strong disagreements about what areas of life or instances of behavior are appropriately protected from governmental intrusion by this constitutional right.

So, what is this right to privacy? Where did it come from? And how did it become a contentious constitutional issue before, during, and after the Supreme Court's deliberations in *Griswold* v. *Connecticut*?

Ever since the founding of the United States, it seems, most Americans have believed in a right to privacy—the right to protection against unwarranted or unlawful government intrusion into certain legally protected areas of private life. The framers of the U.S. Constitution often referred to constitutionally protected personal and private rights. Within several papers of *The Federalist*, the greatest commentary ever written on the meaning and intent of the Constitution, James Madison prominently discusses the public and private rights that a good government should protect. For example, in the tenth paper of *The Federalist*, Madison writes:

> When a majority is included in a faction, the form of popular government…enables it to sacrifice to its ruling passion or interest both the public good and the rights of other citizens. To secure the public good and private rights against the danger of such a faction, and at the same time to preserve the spirit and the form of popular government, is then the great object to which our inquiries are directed.

The very idea of a constitution implies zones of private life that are beyond the reach and regulation of a government limited by law. Indeed, an individual's right to privacy in certain domains of personal life, off-limits to invasive government regulation, is a primary distinction between totalitarian or despotic governments and constitutionally limited and free governments.

Given the long-standing presence of "private rights" (a phrase used often by James Madison, John Adams, and others of the Founding Era) in the political and constitutional traditions of the United States, how did this idea become an object of contention in our time? Louis Brandeis and Samuel Warren, two Massachusetts lawyers who wrote an attention-getting article, "The Right to Privacy," that appeared in the *Harvard Law Review* in 1890, may have laid the ground for this current constitutional controversy. This article stressed the importance of protecting individuals against the violation of their personal dignity and privacy by invasive newspaper and magazine reporters, but it claimed that the "right to be let alone" was also applicable to invasive actions by government.

After becoming an associate justice of the U.S. Supreme Court, Brandeis asserted the right to privacy in a dissent against the Court's 5–4 decision in *Olmstead* v. *United States* (1928). Brandeis based his dissent on a person's presumptive constitutional right to privacy against federal government agents seeking information about illegal behavior by secretly listening to private telephone conversations. Brandeis wrote, "The makers of our Constitution undertook to secure conditions favorable to the pursuit of happiness.... They conferred, as against the Government, the right to be let alone—the most comprehensive of rights and the right most valued by civilized men."

Although Brandeis argued that the Constitution as a whole was a guardian of personal privacy, he pointed particularly to the Fourth Amendment protections against "unreasonable searches and seizures" and the Fifth Amendment guarantees against self-incrimination. He extolled these prime examples, among others, of constitutional barriers against "unjustifiable intrusion by the Government upon the privacy of the individual." For more than thirty years after Brandeis's *Olmstead* dissent, the issue of a constitutional right to privacy lay dormant, as the Court avoided formal discussion of it.

Then, in *Poe* v. *Ullman* (1961), the issue once again came to the forefront. In their dissent, Justices John Marshall Harlan II and William O. Douglas argued for the individual's right to privacy, and against an 1879 Connecticut law banning the use of birth control devices, even by married couples. Harlan pointed to the Fourteenth Amendment's provision that "No State shall make or enforce any law which shall... deprive any person of life, liberty, or property, without due process of law." According to Harlan, the state law at issue unconstitutionally deprived individuals of their liberty, without due process of law, to use birth control devices, which was "an intolerable and unjustifiable invasion of privacy." Thus, Harlan linked the Fourteenth Amendment's guarantee of liberty to an unenumerated (not stated but inferred) substantive right to privacy, which must be protected if there were to be equal justice through due process of law.

As the Court did not rule against the Connecticut law prohibiting the use of contraceptive devices, because it had not been enforced, this issue did not die. The controversy soon returned to the U.S. Supreme Court. Estelle Griswold, executive director of the Planned Parenthood League of Connecticut (PPLC), and her associate Dr. Charles Lee Buxton were arrested for violating their state's anticontraception law. In 1962, they were tried and found guilty of giving married couples advice on birth control and prescribing contraceptive devices. Both of them were fined one hundred dollars for the crime of providing information about contraceptives. In 1963 and 1964, the appellate division of the Connecticut Circuit Court and the Connecticut Supreme Court of Errors upheld the convictions of Griswold and Buxton as justified by the state's "police power." They appealed to the U.S. Supreme Court, which accepted the case of *Griswold* v. *Connecticut* in 1965.

Counsel for Griswold argued that the PPLC's clients had a constitutional right to privacy that enforcement of the 1879 state law violated. The Court sided with Griswold and struck down the state statute as an unconstitutional violation of the right to privacy. However, the seven justices in favor of the petitioner, who agreed to reverse the decision of the Connecticut courts, disagreed markedly about where in the Constitution a right to privacy could be found, and about how it could be justified.

Justice William O. Douglas, who wrote the opinion of the Court, found a general right to privacy, which he believed can be derived from the First, Third, Fourth, Fifth, and Ninth Amendments. These parts of the Bill of Rights, said Douglas, imply "zones of privacy that are the foundation for a general right to privacy." He further held that the unenumerated right to privacy, emanating from several parts of the U.S. Constitution's Bill of Rights, could be applied to a state government through the Fourteenth Amendment's due process clause.

In justification of the Court's opinion, Justice Douglas referred to Court decisions that had alluded to a privacy right, such as *Meyer* v. *Nebraska* (1923), *Pierce* v. *Society of Sisters* (1925), and *DeJonge* v. *Oregon* (1937). Douglas noted that in *Meyer*, for example, the Court had applied the property and liberty interests of the Fourteenth Amendment's due process clause to strike down state laws that had prohibited the teaching of foreign languages to elementary and middle school students. In *Pierce* it had similarly struck down a law that had outlawed private schools. And, Douglas pointed out, in *DeJonge* the Court had recognized freedom of association with others in private groups, a right not mentioned explicitly in the Constitution but derived from the First Amendment's guarantee of the right to assembly, which it applied to the state of Oregon through the liberty and due process clauses of the Fourteenth Amendment. Douglas argued that in all three cases—*Meyer, Pierce,* and *DeJonge*—the Court had prohibited state governments from infringing upon private rights related either to property, personal choice, or civil association, which were applied against state governments through the liberty and due process clauses of the Fourteenth Amendment.

Justice Arthur Goldberg, who concurred in the Court's decision, argued that the basic source of the individual's right to privacy is the Ninth Amendment, which says, "The enumeration in the Constitution of certain rights shall not be construed to deny or disparage others retained by the people." According to Goldberg, the idea of liberty in the Fourteenth Amendment protects unenumerated personal rights, which are listed neither in the Bill of Rights nor in any other part of the Constitution. He claimed that the right to privacy in marital relationships was one of those rights not specified in the Constitution that nonetheless was "retained by the people." Goldberg also said, "To hold that a right so basic and fundamental and so deep-rooted in our society as the right of privacy in marriage may be infringed because the right is not guaranteed in so many words by the first eight amendments to the Constitution is to ignore the Ninth Amendment and to give it no effect whatever."

Justices John Marshall Harlan II and Byron White wrote concurring opinions based solely on the due process clause of the Fourteenth Amendment, which essentially endorsed Harlan's dissent in the 1961 case of *Poe* v. *Ullman*. Harlan, for example, argued that privacy is an unenumerated substantive right at the core of due process. There are two interlocking conceptions of due process: procedural and substantive. Procedural due process is about the fair application of laws to guarantee equal justice for all persons in legal proceedings. Substantive due process refers to unspecified rights, fundamental to the maintenance of liberty and order, that must be guaranteed to all persons in conjunction with fair and equal legal procedures, if equal justice under the law is to prevail. Harlan and White relied on their concept of substantive due process through the Fourteenth Amendment to justify an unenumerated substantive right to privacy, which constitutionally protects an individual's liberty against intrusion from the state government under certain conditions, such as the intimate relations between partners in a marriage.

Justices Hugo Black and Potter Stewart dissented. Both of them disagreed with the 1879 Connecticut law at issue in *Griswold*. Stewart called it "an uncommonly silly law." However, both Stewart and Black argued that enforcement of the 1879 law did not violate anyone's rights under the U.S. Constitution. They insisted there is no right to privacy in the Constitution. Stewart wrote, "With all deference, I can find no such general right of privacy in the Bill of Rights, in any other part of the Constitution, or in any case ever before decided by this Court."

Justice Black wrote, "I like my privacy as well as the next one, but I am nevertheless compelled to admit that government has a right to invade it unless prohibited by some specific constitutional provision." In *Griswold*, Justice Black found no "specific constitutional provision" that prohibited the state government's regulation of the private behavior at issue in this case.

Both Black and Stewart criticized the Court's majority for going beyond the Constitution to use their judicial power willfully to achieve a desired social outcome.

Justice Black concluded, "Use of any such broad, unbounded judicial authority would make of this Court's members a day-to-day constitutional convention." According to Stewart, this unrestrained use of judicial power would lead to a "great constitutional shift of power to the courts" and away from the legislative and executive branches of government, the branches directly accountable to the people through regular elections.

Support for a right to privacy has grown since the *Griswold* decision. In *Katz* v. *United States* (1967), the Court overturned the decision in *Olmstead* v. *United States* (1928). The Court held that the Fourth and Fifth Amendments protect an individual's right to privacy against electronic surveillance and wire-

Estelle Griswold, executive director of the Planned Parenthood League of Connecticut, violated her state's anticontraception law, which led ultimately to the U.S. Supreme Court's recognition of a constitutional right to privacy in Griswold v. Connecticut.

John Lawrence (right) and Tyron Garner celebrate the U.S. Supreme Court decision in Lawrence v. Texas *(2003), which struck down a Texas law that prohibited private and consensual homosexual activity. This decision was based on the constitutional right to privacy recognized by the Court in the 1965* Griswold *case.*

tapping by government agents, even in a place open to the public such as a telephone booth on a city street.

In *Eisenstadt* v. *Baird* (1972), the Court applied the right of privacy in obtaining and using contraceptive devices to individuals in general, rather than limiting it to married couples, as in *Griswold.* Writing for the Court, Justice Brennan said, "If the right of privacy means anything, it is the right of the individual, married or single, to be free from unwarranted governmental intrusion into matters so fundamentally affecting a person as the decision whether to bear or beget a child."

The Court's most controversial applications of the privacy right have been in cases that in one way or another are associated with sexual behavior. For example, in *Roe* v. *Wade* (1973), the Court ruled that the right to privacy included a woman's right to terminate her pregnancy by choice during the first trimester and during the second and third trimester when necessary to protect the life and health of the woman. This use of an unenumerated substantive right to privacy has been used by the Court in series of cases since *Roe* to uphold in general a woman's "right to choose" an abortion while modifying in some respects the Court's 1973 holding about this matter.

Another controversial Supreme Court decision that connected an unenumerated substantive right to privacy with sexual behavior was *Lawrence* v. *Texas* (2003). In this case, the Court found unconstitutional a state law banning certain kinds of consensual sexual behavior between two people of the same sex, because the statute violated the privacy rights of two adult males to engage in sexual relations in a private residence. In his opinion for the Court, Justice Anthony Kennedy emphasized the liberty and due process clauses of the Fourteenth Amendment, which were applied against the state government of Texas to protect the personal choices of consenting adults in a private homosexual relationship. He thus continued a line of reasoning about personal choice and privacy that can be traced to the Court's rulings in *Meyer* v. *Nebraska* and *Pierce* v. *Society of Sisters*.

Supreme Court decisions such as *Roe* and *Lawrence* have been criticized not only by those who refute an explicit right to privacy in the Constitution, but also by some who agree with the idea of a general constitutional right to privacy. The pro–privacy rights critics of the *Roe* decision, for example, claim that it wrongfully uses a valid, if unenumerated, constitutional right to justify behavior that should not be constitutionally protected. As a result, some individuals who strongly disagree with a constitutional right to choose an abortion are staunch defenders of a constitutional right to privacy in other instances.

It appears that a constitutional right to privacy is here to stay. It also seems that the exact meaning, justification, and limits of a constitutional right to privacy will continue to be controversial. Every extension of the right to privacy limits the power of government to regulate behavior for the common good, even though citizens in a democracy expect their government to advance community-wide concerns. By contrast, every expansion of government power to regulate the behavior of individuals diminishes the private domain of personal liberty, which Americans have always cherished. How to justly balance and blend these contending factors, so that both are addressed but neither one is sacrificed to the other, is an ongoing question that the Supreme Court asks when considering the correct uses and limitations of the right to privacy.

"The Right to Be Left Alone"

Following oral arguments about the Griswold *case, the Court met in conference to discuss the issues in the Court's secluded conference room. Reconstructions of the surviving notes made by Justices William O. Douglas and William J. Brennan in conference on April 2, 1965, provide a glimpse into the proceedings. In conformity with the Court's tradition, the conference started with comments from the chief justice. Chief Justice Warren, in the conference at least, rejected the privacy rights argument that he later accepted in voting for the petitioners in this case. He also demonstrated his antipathy to the substantive due process argument, shared by some other justices, that Justice Harlan and Justice White later presented in their concurring opinion in this case. The bracketed comments are notes of Justice Douglas that pertain to the comments attributed to Justice Harlan and Justice Brennan.*

Warren: I am bothered with this case. The Connecticut legislature may repeal the law.... I can't say that this affects the First Amendment rights of doctors, and I can't say that the state has not legitimate interest in the field.... I can't... use equal protection, or use a "shocking" due process standard. I can't accept a privacy argument.

I might rest on... the theory that there is no prohibition on sales and they don't go after doctors as such, but only clinics. I prefer to hold that since the act affects rights of association, it must be carefully and narrowly drawn. Basic rights are involved here— we are dealing with a most confidential association, the most intimate in our life. This act is too loosely

The members of the United States Supreme Court who decided the 1965 case of Griswold v. Connecticut *were (standing from left) Byron White, William J. Brennan Jr., Potter Stewart, and Abe Fortas and (seated from left) Tom Clark, Hugo Black, Chief Justice Earl Warren, William O. Douglas, and John Marshall Harlan II.*

drawn—it has to be clear-cut and it isn't. I am inclined to reverse [the decision against Griswold of the Connecticut courts].

Black: I can't reverse on any ground. Only one of two possible grounds are conceivable for me—the doctors' First Amendment rights. The right of association is for me the right of assembly, and the right of a husband and wife to assemble in bed is a new right of assembly to me.... The [state law at issue] is pretty clear and carefully drawn—it is not ambiguous. So I can't find why it isn't within the state's power to enact. If I can be shown that it is too vague on due process grounds, I can join it.... I am not at rest on it. I am against the policy of the act.

Douglas: The right of association is more than the right of assembly. It is a right to join with and associate with—the right to send a child to a religious school is on the periphery. *Pierce* is such a case. We have said that the right to travel is in the radiation of the 1st Amendment, and so is the right of association. Nothing is more personal than this relationship, and if on the periphery is still within First Amendment protection. I reverse.

Clark: I reverse. I agree with Bill Douglas. There is a right to marry, to have a home, and to have children.

Black: A state can abolish marriage.

Clark: This is an area where I have the right to be left alone. I prefer that ground for reversal.

Harlan: [Douglas: He restates his position in *Poe* v. *Ullman*—he relies on due process and reverses.] I would have difficulty if this were not a "use" act and if not applied to married couples.

Brennan: I reverse. [Douglas: He continues the Chief Justice's and Clark's, and Douglas's views.] I would bring the realm of privacy in. I do not reach the act that applies only to unmarried people.

Stewart: There is nothing in the Bill of Rights that touches this. I can't find anything in the First, Second, Fourth, Fifth, Ninth, or other amendments, so I would have to affirm [the decisions of the Connecticut courts].

White: I reverse.

Goldberg: I reverse. You may regulate this relationship and the state cannot. There is no compelling state reason in that circumstance to justify the statute. I rely on *Meyer* v. *Nebraska, Schware* v. *Board,* and *Pierce* v. *Sisters*. These are all related to First Amendment rights—assembly—as we said in *Aptheker*. If we can form a club, he can join his wife and live with her as he likes.

17

The Right to Remain Silent

Miranda v. *Arizona* (1966)

Miranda v. Arizona

- 384 U.S. 436 (1966)

- Decided: June 13, 1966

- Vote: 5–4

- Opinion of the Court: Earl Warren

- Concurring opinion in part, dissenting in part: Tom Clark

- Dissenting opinions: John Marshall Harlan II (Potter Stewart and Byron White) and Byron White (John Marshall Harlan II and Potter Stewart)

Ever since colonial times, most Americans have believed in an old English saying: "It is better for ninety-nine guilty people to go free than for one innocent person to be punished." In the United States, a person accused of a crime is presumed innocent until proven guilty. Thus the burden of proving the suspect guilty rests upon the government prosecutors.

The U.S. Constitution generally, and especially its Bill of Rights, protects individuals accused of crimes from wrong or unjust accusations and punishments by government officials. But the Constitution and laws made in conformity with it also authorize the federal and state governments to exercise certain powers in order to protect people from criminals intending to harm them. So Americans want their federal and state governments to be simultaneously powerful enough to protect them from criminals and sufficiently limited to prevent the government from abusing anyone, including those accused of criminal behavior.

Constitutional issues inevitably arise when the government's efforts to prevent crime clash with the need to protect those accused of crime. The U.S. Supreme Court confronted such issues in *Miranda* v. *Arizona* (1966). This case arose in 1963 following the arrest of Ernesto Miranda, who was accused of kidnapping and raping a young woman near Phoenix, Arizona. The victim identified Miranda in a lineup at the police station, and the law enforcement officers questioned him intensely for two hours. No one told him that he could refuse to answer questions or seek assistance from a lawyer. Intimidated by the high-pressure tactics of the police, Ernesto Miranda confessed to the crime of which he had been accused.

Miranda was too poor to hire an attorney, so the Maricopa County Court provided a lawyer to assist him at trial. He was duly tried, and near the end of the proceedings the presiding official, Judge Yale McFate, gave instructions to the members of the jury before they departed to meet, deliberate, and decide the defendant's guilt or innocence. The judge said he had allowed Miranda's confession to be presented as evidence in the trail despite objections of the defendant's attorney, who claimed that his client had been forced to admit guilt. The judge emphasized that the jury was free to decide whether Miranda's confession had been voluntary or coerced. However, the judge's final words of instruction raised the constitutional issue that eventually brought Miranda's case to the Supreme Court:

The fact that a defendant was under arrest at the time he made a confession or that he was not at the time represented by counsel or that he was not told that any statement he might make could be or would be used against him, in and of themselves, will not render such a confession involuntary.

After five hours of deliberation, the jury of three women and nine men returned to the courtroom and presented their verdict: Miranda was found guilty of kidnapping and raping the victim. Judge McFate sentenced Miranda to serve twenty to thirty years in the Arizona State Prison at Florence. Miranda appealed to the Arizona Supreme Court, which upheld his conviction.

From his prison cell, Miranda petitioned the U.S. Supreme Court, which accepted his case in 1966 because it raised unresolved issues about the constitutional rights of an accused person that the Court wanted to settle. These issues had surfaced in the wake of *Escobedo* v. *Illinois* (1964), which the Court had decided nearly one year after Miranda's trial.

The Court's *Escobedo* decision expanded the Sixth Amendment right to counsel, which previously had been understood as an accused person's right to have a lawyer at the time of trial. After *Escobedo* this right also covered the time of interrogation by police. But there was confusion among law enforcement officers and trial judges across the country about how to apply the *Escobedo* decision. Questions arose about matters such as when an attorney must be present to assist an accused person and exactly when the suspect had to be informed about his or her rights to counsel. The U.S. Supreme Court planned to use the *Miranda* case to respond to the confusion the *Escobedo* decision raised.

Miranda's chief counselor, John Flynn, was a highly regarded criminal defense lawyer who was recruited for this case by the American Civil Liberties Union (ACLU). In his oral argument and brief presented to the Court, Flynn claimed that the police violated Miranda's Fifth Amendment right to protection against self-incrimination. This part of the Bill of Rights says, "No person...shall be compelled in any criminal case to be a witness against himself."

Flynn said that the police had behaved unconstitutionally because they did not inform the suspect, Miranda, of his right to remain silent, so as not to assume the risk of providing incriminating evidence to his police interrogators. Because the police gained their evidence, Miranda's confession, unconstitutionally, Flynn argued it should be dismissed from consideration. Finally, Flynn linked the denial of Miranda's Fifth Amendment right to protection from self-incrimination to his Sixth Amendment right to a lawyer. Flynn argued that if a

The 1963 arrest report for Ernesto Miranda indicates that he was charged with kidnapping and rape. After his conviction, his appeal to the Supreme Court allowed the justices to clarify exactly when a person has to be informed of his rights, such as the right to remain silent.

lawyer had been present, then Miranda probably would not have so readily provided an incriminating confession, which was the product of subtle, if not overt, intimidation by the police.

Arizona's lawyers argued that Miranda could have asked for a lawyer at any time during questioning. He had not done so. They also said no one had forced him to confess. His interrogators had neither harmed him physically nor threatened to do so. Because Miranda had given his confession voluntarily, the prosecution was justified in using it in court to convict him.

The Supreme Court agreed with John Flynn's arguments for Miranda and struck down his conviction. The police in charge of Miranda's case had violated his Fifth Amendment right to protection against self-incrimination, and, while doing this, they had neglected to make him aware of his Sixth Amendment right to a lawyer. Writing for the Court, Chief Justice Earl Warren said that *Miranda* raised issues that "go to the roots of our concepts of American criminal jurisprudence: the restraints society must observe consistent with the Federal Constitution in prosecuting individuals for crime." He stressed "the necessity for procedures which assure that the individual is accorded his privilege under the Fifth Amendment to the Constitution not to be compelled to incriminate himself."

The chief justice provided strict and clear rules for the police to follow in future cases of this kind. From now on, said Warren's opinion for the Court, law enforcement officers are required to inform suspects that they have the right to remain silent, that anything they say can be held against them, that they have a right to consult a lawyer, and that they may request the attorney to be present during questioning. Further, they must be told that if they cannot afford to hire an attorney, the state will provide one for them. The police must inform the suspect of these rights, the Court said, before any questioning can take place. A defendant can then voluntarily waive the rights communicated to her or him by the police. But if not, the law-enforcement officers must follow the rules exactly as prescribed by the Court. If they fail to do so, then any evidence obtained would be a product of unconstitutional violations of the Fifth and Sixth Amendments, and therefore could not be used against the suspect in a court of law.

Chief Justice Warren's opinion emphasized that if a suspect wants to remain silent or to contact a lawyer, police interrogation must stop until the suspect is ready to talk again or a lawyer is present. And the chief justice insisted that the rules prescribed by the Court in response to this case—later known as Miranda warnings—are an "absolute prerequisite" to interrogation of an accused person. Warren argued that the U.S. system of justice is based on the idea that an individual is innocent until proved guilty. The government, he emphasized, must produce evidence against an accused person. It cannot resort to forcing suspects to prove their own guilt.

The dissent of Justice John Marshall Harlan II began with a sharp criticism: "I believe the decision of the Court represents poor constitutional law and entails harmful consequences for the country at large." He continued in this vein, "One is entitled to feel astonished that the Constitution can be read to produce this result." He found nothing wrong with the procedures used by the law-enforcement officers in this case. "Yet the resulting confessions, and the responsible course of police practice they represent, are to be sacrificed to the Court's own finespun conception of fairness which I seriously doubt is shared by many thinking citizens in this country."

Justice Byron White dissented even more strongly than Harlan. He wrote, "The proposition that the privilege against self-incrimination forbids in-custody interrogation without the warnings specified in the majority opinion and without a clear waiver of counsel has no significant support in the history of the privilege or in the language of the Fifth Amendment." He predicted grim consequences from the Court's requirement that the Miranda warnings must be issued in order to obtain evidence constitutionally from a suspect. Justice White said, "In some unknown number of cases the Court's rule will return a killer, a rapist or other criminal to the streets and to the environment which produced him, to repeat his crime whenever it pleases him."

Miranda, however, was not returned to the streets by the Court's decision, as Justice White had feared. His case was remanded, or sent back, to the court of original jurisdiction for retrial without the inadmissible evidence. Nonetheless, Miranda was convicted again and sent to prison. He was paroled in 1972, but in 1976 he was knifed and killed during a barroom fight in Phoenix. After arresting a suspect in the murder of Miranda, the policemen read the Court-mandated Miranda warning to him. He exercised his right to remain silent and was released from custody. No one was ever charged in the murder of Ernesto Miranda.

At the time *Miranda* was decided, it was controversial. Many law enforcement officials complained that the mandated use of Miranda warnings severely interfered with their ability to gather evidence from suspects. In his successful 1968 campaign for President, Richard Nixon strongly criticized the Court's *Miranda* decision as an unnecessary obstacle to the work of law-enforcement officers. Nixon charged that too many federal judges were "soft" in their judgments of criminals. He pledged that, if elected, he would fill any open seats on the Supreme Court with justices who would overturn the *Miranda* decision and other rulings that favored the rights of criminals more than the rights of their victims and the authority of the police. And so he did, with the appointment of Warren Burger to replace Earl Warren as chief justice in 1969. Burger

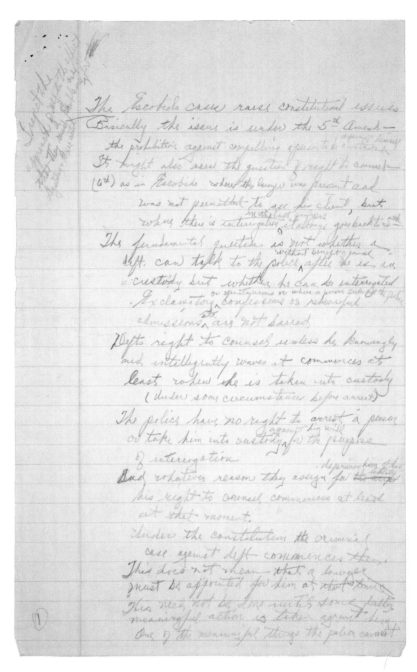

Chief Justice Earl Warren, who wrote the opinion of the Court in the 5–4 Miranda *decision, made these notes as he began to formulate his thoughts about the issues at stake in the case. Cognizant of potential police abuse, he wrote, "The police have no right to arrest a person or take him into custody against his will for the purpose of interrogation."*

WARNING AS TO YOUR RIGHTS

You are under arrest. Before we ask you any questions, you must understand what your rights are.

You have the right to remain silent. You are not required to say anything to us at any time or to answer any questions. Anything you say can be used against you in court.

You have the right to talk to a lawyer for advice before we question you and to have him with you during questioning.

If you cannot afford a lawyer and want one, a lawyer will be provided for you.

If you want to answer questions now without a lawyer present you will still have the right to stop answering at any time. You also have the right to stop answering at any time until you talk to a lawyer.

P-4475

This card contains the words that one police department provides its officers to read to a suspect at the time of his or her arrest. These "Miranda warnings," which vary slightly from one location to another, are the enduring legacy of Chief Justice Warren's opinion in Miranda v. Arizona *(1966).*

had publicly expressed his displeasure with the *Miranda* decision. In a 1968 meeting of the Center for the Study of Democratic Institutions, Burger had said, "Certainly you have heard—and judges have said—that one should not convict a man out of his own mouth [through a confession]. The fact is that we establish responsibility and liability and we convict in all the areas of civil litigation out of the mouth of the defendant."

During Burger's tenure as chief justice, the Court did slightly modify the rules established by the *Miranda* case. In *New York* v. *Quarles* (1984), the Court decided that police officers could, in order to protect themselves, question a suspect about possession of weapons before informing her or him of the Miranda warnings. However, the Court maintained and even strengthened the *Miranda* precedent after Burger retired from the Court in 1986.

In *Dickerson* v. *United States* (2000), the Court reaffirmed, by a 7–2 vote, the Miranda rights of suspects. At issue was a 1968 federal law that held it was not always necessary to read Miranda warnings to suspects before they confessed voluntarily to crimes. This law was made in reaction to the *Miranda* decision. In striking down this statute, Chief Justice William Rehnquist wrote, "*Miranda* has become embedded in routine police practice to the point where the warnings have become part of our national culture." Thus, the Court struck down the 1968 congressional statute and stressed that the police must give the Miranda warnings to suspects or risk having their confessions excluded as evidence against them.

Today, law enforcement officers throughout the United States carry cards with the Miranda warnings printed on them, as they have done since the Supreme Court's pivotal decision of 1966. These cards include four warnings that all suspects need to know: the right to remain silent, the reminder that anything said by the suspect can be used against her or him, the right to a lawyer, and the reminder that a lawyer will be provided free if the suspect cannot afford to hire one.

The *Miranda* case is a standing reminder of the ongoing tensions between liberty and order in the United States. In our free society, there will always be questions about the proper balance between the rights of criminal suspects and the need for safety and security against criminals. The exact meaning and practical applications of due process rights—such as the Miranda warnings—will continue to be debated in community forums and courts of law. Such constructive controversies are vital signs of a healthy constitutional democracy.

Protecting the Rights of the Accused

John Flynn presented the oral argument for Ernesto Miranda before the Supreme Court on February 28, 1966. Flynn described Miranda's arrest and argued that the police had subtly coerced his confession during his interrogation. Flynn emphasized Miranda's vulnerability to manipulation. He pointed to his lack of education, minimal intelligence, and low social status as disadvantages exploited by the questioners to influence Miranda to confess to a crime. Flynn charged that people such as Miranda often do not receive justice on equal terms with the more advantaged members of society. Both Chief Justice Warren and Justice Stewart asked leading questions that prompted Flynn to provide answers that helped his client.

Warren: Mr. Flynn, you may proceed now.

Flynn: Mr. Chief Justice, may it please the Court.

This case concerns itself with the conviction of a defendant of two crimes of rape and kidnapping, the sentences on each count of twenty to thirty years to run concurrently....

Now the issue before the Court is the admission in evidence of the defendant's confession, under the facts and circumstances of this case, over the specific objection of his trial counsel that it had been given in the absence of counsel....

The facts in the case indicate that the defendant was a twenty-three-year-old, Spanish-American extraction, that on the morning of March 13, 1963, he was arrested at his home, taken down to the police station by two officers named Young and Cooley; that at the police station he was immediately placed in a lineup. He was there identified by the prosecutrix [sic] in this case....And immediately after the interrogations, he was taken into the police confessional at approximately 11:30 A.M. and by 1:30 they had obtained from him an oral confession.

He had denied his guilt, according to the officers, at the commencement of the interrogation; by 1:30 he had confessed. I believe that the record indicates that at no time during the interrogation and prior to his confession, his oral confession, was he advised either of his right to remain silent, of his right to counsel, or of his right to consult with counsel....

The defendant was then asked to sign a confession, to which he agreed. The form handed to him to write on contained a typed statement as follows, which precedes his handwritten confession. "I, Ernesto A. Miranda, do hereby swear that I make this statement voluntarily and of my own free will, with no threats, coercion, or promises of immunity, and with full knowledge of my legal rights, understanding any statement I make may be used against me."

The statement was read to him by the officers, and he confessed in his own handwriting. Throughout the interrogation the defendant did not request counsel at any time. In due course, the trial court appointed counsel to defend him....

The further history relating to this defendant found...that he had an eighth-grade education, and ...a prior criminal record and that he was mentally abnormal. He was found, however, to be competent to stand trial and legally sane at the time of the commission of the alleged acts....

Stewart: What do you think is the result of the adversary process coming into being when this focusing takes place [against a particular suspect]? What follows from that? Is there then, what, a right to a lawyer?

Flynn: I think that the man at that time has the right to exercise, if he knows and under the present state of the law in Arizona, if he's rich enough, and if he's educated enough, to assert his Fifth Amendment right, and if he recognizes that he has a Fifth Amendment right, to request counsel. But I simply say that at that stage of the proceeding, under the facts and circumstances in *Miranda* of a man of limited education, of a man who certainly is mentally abnormal, who is certainly an indigent, that when that adversary process came into being that the police, at the very least, had an obligation to extend to this man not only his clear Fifth Amendment right, but to afford to him the right of counsel [provided in the Sixth Amendment]....

Stewart: I don't mean to quibble, and I apologize, but I think it's first important to define what those rights are—what his rights under the Constitution are at that point. He can't be advised of his rights unless somebody knows what those rights are.

Flynn: Precisely my point. And the only person that can adequately advise a person like Ernest Miranda is a lawyer.

Stewart: And what would the lawyer advise him that his rights then were?

Flynn: That he had the right not to incriminate himself, that he had a right not to make any statement, that he had the right to be free from further questioning by the police department, that he had the right, at an ultimate time, to be represented adequately by counsel in court; and that if he was too indigent, too poor to employ counsel, that the state would furnish him counsel....

[Justice Black asked if the Constitution protected all Americans.]

Flynn: It certainly does protect the rich, the educated, and the strong—those rich enough to hire counsel, those who are educated enough to know what their rights are, and those who are strong enough to withstand police interrogation and assert those rights.... In view of the interrogation and the facts and circumstances of *Miranda,* it simply had no application...and that's what I am attempting to express to the Court.

Stewart: Is there any claim in this case that this confession was compelled—was involuntary?

Flynn: No, your Honor.

Stewart: None at all?

Flynn: None at all. We have raised no question that he was compelled to give this statement, in the sense that anyone forced him to do it by coercion, by threats, by promises, or compulsion of that kind.

Black: He doesn't have to have a gun pointed at his head, does he?

White: Of course he doesn't. So he was compelled to do it, wasn't he, according to your theory?

Flynn: Not by gunpoint, as Mr. Justice Black has indicated. He was called upon to surrender a right that he didn't fully realize and appreciate that he had....

Warren: I suppose, Mr. Flynn, you would say that if the police had said to this young man, "Now, you're a nice young man, and we don't want to hurt you, and so forth; we're your friends and if you'll just tell us how you committed this crime, we'll let you go home and we won't prosecute you," that that would be a violation of the Fifth Amendment, and that technically speaking would not be "compelling" him to do it. It would be an inducement, wouldn't it?

Flynn: That is correct.

Warren: I suppose you would argue that that is still within the Fifth Amendment, wouldn't you?

Flynn: It's an abdication of the Fifth Amendment right, simply because of the total circumstances existing at that time....

Warren: That's what I mean.

18

Freedom of Speech in Public Schools

Tinker v. Des Moines Independent Community
School District (1969)

A primary purpose of public schools in the United States is to educate students for competent citizenship within the system of constitutional government. Thus, local school boards throughout the country authorize teachers to instruct students about their constitutional rights and the obligations of citizenship associated with them. Among the rights of citizens and noncitizens in the United States—which citizens are obligated to use responsibly—is a constitutional guarantee of free speech.

Are these rights and responsibilities, which the public expects the schools to convey to students, the same for individuals within the school as for individuals, including students, in the community outside it? During the autumn of 1965, this question was raised dramatically in the city of Des Moines, Iowa, by students who protested in their public schools the escalating participation of the United States in the Vietnam War. The U.S. Supreme Court responded nearly four years later with its decision in *Tinker v. Des Moines Independent Community School District* (1969).

The controversy that led to the *Tinker* decision began at a late-November 1965 antiwar demonstration in Washington, D.C. Among the thousands of protestors at the nation's capital were about fifty Iowans, including two high school students from Des Moines, John Tinker and Christopher Eckhardt. Along with John's sister Mary Beth, they became the principal figures in a lawsuit about the constitutional rights of students. On the return trip from the nation's capital, the passengers on the bus discussed how to protest the Vietnam War back home in Iowa. From this conversation came the idea of wearing black armbands as symbols of opposition to U.S. military involvement in Vietnam.

On December 11, at the Eckhardts' home there was a meeting of antiwar activists, including John and Mary Beth Tinker and their parents. The group agreed that local students should be encouraged to express their antiwar sentiments by wearing black armbands at school.

Christopher Eckhardt and the Tinker children resolved to carry out the group's plan of protest. They would wear black armbands to school. Christopher was a fifteen-year-old tenth-grade student at Theodore Roosevelt High School; John Tinker, a fifteen-year-old eleventh grader, attended North High School; and Mary Beth Tinker, age thirteen, was an eighth-grade student at Warren Harding Junior High School.

Tinker v. Des Moines Independent Community School District

- 393 U.S. 503 (1969)
- Decided: February 24, 1969
- Vote: 7–2
- Opinion of the Court: Abe Fortas
- Concurring opinions: Byron White and Potter Stewart
- Dissenting opinions: Hugo Black and John Marshall Harlan II

Mary Beth Tinker, a thirteen-year-old middle school student, sits with her mother at a school board meeting. She is wearing the black armband that was the cause of her suspension from school.

Heated conversations about imminent antiwar activities spread wildly through the community. Public school officials in Des Moines were alarmed. They imagined scenes of unruly antiwar protestors wreaking havoc in the classrooms and hallways of the schools, and they quickly made rules to prevent such a catastrophe.

The school principals issued a statement informing all teachers, students, and other relevant personnel that wearing black armbands or other symbols of protest in the public schools was prohibited. Students displaying such symbols would be asked to remove them; refusal would be punished by suspension from school, and offenders would not be readmitted until they pledged to comply with the rules.

The statement did not deter Christopher Eckhardt, John Tinker, and Mary Beth Tinker and they went to their respective schools wearing black armbands. When asked to remove them by teachers and principals, they refused and were suspended from school.

The Iowa Civil Liberties Union (ICLU), an affiliate of the American Civil Liberties Union (ACLU), became interested in the freedom of speech issue raised by the confrontation. They had no doubt that the three public school students had a constitutional right to wear the black armbands as a symbol of antiwar protest in the community outside the school. No local, state, or federal government official could have constitutionally prevented their freedom of expression in this manner. At issue here was the place the students chose to express their antiwar opinion, and leaders of both the ICLU and ACLU believed that students had the same constitutional rights inside their public school that they had on the streets outside it.

Leaders of the ICLU contacted the Eckhardt and Tinker families and offered help in responding to the school officials. By this time, the students had returned to school after a very brief suspension, and they agreed not to continue their armband-wearing protest. However, they and their parents were interested in taking this controversy from the classroom to the courtroom, and they accepted the ICLU offer of support. Thus an ICLU lawyer, Dan Johnston, went to the federal district court and filed suit against the Des Moines Independent Community School District in the name of the students' fathers. He sought compensation for damages incurred and an injunction to prevent school authorities from punishing the students. Johnston argued that the school district's rules prohibiting the display of black armbands violated the students' rights to freedom of speech under the First and Fourteenth Amendments to the Constitution.

The federal district court judge, Roy Stephenson, dismissed the suit, and Johnston appealed to the U.S. Court of Appeals for the Eighth Circuit. The Court of Appeals met in full court to consider this case and responded with an evenly divided vote, 4–4. Usually, the federal appellate courts sit in panel to decide cases rather than en banc, or with participation of all members. In the absence of a clear-cut decision, the lower court's ruling was, in effect, affirmed. With support from the Iowa Civil Liberties Union and the American Civil Liberties Union, the Tinkers and Eckhardts appealed to the U.S. Supreme Court.

Oral arguments before the high court took place on November 12, 1968. Dan Johnston of the ICLU again represented the Eckhardts and Tinkers. Counsel for the Des Moines school district was Allan Herrick, the board's long-time attorney. During his presentation, Johnston stressed that the students' antiwar protest caused no disturbances at school. Justice Byron White pressed Johnston with several sharply worded questions about this point. But Johnston held his ground: "I think they [the students] chose a message, chose a method of expression, Your Honor, which would not be distracting."

Later on, Johnston returned to this point, stating that "there was no indication, no testimony by teachers, by administrators or anyone else, of any reason to believe that it [the wearing of armbands] would be disruptive. And when the students in fact did wear the armbands, the record quite clearly shows that it was not in fact disruptive." Johnston concluded with an argument against distinguishing between the right to free speech within and outside of the school.

> I should not think that there would have to be a special rule for schools or any other part of our society for the First Amendment....[A]s far as the principles applied, we'd like to have the same principles applied in the school or perhaps especially in the school that are applied elsewhere.

In his presentation for the school district, Allan Herrick emphasized the need to balance the right to freedom of expression with the maintenance of order. He pointed to precedents for limiting free speech, such as *Adderly* v. *Florida* (1966), in which the Supreme Court had upheld restrictions against the speech of a student group protesting civil rights violations. In that case, the

An anti–Vietnam War protestor offers a flower to military police officers during a large public demonstration at the Pentagon, the headquarters of the U.S. Department of Defense. During the 1960s, such antiwar protests were staged throughout the country.

Court had held that the place of the protest, the grounds outside a jailhouse, was an inappropriate venue for this kind of activity.

Justice Thurgood Marshall interrupted Herrick and the following exchange occurred:

> Marshall: How many students were involved in the *Adderly* case? Several hundred wasn't it?
>
> Herrick: It was quite a large number.
>
> Marshall: How many were involved in this one?
>
> Herrick: Well, there were.... That's a question, Your Honor, what do you mean by involved?
>
> Marshall: How many were wearing armbands?
>
> Herrick: Well, there were five suspended for wearing armbands.
>
> Marshall: Well, were any wearing armbands who were not suspended?
>
> Herrick: Yes, I think there were two.
>
> Marshall: That makes seven.... Seven out of eighteen thousand [students in the entire school district], and the school board was afraid that seven students wearing armbands would disrupt eighteen thousand. Am I correct?
>
> Herrick: I think, if the Court please, that that doesn't give us the entire background that builds up to what was existing in the Des Moines schools at the time the armbands were worn.

Marshall's incisive questioning seemed to raise doubts among the justices about Herrick's claims that the school district's policy, restricting symbolic expression by armband-wearing students, was a reasonable attempt to maintain order in the schools. In response to questions from other justices, Herrick was forced to admit the paucity of evidence to support the school district's policy as necessary to prevent disruption of the educational process.

The Court decided by a vote of 7–2 that the school district officials had violated the students' right to free speech. In his opinion for the Court, Justice Abe Fortas raised the perennial challenge in a free society of balancing the individual's constitutional right to free speech against the community's expectation and need for public order and safety. The Court came down decisively on the side of the individual's right to freedom of speech.

Justice Fortas said that the wearing of black armbands to protest the war in Vietnam was a form of "symbolic speech" protected by the First Amendment and applied against state and local governments through the due process clause of the Fourteenth Amendment. In the opening paragraph of his opinion, Justice Fortas wrote memorably in favor of the students' rights in this case: "First Amendment rights, applied in light of the special characteristics of the school environment, are available to teachers and students. It can hardly be argued that either students or teachers shed their constitutional rights to freedom of speech or expression at the schoolhouse gate."

Fortas acknowledged that school officials are responsible for maintaining an orderly educational environment conducive to teaching and learning. He recognized the school officials' authority to limit a student's constitutional rights to freedom of expression in order to prevent serious disruption of the educational process, which is vital to the continuation and improvement of the community. However, Fortas stressed that the burden of proof was on the school officials. They had to provide compelling evidence to show how a rule enforced by them, which curtailed First Amendment freedoms, was necessary to sustain the school's educational mission. Fortas put forward a "rule of reason" as the governing criterion for the kind of issue raised by this case. For example, a regulation, such as the prohibition against wearing black armbands in school, must be a reasonable means of preventing disorders, which in the absence of the rule, would severely disrupt the educational process.

The school officials had failed to satisfy the "rule of reason" criterion, said Fortas. They could not demonstrate that the regulation against wearing black armbands in school had any reasonable connection to the prevention of disorder that could have seriously interfered with teaching and learning. "There is no indication that the work of the schools or any class was disrupted," wrote Fortas. Therefore, he concluded, "the prohibition cannot be sustained."

Fortas stressed the importance of protecting the constitutional rights of students against any unfounded fear of disruptions that might ensue from their exercise of these rights. "School officials do not possess absolute authority over their students," said Fortas. He believed adolescent students to be rights-bearing individuals, just like adults, both inside and outside the schoolhouse doors. "Students in school as well as out of school are 'persons' under our Constitution. They are possessed of fundamental rights which the State must respect, just as they themselves must respect their obligations to the State," wrote Justice Fortas.

The Court remanded, or sent back, the case to the federal district court for judgments, consistent with Justice Fortas's opinion, about how to compensate the plaintiffs or otherwise provide what was due them. The court ordered the Des Moines Independent Community School District to expunge the students' suspensions from their school records and to pay all costs of the litigation.

Two justices, John Marshall Harlan II and Hugo Black, dissented from the Court's opinion. Harlan's dissent was brief. He disagreed with Fortas that the school officials had the burden of proof in justifying a rule that limited students' freedom of expression. "I would in cases like this cast upon those complaining the burden of showing that a particular school measure was motivated by other than legitimate school concerns," wrote Justice Harlan.

Justice Black's dissent, by contrast, was a long and passionate denunciation of the Court's decision. Here is the nub of his strong disagreement with Fortas:

> While I have always believed that under the First and Fourteenth Amendments neither the State nor the Federal Government has any authority to regulate or censor the content of speech, I have never believed that any person has a right to give speeches or engage in demonstrations where he pleases. This Court has already rejected such a notion....

In 1965, Christopher Eckhardt and his parents attend a Des Moines, Iowa, school board meeting where the free speech rights of public school students were discussed. Christopher and his mother are wearing the black armbands that led to Christopher's suspension and ultimately to the U.S. Supreme Court case Tinker v. Des Moines Independent Community School District.

Mary Beth Tinker participates in a panel on First Amendment struggles hosted by the Freedom Forum in Washington, D.C., in 2000. Tinker, whose father was a Methodist minister, stated during the panel discussion that she decided to protest the Vietnam War as an expression of her religious beliefs.

One does not need to be a prophet or the son of a prophet to know that after the Court's holding today some students in Iowa schools and indeed in all schools, will be ready, able, and willing to defy their teachers on practically all orders....

This case, therefore, wholly without constitutional reasons in my judgment, subjects all the public schools in the country to the whims and caprices of their loudest, but maybe not their brightest students.

Justice Black's dissent in the *Tinker* case surprised and even shocked many civil libertarians, who had revered Hugo Black as a staunch and uncompromising champion of the right to free speech. Had Hugo Black changed his often stated belief that the Constitution's First Amendment was an absolute guarantee of the right to free speech? Justice Black strongly maintained his long-standing belief that there should be no restriction on the content of a person's speech. However, he argued in his *Tinker* dissent, as he had in other instances, that the person's manner of expression may be limited under certain conditions, just as it may be appropriate to regulate the times and places of speaking. In his opinion, the school building, especially during the daily schedule of events, was not an appropriate forum for antiwar protests nor was the wearing of armbands in this place an appropriate form of expression for students.

The Eckhardt and Tinker families expressed great satisfaction with the Court's decision. Both the parents and their children were pleased to receive credit from legal scholars and journalists for their advancement of civil liberties under the Constitution. And they readily responded to the many newspaper reporters, magazine writers, and radio and television broadcasters who rushed them for interviews about their campaign to expand and amplify the rights of students.

In retrospect, the *Tinker* decision represents a high point in the recognition of student rights under the Constitution. This decision continues to protect free expression of students that neither disrupts the educational purposes of the school nor violates the rights of other students. However, subsequent Supreme Court decisions have favored the authority of school officials to impose certain "reasonable" restrictions upon the rights of students in order to protect the school's educational mission against disruption. For example, in *Bethel School District No. 403* v. *Fraser* (1986), the Court ruled in favor of restrictions against vulgar student speech in a school assembly hall. And in *Hazelwood School District* v. *Kuhlmeier* (1989), the Court upheld restrictions and censorship by school authorities of hypersensitive content in a student newspaper produced by a journalism class. The school principal had decided that two articles, one providing information about birth control and the other describing intimate details about the divorce of a student's parents, were not appropriate for the intended readers.

Mary Beth Tinker Recalls Her Stand
for Student Rights

As a middle-aged woman, Mary Beth Tinker remembered vividly and proudly the stand she took as a teenager against the Vietnam War and for the constitutional rights of students in public schools. In the mid-1980s, University of California, San Diego, law professor Peter Irons interviewed her about the case for his book The Courage of Their Convictions, *which includes the stories of sixteen citizens who appealed their cases to the U.S. Supreme Court.*

After the Vietnam War started to escalate and became controversial, we were going to these various demonstrations and pickets against the war. There was a teen group also that had its own activities. I was kind of a hanger-on because I was a little young. I remember sitting at Bill and Maggie Eckhardt's house one night—their son, Chris, was also involved in our group, along with my older brother, John—and we decided to wear these black armbands to school....

After we had our meeting at the Eckhardt's and decided to wear the black armbands, we were all going to do it on the same day. I told this kid at school about it, and the day before we were going to wear the armbands it came up somehow in my algebra class. The teacher got really mad....I went back and told the group and the next thing we knew, the school board made this policy against wearing armbands. They had a special meeting and decided that any student who wore an armband would be suspended from school.

The next day I went to school and I wore the armband all morning. The kids were kind of talking, but it was all friendly, nothing hostile. Then I got to my algebra class, right after lunch and sat down. The teacher came in, and everyone was kind of whispering; they didn't know what was going to happen. Then this guy came to the door of the class and... they called me down to the principal's office.

The girls' counselor was there in the office....I took off the armband because I was intimidated. I was in this office with these people, the principal was there, and they were giving me these threats and I didn't know what was going to happen, so I took it off.

The principal was pretty hostile. Then they suspended me anyway....

The principal sent me home and called my parents. I went home and everyone was getting a little bit hysterical. It was getting to be a big deal. Everyone was sort of milling around the house. My brother John, who was in the eleventh grade at another school didn't wear an armband until the next day, and he got suspended right after he got to school. The two little kids in the family, Hope and Paul, were in elementary school. Hope was in the fifth grade and Paul was in the second grade. They wore black armbands too but nothing happened to them. I don't think the schools thought people would support suspending little kids for something like that.

We got suspended about a week before the Christmas holiday started. We were out of school that week, and every day there was a lot of activity. We were going to meetings, discussing this, figuring out what was going on. The school board had a meeting after we were suspended that hundreds of people went to, and there was a lot of argument and coverage in the newspapers and television. We all went there, wearing these armbands, and they decided to maintain their policy.

After the Christmas holiday, we went back to school but we didn't wear armbands. What we did was to wear black clothes every day for a long time, I think until school ended for the year. We wore all black because there was nothing they could do about that, but it was still this statement. It was our way of fighting back.

19

Standards for Interpreting the Establishment Clause

Lemon v. *Kurtzman* (1971)

Lemon v. Kurtzman

- 403 U.S. 602 (1971)

- Decided: June 28, 1971

- Vote: 8–0

- Opinion of the Court: Warren E. Burger

- Concurring opinions: William Brennan and Byron White

- Not participating: Thurgood Marshall

The First Amendment of the U.S. Constitution states, "Congress shall make no law respecting an establishment of religion. . . ." Americans have always agreed that this "establishment clause" prohibits the government from establishing or promoting a national religion. However, since the earliest years of the republic, Americans have disagreed about whether the establishment clause bans all government involvement with religion. Does the First Amendment require strict separation of church and state, with no involvement or accommodation between the government and religion? Or does the establishment clause permit certain kinds of interaction, cooperation, and accommodation between religious institutions and the government?

Thomas Jefferson, author of the Virginia Statute for Religious Freedom as well as the Declaration of Independence, favored strict separation of religion from government. Jefferson expressed this viewpoint in an 1802 letter to the Baptist Association of Danbury, Connecticut: "I contemplate with sovereign reverence that act of the whole American people which declared that their Legislature should 'make no law respecting an establishment of religion, or prohibiting the free exercise thereof,' thus building a wall of separation between Church & State."

More than 145 years after Jefferson wrote his letter to the Danbury Baptists, the Supreme Court explicitly acknowledged his view of the First Amendment's establishment clause in response to *Everson* v. *Board of Education of Ewing Township* (1947). Writing for the Court, Justice Hugo Black said,

> [N]either a state nor the Federal Government can set up a church. Neither can pass laws which aid one religion, aid all religions, or prefer one religion over another. Neither can force nor influence a person to go to or remain away from church against his will or force him to profess a belief or disbelief in any religion. . . . In the words of Thomas Jefferson, the clause against establishment of religion by law was intended to erect "a wall of separation between Church and State."

In *Everson,* however, the Court permitted a modest accommodation between church and state within the same opinion that incorporated Jefferson's interpretation of the establishment clause. The Court upheld as constitutional a New Jersey statute that provided for publicly funded transportation of students to Catholic parochial schools. This kind of accommodation between church and state was acceptable, said the Court, because the state government law was neutral in regard to religion. Further, the state provided a public service for the common good, which primarily benefited children and only indirectly helped the religious schools, but did not promote religious doctrine.

Although the Court's *Everson* opinion permitted the use of public funds to transport students to a church-affiliated school, it also strongly endorsed Jefferson's opinion on church-state relations: "The First Amendment has erected a wall between church and state. This wall must be kept high and impregnable. We could not approve the slightest breach."

Thomas Jefferson's "wall of separation" metaphor, as rendered by Justice Black in the 1947 *Everson* case, guided the Court's decisions in several subsequent cases, including two cases prohibiting state-sanctioned prayers or readings from the Bible in public schools, *Engel* v. *Vitale* (1962) and *Abington School District* v. *Schempp* (1963).

Students at a private parochial school in Plymouth, Michigan, work on an art project with their teachers, nuns from the order of Dominican Sisters of Mary Mother of the Eucharist. According to standards set forth in several U.S. Supreme Court decisions since 1947, such as Lemon v. Kurtzman *(1971), the government may not directly grant church-related schools funds or other resources that could be used to promote a particular religious doctrine.*

However, the Court earlier had expressed a slight disagreement with Jefferson's view of church-state relations in *Zorach* v. *Clausen* (1952), when it approved a program whereby public school students could be released during school hours to receive religious instruction in church-owned facilities. Writing for the Court in *Zorach*, Justice William O. Douglas said that the First Amendment "does not say that in every and all respects there shall be a separation of Church and State." In that case, the Court clearly supported an accommodation between government and religion under certain limited conditions.

Throughout American history, there have been examples of accommodation between government and religion, such as the traditional tax exemptions provided to religious institutions and the employment of chaplains by the federal government to serve the U.S. military forces. Furthermore, in *Board of Education of Central School District No. 1* v. *Allen* (1968) the Court had upheld a New York State program that provided textbooks on secular subjects to students in private, sectarian, or religious, schools. And, in *Walz* v. *Tax Commission of the City of New York* (1970), the Court upheld property tax exemptions provided to churches.

The *Allen* decision encouraged state governments in several states to pass laws that provided funds to Catholic parochial schools. Rhode Island, for example, enacted a statute in 1969 that allocated public funds to supplement the salaries of Catholic schoolteachers. And Pennsylvania's Non-Public Elementary and Secondary Education Act of 1968 permitted the state to support salaries of teachers who provided instruction on nonreligious subjects in church-run schools, such as Roman Catholic parochial schools. The Pennsylvania law also permitted the state government to reimburse the church-run schools for their purchase of textbooks and other instructional materials used to teach secular subjects. The Pennsylvania law, however, did require sectarian schools receiving state financial aid to keep records, which government inspectors could audit, to demonstrate nonreligious uses of public money.

Both the Rhode Island and Pennsylvania programs of public aid to private parochial schools were challenged as unconstitutional violations of the First Amendment's establishment clause. Joan DiCenso successfully filed suit to stop the Rhode Island programs in two related cases that came to the U.S. Supreme Court in 1971, *Early* v. *DiCenso* and *Robinson* v. *DiCenso*. And, in Pennsylvania, Alton Lemon filed suit against David H. Kurtzman, the state's superintendent of public instruction, to halt the provision of state funds to church-related schools. Lemon appealed the Pennsylvania case, *Lemon v. Kurtzman,* to the Supreme Court in 1971 after the lower court ruled against him. Because the constitutional issues in the two *DiCenso* cases and the *Lemon* case were practically the same, the Court considered all three cases simultaneously.

In the *DiCenso* cases and in *Lemon,* the Court decided that the state programs at issue were unconstitutional. Writing for the Court, Chief Justice Burger constructed a three-part "Lemon Test" named for the petitioner in the Pennsylvania case, Alton Lemon. In order for a statute to be constitutional and not in violation of the First Amendment's establishment clause, it had to meet the three standards of this test. First, it must have a secular or nonreligious purpose. Second, it must neither promote nor restrict religion in its primary effects. Third, it must not bring about an excessive entanglement of government with religion. By these standards, the Court struck down the Rhode Island and Pennsylvania laws that provided payments by the state government to supplement the salaries of parochial-school teachers providing instruction in secular subjects. In particular, the Court found the involvement of state government auditors in monitoring the use of public funds in parochial schools to be an excessive entanglement of the government with church-run schools. Further, the Pennsylvania law was found unconstitutional because financial aid from the state was given directly to the church-related schools.In the *Everson* and *Allen* cases, by contrast, the state aid was constitutional because it went to students and parents and it was not used to promote religious doctrine.

Although the Court had maintained a barrier between church and state in the *Lemon* decision, Chief Justice Burger noted: "Our prior holdings do not call for total separation between church and state; total separation is not possible in an absolute sense. Some relationship between government and religious organizations is inevitable." Referring to Jefferson's phrase, Burger maintained that the state-church separation was "far from being a wall." Burger argued that the separation of church and state is "a blurred, indistinct, and a variable barrier depending on all the circumstances of a particular relationship."

Chief Justice Burger recognized the value of Roman Catholic and other sectarian schools and their significant contributions to education and the common good. He wrote, "[N]othing we have said can be construed to disparage the role of church-related elementary and secondary schools in our national life. Their contribution has been and is enormous." Burger emphasized that the Court's decision was based entirely upon the constitutional issues related to the establishment clause. He concluded:

> Under our system the choice has been made that government is to be entirely excluded from the area of religious instruction and churches excluded from the affairs of government. The Constitution decrees that

religion must be a private matter for the individual, the family, and the institutions of private choice, and that while some involvement and entanglement are inevitable, lines must be drawn.

In the *DiCenso* cases, the Court affirmed the judgment of the Rhode Island District Court in its ruling that the state program of aid to sectarian schools violated the Constitution's establishment clause. In the *Lemon* case, the Court reversed the judgment of the Pennsylvania District Court and the case was remanded, or sent back, to the district court to be reconsidered in light of the Court's ruling.

On remand, the Pennsylvania District Court terminated the state's Non-Public Elementary and Secondary Education Act of 1968 and prohibited payments to church-related schools made under this statute. The judge, however, approved the state government's payments to the church-related schools that had been made before June 28, 1971, when the Supreme Court announced its decision in *Lemon* v *Kurtzman.*

Alton Lemon objected to the district court's ruling that allowed state payments to the parochial schools prior to the Supreme Court's decision. He wanted the church-related schools to reimburse the state government for money paid to them before the Supreme Court's decision in *Lemon* v. *Kurtzman.* His complaint brought about another Supreme Court case known as *Lemon II* (*Lemon* v. *Kurtzman*, 411, U.S. 192, 1973). But this time Lemon was the loser, as the Court upheld the Pennsylvania District Court's decision that money already spent by the schools did not have to be paid back to the state government.

The most important legacy of *Lemon I* has been the "Lemon test" that Chief Justice Warren Burger constructed in his opinion for the Court in the 1971 case. However, these guidelines for interpreting the meaning of the First Amendment's establishment clause were a synthetic product, not an original creation. Burger acknowledged that his three-pronged test was the result of "cumulative criteria developed by the Court over many years."

The first prong, or standard requiring that "the statute must have a secular legislative purpose," can be traced to the Supreme Court's opinions in *Everson* (1947), *Abington* (1963), and *Walz* (1970). Justice Brennan's opinion for the Court in *Walz* v. *Tax Commission of the City of New York* includes these words relevant to the Lemon test's first standard: "The legislative purpose of a property tax exemption is neither the advancement nor the inhibition of religion."

The second prong of the Lemon test, requiring that the statute's "principal or primary effect must be one that neither advances nor inhibits religion," was derived from the Court's opinions in *Everson* and *Abington*. Justice Tom Clark, in his opinion for the Court in *Abington School District* v. *Schempp* (1963), expressed the key idea of the Lemon test's second standard, "that to withstand the strictures of the Establishment Clause there must be a...primary effect that neither advances nor inhibits religion."

The Lemon test's third prong, which says, "The statute must not foster an excessive government entanglement with religion," is taken from the Court's opinion in the *Walz* decision of 1970. Chief Justice Burger's words mirror those of Justice Brennan in *Walz*: "We must...be sure that the end result—the effect—is not an excessive government entanglement with religion."

Public response to the Court's *Lemon* decision was mostly positive. Editorials in the nation's leading newspapers, such as the *New York Times* and *Washington Post,* were favorable. The Lemon test acknowledged the principle of church-state separation, but not strictly because it permitted accommodation between government and religion under some conditions.

Since its construction in 1971, the Court has continued to apply the Lemon test to most, if not all, of its decisions about establishment clause issues. One notable exception was *Marsh* v. *Chambers* (1983), in which the Court upheld the right of the Nebraska state legislature to opens its sessions with a traditional prayer recitation led by a Christian minister. A lower court had used the Lemon test to strike down the prayer ceremony as a violation of the establishment clause. Writing for the Court, Chief Justice Burger said that this case was an exception to the Lemon test because the practice at issue was a tradition deeply rooted in the history and culture of the United States and therefore permissible.

Antonin Scalia presented a mixed review of the Lemon test in his concurring opinion in *Lamb's Chapel* v. *Center Moriches Union Free School District* (1993). This case involved a dispute between a Christian church group and a public school district about the use of school facilities to show and discuss films that provided a religious viewpoint on raising children. The Court used the First Amendment guarantee of free speech to decide that public schools must open their facilities, during after-school hours, to religious organizations on equal terms with other, nonreligious, civic groups. The Court also used the Lemon test to justify equal access of religious groups to pubic school facilities.

In his concurring opinion, Justice Scalia both criticized and recognized the worth of the Lemon test. He wrote,

> Like some ghoul in a late-night horror movie that repeatedly sits up in its grave and shuffles abroad after being repeatedly killed and buried. *Lemon* stalks our Establishment Clause jurisprudence once again... The secret of the Lemon test's survival, I think, is that it is so easy to kill. It is there to scare us... when we wish it to do so, but we can command it to return to the tomb at will.... When we wish to strike down a practice it forbids we invoke it;.. when we wish to uphold a practice it forbids, we ignore it entirely... Such a docile and useful monster is worth keeping around, at least in a somnolent state; one never knows when one might need him.

Scalia's colleagues on the Court provided this rejoinder to his commentary on the Lemon test. "While we are somewhat diverted by Justice Scalia's evening at the cinema,... we return to the reality that there is a proper way to inter an established decision, and *Lemon,* however frightening it might be to some, has not been overruled."

In *Agostini* v. *Felton* (1997), the Lemon test was invoked to approve the use of public funds in New York City to provide remedial education for disadvantaged students in private, religiously affiliated schools. In making this decision, the Court elaborated upon the second prong of the Lemon test: the act at issue must neither promote nor restrict religion in its primary effects. The Court attempted to clarify this second prong of the Lemon test and its relationship with the third prong about excessive entanglement of government with religion with these questions. Does the program of government aid provided to a sectarian school result in religious indoctrination? Does it define the recipients of government aid by reference to religion? If the answers to these questions are negative, then there is no primary effect of promoting religion and there is no excessive entanglement of government with a religious institution. So, the statute at issue is constitutional.

The Court's ruling in *Agostini v. Felton* (1997) reversed its 1985 decision in *Aguilar v. Felton*. In the *Aguilar* case, a slim 5 to 4 majority used the Lemon test to prohibit the New York City public schools from providing federally funded remedial education to students and Roman Catholic church–affiliated schools. The Lemon test, as originally constructed and applied, had guided the Court in its *Aguilar* decision to strike down a program of government-supported remedial education for parochial school children, because it brought about an excessive entanglement of church and state. However, a change in the Court's membership brought a new perspective, and in *Zobrest v. Catalina School District* (1993) the Court undermined its *Aguilar* decision by allowing a government-funded program in Tucson, Arizona, to fund remedial instruction for a physically handicapped child attending a religious school. The Court explained that this kind of public aid directly helps students and not the religiously affiliated school or the church that sponsors them. Thus, it does not violate the First Amendment's establishment clause.

The Lemon test standards were cited in support of another decision, *Zelman v. Simmons-Harris* (2002). In this case, the Court approved a school voucher program that provided public funds to parents who could then choose to send their children to a religiously affiliated school, because the program did not directly support church-run schools. Writing for the Court, Chief Justice William Rehnquist also used the principles of "private choice" and "neutrality" to support the Ohio State government's voucher program. Rehnquist wrote, "The Ohio program is neutral with respect to religion." And it is a program of "true private choice, in which aid reaches religious schools only as a result of the genuine and independent choice of private individuals." Although the *Zelman* decision allows state voucher programs under certain conditions, many state governments throughout the United States, unlike the Ohio State government, are prohibited from enacting such programs because their state constitution explicitly restricts any kind of public support for a church-affiliated school.

Despite criticisms from various detractors, and modifications in its use by the Court, the Lemon test is still good law. This three-pronged set of standards has endured, even though it has not been the Court's exclusive or definitive guide to every one of its establishment clause decisions.

In 1802, Thomas Jefferson replied to the Baptists of Danbury, Connecticut, who had written to congratulate him on his election as President. The letter includes the phrase "a wall of separation between church and state," a concept that has figured in several important Supreme Court decisions. Despite its later significance, the letter was essentially forgotten for a century after it was published in a Massachusetts newspaper.

[fig. 19.1]

A Newspaper Editorial Endorses
the "Lemon Test"

The Supreme Court's 1971 decision in Lemon v. Kurtzman *and two related cases involved construction of the three-part Lemon test. In response, there were numerous commentaries in newspapers and other media, pro and con, throughout the country. The* Washington Post, *for example, published a laudatory editorial titled "Safeguarding Religious Freedom" on June 30, 1971.*

The Supreme Court's decisions forbidding state financial support of church-related parochial schools should be recognized for what they really are—a strengthening of the traditional wall of separation which shields religion in America from governmental intrusion. No doubt these decisions will seem disappointing and perhaps even hostile to many conscientious Catholics who sincerely believe that the valuable contribution their parochial schools have made to public education in this country deserves recompense; no doubt these decisions will be painful to Catholics who believe that their extensive school system will be doomed if state and federal tax money is not made available to sustain it. Nevertheless, the decisions serve the cause of church independence and of the freedom of men of every faith to worship as they wish.

Catholics need only ask themselves why they want their children in parish schools separate from the community's public schools in order to understand why the use of public money to pay their teachers or to support their courses involves what the Chief Justice called an "excessive entanglement between government and religion." The reason they want their children in parish schools is simply that they want schools in which prayer will play a part and in which the doctrines of the church will be stressed. These are entirely legitimate aims; and the right to pursue them

is indisputable. But there is simply no gainsaying the truth of Mr. Justice Douglas's observation that "the *raison d'etre* of parochial schools is the propagation of a religious faith." That is precisely the kind of propagation which the First Amendment was designed to prohibit government from undertaking.

The English experience, from which so many of the authors of the constitution drew their knowledge and inspiration, was an experience in which Protestants were persecuted when a Catholic monarch was on the throne and Catholics were persecuted in turn when Henry VIII and his successors established a national church over which they ruled. The Crown was forever meddling in modes of worship, in the designation of religious orthodoxy and in preferment of clerics. The aim of the First Amendment was to keep Americans free from that kind of interference.

If parochial schools were to receive public funds, a rigorous auditing of their accounts and an extensive supervision of their classroom practices would be necessary; indeed, there was provision for these in the Rhode Island and Pennsylvania laws which came under the court's scrutiny.

Independence is costly. But it is the fundamental condition of religious liberty. In denying the Catholic Church a government subsidy, the court has assured it unrestricted control over its own destiny.

20

Abortion, Privacy, and Values in Conflict

Roe v. *Wade* (1973)

A bortion has roiled the waters of modern American life as few other issues have. Beneath this debate are simmering differences over basic values: the rights of the unborn and the related matter of when life begins, the rights of women to control their reproductive functions and preserve their health, the expectation that women's most important role is to bear children, and the role of the state in selecting among these values.

The resulting conflicts have haunted American history, and today they are an exceptionally tense social and political issue. In colonial times and in the nation's early years, abortion was unregulated, in large measure because giving birth was at least as, if not more, dangerous than having an abortion. Under such circumstances state lawmakers concluded that it made little sense to declare abortion a crime. That position was reinforced by the English common law, which allowed abortions until the point of "quickening," the first time a pregnant woman felt the movement of an unborn fetus, usually in the fourth or fifth month of a pregnancy.

By 1860 this lack of attention began to change, and lawmakers in twenty of the thirty-three states in the Union had criminalized abortion. These new laws, collectively known as the Comstock laws, and named after Anthony Comstock, a politician and postal inspector, did not punish women seeking abortions, but instead levied fines and jail terms against doctors and others who performed the procedure. The reasons for doing so were complex and varied. With the advent of scientific medicine and the rise of the medical profession, doctors sought to burnish their professional image by distancing themselves from the growing ranks of poorly trained abortionists. Doctors also turned increasingly to the portion of the ancient Hippocratic Oath, from the fourth century B.C., which barred them from assisting women "to produce abortion."

Historically, the law had treated abortion and birth control as separate issues. By 1965, for example, all but one of the states, Connecticut, had fully legalized birth control. By the same year, every state in the Union had outlawed abortion in most circumstances. Rather than stopping abortions, however, these stricter laws drove the procedure "underground," so that pregnant women, especially lower-income women, suffered at the hands of unqualified practitioners in often unsanitary conditions. The well-to-do, on the other hand, had other options. In the 1960s, with the advent of the sexual revolution, women—especially those who wanted to terminate an unwanted pregnancy

Roe v. Wade
• 410 U.S. 113 (1973)
• Decided: January 22, 1973
• Vote: 7–2
• Opinion of the Court: Harry A. Blackmun
• Concurring opinions: Warren Burger, William O. Douglas, and Potter Stewart
• Dissenting opinions: Byron R. White and William H. Rehnquist

This proabortion leaflet from about 1973 with the stark image of a coat hanger illustrates one primitive and dangerous device used to end a pregnancy. Although in Roe *the Court accepted that a woman had a constitutional right to an abortion, the justices rejected the pamphlet's advocacy of "abortion on demand" and instead embraced a rule that made it increasingly difficult for a woman to secure an abortion as her pregnancy came to term.*

but who had to do so through clandestine and illegal means—placed increasing public pressure on existing abortion statutes. As a result, some states began to moderate their laws. Between 1965 and 1970 some fourteen legislatures passed laws that permitted abortion when pregnancy resulted from rape or when the child was likely to be severely disabled. Three states, New York, Alaska, and Hawaii, repealed their abortion laws, making the procedure readily available.

The rubella, or German measles, epidemic in the 1960s revived arguments over the abortion issue. Rubella in a pregnant mother often led to birth defects in her baby. Similarly, the use of the sedative thalidomide resulted in serve deformities in children whose mothers had taken the drug while pregnant. However, some women who were pregnant at the time these side effects were being discovered were unable to terminate their pregnancies. In 1967, the American Medical Association, a group that had historically opposed abortion, called for the liberalization of abortion laws to allow more exceptions.

Arrayed against the proabortion advocates were a variety of fundamentalist Protestant groups and, perhaps most important, the Catholic Church. It urged its millions of adherents in the United States to view abortion as a moral issue involving a fetus's right to life. Leaders of the antiabortion movement believed that life begins at conception and that all life is sacred. They also believed that the embryo is supremely important and the mother must make sacrifices to give birth to the child.

The modern constitutional debate over abortion emerged from this powerful cultural brew. By the 1960s the political issue of abortion was transformed into a pivotal constitutional struggle with the right to privacy as its fulcrum.

The concept of a right to privacy had been debated in American law for more than seventy years. Future Supreme Court justice Louis D. Brandeis and his colleague Samuel Warren's influential 1890 essay in the *Harvard Law Review,* "The Right to Privacy," argued that every American had a right "to be let alone," free from the meddling of government and other individuals in a person's private matters.

One of the first important tests of this idea came in the Supreme Court case *Griswold* v. *Connecticut* (1965). The case concerned an 1879 Connecticut statute that prohibited the use of any drug, instrument, or article to prevent contraception. By 1965 the law was unique; it was the last surviving statutory limit on birth control in the nation.

In his majority opinion in *Griswold,* Justice William O. Douglas concluded that the Constitution contained a right to privacy that included access to and use of birth control. His opinion broke new ground through a novel reading of the Bill of Rights. Douglas noted that although there was no right to privacy written into the Constitution, such a right could be implied as part of the First, Third, Fourth, Fifth, and Ninth Amendments. Justice Arthur Goldberg, who was joined in a concurring opinion by Chief Justice Earl Warren and Justice William J. Brennan Jr., staked out an even more expansive view of the right to privacy, finding that the Ninth Amendment's wording ("The enumeration in the Constitution, of certain rights, shall not be construed to deny or disparage others retained by the people") permitted the

Court to protect rights that were "so rooted in the traditions and conscience of our people as to be ranked fundamental."

This new right to privacy had another distinguished constitutional source. For more than a century the Court had developed the idea of substantive due process of law, a concept that emerged first in the mid-nineteenth century and then reached its apogee in *Lochner* v. *New York* (1903). The concept means that certain rights are so fundamental that the state could take them away only under the most extraordinary circumstances. Initially, substantive due process had been applied to strike many state and federal efforts to regulate the economy through, for example, maximum hours and minimum wage laws. In 1937, however, with the ruin of the Great Depression all around, the justices backed away and accepted that government could aggressively regulate economic affairs. Though the justices disposed of the economic uses of substantive due process, they retained the broad concept itself and began to apply it in new areas, notably matters of civil rights and equality generally and privacy and abortion specifically.

The key constitutional issue became centered on the due process clause of the Fourteenth Amendment and its provision that "No State shall make or enforce any law which shall... deprive any person of life, liberty, or property, without due process of law." The question became whether a substantive reading of that due process clause could be used to establish a right to privacy, even though such a right was not explicitly stated. The justices seized the *Griswold* case as an opportunity to define the right to privacy. Eight years later the Court extended it in *Roe* v. *Wade.*

The *Roe* case developed amid a particularly fractious era of American history. The 1960s were years marked by intense social and political ferment. Women entered the workplace in large numbers; blacks and whites engaged in an aggressive civil rights movement; and discontent over the Vietnam War in particular and distrust of government in general grew. New, permissive sexual standards also generated intense intergenerational conflict.

Abortion rights groups had been seeking test cases to challenge the constitutionality of state bans on abortion. In Texas, attorneys Sarah Weddington and Linda Coffee found Norma McCorvey, a pregnant carnival worker who wanted an abortion because she could not afford to raise a child. Weddington and Coffee were young lawyers committed to the advancement of women's rights. Weddington strongly believed in the right to abortion, and years later

Harry Blackmun, the author of the majority opinion in Roe v. Wade *(1973), wrote this note to Justice Potter Stewart on January 16, 1973, to discuss when the decision would be announced, an event that occurred five days later and included a concurring opinion from Stewart. Blackmun hoped his opinion in* Roe *would give greater professional discretion to doctors, but he badly miscalculated the hostility that it would generate from those opposed to abortion.*

Supreme Court of the United States
Memorandum
_____ 1-16 _____, 1973

Potter

Who knows? I doubt now that they will be announced tomorrow. He says he may write. I hope for Monday, the 22nd at the latest.

They must come down

I wholeheartedly agree.
P.S.

The Texas-born lawyer Sarah Weddington represented Norma McCorvey before the Supreme Court in the case Roe v. Wade. *The case was Weddington's first contested case and propelled her into the national limelight; previously she had handled uncontested divorces and had written wills for people with small estates.*

she revealed in her autobiography that she herself had had a secret abortion. Coffee had clerked for federal district court judge Sarah T. Hughes, herself a pioneer in developing the constitutional bases of women's rights.

In her search for a way to end her pregnancy, McCorvey agreed to participate in the suit against the Texas abortion ban, which dated back to 1854, as long as she could be anonymous. In the suit, therefore, she was called Jane Roe. McCorvey originally told Weddington and Coffee that she had been raped, but in fact her pregnancy resulted from a consensual relationship. McCorvey unrealistically believed that her lawsuit would be resolved in time for her to have an abortion. Instead, she had the baby and placed it for adoption before the Supreme Court acted.

In 1970, Roe sued Dallas County district attorney Henry Wade, who was responsible for enforcing the state's abortion laws in Dallas. Wade was widely known for his prosecution of Jack Ruby for the murder of Lee Harvey Oswald, the alleged assassin of President John F. Kennedy. He disliked prosecuting abortion cases and often overlooked the activities of abortion counseling clinics.

The Court consolidated Roe's case with the case of *Doe* v. *Bolton,* which involved a married couple from Georgia who sought an abortion to avoid possible medical difficulties. The couple appealed to the Court to overturn a Georgia statute from 1968 that permitted abortion when, in the judgment of a woman's doctor, backed by two other physicians who had independently examined her, the pregnancy endangered her life or seriously threatened her health. The statute also made an allowance when a newborn would have serious mental or physical defects and when the pregnancy resulted from rape. The 1968 Georgia statute had replaced one from 1876 that was almost identical to the Texas law.

Lower federal courts in Texas and Georgia struck down all or parts of these states' laws. The court in Texas held that single and married persons had the right to decide whether or not to have children based upon the Ninth and Fourteenth Amendments. While these lower courts accepted the constitutional arguments in support of the right to abortion, they refused to issue injunctions—legal orders directing someone to cease doing something—that would actually forbid the states from enforcing their antiabortion laws. They refused because the cases were decided after the children had been born, seemingly making it impossible to provide an injunction. So, even though they had won their constitutional arguments in the lower courts, both Roe and Doe decided to appeal to the Supreme Court. They wanted the justices to affirm the constitutional support for abortion and also to establish the precedent that lower federal courts were required to issue an injunction against the states to block enforcement of the antiabortion laws.

Roe was both Weddington and Coffee's first appearance before the Supreme Court. They argued that pregnancy unduly burdened women, and that the ban on abortion in Texas had a negative impact on their well-being. Drawing on *Griswold,* they also argued that a right to an abortion was included in the Ninth Amendment and extended to McCorvey through the due process and equal protection clauses of the Fourteenth Amendment. Women had a fundamental right to an abortion, and Texas had no compelling interest to deny such a right. Jay Floyd, the assistant attorney general for Texas, represented Wade. Floyd's two superiors, Robert Flowers and Crawford Martin, were outspoken critics of abortion, which they publicly denounced as the equivalent of murder. The case before the Court was moot, Floyd insisted, because Roe was no longer pregnant and the Court had long ago held that it would not decide cases that failed to present an immediate need for a remedy. Moreover, Floyd argued, women made their choice before they became pregnant by deciding to live in Texas and under its abortion laws. States such as Texas had a compelling interest in protecting fetal life at all times, he continued, because life begins at the moment of conception.

Because of two vacancies on the Court, only seven justices heard the first argument in the case on December 13, 1971. Chief Justice Warren Burger initially assigned the task of writing the opinions in both *Roe* and *Doe* to Justice Harry A. Blackmun, who labored on a draft for more than five months. Blackmun's slowness angered Justice Douglas, who had wanted to write the opinion in *Doe* and expected the Court as a whole to take the broadest possible position in support of a woman's right to an abortion. Douglas considered *Doe* to be the more important of the two cases because striking down the new Georgia reform statute would send a stronger message than overturning the antiquated Texas law.

Even Blackmun was not certain why he had been chosen to write the opinion. Burger and Blackmun were childhood friends from Minnesota; they had double-dated in high school, and Burger had lobbied to secure Blackmun's appointment to the high court. They were so personally tied to one another that the press often referred to them as the "Minnesota twins." Blackmun was also the former legal counsel for the Mayo Clinic, where he had worked closely with doctors, an experience that shaped his approach to *Roe*. In the end, however, Burger, whose political instincts made him more sensitive than the other justices to the volatile nature of the cases, probably was counting on his old friend to deliver a narrowly focused and uncontroversial opinion. Burger guessed wrong, and for the rest of their time together on the bench the relationship between the "Minnesota twins" was strained.

Blackmun's first draft opinion pleased Burger because it asserted that the Texas law was unconstitutionally vague and should be set aside on those grounds. Justices Brennan and Douglas, however, were so displeased with the narrow basis of Blackmun's draft and his reliance on the concept of vagueness that they refused to sign it. Unlike Blackmun, they wanted a strong statement in favor of women's rights generally. They believed that the vagueness theory was analytically weak. Unable to gather a significant majority in favor of his opinion, Blackmun successfully urged Burger to set the case for reargument in the fall of 1972, when the Court's two newest justices, William H. Rehnquist and Lewis Powell, could participate. In the meantime, Blackmun returned to the Mayo Clinic during the summer to conduct extensive research on the history of abortion.

The case was argued a second time on October 11, 1972, before a full bench. The Court that decided *Roe* was a mix of Democratic and Republican appointees, senior and junior justices. Brennan and Douglas believed that *Roe* presented an opportunity to grant women a fundamental right to an abortion based on the

In New York City, Planned Parenthood supporters demonstrate against the nomination of Samuel Alito to the Supreme Court because of his earlier statements about limiting abortions. They feared that Alito would push the Court closer to overturning Roe v. Wade.

concept of privacy. Douglas had hoped to persuade Burger to allow him to prepare the opinion for the Court in *Doe,* but his chilly relationship with the chief justice thwarted those ambitions. Thurgood Marshall and Potter Stewart joined them in believing the Court should make abortion a fundamental right. Newly appointed Justice Powell was a moderate, but during the second *Roe* argument a story circulated that at Powell's Richmond law firm he had helped a young man avoid prosecution for assisting an older woman to obtain an illegal abortion. Powell concluded that antiabortion laws simply increased the number of illegal and dangerous abortions.

On the other side of the issue were Byron White and William Rehnquist. Both insisted that there was no constitutional right to privacy, that the justices had fabricated such a right to the detriment of the fetus, and that abortion should be left where it had historically been lodged—in the states. The justices, they concluded, should not substitute their views for those of state legislators.

Chief Justice Burger was of two minds. He supported the broad concept of civil rights but believed that state legislatures were the best places to make decisions about such matters, not courts. At the same time, Burger also concluded that the Texas statute was simply too vague to stand constitutional scrutiny and should be overturned. Burger did not want to go as far as Brennan and Douglas, but he knew that he could not embrace Rehnquist and White's positions and hold his court together.

Burger once again turned to Blackmun. Blackmun's opinion quickly disposed of the question of whether the case was moot. He reasoned that simply because a pregnancy might end before the Court could reach a decision did not mean that the controversy itself would go away. Other pregnancies would occur. The parties and the states were thus owed a decision. Blackmun then proceeded to mix history, science, and a concern for the professional independence of physicians into a decision that overturned the Texas law. Historically, Blackmun noted, the common law had accepted abortion, and well into the nineteenth century women had been able to secure abortions. Even after the act of abortion was criminalized, the punishments visited on those who performed abortions were less if they occurred early in a pregnancy. Nevertheless, the states had regulated abortion, and those regulations worked to the disadvantage of women and limited the professional judgement of physicians.

Was the fetus a person?, Blackmun asked. His answer was clearly "no." After reviewing the history of the word "person" in the Fourteenth Amendment, Blackmun concluded that its framers did not mean to include the unborn. This point was particularly telling, Blackmun noted, because the

Fourteenth Amendment explicitly applied to "all persons born" in the United States, not simply conceived there.

Blackmun refused to take on the question of when life begins. Again, he stepped outside the law for his arguments. After combing works of theology, history, medicine, and philosophy, the justice concluded that there was no consensus on the question. "[T]he judiciary at this point in the development of man's knowledge," Blackmun observed, "is not in a position to speculate as to the answer."

From there Blackmun reached the major point of his opinion. A pregnant woman had a fundamental right to privacy under *Griswold* and control over whether or not to have a baby was part of that right. The right, however, was not absolute; the state did have an interest in protecting the public health. The balance between that interest and the rights of women shifted during the course of a pregnancy, with abortions later in a pregnancy posing a greater threat to the health of the woman and the well being of the fetus. At a certain point in a woman's pregnancy, the interests of the state became compelling and its ability to regulate abortions was firm.

To make his point, Blackmun drew on the old common law concept of quickening. Up to the end of the first trimester, abortion is safer than childbirth in terms of the woman's health. However, as the pregnancy progresses past the first trimester, regulations on the availability of abortion that reasonably related to the mother's health were permitted. When the fetus reached viability, then the state's compelling interest in protecting both the health of the woman and the life of the fetus became paramount. Viability was defined as the ability of the fetus to live outside the mother's womb, somewhere near the end of the second trimester. After viability, Blackmun concluded, states could regulate and even fully ban abortions, unless that procedure was required to protect the life or health of the woman.

Chief Justice Burger worried that by engaging the issue of privacy so directly, Blackmun had gone far beyond the narrow decision he had expected. Burger's concurring opinion emphatically stated that "the Court today rejects any claim that the Constitution requires abortions on demand."

Burger's concurrence was also directed toward the two dissenters, Rehnquist and White. The chief justice feared that the sweeping consequences the dissenters attributed to Blackmun's opinion would in fact make it more significant than it actually was. They charged Blackmun with inventing a right not contained in the Constitution and dividing pregnancy into a trimester scheme that was unsupportable. If the state had a legitimate interest in fetal health, it clearly began at conception and continued throughout the pregnancy. They insisted that Blackmun's opinion placed the convenience of the pregnant woman above the life of the fetus. Such a position was not supported by anything in the Constitution. By dividing pregnancy into three terms and then varying the rights of women accordingly, the Court was acting as a legislative body rather than as a tribunal charged with interpreting the Constitution.

On the same day, with Justice Blackmun again writing for the same 7–2 majority, the Court also struck down the more liberal Georgia abortion statute in *Doe* v. *Bolton*. Burger, who had originally planned to vote in favor of the

Georgia statute, wrote another concurring opinion in which he emphasized the limited scope of the Court's actions.

The *Roe* decision became part of a national dialogue. Most women's rights groups applauded the decision as a step forward for gender equality. Ironically, Justice Blackmun, whose views on gender issues had been very traditional and whose own daughter had become pregnant out of wedlock, found himself suddenly viewed as a defender of women's rights, a role he never sought but one to which he warmed considerably during the remainder of his career. The Catholic Church launched a blistering attack on the decision, on Blackmun, and especially on Justice Brennan, with some Catholic magazines demanding he be excommunicated. Blackmun became the target of demonstrators and death threats, and for the rest of his time on the bench he received round-the-clock security. Even liberal academics who supported a woman's right to abortion blasted the justice's opinion for lacking appropriate support in the text of the Constitution and in legal history. They insisted that the opinion had actually placed civil rights generally and the rights of women especially in greater danger because of its seemingly unprincipled nature.

Roe also generated a grassroots "right to life" movement that lobbied legislatures and gained considerable power within the Republican Party. Republican Presidential candidates beginning with Ronald Reagan promised that they would not appoint justices to the Court who supported *Roe*. Instead of toeing the constitutional line, legislators in many states began passing laws designed to blunt the ruling's impact. They made adult women's access to abortions and their doctors' ability to perform the procedure more burdensome and required that teenage girls notify and receive permission from their parents for an abortion. Antiabortion groups such as the National Right to Life Committee and Operation Rescue began to picket abortion clinics, often resorting to force and intimidation to keep pregnant women from using them.

The number of abortion cases appealed to the Court skyrocketed. From 1973 to 1986, when Rehnquist replaced Burger as chief justice, the Supreme Court followed a predictable pattern: it distinguished between obstacles to the choice of abortion and refusals to facilitate the choice. The justices generally invalidated the former and upheld the later.

In recent years the Court has expanded the government's power to restrict abortion. For example, in *Webster* v. *Reproductive Health Services* (1989), a closely divided Court concluded that a statutory ban the state of Missouri placed on the use of public employees and facilities to perform abortions was constitutional. But the most serious threat to *Roe* emerged in *Planned Parenthood* v. *Casey* (1992). The state of Pennsylvania had passed a law restricting access to abortions. The statute required women to wait at least twenty-four hours for an abortion after a doctor provided them with specific information about the nature of the procedure, the development of the fetus, and the possibility of putting the newborn child up for adoption. The law also required, on threat of criminal penalties for doctors, that a minor have the consent of one parent before a doctor could perform an abortion. It also mandated that married women inform their husbands that they were about to have an abortion.

The administration of President George H. W. Bush joined the case in support of the state of Pennsylvania and asked the justices specifically to overturn *Roe*. By 1992 abortion had become heavily politicized, much beyond anything Justice Blackmun had anticipated. The Court had undergone significant change as well, not only with Rehnquist becoming chief justice but with Antonin Scalia and Clarence Thomas, both strongly antiabortion, joining the bench. A bitterly divided Court voted 5 to 4 in *Casey* to sustain *Roe*. The opinion for the Court was unique. It was authored by three justices: Sandra Day O'Connor, the first woman to sit on the high court and an appointee of Republican President Ronald Reagan, and Justices Anthony Kennedy and David Souter.

For the first time, the Court imposed a new standard to determine the validity of laws restricting abortions. That standard asked whether a state abortion regulation imposed an "undue burden," which it defined as a "substantial obstacle in the path of a woman seeking an abortion before the fetus attains viability." Under this new standard, the only provision to fail the undue-burden test was the Pennsylvania law's requirement that a woman notify her husband. Four of the justices—Rehnquist, Scalia, Thomas, and White—wanted to go even further; they insisted that the Court should overturn *Roe* on constitutional grounds. Since *Casey* the Court has heard other cases involving the abortion issue, although the justices have refused to address directly the constitutional soundness of *Roe*.

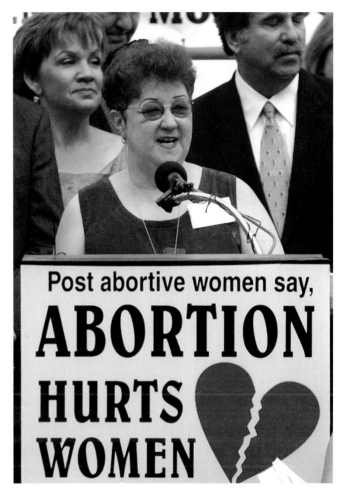

Norma McCorvey, who was the plaintiff "Jane Roe" in Roe v. Wade, *the landmark case legalizing abortion, later became an anti-abortion activist. Here, she addresses supporters in Dallas in 2003. In the highly emotional abortion debate, the Supreme Court mirrors the public in being divided on the issue.*

Abortion remains a vexing constitutional issue. Each new vacancy on the Court raises the possibility that a new justice appointed by a conservative Republican President will form a majority to overturn *Roe*. Perhaps like the desegregation of public schools, this public policy issue will be laid to rest only when the justices can reach an unshakable unanimity that reflects something like a national consensus. Until then the justices, who are themselves divided over the issue of abortion, will continue to shape the constitutional debate over when life begins, the rights of the unborn, the rights of women, and their own power to even decide such matters.

Why *Roe* Should Be Overturned

The Supreme Court systematically limited the scope of Roe *in several cases, the most important of which was* Planned Parenthood of Southeastern Pennsylvania v. Casey *(1992). Planned Parenthood sued Pennsylvania's governor, Robert Casey, claiming that a sate law violated the fundamental right of a woman to have access to an abortion. The law had four important provisions. An "informed consent" rule required doctors to provide woman with information about he health risks of having an abortion before one could be performed. The "spousal notification" rule required women to give prior notice to their husbands; a "parental consent" rule required minors to receive consent from a parent or guardian prior to an abortion. The fourth provision imposed a twenty-four-hour waiting period before obtaining consent.*

Several members of Congress submitted an amicus curiae (friend of the court) brief in Casey *to provide their perspective on the legal basis by which the Court could strike down such a significant precedent as* Roe v. Wade.

The amici, Members of Congress and Senators, have substantial interests in the disposition of this case. Congressional debates on legislation with provisions similar to the challenged sections of the Pennsylvania Abortion Control Act often center on the constitutionality of such requirements.... Congress is keenly interested in the Court's answer as it holds the key to restoring the essential balance between legislative authority and judicial review under the federal Constitution.

This Court's recent decisions have begun the process of dismantling "the mansion of constitutionalized abortion-law, constructed overnight in *Roe v. Wade.*".... A majority of the Court has questioned or repudiated Roe's trimester framework; has recognized compelling state interests in maternal health and fetal life throughout pregnancy; and has employed a more relaxed standard of review in evaluating the constitutionality of abortion regulations. *Roe* is an impaired decision. Some lower federal courts have begun to recognize, and the country increasingly understands, that Roe has been limited. Overruling *Roe v. Wade* would not represent an abrupt about-face in the Court's abortion jurisprudence but rather would be the final step in a journey that began several years ago. [Precedent, as] a doctrine of diminished importance in the field of constitutional law, provides no basis for declining to overrule the multiple errors of *Roe v. Wade*. On 214 occasions this Court has overturned previous decisions. In nearly three-fourths of those cases, the Court overruled because the earlier decision had wrongly interpreted the Constitution.

The reasons for this self-correction—the difficulty of addressing constitutional error through amendment or legislation; the primacy of the text of the Constitution over the interpretations placed upon it; and the inappropriateness of the nation's highest tribunal perpetuating constitutional error—apply with special force to *Roe*. Moreover, the interests furthered by [precedent] are not served by retaining *Roe*; indeed, they are at cross-purposes. The doctrines of *Roe* have caused great instability and unpredictability in the law. Recent decisions of this Court exacerbate this uncertainty. Statements from the lower federal courts, as well as state and federal elected representatives, amply demonstrate the confusion resulting from attempts to read this Court's recent abortion decisions against the backdrop of *Roe* v. *Wade*.

Overruling *Roe* also would be consistent with past willingness to admit error. This Court has corrected decisions which, like *Roe*, have misinterpreted the "liberty" clause of the Fourteenth Amendment by placing an unwarranted strait-jacket on legislative authority. And it has renounced the role of "super-legislature," sitting in judgment on the wisdom of state statutes.

Doctrines on which long-standing social institutions and conventions were established have been overturned, as have doctrines on which scores of criminal convictions were predicated. The overturning of such decisions has often caused change, some of it disruptive. But in appropriate circumstances it also has returned to the political branches of government their rightful authority to respond to the pressing moral and social issues at the root of such change. *Roe*, contrary to this tradition, has usurped the legislative function, and has aggravated the social turmoil over abortion.

Finally, although this Court has shown a proper reluctance to overrule constitutional decisions where a less severe remedy is available, it is appropriate to overrule *Roe* v. *Wade* in this case. *Roe* is no longer viewed as stable or fully intact; this uncertainty concerning a decision so demonstrably unworkable and devoid of constitutional basis divests the decision of any rightful sway over the Court's decision here. *Roe* is constitutional error of the most radical variety, and the traditions of this Court call for such error to be dispatched without ambiguity or equivocation.

Abortion as a Fundamental Right

Both critics and supporters of Justice Harry Blackmun's opinion in Roe v. Wade, *below, have faulted it for being too dependent on non-legal sources of authority and for a problematic reading of the history of abortion and the medical profession. Critics have also charged that Blackmun attempted to establish a fundamental right that was not based on a careful reading of the Constitution. Blackmun, according to his biographers, was most concerned with protecting doctors, with whom he had worked closely his entire professional life, from being treated as criminals in the exercise of their professional judgment about when a woman could have an abortion.*

When most criminal abortion laws were first enacted, the procedure was a hazardous one for the woman.... Modern medical techniques have altered this situation. Appellants and various *amici* [friends of the Court] refer to medical data indicating that abortion in early pregnancy, that is, prior to the end of the first trimester, although not without its risk, is now relatively safe. Mortality rates for women undergoing early abortions, where the procedure is legal, appear to be as low or lower than the rates for normal childbirth. Consequently, any interest of the State in protecting the woman from an inherently hazardous procedure, except when it would be equally dangerous for her to forgo it, has largely disappeared. Of course, important state interests in the areas of health and medical standards do remain. The State has a legitimate interest in seeing to it that abortion, like any

other medical procedure, is performed under circumstances that insure maximum safety for the patient. This interest obviously extends at least to the performing physician and his staff, to the facilities involved, to the availability of after-care, and to adequate provision for any complication or emergency that might arise.... Moreover, the risk to the woman increases as her pregnancy continues. Thus, the State retains a definite interest in protecting the woman's own health and safety when an abortion is proposed at a late stage of pregnancy.

The...State's interest—some phrase it in terms of duty—[is also] in protecting prenatal life. Some of the arguments for this justification rest on the theory that a new human life is present from the moment of conception. The State's interest and general obligation to protect life then extends, it is argued, to prenatal life. Only when the life of the pregnant mother her-self is at stake, balanced against the life she carried within her, should the interest of the embryo or fetus not prevail. Logically, of course, a legitimate state interest in this area need not stand or fall on accept-ance of the belief that life begins at conception or at some other point prior to live birth. In assessing the State's interest, recognition may be given to the less rigid claim that as long as at least *potential* life is involved, the State may assert interests beyond the protection of the pregnant woman alone.…

The Constitution does not explicitly mention any right of privacy. In a line of decisions, however,…the Court has recognized that a right of personal privacy, or a guarantee of certain areas or zones of privacy, does exist under the Constitution.…

This right of privacy, whether it be founded in the Fourteenth Amendment's concept of personal liberty and restrictions upon state action, as we feel it is, or… in the Ninth Amendment's reservation of rights to the people, is broad enough to encompass a woman's deci-sion whether or not to terminate her pregnancy. The detriment that the State would impose upon the pregnant woman by denying this choice altogether is apparent. Specific and direct harm medically diag-nosable even in early pregnancy may be involved. Maternity, or additional offspring, may force upon the woman a distressful life and future. Psychological harm may be imminent. Mental and physical health may be taxed by child care. There is also the distress, for all concerned, associated with the unwanted child.…In other cases, as in this one, the additional difficulties and continuing stigma of unwed mother-hood may be involved. All these are factors the woman and her responsible physician necessarily will consider in consultation.

On the basis of elements such as these, appellant and some *amici* argue that the woman's right is absolute and that she is entitled to terminate her pregnancy at whatever time, in whatever way, and for whatever rea-son she alone chooses. With this we do not agree. Appellant's arguments that Texas either has no valid interest at all in regulating the abortion decision, or no interest strong enough to support any limitation upon the woman's sole determination, are unpersuasive. The

Court's decisions recognizing a right of privacy also acknowledge that some regulation in areas protected by that right is appropriate.…At some point in preg-nancy, these respective interests become sufficiently compelling to sustain regulation of the factors that govern the abortion decision. The privacy right involved, therefore, cannot be said to be absolute.…

We, therefore, conclude that the right of personal privacy includes the abortion decision, but that this right is not unqualified and must be considered against important state interests in regulation.… [This] right, nonetheless, is not absolute and is sub-ject to some limitations; and…at some point the state interests as to protection of health, medical stan-dards, and prenatal life, become dominant.…

While certain "fundamental rights" are involved, the Court has held that regulation limiting these rights may be justified only by a "compelling state interest"…and that legislative enactments must be narrowly drawn to express only the legitimate state interests at stake.…

In the recent abortion cases, courts have recog-nized these principles. Those striking down state laws have generally scrutinized the State's interests in pro-tecting health and potential life, and have concluded that neither interest justified broad limitations on the reasons for which a physician and his pregnant patient might decide that she should have an abortion in the early stages of pregnancy. Courts sustaining state laws have held that the State's determinations to protect health or prenatal life are dominant and con-stitutionally justifiable.…

The appellee and certain *amici* argue that the fetus is a "person" within the language and meaning of the Fourteenth Amendment. In support of this, they outline at length and in detail the well-known facts of fetal development. If this suggestion of personhood is established, the appellant's case, of course, collapses, for the fetus' right to life would then be guaranteed specifically by the Amendment…[but] no case [can] be cited that holds that a fetus is a person within the meaning of the Fourteenth Amendment.

The Constitution does not define "person" in so many words. Section 1 of the Fourteenth Amendment contains three references to "person." The first, in defining "citizens," speaks of "persons born or naturalized in the United States." "person" is used in other places in the Constitution. But in nearly all these instances, the use of the word is such that it has application only postnatally. None indicates, with any assurance, that it has any possible pre-natal application.

All this, together with our observation... that throughout the major portion of the nineteenth century prevailing legal abortion practices were far freer than they are today, persuades us that the word "person," as used in the Fourteenth Amendment, does not include the unborn....

The pregnant woman cannot be isolated in her privacy. She carries an embryo and, later, a fetus.... The situation therefore is inherently different from marital intimacy, or bedroom possession of obscene material, or marriage, or procreation, or education.... As we have intimated above, it is reasonable and appropriate for a State to decide that at some point in time another interest, that of health of the mother or that of potential human life, becomes significantly involved. The woman's privacy is no longer sole and any right of privacy she possesses must be measured accordingly.

Texas urged that, apart from the Fourteenth Amendment, life begins at conception and is present throughout pregnancy, and that, therefore, the State has a compelling interest in protecting that life from and after conception. We need not resolve the difficult question of when life begins. When those trained in the respective disciplines of medicine, philosophy, and theology are unable to arrive at any consensus, the judiciary, at this point in the development of man's knowledge, is not in a position to speculate as to the answer....

In view of all this, we do not agree that, by adopting one theory of life, Texas may override the rights of the pregnant woman that are at stake. We repeat, however, that the State does have an important and legitimate interest in preserving and protecting the health of the pregnant woman,... and that it has still *another* important and legitimate interest in protecting the potentiality of human life. These interests are separate and distinct. Each grows in substantiality as the woman approaches term and, at a point during pregnancy, each becomes "compelling."

With respect to the State's important and legitimate interest in the health of the mother, the "compelling" point, in the light of present medical knowledge, is at approximately the end of the first trimester. This is so because of the now-established medical fact, referred to above, that until the end of the first trimester mortality in abortion may be less than mortality in normal childbirth. It follows that, from and after this point, a State may regulate the abortion procedure to the extent that the regulation reasonably relates to the preservation and protection of maternal health. Examples of permissible state regulation in this area are requirements as to the qualifications of the person who is to perform the abortion; as to the licensure of that person; as to the facility in which the procedure is to be performed....

This means, on the other hand, that, for the period of pregnancy prior to this "compelling" point, the attending physician, in consultation with his patient, is free to determine, without regulation by the State, that, in his medical judgment, the patient's pregnancy should be terminated. If that decision is reached, the judgment may be effectuated by an abortion free of interference by the State.

With respect to the State's important and legitimate interest in potential life, the "compelling" point is at viability. This is so because the fetus then presumably has the capability of meaningful life outside the mother's womb. State regulation protective of fetal life after viability thus has both logical and biological justifications. If the State is interested in protecting fetal life after viability, it may go so far as to proscribe abortion during that period, except when it is necessary to preserve the life or health of the mother.

Measured against these standards... the Texas Penal Code, in restricting legal abortions to those "procured or attempted by medical advice for the purpose of saving the life of the mother," sweeps too broadly. The statute made no distinction between abortions performed early in pregnancy and those performed later, and it limits to a single reason, "saving" the mother's life, the legal justification for the procedure. The statute, therefore, cannot survive the constitutional attack made upon it here.

21

Presidential Immunity and the Watergate Crisis

United States v. *Nixon* (1974)

United States v. Nixon

- 418 U.S. 683 (1974)

- Decided: July 24, 1974

- Vote: 8–0

- Opinion for the Court: Warren E. Burger

- Not participating: William H. Rehnquist

On August 8, 1974, Richard M. Nixon announced that the following day he would resign as President of the United States, becoming the first chief executive to do so. Nixon acted in order to avoid impeachment and, in his words, to begin "that process of healing which is so desperately needed in America."

President Nixon abandoned the White House after five years of service that were marked by unparalleled success amid deepening controversy. His accomplishments included revenue sharing between the states and the national government, the end of the draft, new anticrime laws, and a broad environmental protection program. In 1969, during his first term, American astronauts landed on the moon. Back on Earth, Nixon opened China to the West, reduced tensions with the Soviet Union, and orchestrated a landmark treaty limiting testing of strategic nuclear weapons. In January 1973, he announced that an accord had been reached with North Vietnam to end American involvement in Indochina. A year later, with the assistance of Secretary of State Henry Kissinger, Nixon spurred negotiations that produced disengagement agreements between Israel and its opponents, Egypt and Syria.

Nixon was also a controversial President, in part because of his policies, in part because of his style, and in part because of the fallout from what came to be known as Watergate. Nixon steadily battled Congress over a host of issues throughout his Presidency, and he suffered through the embarrassment of having his Vice President, Spiro T. Agnew, resign over charges of accepting bribes and filing false federal income tax returns in 1973.

The Vietnam War was at the root of Nixon's political frustration. In the 1972 Presidential election, with protests over the Vietnam War raging around the country, Nixon's Democratic challenger, Senator George McGovern of South Dakota, urged a timetable for withdrawal from Vietnam. To counter McGovern and the Democrats, some members of Nixon's election team resorted to efforts to disrupt the campaigns of Nixon's opponents, including the primary campaign of Senator Edmund Muskie. The most damaging of these efforts resulted in the Watergate scandal.

On June 17, 1972, Frank Willis, a security guard at the Watergate building in Washington, D.C., discovered that five men had illegally entered the offices of the Democratic National Committee. The men, Bernard Barker, Virgilio González, Eugenio Martínez, James W. McCord Jr., and Frank Sturgis, were caught inside the office carrying various suspicious items, including camera equipment and telephone bugging devices. It was later revealed that they had broken in three weeks earlier and then returned for another visit in order to remedy improperly functioning eavesdropping equipment. The men were found to be linked to the CIA and, even more importantly, to the White House through the Committee to Re-elect the President (CRP), which people gave the ironic acronym of CREEP. Among the telephone numbers discovered in the records of the burglars was that of E. Howard Hunt, a White House aide and CREEP official. White House spokespersons characterized the affair as a "third rate burglary"; most Americans refused to believe that President Nixon was involved.

While publicly showing an attitude of indifference toward the burglary, Nixon and his top aides scrambled to cover up White House involvement. Their efforts to do so were captured by tape recorders that the President had secretly ordered placed in the Oval Office. Nixon's intent had been to make a thorough record of events during his administration so he could subsequently write its definitive history. The tapes, however, came to be his undoing.

On January 8, 1973, the burglars went to trial for conspiracy, breaking and entering, and wiretapping, along with Hunt and G. Gordon Liddy, who had directed the White House's Special Investigations Unit, a secret operation that came to be known as the Plumbers. This group ran various operations against the Democrats and Vietnam War protestors with the approval of John Mitchell, Nixon's attorney general and the head of CREEP. These included the break-in at the Watergate, and another break-in at the office of a psychiatrist who was treating Daniel Ellsberg, a former Pentagon employee who had leaked a secret

The burglars who broke into the Democratic Party headquarters in the Watergate Hotel placed surveillance equipment such as these hidden microphones disguised as Chap Stick tubes, which police later photographed as evidence. President Richard Nixon's press secretary, Ron Ziegler, who was attempting to shield the President from any connection to Watergate, described it as "a third-rate burglary," which in many ways it was.

and highly critical account of the war to the *New York Times*. The struggle over whether to allow publication of those documents resulted in the landmark Supreme Court case *New York Times Co. v. United States* (1971), in which the justices blocked the President's attempts to prevent publication of the classified papers.

Four of the five Watergate burglars pleaded guilty, but Hunt and McCord went to trial. Because the burglars and the others refused to cooperate, presiding judge John Sirica, who was known for his harsh sentencing policies, gave them all thirty-year sentences. Sirica also told them that he would reduce their sentences if they cooperated. McCord did so and implicated CREEP in the burglary.

The affair might well have ended there had not the *Washington Post* delved more fully into it. Reporters Carl Bernstein and Bob Woodward tapped a host of government sources, including Mark W. Felt, at the time the second-ranking official in the FBI. Felt, whom Bernstein and Woodward assigned the code name Deep Throat, was not publicly identified until 2005. The reporting in the *Post* as well as the *New York Times*

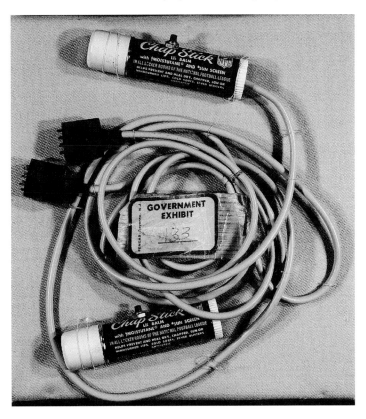

brought mounting pressure on the administration and eventually prompted the Senate to create a special committee, the Watergate Committee, led by Sam Ervin, a North Carolinian with a homespun style.

On April 30, 1973, Nixon requested the resignations of his two top aides, Chief of Staff H. R. Haldeman and Assistant to the President for Domestic Affairs John Ehrlichman. Nixon also fired his White House counsel, John Dean, who in testimony before the Senate Watergate Committee said he had warned Nixon against trying to cover up the Watergate affair. Nixon also named Elliot Richardson attorney general to replace John Mitchell. Richardson then appointed Harvard law professor Archibald Cox to be a special prosecutor charged with conducting an independent investigation of Watergate. These developments occurred just as televised hearings before the Senate committee began. The hearings became an absorbing national spectacle that drew more than 85 percent of the viewing public to one or more sessions.

The defining moment in the hearings came on July 13. Deputy Assistant to the President Alexander Butterfield made a startling disclosure: the President had a secret system for recording everything said in the Oval Office. The existence of tape recordings opened the possibility for the Senate to learn, in the words of Senator Howard Baker of Tennessee, "[w]hat did the president know and when did he know it."

President Nixon, however, refused to turn over the tapes, either to the Senate or to Special Prosecutor Cox. The tension mounted until on Saturday, October 20, 1973, at about 8:30 P.M., Nixon forced the resignations of Richardson and his deputy attorney general, William Ruckelshaus, for refusing to fire Cox. The so-called Saturday Night Massacre ended only when Solicitor General Robert Bork, who became by default the acting head of the Department of Justice, fired Cox. Stunned reporters on network television covered these events on a minute-by-minute basis. "Whether ours shall continue to be a government of laws and not of men is now for Congress and ultimately the American people," Archibald Cox stated after he was fired. Ten days later, the House of Representatives began impeachment proceedings against the President, as the House Judiciary Committee, chaired by Representative Peter Rodino, started its preliminary investigation.

Nixon had no choice but to replace Cox with another special prosecutor; this time he appointed Leon Jaworski, a prominent Texas lawyer and recent American Bar Association president, to continue the investigation. A federal grand jury indicted seven of the President's top aides and campaign officials for conspiracy to obstruct justice. Nixon was named as an "unindicted co-conspirator." The President publicly dismissed allegations of wrongdoing by stating before a large audience at Disneyland in his home state of California, "I am not a crook."

The question of Nixon's guilt or innocence turned on the tapes. In response to a subpoena for the tapes issued by Judge Sirica, Nixon again refused, on the grounds of executive privilege, to furnish them. He also refused to comply with Judge Sirica's order to deliver the tapes for an in camera (private) inspection by the court. Although Nixon's lawyers had planned to take the issue to the federal court of appeals, with July 1974 impeachment hearings against Nixon looming, Jaworski asked the Supreme Court to take up the matter on an expedited review. The Court agreed to hear the case because of its immediate importance and the profound constitutional issues it raised. Spectators lined up two days in advance hoping to witness the oral arguments.

Nixon insisted that because he was President he was immune from court orders to produce documents and other materials. Nixon also claimed that the tapes contained highly sensitive national security and intelligence information. The President attempted to combat growing public suspicion by releasing heavily edited transcripts of the tapes; these efforts did disclose that the tapes were punctuated with profane language and racial and ethnic slurs. The transcript also noted that the tapes contained an eighteen-and-one-half-minute gap that the White House claimed Nixon's secretary, Rosemary Woods, had made accidentally. Subsequent analysis of the tapes suggested, although it could not be proven definitively, that the erasure had been intentional.

Nixon's conduct raised some of the most serious issues of separation of powers and rule of law in American history. Was there, for example, a constitutionally supported doctrine of executive privilege, and if so, how far did it extend? Did the separation of powers prevent the Court from hearing a matter that is contained within one branch of the federal government? Can a subordinate, the special prosecutor, prosecute the President under whom he serves? Which takes precedence, the confidentiality of the President's work or the availability of evidence in a criminal investigation? And are acts of the President subject to review by the courts, or is he supreme in his interpretation of his constitutional duties and powers?

Leon Jaworski, whose varied experience and professional reputation protected him from any accusations of being either partisan or ideologically motivated, argued to the justices that the President had far exceeded his authority. Nixon was acting, Jaworski observed, as the sole judge of the Constitution, a position that conflicted with the powers and responsibilities he had been delegated under the Constitution. Executive privilege was not, Jaworski insisted, a constitutional power, but instead a power derived from practice and custom. That meant it had to be defined in a narrow way that limited the powers of the President. Such privilege should not, and historically had not, included withholding evidence in a criminal matter. President Nixon, Jaworski insisted, was attempting to place himself beyond the law, a position incompatible with the grand concept of the rule of law, which asserts that no person can be above it.

James St. Clair, an experienced trial lawyer and partner in a prestigious Boston law firm, represented Nixon. St. Clair told the justices that the conflict over the subpoena was an issue between two members of the executive branch (the President and the special prosecutor), and that it was therefore not within the Court's jurisdiction. The question of whether a subordinate of the President could force a subpoena on him was entirely for the President, not the courts, to decide. Moreover, St. Clair argued that the President alone could determine the scope of executive privilege and that he had no need to seek the approval of the judicial branch in general and the Supreme Court in particular. The possible impeachment of the President, which was a political rather than a legal proceeding, made the disposition of the Watergate tapes a political issue that should be resolved politically.

SUBPOENA DUCES TECUM
United States District Court
For the District of Columbia

Misc. #47-73

THE UNITED STATES
vs.

JOHN DOE

REPORT TO UNITED STATES DISTRICT
COURT HOUSE
Between 3d Street and John Marshall Place
and on Constitution Avenue NW.
~~ROOM 3232~~ Grand Jury Room 3
Washington, D.C.

To: Richard M. Nixon, The White House, Washington, D. C., or any
subordinate officer, official, or employee with custody or
control of the documents or objects hereinafter described on
the attached schedule.

FILED

JUL 24 1973

JAMES F. DAVEY, Clerk

You are hereby commanded to attend before the Grand Jury of said Court on Thursday
the 26th day of July, 19 73, at 10 o'clock A. M., to testify
~~on behalf of the United States, and not depart the Court without leave of the Court or District Attorney.~~
and to bring with you the documents or objects listed on the attached
sched- WITNESS: The Honorable John J. Sirica, Chief Judge of said Court, this
ule.
23rd day of July, 19 73.
JAMES F. DAVEY, Clerk.

Archibald Cox
ARCHIBALD COX
Attorney for The United States

By *Robert L. Line*
Deputy Clerk.

Form No. USA-9x-184 (Rev. 7-1-71)

34

This subpoena issued by special prosecutor Archibald Cox to the President of the United States on July 23, 1973, requested that Richard Nixon hand over the tapes of conversations that he had secretly made in his office. Nixon refused and fired both Cox and Attorney General Elliot Richardson in an unsuccessful attempt to demonstrate that he could not be ordered to produce materials required in a criminal investigation.

The future of the Presidency and of the nation turned on the high court's decision. Of its justices, the justice who most strongly supported the President was Potter Stewart. Like Chief Justice Warren Burger, Stewart believed that the special prosecutor lacked a sufficient connection to the harm done by Nixon, or standing in lawyer's terms, to present a case against the President. The Court, therefore, could not hear the case. Byron R. White agreed that the case should be heard and decided but, like Lewis Powell, he wanted a narrow ruling.

The rest of the Court, however, lined up against Nixon's position. William O. Douglas pressed Burger in conference to avoid an expansive reading of Presidential powers. William Brennan, after realizing that all the justices agreed that Nixon should furnish the tapes, despite their differing views on the merits of the case, pushed for a unanimous decision that would underscore the Court's determination to sustain the rule of law. Thurgood Marshall favored writing a broad opinion that would limit the concept of executive privilege.

The final decision was unanimous, 8–0, and required that Nixon turn over the tapes. The entire Court agreed that it could hear the case because Attorney General Bork had contact not only with the President but with Congress. Writing for the Court, Chief Justice Burger rejected the idea that the President alone could establish the scope of his powers and affirmed that no one, including the President, was above the law. Burger also noted that Nixon himself had weakened his own case for the tapes' confidentiality by releasing partial contents of the subpoenaed material.

United States v. *Nixon* was a landmark in the history of the nation for three reasons. First, the public hailed the Court's ruling because it broke the political and legal knots into which the nation had been tied. The decision permitted the legal investigation of Watergate affair to move forward and, as a result, clarified the President's vulnerability to the political process of impeachment. By requiring the President to turn over the tapes, Jaworski was able to affirm that a cover-up of criminal behavior had occurred and that Nixon was involved in it. Nixon ended the threat of impeachment by resigning and he escaped any future legal liability when his successor, President Gerald Ford, pardoned him of any criminal wrongdoing. More than twenty of his most trusted advisers, however, including Attorney General John Mitchell, received prison sentences.

Second, the justices reaffirmed the twin concepts of judicial review and judicial sovereignty. To do so, the Court restated the principle finding of

Marbury v. *Madison* (1803): that it is the exclusive duty of the Court to review the law, "to say what the law is," and that it is sovereign, has the last word, when it interprets the Constitution.

Third, the decision was a milestone in the history of the separation of powers. That doctrine requires each of the three branches of government to refrain from infringing or disregarding the constitutionally based prerogatives of the other branches. President Nixon claimed that the President should be able to determine conclusively what information was protected by executive privilege when he communicated with his advisers. The Supreme Court rejected that sweeping claim; instead, it reaffirmed that it is the duty of the judiciary to determine whether the purposes and scope of executive privilege are constitutional. The Supreme Court concluded that final interpretation of the Constitution can no more be shared with the executive branch than the chief executive, for example, can share with the judiciary the veto power, or the Congress can share with the judiciary the power to override a Presidential veto. "Any other conclusion," the Court wrote, "would be contrary to the basic concept of separation of powers and the checks and balances that flow from the scheme of a tripartite government."

But Burger stopped far short of pulling all the teeth of Presidential powers. The chief justice quoted twice from John Marshall's opinion in *United States* v. *Burr* (1807) to make the point that the courts cannot treat the President as merely another citizen. The principle of separation of powers made the Court responsible for determining the law regarding executive privilege, just as the Court had previously defined the limits of congressional immunity. On the critical question of executive privilege, the justices held that executive powers were not absolute, but instead the legitimate demands of a criminal investigation could supersede Presidential privilege. Burger made clear that the framers of the Constitution knew that confidentiality was necessary for the operation of government, but they balanced that requirement against the framers' equally strong insistence that full evidence be available in criminal and other judicial proceedings. Due process, as prescribed by the Fifth Amendment, Burger argued, required that all relevant and admissible evidence be produced.

Still, he wrote, the President was entitled to great deference, especially in matters involving defense and national security. All presumptions about the scope of executive privilege were to be interpreted in favor of the President. However, in this instance, Jaworski had particularized and precisely stated a need for the tapes, both with respect to the credibility of witnesses and for establishing the alleged crime. Burger's carefully crafted opinion limited the sweep of executive privilege and immunity from prosecution while leaving the President with considerable powers.

The Court's decision posed a harsh choice for President Nixon: he could either repudiate the federal courts by refusing to surrender the tapes or give them up and face certain impeachment by the House of Representatives. After Nixon's counsel reviewed the tape made on June 23, 1972, there was no doubt of his complicity to cover up the affair. The President was recorded ordering his staff to use the CIA to abort the FBI's probe, clear evidence of the crime of obstruction of justice. On another tape made on March 21, 1973, Nixon said to his legal counsel, John Dean: "We could get that. On the money, if you need the money you could get that. You could get a million dollars. You could get it in cash. I know where it could be gotten. It is not easy, but it could be done. But the question is, Who would handle it? Any ideas on that?'"

In the meantime, the House Committee on the Judiciary was preparing to impeach the President. It voted three articles of impeachment against Nixon on the theory that he had abused his constitutional power. Whether the committee had adopted a proper constitutional view of the impeachment power was a matter of sharp debate, because there was disagreement about the meaning of "high crimes and misdemeanors," the grounds for impeaching the President in Article II, Section 4. But it was clear in the wake of *Nixon* that the President was vulnerable to impeachment by the full House and conviction by the Senate on the basis of his criminal wrongdoing. Faced with the reality that his "silent majority" was deserting him, the President resigned.

The decision in *Nixon* and the Watergate scandal were inseparably linked. Journalists, for example, placed the chief executive and all politicians under intense scrutiny. Woodward and Bernstein became the role models for a new generation of investigative journalists, each determined to get the goods on public figures.

The *Nixon* decision and the Watergate scandal also temporarily eroded the "imperial Presidency," the idea that the President is a power unto himself. This vision of Presidential authority began to develop when Franklin D. Roosevelt entered the White House and boldly asserted his prerogatives, first to end the Great Depression and later to support England against Germany in the early days of World War II. Yet strong Presidents have dotted American history. George Washington, Abraham Lincoln, and Woodrow Wilson each asserted extraordinary Presidential powers to deal with the crises of their own times. The modern imperial Presidency was notable, however, because the escalating threat of a nuclear exchange with the Soviet Union during Cold War placed a premium on strong executive leadership that in turn depended on secrecy.

The increased accountability of the Presidency, following Watergate and *Nixon,* was a new fact of political life. The press, for example, winked at the personal indiscretions of President John Kennedy while in the White House. Bill Clinton, however, came of political age in a new media era. That point was driven home by the case of *Clinton* v. *Jones* (1997). The justices permitted Paula Corbin Jones, an employee of the state of Arkansas while Bill Clinton was governor, to pursue a civil law suit against the President while he was still in office. Clinton was subsequently impeached in the House of Representatives but not convicted in the Senate for giving false grand jury testi-

Rosemary Woods, President Nixon's secretary, demonstrates to reporters how she might have erased a critical eighteen and one-half minutes of tape before it could be turned over to congressional investigators seeking to impeach the President for his role in Watergate. Some scholars have portrayed the erasure as an intentional act by a Nixon loyalist done in order to protect the President, an assertion that Woods rejected.

mony about his relationship with White House intern Monica Lewinsky while he was President. He apologized to the nation, agreed to pay a $25,000 court fine, settled his sexual harassment lawsuit with Paula Jones for $850,000, and was temporarily disbarred from practicing law in Arkansas and before the U.S. Supreme Court.

Still, the perception that Presidential authority had been eroded by the *Nixon* case was relative and short-lived. Chief Justice Burger's opinion, by acknowledging that a high degree of discretion was due the President, laid the constitutional ground for this reemergence. Presidents Ronald Reagan and George H. W. Bush reasserted the prerogatives of the chief executive to interact confidentially with his advisers in order to conduct the nation's foreign policy.

President Richard M. Nixon holds a news conference in April 1974 to announce that he will release edited transcripts of the White House tapes he had secretly made. Nixon tried to substitute the transcripts for the actual tapes, citing national security concerns, but the bad language and ethnic and racial slurs sprinkled throughout the transcripts only damaged his case further.

America clearly required strong Presidential leadership in a hostile world, a point made forcefully as a result of the attacks on the United States of September 11, 2001. In response to the terrorist threat, President George W. Bush made claims in favor of Presidential power that were as broad or broader than those made by Nixon, including the right to withhold from the public, on national security grounds, communications with his advisers. President Bush ordered suspected terrorists to be held without charges and without any limit on their incarceration. He ordered the creation of military tribunals to try alleged terrorists that did not adhere to traditional American judicial practices and established a program of electronic eavesdropping that mirrored similar Cold War programs. He did so under what he considered the inherent authority of the President to conduct war and provide for the nation's defense and the authorization by Congress for him to use military force to prosecute the war on terror. In *Hamdan* v. *Rumsfeld* (2006), however, the Supreme Court found the President had exceeded his authority to create the military tribunals without explicit authorization by Congress. As was true in *Nixon*, the high court declared that the "executive is bound to comply with the rule of law."

Although the actions of President Bush have served to remind the nation that the Court's decision in *Nixon* was limited, President Nixon's experience before the Supreme Court made it clear that the most powerful office and the most powerful person on Earth are not above the law. As has no other decision in the history of the Court, *United States* v. *Nixon* taught that basic constitutional lesson to an entire nation.

Articles of Impeachment

The House Committee on the Judiciary considered five articles of impeachment against President Richard M. Nixon. The committee ultimately agreed on three, all of which turned on Nixon's abuse of his Presidential power. It rejected two articles: one on his secret bombing of Cambodia and another on the corruption in the President's personal and Republican Party finances. Nixon was vulnerable to impeachment by the full House and conviction before a trial in the Senate based on his criminal wrongdoing. Faced with that reality, he resigned on August 8, 1974.

I. RESOLVED, That Richard M. Nixon, President of the United States, is impeached for high crimes and misdemeanors, and that the following articles of impeachment to be exhibited to the Senate:

ARTICLES OF IMPEACHMENT EXHIBITED BY THE HOUSE OF REPRESENTATIVES OF THE UNITED STATES OF AMERICA IN THE NAME OF ITSELF AND OF ALL OF THE PEOPLE OF THE UNITED STATES OF AMERICA, AGAINST RICHARD M. NIXON, PRESIDENT OF THE UNITED STATES OF AMERICA, IN MAINTENANCE AND SUPPORT OF ITS IMPEACHMENT AGAINST HIM FOR HIGH CRIMES AND MISDEMEANORS.

Article 1: Obstruction of Justice. In his conduct of the office of the President of the United States, Richard M. Nixon, in violation of his constitutional oath faithfully to execute the office of President of the United States and, to the best of his ability, preserve, protect, and defend the Constitution of the United States, and in violation of his constitutional duty to take care that the laws be faithfully executed, has prevented, obstructed, and impeded the administration of justice, in that: On June 17, 1972, and prior thereto, agents of the Committee for the Re-Election of the President committed unlawful entry of the headquarters of the Democratic National Committee in Washington, District of Columbia, for the purpose of securing political intelligence. Subsequent thereto, Richard M. Nixon, using the powers of his high office, engaged personally and through his subordi-

nates and agents in a course of conduct or plan designed to delay, impede and obstruct investigations of such unlawful entry; to cover up, conceal and protect those responsible and to conceal the existence and scope of other unlawful covert activities. The means used to implement this course of conduct or plan have included one or more of the following:

(1) Making or causing to be made false or misleading statements to lawfully authorized investigative officers and employees of the United States.

(2) Withholding relevant and material evidence or information from lawfully authorized investigative officers and employees of the United States.

(3) Approving, condoning, acquiescing in, and counseling witnesses with respect to the giving of false or misleading statements to lawfully authorized investigative officers and employees of the United States and false or misleading testimony in duly instituted judicial and congressional proceedings.

(4) Interfering or endeavoring to interfere with the conduct of investigations by the Department of Justice of the United States, the Federal Bureau of Investigation, the office of Watergate Special Prosecution Force and congressional committees.

(5) Approving, condoning, and acquiescing in, the surreptitious payments of substantial sums of money for the purpose of obtaining the silence or influencing the testimony of witnesses, potential witnesses or individuals who participated in such unlawful entry and other illegal activities.

(6) Endeavoring to misuse the Central Intelli-

gence Agency, an agency of the United States.

(7) Disseminating information received from officers of the Department of Justice of the United States to subjects of investigations conducted by lawfully authorized investigative officers and employees of the United States for the purpose of aiding and assisting such subjects in their attempts to avoid criminal liability.

(8) Making false or misleading public statements for the purpose of deceiving the people of the United States into believing that a thorough and complete investigation has been conducted with respect to allegation of misconduct on the part of personnel of the Executive Branch of the United States and personnel of the Committee for the Re-Election of the President, and that there was no involvement of such personnel in such misconduct; or

(9) Endeavoring to cause prospective defendants, and individuals duly tried and convicted, to expect favored treatment and consideration in return for their silence or false testimony, or rewarding individuals for their silence or false testimony.

In all of this, Richard M. Nixon has acted in a manner contrary to his trust as President and subversive of constitutional government, to the great prejudice of the cause of law and justice and to the manifest injury of the people of the United States.

Wherefore Richard M. Nixon, by such conduct, warrants impeachment and trial, and removal from office.

[Approved by a vote of 27-11 by the House Judiciary Committee on Saturday, July 27, 1974.]

Article 2: Abuse of Power.

Using the powers of the office of President of the United States, Richard M. Nixon, in violation of his constitutional oath faithfully to execute the office of President of the United States and, to the best of his ability, preserve, protect, and defend the Constitution of the United States, and in disregard of his constitutional duty to take care that the laws be faithfully executed, has repeatedly engaged in conduct violating the constitutional rights of citizens, imparting the due and proper administration of justice and the conduct of lawful inquiries, or contravening the laws gov-

erning agencies of the executive branch and the purposes of these agencies. This conduct has included one or more of the following:

(1) He has, acting personally and through his subordinates and agents, endeavored to obtain from the Internal Revenue Service, in violation of the constitutional rights of citizens, confidential information contained in income tax returns for purposes not authorized by law, and to cause, in violation of the constitutional rights of citizens, income tax audits or other income tax investigation to be initiated or conducted in a discriminatory manner.

(2) He misused the Federal Bureau of Investigation, the Secret Service, and other executive personnel, in violation or disregard of the constitutional rights of citizens, by directing or authorizing such agencies or personnel to conduct or continue electronic surveillance or other investigations for purposes unrelated to national security, the enforcement of laws, or any other lawful function of his office; he did direct, authorize, or permit the use of information obtained thereby for purposes unrelated to national security, the enforcement of laws, or any other lawful function of his office; and he did direct the concealment of certain records made by the Federal Bureau of Investigation of electronic surveillance.

(3) He has, acting personally and through his subordinates and agents, in violation or disregard of the constitutional rights of citizens, authorized and permitted to be maintained a secret investigative unit within the office of the President, financed in part with money derived from campaign contributions to him, which unlawfully utilized the resources of the Central Intelligence Agency, engaged in covert and unlawful activities, and attempted to prejudice the constitutional right of an accused to a fair trial.

(4) He has failed to take care that the laws were faithfully executed by failing to act when he knew or had reason to know that his close subordinates endeavored to impede and frustrate lawful inquiries by duly constituted executive; judicial and legislative entities concerning the unlawful entry into the headquarters of the Democratic National Committee, and the cover-up thereof, and concerning other unlawful

activities including those relating to the confirmation of Richard Kleindienst as attorney general of the United States, the electronic surveillance of private citizens, the break-in into the office of Dr. Lewis Fielding, and the campaign financing practices of the Committee to Re-elect the President.

(5) In disregard of the rule of law: he knowingly misused the executive power by interfering with agencies of the executive branch: including the Federal Bureau of Investigation, the Criminal Division and the Office of Watergate Special Prosecution Force of the Department of Justice, in violation of his duty to take care that the laws by faithfully executed.

In all of this, Richard M. Nixon has acted in a manner contrary to his trust as President and subversive of constitutional government, to the great prejudice of the cause of law and justice and to the manifest injury of the people of the United States.

Wherefore Richard M. Nixon, by such conduct, warrants impeachment and trial, and removal from office.

[Approved 28-10 by the House Judiciary Committee on Monday, July 29, 1974.]

Article 3: Contempt of Congress.

In his conduct of the office of President of the United States, Richard M. Nixon, contrary to his oath faithfully to execute the office of the President of the United States, and to the best of his ability preserve, protect and defend the Constitution of the United States, and in violation of his constitutional duty to take care that the laws be faithfully executed, had failed without lawful cause or excuse, to produce papers and things as directed by duly authorized subpoenas issued by the Committee on the Judiciary of the House of Representatives, on April 11, 1974, May 15, 1974, May 30, 1974, and June 24, 1974, and willfully disobeyed such subpoenas. The subpoenaed papers and things were deemed necessary by the Committee in order to resolve by direct evidence fundamental, factual questions relating to Presidential direction, knowledge or approval of actions demonstrated by other evidence to be substantial grounds for impeachment of the President. In refusing to produce these papers and things, Richard M. Nixon, substituting his judgement as to what materials were necessary for the inquiry, interposed the powers of the Presidency against the lawful subpoenas of the House of Representatives, thereby assuming to himself functions and judgments necessary to the exercise of the sole power of impeachment vested by Constitution in the House of Representatives.

In all this, Richard M. Nixon has acted in a manner contrary to his trust as President and subversive of constitutional government, to the great prejudice of the cause of law and justice, and to the manifest injury of the people of the United States.

Wherefore, Richard M. Nixon, by such conduct, warrants impeachment and trial and removal from office.

[Approved 21-17 by the House Judiciary Committee on Tuesday, July 30, 1974.]

22

Affirmative Action and the Boundaries of Discrimination

Regents of the University of California v. Bakke (1978)

T he Supreme Court's decision in *Brown* v. *Board of Education* (1954, 1955) ended the practice of "separate but equal" treatment for blacks and whites in the United States and heralded a new age in constitutional law, but a decade passed before Congress addressed the question of how to broaden legal protections against discrimination. As President John F. Kennedy noted before his death in 1963, "Simple justice requires that public funds, to which all taxpayers of all races [colors, and national origins] contribute, not be spent in any fashion which encourages, entrenches, subsidizes or results in racial discrimination." The Civil Rights Act of 1964 turned Kennedy's words into a legal legacy.

President Lyndon B. Johnson, a Texan elevated to the nation's highest office following the assassination of Kennedy, made passage of the Civil Rights Act a priority for his administration. Johnson cajoled and arm wrestled previously hostile southern Democrats to join with their liberal northern counterparts to enact the legislation, the most significant in the nation's history. Its most important provision, Title VI, ended legally sanctioned discrimination and specifically prohibited preferences based on race, ethnicity, or national origin in programs supported by federal funds. Another provision prohibited discrimination based on sex.

Simply stating that discrimination would no longer be tolerated did not translate into bringing new opportunity to those people who had suffered prejudicial treatment. The question became how to overcome the tension between an individual's claim to equal treatment by a state, and that state's responsibility to foster equality among its citizens. In June 1965, President Johnson spoke to the graduating class of Howard University about the need to bring the ideal of equal opportunity into balance with equality of results. For Johnson the answer was with what he termed "affirmative action" programs. Johnson noted that "You do not take a person who, for years, has been hobbled by chains and liberate him, bring him up to the starting line of a race and then say, 'you are free to compete with others' and still justly believe that you have been completely fair." Johnson went on to explain that "[i]t is not enough to open the gates of opportunity. All our citizens must have the ability to walk through those gates."

> ## Regents of the University of California v. Bakke
>
> - 438 U.S. 265 (1978)
> - Decided: June 28, 1978
> - Vote: 5–4
> - Opinion of the Court: There were multiple opinions filed by several justices, of which the most important was that of Lewis F. Powell, whose views represented the majority with regard to the description of the facts in the case and the remedy.

Allan Bakke sat for this admissions photograph at the University of California, Davis, after he successfully sued the Regents of the University for denying him entry to medical school under an affirmative action plan. The thirty-two-year-old aerospace engineer was denied admission to more than twenty medical schools because of his age. In one admissions essay he wrote, "More than anything else in the world, I want to study medicine."

Affirmative action policies awarded public contracts, jobs, admission to higher education, and other social benefits on the basis of membership in designated groups, or protected classes as the law calls them, who were victims of past discrimination. Affirmative action is premised on the idea of group rather than individual rights, and emphasizes equality of results rather than equality of opportunity. The racial and gender preferences inherent in affirmative action have been repeatedly challenged by individuals, often white males, who are not members of a protected class. They claim what is called reverse discrimination. The "reverse" in reverse discrimination means discrimination directed against white people. The problem, critics of the policy argue, is that discrimination is discrimination, no matter who it is directed against, white or black.

These critics insist that the government should never chose sides based on race and ethnicity. Affirmative action is a retreat from the goal of a color-blind society in which each individual is judged on his or her merit. People opposed to affirmative action assert that any preferences based on race or gender violate the equal protection clause of the Fourteenth Amendment, which orders that "No State shall...deny to any person within its jurisdiction the equal protection of the laws." They also argue that affirmative action flies in the face of the words of Title VI itself, which provides that "[n]o person in the United States shall, on the ground of race, color, or national origin, be excluded from participation in, be denied the benefits of, or be subjected to discrimination under any program or activity receiving Federal financial assistance."

Clearly, values were in conflict. Title VI of the Civil Rights Act of 1964 encouraged greater opportunity for people of all races; it also sought to remedy past racial bias by spending federal funds in ways that would benefit particular racial or other minority groups. A private institution, such as a university or college, was not required to practice affirmative action as long as it did not accept federal funds. If it did, however, then it was required to adopt and follow an affirmative action plan. The Supreme Court has addressed affirmative action in such diverse matters as voting rights, housing sales and rentals, employment, contracts for public works projects, and university admissions and financial aid. It has considered not only the use of race but also sex as a basis on which to distribute certain benefits. At the center of the Court's deliberations has been the hotly contested issue of whether an affirmative action program can specify a quota for any group, such as a racial minority or women, to receive a particular benefit. A sharply divided Court has generally accepted affirmative action programs and the limited use of quotas, although it struggled to do so.

Nowhere is the clash of competing values more apparent than in admissions to college. A college degree has become economically valuable; a college graduate will earn on average one million dollars more than the average high school graduate in his or her lifetime. Historically people from certain minority groups have been denied admission to higher education. Beginning in the 1970s, many universities adopted programs that were intended to make it easier for minorities to gain admission. That goal came into sharp conflict with the aspirations of white, majority candidates who, according to the traditional tests for admission, were often as well qualified or better qualified than the minority candidates.

The medical school of the University of California at Davis, which accepted federal funding, adopted an affirmative action program in 1970. The faculty decided to address the longstanding absence of Latino, African American, and Native American students through a special admissions policy. Of its one hundred annual slots for admission, the school designated sixteen—a quota—to be filled through a special admission process. Individuals claiming special admissions had to come from one of these historically underrepresented groups, and they could present much lower grade point averages and test scores than those candidates admitted through the regular process. Admission to the medical school was a highly competitive process; about 2,600 candidates applied annually for the one hundred places.

Allan Bakke, a white male aerospace engineer in his mid-thirties, applied in 1973 and 1974. He was rejected for admission twice even though his grades and admission scores were significantly better than those of the sixteen people who filled the minority slots. Bakke filed suit in state court claiming "reverse discrimination." Bakke's legal counsel insisted that the Davis program violated Title VI because it used race as a basis by which to admit some students and not others. Bakke's counsel also argued that the Davis policy violated the equal protection clause of the Fourteenth Amendment, once again noting that the state of California through its university system had discriminated against him because he was white.

The Regents of the University of California agreed that using racial designations as criteria for admissions was inappropriate because they had no relevance to the actual performance of medical students or doctors. But they argued that the Davis program was directed toward "disadvantaged citizens" and minorities. In theory, they argued, a white person could be admitted through the special program. The university defended its special program, noting that simply because some of the minority applicants had lower scores than the general pool of candidates it did not mean that they were unqualified. The university also stressed that although historically it had not discriminated, it had an obligation to address the effects of past and continuing societal discrimination. Bringing about such justice was a legitimate and compelling concern of the state. The policy would also, they argued, have other benefits. It would create a richer and more diverse environment for all medical students, improve medical services to minority communities, and provide role models for the next generation of minority youths The university lost in both the state trial court and on appeal to the California Supreme Court. It then turned to the U.S. Supreme Court for relief.

Bakke's case sparked extensive national attention. The Supreme Court received fifty-seven amici curiae (friends of the court) briefs, an extraordinarily large number, from both supporters and opponents of Bakke. These briefs vividly demonstrated how divisive the affirmative action debate had become. Hundreds of people lined up at dawn outside the Supreme Court in order to hear the oral arguments, and demonstrators marched in front of the building.

Several minority organizations tried to stop the university from appealing the case. They believed that it was a poor vehicle with which to test the constitutionality of affirmative action, in large measure because the policy of the UC

In 1978, activists protest the Court's decision in Bakke. One sign equates the outcome in Bakke *with apartheid, the system of racial segregation in South Africa.*

Davis Medical School itself was suspect. Though directed at "disadvantaged citizens," the special admissions program, they noted, had admitted only nonwhite applicants. Groups representing Asian Americans had another concern. They complained that the affirmative action policy at Davis worked against them, as they had among the highest grade point averages and test scores, yet were not admitted in numbers commensurate with their academic success.

Reynold Colvin argued Bakke's case before the Court. He was the senior member of a small general practice law firm in San Francisco, and most observers concluded that Colvin was in over his head. Colvin's oral argument did little to assuage their concerns. Several of Bakke's supporters had urged Colvin to allow University of Chicago law professor Phillip B. Kurland, an experienced high court litigator and distinguished constitutional scholar, to do some or all of the argument. Colvin refused, and simply pounded home one message: "to the extent that the preference is on the basis of race, we believe that is an unconstitutional advantage." The sixteen slots set aside for "disadvantaged citizens" amounted to nothing more than a racial quota, an act of reverse discrimination that should be held unconstitutional under the equal protection clause of the Fourteenth Amendment. Colvin insisted that any quota was illegal under Title VI of the Civil Rights Act.

The Regents of the University of California retained Archibald Cox, a Harvard law professor and one of the most distinguished figures in American law. Cox was a former solicitor general who had argued more than sixty cases before the Supreme Court.

Cox sketched his case in epic terms. He observed,

> The answer which the Court gives [in this case] will determine, perhaps for decades, whether members of these minorities are to have the kind of meaningful access to higher education in the professions, which the universities have accorded them in recent years, or are to be reduced to the trivial numbers which they were prior to the adoption of minority admission programs.

The special admissions program, he noted, had the welcome benefit of bringing greater numbers of minorities into medical education. More diversity in the classroom would promote more diversity in the profession, which would in turn mean the better delivery of health services.

Cox also argued that the sixteen slots reserved for "disadvantaged citizens" did not create a quota, an assertion that encountered immediate, skeptical questioning from the justices. Cox replied that any program that did not take race into account would not work and the state had, in any case, a compelling interest in addressing in society the wrongs of past discrimination, even if the UC Davis Medical School had not itself engaged in racial discrimination.

The Court that Cox addressed had become consistently more conservative on a host of issues, including race, but it was also seriously fractured internally. The court voted 5 to 4 to admit Bakke to the UC Davis Medical School. It held further that a university may consider racial criteria as part of the admissions process but that it cannot do so through fixed quotas and in such a way that made race the determining factor in the process.

The justices reached this conclusion through six separate opinions. Draft opinions circulated among the justices for eight months, but none of these was capable of commanding a majority. Finally, on June 28, 1978, at the end of the term, the Court rendered its decision. In announcing that decision, Justice Lewis F. Powell Jr. said, "we speak today with a notable lack of unanimity."

The *Bakke* decision is best understood as two decisions. One part of the Court preferred to consider only the statutory, not the constitutional, basis of the issues; that is, they addressed only the question of whether Title VI prohibited the kind of policy adopted at Davis. Four of the justices (John Paul Stevens, Warren Burger, Potter Stewart, and William H. Rehnquist) agreed that, in the words of Justice Stevens, the "plain meaning" of Title VI and its "broad prohibition against the exclusion of any individual" from a federally funded program based on race was enough to order Bakke admitted. A second bloc of the Court, also composed of four justices (William J. Brennan Jr., Thurgood Marshall, Byron White, and Harry Blackmun) believed that the issue should be addressed as a constitutional matter. It was possible to use race as a basis for helping groups that had suffered discrimination as long as there was an important public purpose in doing so. Race could be used, these four insisted, as long as it did not put the weight of the government behind policies that either stigmatized an individual or fostered hatred and separation.

Powell cast the deciding vote, and he sided with different justices in doing so. Powell's opinion stated, "On the first question—whether the special admission program is invalid... there are five votes to affirm the judgment invalidating the special program. Under this judgment, Bakke will be admitted to the medical school." Powell wrote, "When classification denies an individual opportunities or benefits enjoyed by others solely because of his race or ethnic background, it must be regarded as suspect. There are serious problems of justice," he continued, "connected with the idea of preference." "[C]ourts may be asked, to validate the burdens imposed upon individual members of a particular group in order to advance the group's general interest. Nothing in the Constitution supports the notion that individuals may be asked to suffer otherwise impermissible burdens in order to enhance the societal standing of their ethnic groups."

In answering the second issue, whether race may be considered as a factor in an admissions program, Powell said that some programs can legally take race into account. This approach meant, given previous Court decisions on issues such as contracts set aside for minority business people, that race could be used as a basis upon which to rest state policy, but such policies would be subject to the most intense review. Powell concluded by drawing on Justice Brennan's separate opinion, which argued for less scrutiny to be applied to the affirmative action programs: "Government may take race into account when it acts not to demean or insult any racial group, but to remedy disadvantages cast on minorities by past racial prejudice."

Powell concluded that the state's goal of educational diversity was the only constitutionally permissible justification. Universities had the power to exercise affirmative action based on the academic freedom granted them under the First Amendment.

> An otherwise qualified medical student," he wrote, "with a particular background—whether it be ethnic, geographic, culturally advantaged or disadvantaged—may bring to a professional school of medicine experiences, outlooks, and ideas that enrich the training of its student body and better equip its graduates to render with understanding their vital service to humanity.

Powell, perhaps with an eye to Archibald Cox's arguments, cited the Harvard admissions program as an example in which "race is considered in a flexible program designed to achieve diversity, but it is only one factor—weighed competitively—against a number of factors deemed relevant."

In separate opinions, Justices Marshall and Blackmun expressed their support for affirmative action and their displeasure at the narrow holding. "After several hundred years of class-based discrimination against Negroes," Marshall observed, "the Court is unwilling to hold that a class-based remedy for that discrimination is permissible." Blackmun wrote of his desire that affirmative action would be only a temporary fix and would become unnecessary within a decade. However, he conceded that "in order to get beyond racism, we must first take account of race. There is no other way. And in order to treat some persons equally, we must treat them differently."

Judicial division fueled public confusion. The *New York Times* summarized the decision in a headline that read: "No One Lost." Perhaps no one won either. Attorney General Griffin Bell hailed the decision as "a great victory for affirmative action"; the civil rights leader Jesse Jackson declared it "a devastating blow to our civil-rights struggle." The divisions in the courts reflected divisions in society. Two of the nation's largest states, California and Florida, passed ballot initiatives to prohibit the use of race as a consideration in college admissions. The issue was far from settled.

In 2003, the Court returned to the issue of affirmative action in college admissions when it decided, by votes of 5 to 4, two cases involving the University of Michigan, *Grutter* v. *Bollinger* and *Gratz* v. *Bollinger*. As in the *Bakke* case, friends of the court piled on a record number of briefs. More than

one hundred amicus briefs were filed in the two cases in support of the University of Michigan and its president, Lee Bollinger, who had vigorously pushed affirmative action. Corporate and military leaders filed briefs arguing that the increasingly diverse racial make-up of the nation and the globalization of business and national defense required universities to educate leaders of the next generation drawn from all segments of society. Diversity, in their view, was essential to America's national security and economic competitiveness. Another fifteen amicus briefs were filed in support of the plaintiffs, Jennifer Gratz and Barbara Grutter.

Grutter involved the admissions policy of the University of Michigan Law School; *Gratz* considered the admissions policy for the university's undergraduate program. The goal of the university's admissions policy in both instances was to achieve greater racial diversity, but these two different schools attempted to accomplish this in different ways. The law school's policy required that admissions officers evaluate each applicant individually based on his or her undergraduate grade point average, law school admissions test scores, a personal statement, letters of recommendation, and an essay describing the way in which the applicant would contribute to the life and diversity of the law school. The program aimed to "achieve that diversity which has the potential to enrich everyone's education and thus make a law school class stronger than the sum of its parts." To achieve this goal, admissions officers were directed to give special attention to students from groups historically discriminated against, such as African Americans, Hispanics, and Native Americans. Without such attention, the program assumed, students in these groups would never be admitted in meaningful numbers. What was that critical number? The answer was a "critical mass" sufficient to "ensure their ability to make unique contributions to the character of the Law School."

The undergraduate policy operated differently. Applicants were evaluated using a point system, in which one hundred points were needed to gain admission. Every applicant from a minority group was automatically given twenty points, more points than were assigned to any other attribute, such as high school class standing.

In *Grutter*, the Court approved the law school's "narrowly tailored" approach and reiterated the *Bakke* finding that fostering diversity in higher education was a compelling state interest. As Justice Sandra Day O'Connor explained in her opinion for the Court, "The Law School engages in a highly individualized, holistic review of each applicant's file, giving serious consideration to all the ways an applicant might contribute to a diverse educational environment." Justice O'Connor, however, also believed that such a policy could and should not continue indefinitely. "We expect that twenty-five years from now, the use of racial preferences will no longer be necessary to further the interest approved today."

In *Gratz*, the Court reached the opposite conclusion. With Justice O'Connor now on the other side of the issue, the Court held that the undergraduate admissions policy was not narrowly tailored to meet the goal of promoting diversity and failed to provide for a "meaningful individualized review of applicants." The automatic assignment of twenty points to each minority applicant meant that race became the decisive factor rather than one of many factors used to settle on who was admitted.

Four members of the Court, Chief Justice William Rehnquist and Justices Antonin Scalia, Clarence Thomas, and Anthony Kennedy, would have voted to hold both policies unconstitutional. The chief justice described the law school's policy as a "sham" to cover a scheme of racially proportionate admissions. Both Scalia and Thomas insisted that the equal protection clause prohibited any consideration of race in admissions. Quoting the antislavery orator Frederick Douglass, Thomas, himself African American, denounced negative stereotyping as the inevitable outcome of using race to decide who is admitted to prestigious colleges.

The debate over affirmative action remains unsettled. In *Bakke* the high court recognized that a definitive ruling on the matter would create a powerful political backlash from one end of the political spectrum or the other. Though the decision has come under fire in recent years for failing to come to grips with the issue, this case serves as an important reminder that, often, precise resolutions of constitutional matters by the high court do not necessarily best serve the public interest. The *Grutter* and *Gratz* decisions affirmed by a narrow margin that diversity should be upheld as a matter of diversity but race should not be the deciding factor in awarding social benefits.

The unprecedented support that corporate America and the military gave to the University of Michigan and its admissions policies provided a reminder that diversity was not just a social justice issue but a necessity for a strong national economy and defense. And, yet, while affirmative action stands on firmer legal ground, the Court's work in *Bakke* and the Michigan cases also leaves mixed messages and considerable uncertainty about whether the Constitution values more highly equality of opportunity or equality of results. Critics of affirmative action also continue to complain that the real differences in American life result from the unequal distribution of income and wealth, matters not covered by diversity policies. Most likely, the constitutional debate over affirmative action and the troubling conditions that it attempts to address will linger well beyond Justice O'Connor's quarter-century deadline.

"Equal Opportunity Is Essential but Not Enough"

Dissenting in Plessy *v.* Ferguson *(1896) Justice John Marshall Harlan declared, "Our Constitution is color-blind and neither knows nor tolerates classes among citizens." Yet by the 1960s some observers had concluded that it was insufficient to remove prior legal barriers for racial minorities. They insisted that affirmative steps were required to rectify past racial discrimination and to ensure greater economic opportunities for minorities. President Lyndon B. Johnson articulated this view in a 1965 commencement address at historically black Howard University. The speech's title was "To Fulfill These Rights." Johnson was the first President to suggest that the government had a duty to provide for equality of outcomes, not just of opportunities. First used to assist disadvantaged racial minorities, affirmative action programs were subsequently extended to women.*

Freedom is not enough. You do not wipe away the scars of centuries by saying: Now you are free to go where you want, and do as you desire, and choose the leaders you please.

You do not take a person who, for years, has been hobbled by chains and liberate him, bring him up to the starting line of a race and then say, "you are free to compete with all the others," and still justly believe that you have been completely fair.

Thus it is not enough just to open the gates of opportunity. All our citizens must have the ability to walk through those gates.

This is the next and the more profound stage of the battle for civil rights. We seek not just freedom but opportunity. We seek not just legal equity but human ability, not just equality as a right and a theory but equality as a fact and equality as a result.

For the task is to give 20 million Negroes the same chance as every other American to learn and grow, to work and share in society, to develop their abilities—physical, mental and spiritual, and to pursue their individual happiness.

To this end equal opportunity is essential, but not enough, not enough. Men and women of all races are born with the same range of abilities. But ability is not just the product of birth. Ability is stretched or stunted by the family that you live with, and the neighborhood you live in—by the school you go to and the poverty or the richness of your surroundings. It is the product of a hundred unseen forces playing upon the little infant, the child, and finally the man.

Racial Preferences Are Always Unconstitutional

In Grutter v. Bollinger *the Court upheld the University of Michigan Law School's use of race, along with other factors, to evaluate applicants in an attempt to foster a diverse educational community. Justice Sandra Day O'Connor, writing for a 5–4 majority, endorsed the diversity rationale first set forth by Justice Powell in* Bakke. *Justice Antonin Scalia, however, issued this biting dissent (with which Justice Clarence Thomas concurred), which summed up the argument against affirmative action.*

The University of Michigan Law School's mystical "critical mass" justification for its discrimination by race challenges even the most gullible mind. The admissions statistics show it to be a sham to cover a scheme of racially proportionate admissions.

I find particularly unanswerable [this] central point: that the allegedly "compelling state interest" at issue here is not the incremental "educational benefit" that emanates from the fabled "critical mass" of minority students, but rather Michigan's interest in maintaining a "prestige" law school whose normal admissions standards disproportionately exclude blacks and other minorities. If that is a compelling state interest, everything is.

The "educational benefit" that the University of Michigan seeks to achieve by racial discrimination consists, according to the Court, of "cross-racial understanding," and "better prepar[ation of] students for an increasingly diverse workforce and society," all of which is necessary not only for work, but also for good "citizenship." This is not, of course, an "educational benefit" on which students will be graded on. . . . For it is a lesson of life rather than law. . . . If properly considered an "educational benefit" at all, it is surely not one that is either uniquely relevant to law school or uniquely "teachable" in a formal educational setting. *And therefore*: If it is appropriate for the University of Michigan Law School to use racial discrimination for the purpose of putting together a "critical mass" that will convey generic lessons in socialization and good citizenship, surely it is no less appropriate—indeed, *particularly* appropriate—for the civil service system of the State of Michigan to do so. There, also, those exposed to "critical masses" of certain races will presumably become better Americans,

better Michiganders, better civil servants. And surely private employers cannot be criticized—indeed, should be praised—if they also "teach" good citizenship to their adult employees through a patriotic, all-American system of racial discrimination in hiring. The nonminority individuals who are deprived of a legal education, a civil service job, or any job at all by reason of their skin color will surely understand.

Unlike a clear constitutional holding that racial preferences in state educational institutions are impermissible, or even a clear anticonstitutional holding that racial preferences in state educational institutions are OK, today's *Grutter-Gratz* split double header seems perversely designed to prolong the controversy and the litigation. . . . [S]uits may challenge the bona fides of the institution's expressed commitment to the educational benefits of diversity that immunize the discriminatory scheme in *Grutter.* (Tempting targets, one would suppose, will be those universities that talk the talk of multiculturalism and racial diversity in the courts but walk the walk of tribalism and racial segregation on their campuses—through minority-only student organizations, separate minority housing opportunities, separate minority student centers, even separate minority-only graduation ceremonies.) And still other suits may claim that the institution's racial preferences have gone below or above the mystical *Grutter*-approved "critical mass." Finally, litigation can be expected on behalf of minority groups intentionally short changed in the institution's composition of its generic minority "critical mass.". . . The Constitution proscribes government discrimination on the basis of race, and state-provided education is no exception.

23

The Judicial Path to the White House

Bush v. *Gore* (2000)

The Presidential election of 2000 was a cliffhanger that was ultimately decided by a few hundred contested ballots in Florida. In order to win, either Vice President Al Gore, a Democrat, or Texas governor George W. Bush, a Republican and the son of former President George H. W. Bush, had to secure at least 270 electoral votes. During the evening of Election Day, November 7, most of the television networks placed Florida in Gore's column. Whoever won in Florida would be President. Later in the evening, however, this early prediction began to crumble; Bush gained a slim lead and the networks reversed their projections. Gore prepared to give a concession speech in Nashville, Tennessee. But under intense pressure from his aides, Gore decided at the last minute not to do so.

The Vice President believed that only a few hundred votes out of more than 6 million cast separated him and Bush. Gore's campaign operatives in Florida reported to the candidate that there were allegations of voting irregularities. For example, reports surfaced that in voting districts with black majorities, which were likely to go to Gore, either the polls had closed before everyone could vote or voters were inappropriately turned away. There were also reports that in some counties, notably Palm Beach County in south Florida, the use of the so-called butterfly ballot had confused voters, many of them elderly, which may have resulted in votes that were intended for Gore going to Reform Party candidate Pat Buchanan. Further, the Gore campaign feared that the voting rolls in Florida had been purged of some 50,000 alleged felons, including some who were again eligible to vote under Florida law.

Allegations of voting irregularities, however, were not all on the Democratic side. Bush forces feared that overseas absentee votes, primarily from military personnel, most of whom were thought to be Bush supporters, were not being counted. They also believed an unfair advantage was given to Gore when all the major news networks incorrectly projected Gore as the winner at 7:52 P.M. eastern standard time, before the polls closed in ten counties in the heavily Republican western panhandle. They claimed that the Bush vote would have been greater had his supporters concluded that their votes would indeed count.

Both sides also became painfully aware that Florida's use of machine readable punch card ballots had a high rate of error. These ballots required a voter to use a stylus to push out a perforated section of the ballot to indicate his or her choice. In some instances the voter did not push hard enough to perforate the

Bush v. Gore

- 531 U.S. 98 (2000)
- Decided: December 12, 2000
- Vote: 5–4
- Opinion of the Court: Per Curiam (by the Court and unsigned)

A protestor in front of the Supreme Court on December 11, 2000, the day the justices heard oral arguments in the case of Bush v. Gore, *carries a sign that speaks to Democrats' frustrations with the period of political turmoil that began with public revelations of President Clinton's affair with White House intern Monica Lewinsky and his subsequent impeachment for lying to a grand jury about his misconduct. Despite such howls of protest, most Americans accepted the Court's decision a day later to award the electoral votes of Florida to George W. Bush, thus making him President.*

card and indicate a vote conclusively (resulting in a "dimpled chad") or a bit of paper remained attached to the ballot (a "hanging chad") that could potentially be read incorrectly by the counting machine.

The Gore campaign believed that it could find enough incorrectly counted ballots to close the gap and decide the election in its favor, and its representatives requested a hand recount of ballots in four counties. What constituted a legally counted ballot became a subject of intense dispute. The Bush forces, on the other hand, wanted the recounts stopped, the election declared legal, and the state's twenty-five electoral votes placed in their column.

Over the next five weeks the nation was treated to an intense political and legal struggle. The predicament was hardly new. On fifteen different occasions the nation had selected plurality Presidents, those who captured less than 50 percent of the popular vote but more than 50 percent of the Electoral College vote. Three candidates who received the greater share of the popular vote—Andrew Jackson in 1824, Samuel J. Tilden in 1876, and Grover Cleveland in 1888—failed to gain a majority in the Electoral College. As it turned out, Gore would be the fourth.

Gore won the national contest by more than 500,000 popular votes, but ultimately lost in the Electoral College by 266 to 271. Gore actually should have received 267 electoral votes, but an elector from the District of Columbia abstained from voting to protest the District's lack of representation in Congress.

What was unique about the election was the closeness of the vote and the remarkable role that the Supreme Court played in deciding it. The election culminated in *Bush* v. *Gore,* the only time in our history that a Supreme Court decision determined the outcome of a Presidential election. Historically, the justices had shunned deciding so-called political questions. These were controversies that the Court regarded as inappropriate for judicial resolution. It has often decided not to decide political cases, preferring instead to allow the executive and legislative branches and the political process to resolve them. In this instance, however, the Court thought it necessary to hear the case in order to resolve the significant constitutional issues at stake.

Florida law seemed to favor Gore. It provided that a candidate could request a hand recount in any county and that, if the election were close enough, as this one was, an automatic recount would be triggered statewide. But the Republicans, led by James Baker, the former secretary of state for President George H. W. Bush, decided to contest these recount efforts. They filed suit in federal court asking for an injunction to block them. The judge refused to grant the injunction and instead directed the Republicans to plead their case before the Florida courts. They found an unreceptive audience. The Florida Supreme Court rebuffed attempts by Florida secretary of state Katherine Harris to order an end to the recounts. Nevertheless, Harris proceeded on her own authority to declare that any recounted ballot would not be accepted after a specified time. Gore's lawyers challenged her order in the state courts, and on November 21, 2000, the Florida Supreme Court again rejected Harris's actions and ordered that the recounts continue through the Thanksgiving weekend. Harris also ignored these findings and declared Bush the winner.

The Bush team again turned to the lower federal courts and ultimately the Supreme Court, which held an expedited review of the case. The Bush team argued that the Florida court had erred in two ways. First, it had violated the equal protection clause of the Fourteenth Amendment by permitting the recounts. Bush claimed that because there was no standard that could be applied statewide to what constituted a legal ballot, some counties would have more liberal standards than others. A vote in one county might be counted while in another, a ballot marked in an identical way would be rejected. Second, the Bush team insisted that the determination of Presidential electors was a political matter that rested with the legislature, not the courts. On November 27, the justices in a unanimous and unsigned opinion in the case of *Bush* v. *Palm Beach County Canvassing Board* remanded the case back to the Florida Supreme Court. The justices specifically asked the Court to clarify whether its ruling rested on the Florida constitution or Florida statutes. The U.S. Supreme Court was concerned that if the Florida judges had acted on the basis of the Florida constitution, which was not written by the Florida legislature, then their finding would be unconstitutional under Article II, Section 1, Clause 2 of the federal Constitution. It provides that "each state shall appoint, in such a manner as the Legislature thereof may direct, a number of electors."

By this time the entire nation had become focused not just on who would be elected President but on who ultimately would decide that question. There was also a sense of immediacy, even urgency, not just to resolve who would be President but to do so within the time frame specified by law. Under a federal law dating from the Reconstruction era, each state is provided a "safe harbor" during which period the state has to select its electors. This safe harbor ends six days prior to the meeting of the Electoral College; in the 2000 election, the safe harbor deadline was December 12.

The safe harbor provision was introduced into federal law following the 1876 Presidential election, perhaps the most bitterly disputed contest in American history. Democrat Samuel Tilden handily beat Rutherford B. Hayes in the popular vote, but twenty electoral votes were in dispute among three states—Florida, Louisiana, and South Carolina. A backroom deal in Congress sealed Tilden's fate and sent Hayes to the White House, despite the wishes of the electors from the three Democratic states. For more than a decade following the election, Congress tried to fashion federal rules that would make a similar occurrence unlikely. They settled on the "safe harbor" provision as one way of protecting the decisions states made about their electors. It provided that if states resolved disputes within six days of the time the electors were to cast their ballots, then Congress could not interfere. The provision invited the states to establish means of settling disputes that would make the states' own resolutions of election controversies conclusive and prevent a debacle like the one following the 1876 election.

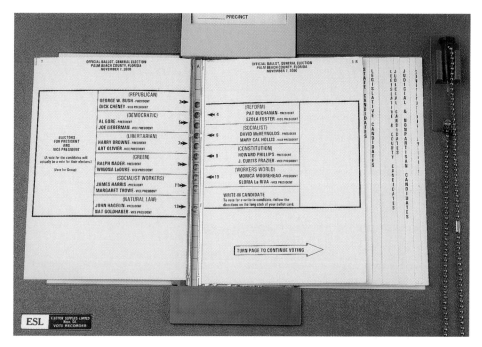

OFFICIAL BALLOT, GENERAL ELECTION
PALM BEACH COUNTY, FLORIDA
NOVEMBER 7, 2000

OFFICIAL BALLOT, GENERAL ELECTION
PALM BEACH COUNTY, FLORIDA
NOVEMBER 7, 2000

This type of "butterfly ballot" was used in Palm Beach County, Florida, during the 2000 Presidential election. These ballots produced an unexpectedly large number of votes for third-party candidate Patrick Buchanan, votes that Democratic candidate Al Gore contended would have gone to him had older voters not been confused by the alignment of the names on the ballot.

When the Florida Supreme Court heard *Bush* v. *Palm Beach County Canvassing Board* a second time, it again sided with Gore. The judges ordered the election authorities in Florida to continue a statewide recount of all ballots. The Bush forces feared that such a recount would undermine the thin margin of victory they commanded and pointed to the fact that Secretary of State Harris had declared their candidate the victor. The case again went to the U.S. Supreme Court, this time titled *Bush* v. *Gore*. By a 5–4 vote, the justices decided to issue a controversial emergency injunction halting the recount.

Justice Antonin Scalia explained that the injunction was appropriate because if the recount continued it would, in his words, "do irreparable harm to [Bush], and to the country, by casting a cloud upon what he claims to be the legitimacy of his election." The dissenters argued, in the words of Justice John Paul Stevens, that "counting every legally cast vote cannot constitute irreparable harm." The decision to issue the injunction did not, however, settle the larger constitutional issues but only set the stage for the final arguments before the justices, which were held two days later.

The arguments before the Supreme Court in *Bush* v. *Gore* received an extraordinary level of public attention. On the day the case was argued, hundreds of demonstrators from both parties shouted and carried placards outside the court building. By and large, public opinion polls suggested that the high court was the appropriate venue through which to settle the matter, underscoring the extent to which the Court had, over the previous two centuries, come to be viewed by the public as the final arbiter of the Constitution and an honest voice amid self-interested politicians.

David Boies, one of the nation's most successful litigators, aided by Laurence Tribe, a Harvard Law School professor, argued the case for Vice President Gore. Theodore B. Olson, a partner in a leading Los Angeles law firm who had served as an assistant attorney general in the Reagan administration, represented Bush. The justices had to resolve two different questions in *Bush* v. *Gore*. The first involved the constitutionality of recounts. If they were not constitutional, the justices had to decide on a remedy for the contested election. And they had to do so swiftly. The safe harbor provision would become operative in Florida the day after the Court was to hear the case.

Against this background, Theodore Olson rested part of his case on the equal protection clause of the Fourteenth Amendment. The problem created by the Florida Supreme Court's order, Olson insisted, was that it failed to provide a statewide standard for recounts. That meant that each county election board could follow whatever standard it chose to determine whether a ballot was legal or not. Two similarly marked ballots in two different counties could be judged in different ways. What was accepted in one county could be rejected in another; dimpled and hanging chads might pass muster in one place but fail in another.

Boies responded that there were already statewide standards in place. In Florida, persons known as canvassers checked the authenticity of ballots. They did so by applying the "intent of the voter" standard, which had been used for years and was compatible with the equal protection clause. Boies reminded the justices that the issues in Florida were not unique. If the justices ruled the Florida recount unconstitutional simply on the unproven view that it treated different voters differently, then they would effectively render every state election unconstitutional. Boies insisted that the states had the right to set their own systems of casting, counting, and recounting votes. One state might use hand-pulled voting machines; another state, like Florida, could choose to rely on the punch-card system.

Olson also argued that the Florida Supreme Court's ruling that the statewide recount should continue violated Article 2, Section 1, Clause 2 of the U.S. Constitution, which requires that each state appoint electors "in such Manner as the Legislature thereof may direct." In simplest terms, the Florida Supreme Court judges could not supersede the role of the legislature and thereby violate Article 2. This portion of Olson's argument was controversial. Under the Supreme Court's own precedents, the rule had held that when a state's highest court interprets state law, that interpretation is final and a federal court, even the Supreme Court, must defer to it. Olson agreed that this was established precedent, but that the circumstances in this case were different. Article 2, Olson insisted, gave the federal judiciary the power to interpret state election law in order to make sure that state courts were actually following the intent of the state legislature. Without such a check, the state courts could improperly intervene, as the Florida Supreme Court was doing, in the results of a federal election. In response, Boies claimed that such a ruling would give new powers to the federal courts and that the power to interpret state election laws should remain, as it been historically, with the states and state judges, who were ideally suited to understand the intent of the legislature.

The justices embraced only part of Olson's arguments, but in the end sided with Bush. Only three justices, Rehnquist, Scalia, and Clarence Thomas—all Republican appointees and all conservatives committed to state rights, accepted Olson's efforts to expand federal supervision of the state courts. On the other hand, seven of the justices, with varying degrees of intensity, embraced some or all of his equal protection argument. Only Justices John Paul Stevens and Ruth Bader Ginsburg refused to go along with it at all.

Having found a violation of equal protection of the laws, the justices had to decide what remedy was appropriate. The calendar complicated the answer. Oral arguments were held on December 11; the safe harbor provision involving Florida became effective the following day; and the electors were required by federal law to meet and cast their ballots on December 18. The irony for the nation was that a recount probably would have been completed had the justices not stayed it on December 9, but it was impossible to complete, especially with the new equal protection requirements, in the two hours that remained when the justices issued their decision at 10:00 PM on December 12.

Moreover, a bewildering set of concurrences and dissents complicated the matter further, so much so that television reporters struggled in front of their cameras to explain to an anxious nation exactly what the justices had done. Nevertheless, the import of the Court's decision soon became clear: a further recount was unworkable and illegal, and Bush had won. The 5–4 majority ordered that the results certified by Secretary of State Harris on November 26 be made official. The justices issued a brief, thirteen-page, per curiam (unsigned) opinion. In an additional fifty-two pages they clashed with one another. What had gone on inside the conference as the justices wrestled with the case splintered the Court.

On the question of the appropriate remedy, Chief Justice Rehnquist wrote for a majority of the justices apart from the unsigned portion of the opinion. He noted that intervention by the Court was an "unsought responsibility." He concluded, along with five other members of the Court, that the methods of counting ballots in Florida violated the equal protection clause of the Fourteenth Amendment because the state had no uniform standard, just as Olson had argued. The majority also noted that it would be impossible to conduct a constitutionally acceptable recount in the time left to do so. Though it was true that Florida had adopted the "intent of the voter" standard, in practice this standard failed to guarantee that each county would treat ballots in the same way. "When a [state] court orders a statewide remedy, there must be at least some assurance that the rudimentary requirements of equal treatment and fundamental fairness are satisfied," Rehnquist observed.

Chief Justice Rehnquist attempted to limit the sweep of the decision and forestall criticism by explaining that "[o]ur consideration is limited to the present circumstances, for the problem of equal protection in election processes generally presents many complexities." The Court apparently agreed on this wording because it recognized that time was so short in reaching a decision and that it would be inappropriate to extend its larger implications to other states or other matters. For the critics of the Court, however, the sentence seemed to suggest that a bare majority of the justices had fabricated a standard to be applied only once that conveniently assured George Bush's victory. If, critics complained, the decision was not sufficient to be a precedent in the future, then it followed that it was not sufficient to decide the case.

Moreover, critics argued the majority had improperly favored Bush when it halted the recount on the grounds that one candidate, George Bush, faced irreparable harm. Moreover, liberals who had viewed judicial power as a way of restoring rights and promoting equality through the Fourteenth Amendment denounced the justices for playing politics that favored the Republican Party, with which the majority of them had been associated.

In its opinion, the Court also reminded the nation that its voting procedures were badly in need of revision. "This case has shown," the Court observed, "that punch card balloting machines can produce an unfortunate number of ballots which are not punched in a clean, complete way by voters."

The justices expected that following *Bush* v. *Gore,* state legislatures would "improve the mechanisms and machinery for voting." While the critics wailed, opinion polls in the wake of the decision revealed broad support for the actions of the Court. Most Americans seemed grateful that the justices had stepped into this particular political thicket.

There was no denying, however, the real differences inside the Court. Ironically, conservative justices, who had clamored for the federal courts to stay out of political matters and defer to the states, resorted to judicial power to override Florida's high court and to resolve one of the most important political questions in American history. The four dissenters (David Souter, Stephen Breyer, Ruth Bader Ginsburg, and John Paul Stevens) charged that the outcome was unfair and that the recount should have been allowed to go forward until December 18, when the electors were to cast their ballots. Perhaps the harshest judgment passed on the decision came from Justice Stevens, an appointee of Gerald Ford who had become increasingly liberal. Stevens concluded:

> What must underlie petitioners' entire federal assault on the Florida election procedures is an unstated lack of confidence in the impartiality and capacity of the state judges who would make the critical decisions if the vote count were to proceed. Otherwise, their position is wholly without merit. The endorsement of that position by the majority of this Court can only lend credence to the most cynical appraisal of the work of judges throughout the land. It is confidence in the men and women who administer the judicial system that is the true backbone of the rule of law. Time will one day heal the wound to that confidence that will be inflicted by today's decision. One thing, however, is certain. Although we may never know with complete certainty the identity of the winner of this year's Presidential election, the identity of the loser is perfectly clear. It is the Nation's confidence in the judge as an impartial guardian of the rule of law.

Justice Stevens's fears were not fulfilled, as public opinion surveys conducted after the *Bush* v. *Gore* decision did not reveal a loss of confidence in judges and courts of law. Although the decision remained controversial, most Americans were relieved that it brought an orderly and peaceful conclusion to a politically divisive dispute.

Bush v. *Gore* left an indelible mark on the history of the Court and the nation. The official vote tally in Florida made Bush the winner by 537 votes and gave him the state's twenty-five electoral votes. Al Gore had 543,816 more votes nationally than George Bush. Predictably, reformers demanded an amendment to the Constitution that would end the Electoral College system. These pleas fell on deaf ears. Congress did pass the Help America Vote Act, an electoral reform measure that authorized the federal government to provide funds to the states to replace their mechanical voting equipment with electronic equipment. Most importantly, however, the decision represented the extraordinary exertion of judicial power that determined no less than who would lead the world's most powerful nation.

Al Gore's Concession Speech

On December 13, 2000, Vice President Al Gore conceded defeat in the face of the Supreme Court's ruling in an eight-minute televised speech from his ceremonial office next to the White House. Gore was gracious in defeat, although certain that the Court had acted incorrectly. His remarks drew high praise from the media and Republicans as well as Democrats. Gore underscored the importance of abiding by the decision of the Court even though he disagreed with it.

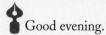 Good evening.

Just moments ago, I spoke with George W. Bush and congratulated him on becoming the 43rd president of the United States, and I promised him that I wouldn't call him back this time.

I offered to meet with him as soon as possible so that we can start to heal the divisions of the campaign and the contest through which we just passed.

Almost a century and a half ago, Sen. Stephen Douglas told Abraham Lincoln, who had just defeated him for the presidency, "Partisan feeling must yield to patriotism. I'm with you, Mr. President, and God bless you."

Well, in that same spirit, I say to President-elect Bush that what remains of partisan rancor must now be put aside, and may God bless his stewardship of this country.

Neither he nor I anticipated this long and difficult road. Certainly neither of us wanted it to happen. Yet it came, and now it has ended, resolved, as it must be resolved, through the honored institutions of our democracy.

Over the library of one of our great law schools is inscribed the motto, "Not under man but under God and law." That's the ruling principle of American freedom, the source of our democratic liberties. I've tried to make it my guide throughout this contest as it has guided America's deliberations of all the complex issues of the past five weeks.

Now the U.S. Supreme Court has spoken. Let there be no doubt, while I strongly disagree with the court's decision, I accept it. I accept the finality of this outcome which will be ratified next Monday in the Electoral College. And tonight, for the sake of our unity of the people and the strength of our democracy, I offer my concession.

I also accept my responsibility, which I will discharge unconditionally, to honor the new president elect and do everything possible to help him bring Americans together in fulfillment of the great vision that our Declaration of Independence defines and that our Constitution affirms and defends....

This has been an extraordinary election. But in one of God's unforeseen paths, this belatedly broken impasse can point us all to a new common ground, for its very closeness can serve to remind us that we are one people with a shared history and a shared destiny.

Indeed, that history gives us many examples of contests as hotly debated, as fiercely fought, with their own challenges to the popular will.

Other disputes have dragged on for weeks before reaching resolution. And each time, both the victor and the vanquished have accepted the result peacefully and in the spirit of reconciliation.

So let it be with us.

I know that many of my supporters are disappointed. I am, too. But our disappointment must be overcome by our love of country.

And I say to our fellow members of the world community, let no one see this contest as a sign of American weakness. The strength of American democracy is shown most clearly through the difficulties it can overcome.

Some have expressed concern that the unusual nature of this election might hamper the next president in the conduct of his office. I do not believe it need be so.

President-elect Bush inherits a nation whose citi-

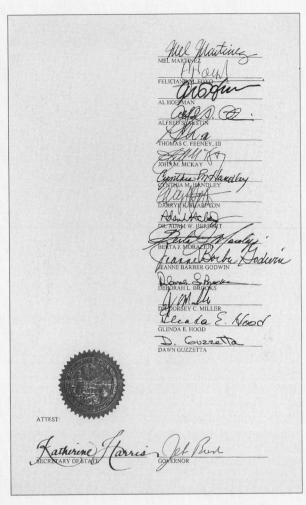

This official certificate of the Florida vote electing George W. Bush and Dick Cheney as President and Vice President of the United States was signed by the electors; the Secretary of State, Katherine Harris, co-chair of Bush's campaign in Florida; and Jeb Bush, the governor of Florida and the President-elect's brother. Bush won Florida's hotly disputed twenty-five electoral votes by a razor-thin margin of 537 popular votes while losing the national popular vote by more than 500,000 votes.

zens will be ready to assist him in the conduct of his large responsibilities.

I personally will be at his disposal, and I call on all Americans—I particularly urge all who stood with us to unite behind our next president. This is America. Just as we fight hard when the stakes are high, we close ranks and come together when the contest is done.

And while there will be time enough to debate our continuing differences, now is the time to recognize that which unites us is greater than that which divides us.

While we yet hold and do not yield our opposing beliefs, there is a higher duty than the one we owe to political party. This is America and we put country before party. We will stand together behind our new president....

Now the political struggle is over and we turn again to the unending struggle for the common good of all Americans and for those multitudes around the world who look to us for leadership in the cause of freedom.

In the words of our great hymn, "America, America": "Let us crown thy good with brotherhood, from sea to shining sea."

And now, my friends, in a phrase I once addressed to others, it's time for me to go.

Thank you and good night, and God bless America.

President-Elect George W. Bush
Addresses the Nation

On December 13, 2000, one day after the Supreme Court's decision in Bush *v.* Gore, *George W. Bush addressed the nation, seeking to bind it together. He delivered the speech on national television from the Texas Capitol, in Austin. Bush's comments were welcomed by a nation exhausted by the drama surrounding who would be the new President.*

Good evening, my fellow Americans. I appreciate so very much the opportunity to speak with you tonight.

Mr. Speaker, Lieutenant Governor, friends, distinguished guests, our country has been through a long and trying period, with the outcome of the presidential election not finalized for longer than any of us could ever imagine.

Vice President Gore and I put our hearts and hopes into our campaigns. We both gave it our all. We shared similar emotions, so I understand how difficult this moment must be for Vice President Gore and his family.

He has a distinguished record of service to our country as a congressman, a senator and a vice president.

This evening I received a gracious call from the vice president. We agreed to meet early next week in Washington and we agreed to do our best to heal our country after this hard-fought contest.

Tonight I want to thank all the thousands of volunteers and campaign workers who worked so hard on my behalf.

I also salute the vice president and his supports for waging a spirited campaign. And I thank him for a call that I know was difficult to make. Laura and I wish the vice president and Senator Lieberman and their families the very best.

I have a lot to be thankful for tonight. I'm thankful for America and thankful that we were able to resolve our electoral differences in a peaceful way.

I'm thankful to the American people for the great privilege of being able to serve as your next president.

I want to thank my wife and our daughters for their love. Laura's active involvement as first lady has made Texas a better place, and she will be a wonderful first lady of America.

I am proud to have Dick Cheney by my side, and America will be proud to have him as our next vice president.

Tonight I chose to speak from the chamber of the Texas House of Representatives because it has been a home to bipartisan cooperation. Here in a place where Democrats have the majority, Republicans and Democrats have worked together to do what is right for the people we represent.

We've had spirited disagreements. And in the end, we found constructive consensus. It is an experience I will always carry with me, an example I will always follow....

I believe things happen for a reason, and I hope the long wait of the last five weeks will heighten a desire to move beyond the bitterness and partisanship of the recent past.

Our nation must rise above a house divided. Americans share hopes and goals and values far more important than any political disagreements.

Republicans want the best for our nation, and so do Democrats. Our votes may differ, but not our hopes.

I know America wants reconciliation and unity. I know Americans want progress. And we must seize this moment and deliver.

Together, guided by a spirit of common sense, common courtesy and common goals, we can unite and inspire the American citizens....

Two hundred years ago, in the election of 1800, America faced another close presidential election. A tie in the Electoral College put the outcome into the hands of Congress.

After six days of voting and 36 ballots, the House of Representatives elected Thomas Jefferson the third president of the United States. That election brought the first transfer of power from one party to another in our new democracy.

Shortly after the election, Jefferson, in a letter titled "Reconciliation and Reform," wrote this. "The steady character of our countrymen is a rock to which we may safely moor; unequivocal in principle, reasonable in manner. We should be able to hope to do a great deal of good to the cause of freedom and harmony."

Two hundred years have only strengthened the steady character of America. And so as we begin the work of healing our nation, tonight I call upon that character: respect for each other, respect for our differences, generosity of spirit, and a willingness to work hard and work together to solve any problem.

I have something else to ask you, to ask every American. I ask for you to pray for this great nation. I ask for your prayers for leaders from both parties. I thank you for your prayers for me and my family, and I ask you pray for Vice President Gore and his family.

I have faith that with God's help we as a nation will move forward together as one nation, indivisible. And together we will create an America that is open, so every citizen has access to the American dream; an America that is educated, so every child has the keys to realize that dream; and an America that is united in our diversity and our shared American values that are larger than race or party.

I was not elected to serve one party, but to serve one nation.

The president of the United States is the president of every single American, of every race and every background.

Whether you voted for me or not, I will do my best to serve your interests and I will work to earn your respect.

I will be guided by President Jefferson's sense of purpose, to stand for principle, to be reasonable in manner, and above all, to do great good for the cause of freedom and harmony.

The presidency is more than an honor. It is more than an office. It is a charge to keep, and I will give it my all.

Thank you very much and God bless America.

Epilogue
"We Are All Slaves of the Law"

The pivotal Supreme Court cases described in this book remind us that our constitutional system places change and continuity in constant tension. And that is just what the framers of the Constitution intended. They wanted the Constitution to be difficult to change because its predictability is essential to its legitimacy. We believe in the Constitution when we know that it will be applied in a stable, routine way. But the framers, faced in Philadelphia with the need to compromise over issues such as slavery and the representation of the states in the new government, purposefully crafted a short, incomplete document. The original U.S. Constitution was one of the briefest in the history of the world, only 4,069 words exclusive of the signers' names and subsequent amendments. Today, with twenty-seven amendments, it is only 7,606 words long.

The framers also knew that those areas of government they did not address when they wrote the Constitution would have to be considered as the document was adapted to changing circumstances. A static constitution was as sure to lose its base of popular support as one that was constantly undergoing change. The device they provided for adapting the Constitution was the amendment process outlined in Article 5. In order to change the Constitution, Congress has to pass a proposed amendment by a two-thirds majority and then have it ratified by three-quarters of the states, a very demanding and time-consuming process. In the nation's more than two-hundred-year history, only thirty-three such proposals, including the twenty-seven that were ultimately ratified, have been sent to the states. Of the twenty-seven amendments, ten, collectively called the Bill of Rights, were ratified in 1791. Today, members of Congress propose an average of two hundred amendments each term, with the vast majority dying in the same place they were born.

The framers did provide an even more dramatic means of changing the Constitution—a constitutional convention that would meet if two-thirds of the state legislatures applied to Congress to hold one. Efforts to hold a second convention have routinely failed, largely because of fears that a new convention might get out of control and go beyond the purpose for which it was originally called. The most serious attempt occurred on the eve of the Civil War. Outgoing President James Buchanan urged a convention to deal with the future of slavery, as a way of preventing the secession of the southern states, but incoming President Abraham Lincoln and the Congress rejected his plea.

Despite the difficulties associated with amending the Constitution by means of Article 5, the nation's ruling document has been adapted, sometimes dramatically, to social circumstances the framers did not contemplate. The instrument for doing so has been the Supreme Court, making it, for better or worse, a kind of continuing constitutional convention.

The justices have made themselves indispensable to the American scheme of government by establishing three broad concepts. These are: judicial review (the right to review and, if necessary, set aside not only acts of Congress and the President, but also those of state governments, including state courts and legislatures); judicial independence (the concept that the Court is free of political entanglements and that its actions are controlled by principles of law not politics); and, perhaps the most important of all, judicial sovereignty (the idea that what the justices say about the Constitution is final and authoritative).

Because the justices have successfully established their right to decide conclusively the meaning of the Constitution and because their decisions almost always leave one party unhappy, critics of the Court have argued that it has become too powerful. They typically complain that the Court has been too activist, meaning that it has been willing to substitute its views for those of the elected branches of government. It would be far better, these critics argue, for the justices to adhere to the intentions of the framers of the Constitution. Others, however, insist that the Court cannot be restrained by what they describe as the dead hand of the past; in their view, the nation's ruling document has to fit the times if it is to be legitimate.

As a matter of history, the Court has actually embraced a bit of both of these views, as its landmark decisions remind us. The justices are not free to exercise their power any way they wish; even though the Court's power has grown, it remains constrained in what it can do. For example, in order to render a decision, a litigant has to bring them a dispute. They cannot simply issue opinions on their own without first hearing a case. Moreover, the justices must rely on others to enforce those decisions. As Alexander Hamilton wrote in *The Federalist No. 78*, the justices command neither the power of the sword nor of the purse. And the Court cannot perpetuate itself; instead, the President nominates its members, with the advice and consent of the Senate.

The justices are also beholden to Congress for most of their jurisdiction to hear cases. While the Constitution in Article 3 outlines the jurisdiction of the Court, it places in the hands of Congress considerable authority to specify the circumstances under which that power can be exercised. Article 3 of the Constitution provides that "The Judicial Power of the United States, shall be vested in one supreme Court, and in such inferior Courts as the Congress may from time to time ordain and establish." Congress can limit or expand the jurisdiction of the Court; Congress can add or subtract justices.

Using its power of judicial review, the Supreme Court threw out the Agricultural Adjustment Act in 1936, claiming that agriculture is not an interstate business that can be regulated by the federal government. Chief Justice John Marshall first established the principle of judicial review in 1803 in Marbury v. Madison, *but the power was used most extensively during the 20th century.*

Over two centuries the Court as an institution has changed, almost always with the blessing of Congress. The size of the Court has grown, from six to nine justices. The Court has had many homes, from its quarters in the old Senate chamber in the Capitol to the marble palace of today. As in the federal government as a whole, the work of the Court has grown to meet the demands of an expanding nation. In the first decade of the Court's history the justices decided just one hundred cases; today the Court has as many as ten thousand cases brought to it annually. An equally important development has been the willingness of Congress to expand the certiorari jurisdiction of the Court, which has given the justices greater control over the cases they ultimately decide. Out of the thousands of cases it could potentially decide, the Court today usually issues written opinions in seventy to eighty. As its discretion to pick and choose among those cases has grown so, too, has its power and visibility.

Many of its pivotal decisions, such as *Brown* v. *Board of Education* (1954, 1955), reveal that the justices have understood that if they try to reach too far and too fast, they are likely to suffer a backlash. Indeed, that is exactly what happened in response to their decisions involving slavery in the territories, *Scott* v. *Sandford* (1858), and the New Deal. The latter produced President Franklin Roosevelt's ill-fated court-packing scheme.

Although there are some who might wish that the Court would remain anchored in the past, its history has been one of adapting American constitutional law to changing social circumstances, often in subtle ways. Take for example the authority that the justices cite to make decisions. Although the Court is above all an institution of law that relies on legal precedents, its justices in the twentieth century turned increasingly to fields outside the law (sociology, psychology, statistics, and the social sciences generally) to support their opinions. The groundbreaking Brandeis brief in *Muller* v. *Oregon* (1908), which relied heavily on statistics about the impact of factory work on women, established a pattern of using nonlegal materials that was amplified in *Brown* and other cases.

The Court has changed its views on critical matters, as the cases in this volume so often remind us. And when the Court has changed its mind, it has produced some of the most memorable moments in the history of the nation. We might prefer a Supreme Court founded on the idea of original intent, that is, a Court that constantly refers to the wishes of the framers of the Constitution. But its most important decisions reveal that while the justices have kept an eye to precedent and the work of the Philadelphia convention, they have also been willing to gaze decisively into the future when confronted with new realities, such as abortion and affirmative action, that the framers did not envision.

The high court has been something of a magic mirror that reflects back to us the assumptions and values of earlier times. It decisions remind us how important it is that the Court has the power and opportunity to change its mind. In the *Scott* decision (1857), the justices approved the institution of slavery and issued the sobering declaration that "persons of African descent have no rights which the white man is bound to respect." A century later, in *Brown*, the justices ended the practice of racial segregation in public schools and challenged America to live up to the pledge of "equal justice under law," words that are carved above the entrance to the Supreme Court.

These historic cases also remind us that disputes in society about how to deal with controversial issues are repeatedly framed through constitutional arguments. Ours is truly a dynamic constitutional order. Alexis de Tocqueville, a French writer who traveled across early nineteenth-century America, wrote one of the great surveys of American life, *Democracy in America* (1835, 1840). He slyly observed that "there is hardly a political question in the United States which does not sooner or later turn into a judicial one." Congress has often found it useful to expand the powers of the Court so that the justices can address legally matters, such as slavery in the territories and apportionment of legislative districts, that would be difficult to compromise on politically.

Social change has often meant new challenges (and opportunities) for the justices. The Civil War left a bloody wound in America's heart, but it also produced the Thirteenth, Fourteenth, and Fifteenth Amendments. These amendments, especially the Fourteenth, gave the justices new opportunities to reassess such critical issues as federalism, the rights of the accused, the scope of freedoms of speech and press, the relationship between church and state, and race relations. The justices also seized the wording in the due process clause of the Fourteenth Amendment to develop through substantive due process whole new areas of law involving privacy, women's rights, and the related issues of birth control and abortion.

The Court is not today and historically never has been a runaway train. It is, at its heart, a legal institution, one shaped by the institutions and traditions of the law. The Court listens to lawyers who typically frame their arguments through the law's language and processes, crafts its decision through that same language and those same processes, and sustains itself through the idea that it above all other institutions embodies the rule of law, meaning that no person is above the law.

The Supreme Court is a powerful institution and its justices have become an integral part of American government. The closely fought Presidential election of 2000 turned on a decision by the high court about who would become the nation's chief executive. Although many commentators condemned the Court for tackling a political question, the American people as a whole embraced the Court's decision, in part because they held the justices in such high regard and in part because they so distrusted the political process that might have otherwise resolved the election results. As Justice Robert H. Jackson once observed, the justices "are not final because we are infallible, but we are infallible only because we are final."

The Court's most significant decisions also affirm the pragmatism of the framers and of the justices who interpret the Constitution they created. The framers knew they were creating a legal institution with a human dimension. It makes a difference who sits on the Court. The nation's most important legal body is, after all, composed of human beings who bring a variety of experiences and talents to the bench, although they are bound together by being trained in the law. The process by which Supreme Court justices are selected (appointment by the President with the advice and consent of the Senate) has always been political. For example, the selections of John Roberts and Samuel Alito, both made by George W. Bush, would be unthinkable had Al Gore been President.

Yet the justices have not been mere extensions of the Presidents who selected them. Tenure during good behavior and freedom from having their salaries reduced gives them a high degree of independence. We should not be surprised that they have often behaved accordingly. Former President Dwight Eisenhower, when asked what his biggest mistakes had been, reputedly replied: the appointments of Earl Warren and William J. Brennan Jr. Both justices proved far more liberal than either Eisenhower or his Republican Party would have liked. President Richard Nixon appointed Warren Burger in the hope that he would be a social conservative and a supporter of Presidential power. Burger ended up voting in favor of women having a right to an abortion in *Roe* v. *Wade* (1978) and ordering Nixon to turn over the Watergate tapes in *United States* v.

Nixon (1974). And the list could go on. Scholars estimate that about half of the justices who have served have taken positions consistently at odds with the Presidents who appointed them.

The question of what qualities make for great or failed Supreme Court justices has stirred considerable debate. Some commentators insist that the intellectual ability to deal with the complex legal issues that come before the Court is critical. That means that a great justice must also be a great lawyer, but one of a special sort. A vision for what law can be rather than for what it is seems to be critical, especially in eras marked by powerful social change, such as the Civil War and the Great Depression. An old Yugoslav proverb holds that "If you want to know what a man is, place him in a position of authority." The greatest of our justices have, in the end, been those who have grown in response to and have been shaped by the authority vested in them. Some of the greatest justices in the Court's history, notably Oliver Wendell Holmes Jr. and John Marshall Harlan, were important as much for their dissents, which were later embraced by the majority, as for the majority opinions they wrote for the Court. Leadership and persuasiveness, the ability to encourage fellow justices to see in new ways and then to lead them there, have also been valuable talents. A justice has to be able to write not only clearly but persuasively and to argue in the close quarters of the conference in a way that can build and hold the votes necessary to forge a majority.

In order to be a great justice, it is also necessary to have spent an extended period of time on the Court. A justice may be a quick study, but in order to have a lasting impact he or she must persist for at least a decade. John Marshall, for example, was the Court's greatest chief justice not only because he had extraordinary leadership skills but because he exercised those skills over thirty-four years of service (1801–1835). Learning to be a justice, whether for better or worse, takes time, but it is equally true that, because change in the law often comes gradually, endurance is important in shaping it.

These great cases also remind us that the justices mix pragmatism with nobility. The justices have not left an unalloyed legacy of support for equality, freedom, and fairness. During periods of national crisis the Court has frequently deferred to the executive branch to the detriment of individual liberty, as its decisions in *Schenck* v. *United States* (1919) and *Abrams* v. *United States* (1919) during World War I underscore. In the Japanese American internment cases of World War II, the Court tragically permitted the detention of thousands of Japanese American citizens in one of the worst moments in its history. Perhaps the best we can say is that the high court is, like every other feature of American government, imperfect, an institution that, like the American people, is fully capable of holding contradictory views simultaneously.

Yet, its imperfections notwithstanding, the Court has had the unique role of being America's most visible manifestation of the rule of law. The Constitution has evolved into America's civic religion, a collection of words whose noblest principles rally a nation. The justices who interpret those words are its high priests; their opinions shape the contours of American life For these efforts the justices and their Court have earned praise, provoked criticism, and generated controversy.

There is no doubt that the Supreme Court's principal role has been to remind us that the law generally and constitutional law in particular cannot be a game of roulette. We depend on the justices and the high court to exercise a limited degree of discretion in return for a high degree of certainty. As a matter of history, the justices have performed this task sufficiently well that there has been no need for a second constitutional convention. It is left to the justices to wrestle with applying the rule of law while acknowledging that the Constitution rests on a base of popular will that is articulated in its Preamble with the words "We the People."

The Roman philosopher Cicero summed matters up nicely with the observation that "We are all slaves of the law that we may enjoy freedom." The framers of the Constitution, schooled as they were in the classics, knew and appreciated this basic insight. One of the most important reasons that they created the Court—and one of the most important reasons it has played such a critical role in our history—is that it has maintained the concept of the rule of law as an essential, if sometimes not fully realized, element of our liberty.

Appendix
An Annotated List of Important Supreme Court Decisions

This annotated list provides citations and brief descriptions of important Supreme Court decisions, presented in an A–Z format. Most of the cases are related in some way to the topics and cases treated in the chapters of this book. In addition, this list includes every case—except those already emphasized in the chapters—mentioned in the social studies standards of the state departments of education throughout the United States. This appendix is a supplement to the chapters, so the major cases treated centrally in the book's chapters are *not* included here.

Minimal information is provided about each case, just enough to help readers decide whether they want to learn more about it from another source. If so, they can use the citation of the case to look it up on one or more of the websites listed in the section of this book called Websites, or in another reference source.

Each citation includes the name of the parties to the case: for example, *Abington School District* v. *Schempp*. The citation also includes numbers in the following format: 374 U.S. 203 (1963). The numbers mean that the opinion in this case is published in volume 374 of *United States Reports,* beginning on page 203. The year the case was decided follows in parentheses. During most of the first one hundred years of Supreme Court history, official reports of the cases were published under the names of the Court reporters. Thus, these names (full or abbreviated) appear in the citations of the Court's decisions. For example, the citation for *Barron* v. *Baltimore* (1833) includes this information: 7 Pet. 243. This citation indicates that the case can be found in the seventh volume compiled by Richard Peters (Pet.), and that it begins on page 243. Some of the annotated websites present unofficial copies of the records about the Supreme Court cases that appear officially in the bound volumes of *United States Reports.*

Abington School District v. Schempp
374 U.S. 203 (1963)

The Schempp family challenged a Pennsylvania law requiring public school students to read from the Bible at the start of the school day. The Supreme Court overturned the law because it violated the First Amendment's establishment clause, which was applied against the state through the due process clause of the Fourteenth Amendment. The establishment clause was originally incorporated under the Fourteenth Amendment's due process clause in *Everson* v. *Board of Education of Ewing Township* (1947).

Adderly v. Florida
385 U.S. 39 (1966)

More than two hundred students assembled in front of a prison to protest the arrests of their schoolmates and the racial segregation policies of Florida's state prison system. During their boisterous demonstration, they blocked access to a prison driveway. The sheriff told the demonstrators to disperse, because they were violating a state law against "trespass with a malicious and mischievous intent." More than half the students departed, but others who continued to protest were arrested and convicted of violating a state law, which the U.S. Supreme Court upheld. The Court concluded that the state had not violated the protesters' rights to freedom of speech, assembly, and petition, because the state had the authority to maintain order on its own property in a manner that was lawful and nondiscriminatory. The protesters were free to assemble in other places to express their dissent against state and county prison policies. But they were restricted from demonstrating in the place and manner they had chosen, which violated a clearly defined and constitutionally applied state law.

Adkins v. Children's Hospital
261 U.S. 525 (1923)

The Court overturned a 1918 federal minimum wage law for working women in the District of Columbia because the law violated the liberty of contract guaranteed by the Fifth Amendment's due process clause. The Court's decision followed the liberty of contract principle established in *Lochner* v. *New York* (1907). The *Adkins* decision, however, disregarded the Court's 1908 ruling in *Muller* v. *Oregon* that had recognized the need for state governments to protect certain vulnerable groups of people, such as women, through workplace regulations. Chief Justice Taft and Associate Justice Holmes wrote stinging dissents that presaged the Court's overruling of the *Adkins* decision in *West Coast Hotel* v. *Parrish* (1937).

Agostini v. Felton
521 U.S. 203 (1997)

The Court ruled that New York City could use public funds granted by the federal government to support remedial programs that directly aid students in church-run schools, if the programs are secular. The establishment clause of the Constitution's First

Amendment, applied to the states through the due process clause of the Fourteenth Amendment, is not violated as long as the government-funded program neither advances nor obstructs the religious mission of the private school. This decision overturned the Court's ruling in *Aguilar* v. *Felton* (1985).

Aguilar v. *Felton*
473 U.S. 402 (1985)

The Court struck down a New York City program that used federal funds, granted through the Title I Elementary and Secondary Education Act, to pay public school employees who provided remedial education to students in private, church-run schools. The Court ruled that the New York City program violated the First Amendment's establishment clause, because it involved an excessive entanglement of church and state, the third prong of the Lemon test from *Lemon* v. *Kurtzman* (1971). In 1997, the Court modified its interpretation of the Lemon test in *Agostini* v. *Felton*

Alden v. *Maine*
527 U.S. 706 (1999)

Probation officers in Maine sued the state to collect overtime pay under the terms of a federal law, the Fair Labor Standards Act of 1938. The Court ruled that private parties seeking damages resulting from a state's violation of a federal statute cannot sue the state for monetary damages in its own state courts or in a federal court. The Court held that the states have sovereign immunity from such private lawsuits under the Constitution's principle of federalism.

Aptheker v. *Secretary of State*
378 U.S. 500 (1964)

Herbert Aptheker, chairman of the Communist Party of the United States, sued to have Section 6 of the Subversive Activities Control Act declared unconstitutional. This federal law prohibited him from obtaining a passport in order to travel outside the United States, because he belonged to an organization that the U.S. Department of State identified as a threat to the security and safety of the nation. However, the Supreme Court ruled that the liberty interest of the due process clause in the Constitution's Fifth Amendment protects a U.S. citizen's right to travel internationally. Therefore, a citizen cannot be denied a passport and deprived of his or her liberty to travel abroad solely because of membership in a so-called subversive political organization, in this instance the Communist Party of the United States.

Barron v. *Baltimore*
32 U.S. 243 [7 Pet. 243] (1833)

Prior to the enactment of the Fourteenth Amendment in 1868, the Bill of Rights restrained only the federal government. Thus, the Court did not recognize the claim of John Barron, the owner of docks and warehouses, against the city of Baltimore, which had damaged his property through public works projects. Barron claimed that the city had violated the portion of the Fifth Amendment that states "private property" shall not "be taken without just compensation," but the Court determined that the amendment only applied to the actions of the federal government.

Benton v. *Maryland*
395 U.S. 784 (1969)

The state of Maryland charged John Dalmer Benton with two crimes, larceny and burglary; he was acquitted of the first charge but found guilty of the second. When he appealed his burglary conviction, his larceny case was reopened and he was found guilty of both crimes. When his case came before the Supreme Court, the Court ruled that the Fifth Amendment protection against "double jeopardy" could be applied against state governments through the due process clause of the Fourteenth Amendment. This ruling overturned the Court's decision in *Palko* v. *Connecticut* (1937).

Bethel District No. 403 v. *Fraser*
478 U.S. 675 (1986)

In a school assembly speech, Matthew Fraser made sexually suggestive comments and gestures, which amused some students and shocked others. Fraser, after being suspended, sued the school district for violating his First Amendment right to free speech. The Court ruled that school officials may limit the free speech rights of students in a public school in order to prevent disruptions of the school's educational mission.

Board of Education of Central School District No. 1 v. *Allen*
392 U.S.236 (1968)

A New York State law required the state to loan textbooks on secular subjects to all school children in grades seven through twelve in public and private schools, including church-run schools. The Court ruled that this law was not a violation of the First Amendment's prohibition of an establishment of religion primarily because the funds were not used to advance the religious mission of the private, church-run schools, and the students and their parents were the beneficiaries, not the schools themselves.

Bradwell v. *Illinois*
83 U.S. 130 [16 Wall. 130] (1873)

Myra Bradwell was well qualified to be a lawyer, but Illinois denied her the right to practice law solely because of her gender. She based her appeal of the Illinois Supreme Court's decision on the "privileges and immunities" clause of the Fourteenth

Amendment, but the U.S. Supreme Court upheld the state court's ruling against her. In a concurring opinion, Justice Joseph P. Bradley argued that women in general were by nature unfit to perform the public duties of professional occupations. By the early years of the twentieth century, most states had permitted women to practice law. However, not until *Reed* v. *Reed* (1971) did the Court interpret the Constitution's Fourteenth Amendment to protect the rights of women against sex-based discrimination.

Brandenburg v. *Ohio*
395 U.S. 444 (1969)

Clarence Bradenburg, a Ku Klux Klan leader, was convicted of violating an Ohio state law banning speech that advocated violence as a means of bringing about social reform. The Court ruled that the content of speech can be restricted only when the speech can be directly and immediately linked to specific actions that could result in lawless behavior, such as harm to persons or property. The Court defined the right to free speech so broadly that even hateful speech by a despicable person is permitted, unless it can be linked to imminent lawless behavior.

Bush v. *Palm Beach County Canvassing Board*
531 U.S. 70 (2000)

The 2000 Presidential election remained in doubt on November 8, the day after voters throughout the United States had cast their ballots. The outcome of this very close election hinged on the resolution of disputes about the counting of votes cast in Florida. The official count favored the Republican candidate George W. Bush by a very slim margin over the Democrat Al Gore, who filed suit in a Florida court to force a manual recount of votes in certain counties, including Palm Beach County. The state supreme court ruled in favor of Gore, but Bush challenged the decision, and the issue went on appeal to the U.S. Supreme Court. On December 4, the Court decided unanimously to vacate the state supreme court's decision and remanded (returned) it to the state court for clarification. The issue of a contested election and how to resolve it constitutionally came back to the U.S. Supreme Court, which ruled on December 12, in *Bush* v. *Gore*, to immediately end the recount of ballots that the state supreme court had once again approved in the contested counties. The U.S. Supreme Court held in a narrow decision that the recount procedures were being conducted unconstitutionally, ordered an immediate halt to the recounting of ballots, and once again remanded the case to the state supreme court. This time, however, the state court did not take further action, and Al Gore publicly conceded the election to George Bush.

Cantwell v. *Connecticut*
310 U.S. 296 (1940)

Newton Cantwell was arrested and convicted because of his intrusive and offensive door-to-door soliciting on behalf of his religious group, the Jehovah's Witnesses. He had not obtained from the state the necessary permit to conduct his activities, which included distributing reading material and audio records considered derogatory to the Roman Catholic Church. The Court ruled that a state may regulate the time, manner, and place of speech by members of a religious organization seeking support for or converts to their religion. The opinion also stated, however, that if the state comprehensively prohibits such proselytizing actions or censors the content of the speech associated with them, then the state violates one's First Amendment rights to free exercise of religion and free speech, which are applied to the states through the due process clause of the Fourteenth Amendment. This was the first time that the Court incorporated the First Amendment right to free exercise of religion under the Fourteenth Amendment's due process clause in order to apply this right against a state.

Charles River Bridge v. *Warren Bridge*
36 U.S. 420 [11 Pet. 420] (1837)

In 1828, when Massachusetts granted a permit for the Warren Bridge to be built across the Charles River in Boston, the owners of the Charles River Bridge, who had an earlier charter, objected on the grounds that the new permit violated the contract clause of the Constitution (Article 1, Section 10). The Court ruled that a state may interpret public charters for the benefit of the public and to meet community needs. According to this ruling, the state government of Massachusetts did not violate the contract clause when it chartered the new bridge.

Chicago, Burlington & Quincy Railroad v. *Chicago*
166 U.S. 226 (1897)

The city of Chicago took private property of the Chicago, Burlington & Quincy Railroad in order to build a street for public use and compensated the railroad company with the nominal sum of one dollar. The U.S. Supreme Court ruled against Chicago. Through the due process clause of the Fourteenth Amendment the Court incorporated the Fifth Amendment right of "just compensation" and thereby required the city, an agent of the state government of Illinois, to make an equitable payment to the railroad company because its private property had been taken for public use without an equitable payment.

City of Boerne, Texas v. *Flores*
521 U.S. 507 (1997)

Archbishop P. F. Flores of San Antonio sued the small Texas city of Boerne when the city refused to grant Catholic Church officials a permit to expand the building that housed St. Peter's Church, located in the city's historic district, where construction was severely restricted. Flores argued that the city was violating the Religious Freedom Restoration Act (RFRA), which limited government from enforcing laws that "substantially burden" the free exercise of religion. The Court struck down this federal statute, holding that Congress had violated the Constitution's separation of powers and federalism principles. By enacting this law, Congress had usurped the Court's power, under the separation of powers principle, to decide what is or is not a violation of religious liberty guarantees in the First and Fourteenth Amendments. Further, the Court also ruled that Congress's enactment of the RFRA had infringed upon the traditional authority of a state government, under the constitutional principle of federalism, to regulate matters pertaining to the general welfare of the state's people.

Civil Rights Cases
109 U.S. 3 (1883)

In these five cases that were decided as a group, the Court considered whether federal government, under the Civil Rights Act of 1875, had the right to force private facilities to provide blacks the same access as whites. The Court decided was the act was unconstitutional because it regulated the private conduct of individuals with regard to racial discrimination—an action beyond the scope of the Fourteenth Amendment. The Court held that the Fourteenth Amendment only banned the state governments' violation of individual rights and had nothing to do with racial discrimination by owners of private hotels, restaurants, theaters, and so forth. This type of discrimination would be illegal today under the Civil Rights Act of 1964.

Clinton v. City of New York
524 U.S. 417 (1998)

In 1986, Congress passed the Line Item Veto Act, giving the President the power to veto particular items in a bill, rather than the bill as a whole. President Clinton used this new power to reject items in the budget that benefited hospitals and health-care workers in New York City, and representatives of these groups filed suit. The Court found that the President cannot constitutionally veto part of a bill Congress sends him for his signature, and the line-item veto power was nullified.

Clinton v. Jones
520 U.S. 681 (1997)

The Court unanimously decided that the U.S. President does not have a constitutionally based immunity from civil litigation. Thus, a civil suit brought by Paula Jones against President William J. Clinton was allowed to proceed. Clinton settled the suit in 1998 by agreeing to pay Jones $850,000.

Cohens v. Virginia
19 U.S. 264 [6 Wheat. 264] (1821)

Philip and Mendes Cohen were convicted of selling lottery tickets in Virginia, in violation of state law. The brothers claimed that their lottery had been incorporated in Washington, D.C., and was therefore conducted under federal law, which takes precedence over state law. The Supreme Court asserted its jurisdiction and authority to review decisions of state courts when they involve issues about federal law or the U.S. Constitution, but upheld the Cohens' conviction.

Colegrove v. Green
328 U.S. 549 (1946)

In this case involving voting districts in Illinois, the Court held that districting issues were political questions and therefore beyond the jurisdiction of the judicial branch of government. This decision was overturned in *Baker* v. *Carr* (1962).

Cooper v. Aaron
358 U.S. 1 (1958)

In 1958, the Arkansas legislature enacted measures to postpone the desegregation of the state's public schools, in defiance of the Court's ruling in *Brown* v. *Board of Education*. The NAACP filed suit against William Cooper, president of the Little Rock school board, on behalf of John Aaron and twelve other black students. The Court affirmed its 1954 decision in *Brown*, declaring that a state government could not ignore or oppose a Supreme Court decision and asserting its primacy as the final interpreter of the Constitution.

Craig v. Boren
429 U.S. 190 (1976)

The Court ruled that a government classification that discriminates against a female would have to serve an important government interest for the public good in order to be judged constitutional under the Fourteenth Amendment's equal protection clause. Thus, the Court expressed for the first time its doctrine of "intermediate scrutiny." Henceforth, gender-based discrimination in government classifications would be held to a higher standard of justification than any other kind except that based on race, which is always subject to "strict scrutiny" and thereby practically disallowed.

Dartmouth College v. Woodward
17 U.S. 518 [4 Wheat. 518] (1819)

New Hampshire's state legislature passed several amendments to the charter of Dartmouth College, effectively changing the private institution into a state college. The lawyer and politician Daniel Webster, a graduate of Dartmouth, represented his alma mater before the Supreme Court, arguing that the charter of a private corporation (in this case, Dartmouth College) is a contract, which a state government is prohibited from abridging by the contract clause of the U.S. Constitution's Article 1, Section 10. The Court sided with Dartmouth, and the state of New Hampshire was prevented from violating the original charter of the private educational institution.

DeJonge v. Oregon
299 U.S. 353 (1937)

Dirk DeJonge, a member of the Communist Party, was prevented by Oregon state law from advertising and conducting public meetings to promote his party's agenda of revolution against the U.S. government. The Court struck down the Oregon law, because it deprived certain individuals of their rights to freedom of speech and assembly under the First and Fourteenth Amendments of the U.S. Constitution. For the first time, the Court incorporated the First Amendment right to assembly under the due process clause of the Fourteenth Amendment and applied it against a state government.

Dennis v. United States
341 U.S. 494 (1951)

The Court upheld the convictions of eleven members of the U.S. Communist Party for violating the Smith Act. This act, a response to national security concerns during the Cold War era, made it a crime for anyone to form or participate in a political party or other organization with the publicly expressed mission of violently overthrowing the U.S. government. Dissenting opinions by Justices Hugo Black and William O. Douglas argued that the Court's ruling contradicted First Amendment guarantees of free speech and assembly, including by implication, the right of association. A few years later, in *Yates* v. *United States* (1957), the Court declined to uphold convictions of Communist Party members for violations of the Smith Act. And in *Brandenburg* v. *Ohio* (1969), the Court set forth the precedent that the government may not constitutionally restrict speech unless it is connected immediately and directly to lawless behavior that threatens public safety and property.

Dickerson v. United States
530 U.S. 428 (2000)

In 1968, Congress attempted to weaken the protections of the Miranda warnings, established in *Miranda* v. *Arizona* (1966), by enacting a law to provide that a voluntarily made confession is admissible in federal court. In the case of Charles Dickerson, an alleged bank robber, his purported confession of criminal behavior was used to convict him under the terms of the 1968 federal law, even though he had not been read the Miranda warnings. However, the Supreme Court held that Congress cannot enact legislation to overrule or modify the long-standing Miranda warnings, which protect a suspect against infringement of her or his Fifth Amendment right to protection against self-incrimination and which are applied against a state government through the due process clause of the Fourteenth Amendment.

Edwards v. Aguillard
482 U.S. 578 (1987)

A Louisiana state law that required science teachers in the public schools to teach creationism, a religious doctrine, was ruled to be an unconstitutional violation of the First Amendment's establishment clause, applied against a state government through the due process clause of the Fourteenth Amendment.

Eisenstadt v. Baird
405 U.S. 438 (1972)

At issue was a Massachusetts law that prohibited the distribution of contraceptives to unmarried men or women. The U.S. Supreme Court struck down the state law because it violated the Fourteenth Amendment's equal protection clause. Under the Court's *Griswold* v. *Connecticut* (1965) decision, married couples could legally obtain contraceptive devices. The Court held that withholding this right from unmarried persons without a rational basis violated the constitutional provision for equal protection of the laws. This decision buttressed the right to privacy established in *Griswold*.

Engel v. Vitale
370 U.S. 421 (1962)

The Court ruled that an official prayer prescribed by an agency of the New York State government for students in public schools to recite daily was an unconstitutional violation of the First Amendment's establishment clause, applied against a state government through the due process clause of the Fourteenth Amendment.

Escobedo v. Illinois
378 U.S. 478 (1964)

Danny Escobedo was detained and questioned by police about the fatal shooting of his brother-in-law. Escobedo repeatedly asked to see his attorney during the interrogation, but the police refused this request. Thus, Escobedo gave answers to police questions that incriminated him in the shooting. After Escobedo had incriminated himself, he was allowed to see his lawyer. The U.S. Supreme Court decided that the police had treated Escobedo unconstitutionally. The Court ruled that the Sixth Amendment right to counsel applies not only to the trial of a person accused of a crime but also during the interrogation phase of an investigation of criminal behavior.

Everson v. Board of Education of Ewing Township
330 U.S. 1 (1947)

Arch Everson sued the Ewing, New Jersey, board of education claiming that a state law that allowed school boards to use state funds to transport students to parochial schools violated the establishment clause of the First Amendment. The Court decided for the first time to apply the establishment clause against a state through the due process clause of the Fourteenth Amendment. While the Court asserted the constitutional principle of church-state separation, it permitted the use of public funds for transporting private, religious school students on equal terms with public school students.

Frontiero v. Richardson
411 U.S. 677 (1973)

Sharon Frontiero, an officer in the U.S. Air Force, challenged a federal law that provided lesser benefits to married women in the armed services than to their married male counterparts. The Supreme Court ruled that the Fifth Amendment's due process clause protects women from discrimination by the federal government based solely on gender. Thus, married women in the armed forces are entitled to the same medical benefits and housing allowances provided to married men.

Gault, In re
387 U.S. 1 (1967)

Gerald Gault, a fifteen-year-old boy, made obscene telephone calls to a neighbor. At the time, he was on court-ordered probation for a different act of juvenile delinquency, and was given a rather severe punishment for his errant behavior. As a juvenile, Gault did not have the standard constitutional guarantees of due process of law, and his father hired counsel that appealed Gault's conviction. The Supreme Court ruled in favor of Gault and held that constitutional rights of due process of law are guaranteed to juveniles accused of criminal behavior. Prior to the *Gault* decision, the state courts treated juvenile offenders differently from adults accused of crime. The juvenile justice system—although it provided special, benevolent consideration for minors—withheld constitutional protections normally afforded adults.

Gideon v. Wainwright
372 U.S. 335 (1963)

When a Florida drifter named Clarence Earl Gideon was arrested for robbing a pool hall, he requested that the court appoint a lawyer for his defense. The court refused his request and Gideon was found guilty. Gideon appealed to the Supreme Court and the Court ruled that the Sixth Amendment right to counsel applies to the states through the due process clause of the Fourteenth Amendment. Prior to the *Gideon* decision, states were required to provide counsel only when the accused faced the death sentence or in special cases such as youth or mental incompetence. *Gideon* ensured that any person accused of a crime is entitled to legal representation, and if they cannot afford an attorney one will be appointed and paid for by the government.

Gitlow v. New York
268 U.S. 652 (1925)

Benjamin Gitlow, a member of the Commnist Labor Party, wrote a pamphlet that encouraged Americans to overthrow the U.S. government, and he was convicted for violating the state of New York's Criminal Anarchy Law. The Court upheld his conviction. However, the majority opinion said that in principle the U.S. Constitution's First Amendment guarantee of free speech is applicable to state governments through the due process clause of the Fourteenth Amendment. This was the Court's first formal acknowledgment that the First Amendment's protection of free speech could be applied against a state.

Goss v. Lopez
419 U.S. 565 (1975)

Dwight Lopez and other students of public schools in Columbus, Ohio, sued because they were suspended from school without due process of law protections normally extended to adults accused of wrongful behavior. The U.S. Supreme Court decided in favor of Lopez and held that students in public schools must be afforded rights to due process of law when they are accused of violating rules that could bring a suspension from school.

Gratz v. Bollinger
539 U.S. 244 (2003)

The Court struck down an affirmative action admissions policy of the University of Michigan's College of Literature, Science, and the Arts, because it involved group-based considerations that broadly and unfairly discriminated against individuals outside the preferred racial or ethnic categories and thereby violated the Fourteenth Amendment's equal protection clause.

Gray v. Sanders
372 U.S. 368 (1963)

The Court struck down the state of Georgia's system of apportionment for representation of districts in the state legislature, because it heavily favored residents of rural counties relative to those in urban counties. Thus, the Court decided the state law at issue violated the equal protection clause of the Constitution's Fourteenth Amendment. Writing for the Court, Justice William O. Douglas stated, for the first time, the principle of "one person, one vote" that governed decisions in subsequent cases about apportionment and representation of voters.

Grutter v. Bollinger
539 U.S. 306 (2003)

The Court upheld the University of Michigan Law School's affirmative action policy, because racial or ethnic identity was only one among several factors considered for admission to the school. Thus, this narrowly designed policy to achieve diversity among the students did not violate the Fourteenth Amendment's equal protection clause

Hague v. Committee for Industrial Organization
307 U.S. 496 (1939)

The Committee for Industrial Organization (CIO) distributed pamphlets and conducted meetings in Jersey City, New Jersey, to promote the unionization of workers. The local government stopped the CIO's activities as a violation of its law prohibiting public assemblies without a permit from the city. In response to the CIO's appeal, the U.S. Supreme Court ruled that the First Amendment protections of rights to free speech, petition, and assembly are applicable to the states and the local governments within them through the due process clause of the Fourteenth Amendment. Further, these First Amendment rights cannot be denied to members of a labor union seeking to advance their economic interests through freedom of association and expression in public places.

Hazelwood School District v. Kuhlmeier
484 U.S. 260 (1988)

When a high school principal deleted two pages from a student newspaper because they contained stories about a student pregnancy, birth control, and the divorce of a student's parents, the student journalists claimed that their First Amendment right to freedom of the press was denied. The Court ruled that students in a public high school do not have the same First Amendment protections as individuals in the community outside the school. For example, public school administrators and teachers may restrict the content of a school newspaper in order to serve a valid educational purpose.

Heart of Atlanta Motel v. United States
179 U.S. 241 (1964)

The owner of the Heart of Atlanta motel refused to rent rooms to blacks, claiming that Congress had overstepped its authority when it passed the Civil Rights Act of 1964, which made such discrimination by private businesses illegal. The Court ruled that Congress has the power under the commerce clause in Article 1, Section 8 of the U.S. Constitution to prohibit racial discrimination in privately owned accommodations, such as hotels and restaurants within a state, which are involved with interstate travel or trade.

Helvering v. Davis
301 U.S. 619 (1937)

George P. Davis, a shareholder in Edison Illuminating Company, challenged the constitutionality of the Social Security Act on the grounds that the U.S. Constitution does not explicitly grant the federal government the power to tax a private business in order to fund a public pension plan for its employees. However, the U.S. Supreme Court upheld the Social Security Act, ruling that Congress's power to regulate commerce and provide for the general welfare provided a constitutional basis for the tax.

Herndon v. Lowry
301 U.S. 242 (1937)

Angelo Herndon was an organizer and promoter of the Communist Party of the United States, who traveled throughout the country distributing his party's literature and conducting meetings to recruit new members. While in Georgia, he was arrested and convicted for attempting to incite an uprising against the government in violation of the state's anti-insurrection law. He appealed his conviction to the U.S. Supreme Court, which applied the First Amendment rights to free speech and assembly through the due process clause of the Fourteenth Amendment against the state government. Thus, a state government cannot deprive an individual of these rights merely due to his expression of offensive ideas or his membership in a reviled political party.

Humphrey's Executor v. United States
295 U.S. 602 (1935)

President Franklin Roosevelt wanted to dismiss William Humphrey from his position on the Federal Trade Commission, an independent regulatory agency within the executive branch, because he disagreed with the commissioner's conservative political philosophy. However, the Federal Trade Commission Act only permitted the President to remove a commissioner for "inefficiency, neglect of duty, or malfeasance in office." The President relied on the Court's 1926 decision in *Myers* v. *United States,* which permitted the President to remove one of his appointees to the executive department position of postmaster. The Court prohibited President Roosevelt from dismissing Humphrey, holding that an official working purely within the executive branch of government, such as the post office, was not the same as one within an independent regulatory agency, such as the FTC, which has quasi-legislative and quasi-judicial functions, established by federal law, and therefore is not wholly under the authority of the chief executive.

Hylton v. United States
3 U.S.171 [3 Dall.171] (1796)

A Virginia man, Daniel Hylton, refused to pay a federal tax on horse-drawn carriages that were used as passenger vehicles, claiming that, as a direct tax, it was prohibited under Article 1, Section 9 of the Constitution. For the first time, the Court considered the constitutionality of a federal statute, and upheld the tax. In the opinion, however, the justices recognized that they had the authority to declare a federal law invalid if it violated any part of the U.S. Constitution.

Johnson v. Transportation Agency of Santa Clara
480 U.S. 616 (1987)

Paul Johnson and Diane Joyce were the two lead candidates for a skilled position with the Transportation Agency of Santa Clara, California. Although Johnson scored slightly higher in his interview, Joyce was given the job. Santa Clara had an affirmative action plan that recognized gender as one of several factors to be considered in the hiring of employees, in order to overcome past discrimination against female applicants for jobs. The Court ruled that the plan was legal under the terms of Title VII of the Civil Rights Act of 1964.

Katz v. *United States*
389 U.S. 347 (1967)

The FBI placed electronic surveillance equipment outside a telephone booth regularly used by Charlie Katz, whom the agents suspected of illegal gambling activity. Katz claimed that the FBI had violated his Fourth Amendment right "to be secure" with respect to his person, papers, and belongings from "unreasonable search and seizure." The Court expanded its interpretation of the Fourth Amendment to include protection against certain kinds of electronic invasions in places open to the public, where someone might expect a certain degree of privacy.

Kimel v. *Florida Board of Regents*
528 U.S. 62 (2000)

Professor J. Daniel Kimel was one of several state university employees in Florida who claimed age-based discrimination and sued the state for compensation. The Court ruled that a federal law, the Age Discrimination in Employment Act, cannot be the basis for a private lawsuit seeking damages against a state government. In this decision, the Court acknowledged the power reserved to the states according to the constitutional principle of federalism.

Lamb's Chapel v. *Center Moriches Union Free School District*
508 U.S. 384 (1993)

Lamb's Chapel, an evangelical Christian church asked the town government of Center Moriches for permission to use public school buildings, after hours, to show films that promoted their religious values in family life and child raising. The local school board rejected the request. The Supreme Court, however, ruled that a public school district that permitted various kinds of community groups to use its buildings after school hours for meetings could not deny the same access to a religious organization for sectarian purposes. The justices held that discrimination against religious groups in the use of school district facilities on equal terms with other community groups was a violation of rights to freedom of speech and free exercise of religion. Granting permission to use facilities on equal terms with others does not violate the establishment clause of the First Amendment.

Lawrence v. *Texas*
539 U.S. 558 (2003)

The Court ruled that a Texas law criminalizing homosexual behavior between two consenting adults in a private residence was an unconstitutional violation of the rights to privacy and liberty under the due process clause of the Fourteenth Amendment.

Lee v. *Weisman*
505 U.S. 577 (1992)

The principal of a public middle school in Providence, Rhode Island, invited a Jewish religious leader, Rabbi Leslie Gutterman, to offer benediction at the school's annual graduation ceremony. The father of a graduating student, Daniel Weisman, brought suit against the principal for violating of the First Amendment's establishment clause. The Supreme Court decided that the First Amendment's establishment clause, applied to the states through the due process clause of the Fourteenth Amendment, prohibits clergy from saying prayers as part of an official public school ceremony, such as graduation.

Loving v. *Virginia*
388 U.S. 1 (1967)

The Court ruled that a Virginia law prohibiting marriage between persons of different races was unconstitutional, because such a racial classification violates the equal protection clause of the Fourteenth Amendment.

Lynch v. *Donnelly*
465 U.S. 668 (1984)

The Court ruled that the display of a Christian nativity scene on public property during the Christmas season does not violate the First Amendment's establishment clause, if it is placed within a context of secular or nonreligious objects.

Malloy v. *Hogan*
378 U.S. 1 (1964)

When William Malloy was called to be a witness in a Connecticut state government investigation of illegal gambling, he refused to answers questions on grounds of the constitutional protection against self-incrimination. The Supreme Court agreed with Malloy and decided, for the first time, that the Fourteenth Amendment incorporates through its due process clause the Fifth Amendment protection against self-incrimination and applies this right against the state governments.

Mapp v. Ohio
367 U.S. 643 (1961)

In 1957 police searched the home of Dollree Mapp without a warrant, and seized incriminating evidence that resulted in her imprisonment. The Court ruled that evidence obtained in violation of the Fourth Amendment's protection against unlawful searches and seizures must be excluded from use in state as well as federal criminal trials.

Marsh v. Chambers
463 U.S. 783 (1983)

The Nebraska legislature traditionally opened its sessions with a prayer recited by a Protestant chaplain, whose services were paid for by the state government. The Court ruled that this practice did not violate the First Amendment's establishment clause, even though it clearly violated precedents in constitutional law, including the Lemon test, established in *Lemon* v. *Kurzman* (1971). The Court considered this decision to be an acceptable exception to the Lemon test, because the practice at issue was a deeply rooted historical tradition.

Martin v. Hunter's Lessee
14 U.S. 304 [1 Wheat. 304] (1816)

When a Virginia judge refused to carry out the decision of the U.S. Supreme Court in a dispute about the ownership of a large tract of land in the state, the Court asserted the supremacy of its decisions over the states in cases pertaining to the U.S. Constitution, federal laws, and treaties.

McLaurin v. Oklahoma State Board of Regents
339 U.S. 637 (1950)

George McLaurin, a nonwhite resident and citizen of Oklahoma, was denied admission to the University of Oklahoma on the basis of his skin color. A state court ordered his admission to the university. However, while attending the university as a fully admitted student, he was forced to sit apart from the white students in the classroom and the lunchroom. McLaurin appealed to the U.S. Supreme Court, which decided unanimously against the personal segregation imposed upon him, because it violated the equal protection clause of the Constitution's Fourteenth Amendment.

Meyer v. Nebraska
262 U.S. 390 (1923)

The Court struck down a Nebraska law that banned schools from teaching any modern language other than English to children who had not passed the eighth grade, because this law violated the private property and liberty rights of teachers and children guaranteed through the due process clause of the

Fourteenth Amendment. The decision in this case was used later to justify the constitutional right to privacy set forth in *Griswold* v. *Connecticut* (1965).

Minor v. Happersett
88 U.S. 162 [21 Wall. 162] (1875)

In this case involving a woman's right to vote, the Court ruled that the U.S. Constitution does not confer the right to vote upon anyone. The right to vote is a matter left to the states, which may decide to deny this right to women. The Court recognized that women were citizens, but decided that citizenship does not automatically convey the right to vote.

Missouri ex rel. Gaines v. Canada
305 U.S. 337 (1938)

When the University of Missouri denied Lloyd Gaines admission to its law school because of its policy of racial discrimination, the Court ruled that the state's failure to provide a law school for black students within Missouri was a violation of the Court's "separate but equal" ruling in *Plessy* v. *Ferguson* (1896). The Court rejected Missouri's proposal to pay Lloyd Gaines's tuition at a law school outside the state and ordered his admission to the state university's law school until the state provided a "substantially equal" law school for black students. As a citizen of Missouri, Gaines was entitled to the same opportunities for education that white citizens enjoyed.

Mitchell v. Helms
530 U.S. 793 (2000)

Under the 1981 Education Consolidation and Improvement Act, Congress provided funds to the states for instructional materials and equipment that was to be made available to public and private schools, including religiously affiliated schools. The Court ruled that the federal program did not violate the First Amendment's establishment clause because the federal aid conformed to the Lemon test, established in *Lemon* v. *Kurtzman* (1971).

Morehead v. New York ex rel. Tipaldo
298 U.S. 587 (1936)

The Court struck down a New York State minimum wage law for women and children, because it violated the liberty of contract principle and the due process clause of the Constitution's Fourteenth Amendment. This was the last time the Court declared a minimum wage law to be unconstitutional.

Munn v. Illinois
94 U.S. 113 (1877)

In the late nineteenth century, railroads and grain warehouses were at liberty to set very high fees for hauling and storing grain, and farmers formed an alliance to encourage state legislatures to regulate the prices. The Court ruled that Illinois could fix maximum rates for grain storage within the state, on the grounds that a state could constitutionally regulate private business activities for the common good of the community. The Court recognized that under the constitutional principle of federalism, the state retains police power to regulate private businesses located within its boundaries.

National Labor Relations Board v. Jones & Laughlin Steel Corp.
301 U.S. 1 (1937)

In 1935 the Jones & Laughlin Steel Corporation fired ten workers who were the leaders of a labor union. The Court upheld the Wagner Act of 1936, which made it illegal for an employer to fire a worker for belonging to a labor union, as a constitutional exercise of Congress's commerce power, which did not violate the liberty interest of the Fifth Amendment's due process clause.

Near v. Minnesota
283 U.S. 697 (1931)

Jay Near, the bigoted publisher of the *Saturday Press,* published a series of articles attacking Floyd Olson, a county prosecutor. A county judge issued a restraining order against the paper, which the publisher fought as unconstitutional. The Court ruled that the First Amendment's guarantee of freedom of the press, applied to the states through the due process clause of the Fourteenth Amendment, prohibited a state government from exercising prior restraint, that is, censoring the content of a publication before it is distributed.

Nebbia v. New York
291 U.S. 502 (1934)

The Court upheld the New York Milk Control Act of 1934 against Leo Nebbia's claim that the due process clause of the Constitution's Fourteenth Amendment prohibited the state from regulating retail prices for milk. The state law at issue, said the Court, would be unconstitutional only if it unreasonably or arbitrarily regulated the practices of a private business. In this case, held the Court, a state law enacted on behalf of the public interest was justified despite its interference with traditional private property rights of certain individuals. In this instance, the general good of the community outweighed the property rights of a relatively small number of individuals.

New Jersey v. T.L.O.
469 U.S. 325 (1985)

When a school official searched a student's purse and found evidence that she had been dealing marijuana, resulting in the student's conviction as a delinquent, the student, called T.L.O. in the case, asserted that the school official had violated her Fourth Amendment protection against unreasonable search and seizure. The Court ruled that this right could be modified to permit school officials to conduct a search of a student's possessions without a warrant, if there is reason to suspect that evidence will be found that the student has violated school rules. Thus, the Court determined that a student's Fourth Amendment rights on school grounds are not equivalent to the constitutional protection of these rights on the streets outside the school, in the interest of the public schools' educational mission.

New York v. Quarles
467 U.S. 649 (1984)

In this case, a police officer confronted a suspect in a supermarket and frisked him, finding an empty shoulder holster. The officer asked the suspect where the gun was, and he responded. At this point, the suspect was arrested and the officer read him the Miranda warnings. The Court ruled that the officer had not violated the suspect's constitutional rights because he acted to protect the safety of bystanders in a public place when he delayed reading the Miranda warnings to the suspect. The Court decided there is a public safety exception to the requirement that law enforcement officers must communicate Miranda warnings to individuals suspected of criminal behavior.

New York Times Company v. United States
403 U.S. 713 (1971)

This case, often called the "Pentagon Papers" case, involved the *New York Times's* publication of documents about military operations in the Vietnam War, which an employee of the U.S. Department of Defense had secretly taken from the Pentagon. The federal government sought to prevent the paper from publishing the documents, which it claimed were top secret. The Court ruled that prior restraint by the federal government to censor the content of a publication before its distribution violated the First Amendment's protection of a free press. The Court held that even national security concerns did not justify prior restraint.

Northern Securities Co. v. United States
193 U.S. 197 (1904)

The powerful investors J. P. Morgan, James J. Hill, and Edward H. Harriman joined their interests in three major railroads to create the Northern Securities Company in 1901. The U.S. government argued that the company violated the Sherman Antitrust Act, which prohibited trusts, or combinations of businesses, that restrained "trade or commerce among the several States." The Court upheld Congress's power to regulate interstate commerce for the purpose of maintaining competition in the railroad industry and blocking a monopoly.

Olmstead v. United States
277 U.S. 438 (1928)

During the Prohibition era, Roy Olmstead operated a large-scale business transporting liquor through Washington State to Canada. Federal agents gained evidence of his illegal activities by tapping the phone lines of one of his customers and several workers. Olmstead claimed that the law enforcement officers violated his Fourth Amendment right to protection against "unreasonable search and seizure." The Court upheld the agents' right to wiretap the telephones of persons suspected of criminal behavior. Justice Brandeis's dissent argued for a right to privacy protected by the Fourth Amendment, which in the 1960s influenced the Court to overturn the *Olmstead* decision.

Oregon v. Mitchell
400 U.S. 112 (1970)

The state of Oregon challenged a 1970 amendment to the federal Voting Rights Act enfranchising eighteen-year-olds in all state and federal elections by claiming that this federal act usurped a power reserved to the states by the U.S. Constitution. The Court ruled that the federal act could only apply to national elections, but a few months later the Twenty-sixth Amendment superseded this decision by guaranteeing the right to vote of eighteen-year-olds in all elections, federal and state.

Palko v. Connecticut
302 U.S. 319 (1937)

Frank Palko was tried for the crimes of robbing a liquor store and shooting and killing two police officers and convicted of second-degree murder. The state conducted a second trial at which the judge allowed as evidence a confession that was not admitted in the first trial; as a result, Palko was convicted of the more serious charge of first-degree murder and sentenced to death. Palko claimed that the state had violated his Fifth Amendment right to protection against "double jeopardy," that is, being put on trial for the same crime twice. The Court denied Palko's appeal and set forth the "fundamental rights" test to guide decisions about incorporating particular rights in the federal Bill of Rights under the due process clause of the Fourteenth Amendment and thereby applying them against state governments. By this test, the Court did not incorporate the Fifth Amendment's protection against "double jeopardy" in the *Palko* case.

Pierce v. Society of Sisters
268 U.S. 510 (1925)

Roman Catholic parochial schools were a particular target of the Oregon Compulsory Education Act, which outlawed all private schools in the state. The Court ruled that this state statute violated the private property rights of school owners and teachers and the liberty of parents to choose between private and public schools for the education of their children. These rights to private property and liberty, said the Court, are parts of the due process clause in the Fourteenth Amendment, which Oregon was prohibited from violating by establishing a public school monopoly. The Court's decision in *Pierce* was used later in support of a constitutional right to privacy, established in *Griswold* v. *Connecticut* (1965).

Planned Parenthood of Southeastern Pennsylvania v. Casey
505 U.S. 833 (1992)

The Court upheld certain state government regulations of the right to an abortion and thereby recognized greater latitude for states to restrict abortion. For example, the Court upheld a Pennsylvania regulation requiring a woman to wait twenty-four hours before having an abortion after receiving information from a doctor about possible medical complications associated with this procedure. However, the Court also upheld the core of the *Roe* v. *Wade* (1973) decision that established the right of a woman to choose an abortion.

Pollock v. Farmers' Loan and Trust Co.
157 U.S. 429 (1895)

A federal income tax statute, enacted in 1894, was struck down by the Court. This decision was superseded in 1913 by ratification of the Sixteenth Amendment to the Constitution, which granted Congress the power to enact federal income tax laws.

Powell v. Alabama
287 U.S. 45 (1932)

In 1931, nine African American youths were arrested near Scottsboro, Alabama, and accused of raping two white women. Their case was rushed to trial and, when the judge refused to assign an attorney to defend the youths, two lawyers volunteered for the task only moments before the trial. These lawyers asked the judge to delay the trial so they could confer with their clients, and the judge allowed the lawyers thirty minutes to prepare. Eight of the nine "boys" were found guilty and sentenced to death, and the case was appealed to the Supreme Court. The Court ruled, based on the due process clause of the Fourteenth Amendment, that defendants in a criminal case involving capital punishment must be provided with counsel by the state if they are too poor to provide it for themselves, and the convictions of the "Scottsboro boys" were overturned.

Printz v. United States
521 U.S. 898 (1997)

The Court struck down part of a federal gun control law that required local officials to do a background check on a customer before a gun sale could be completed. The Court held that the principle of federalism expressed in the Constitution's Tenth Amendment prohibits the federal government from controlling certain acts of state or local officials that are carried out in terms of powers reserved to the states.

Reed v. Reed
404 U.S. 71 (1971)

Sally and Cecil Reed petitioned the Idaho court for permission to administer their deceased son's estate. The Idaho court decided on behalf of Cecil based on a state statute that preferred men to women as the administrators of estates. The Supreme Court decided in favor of Sally Reed, and this case was the first to rule that a law mandating gender discrimination against a female violates the equal protection clause of the Fourteenth Amendment, if there is no rational basis on behalf of the public good to justify such discrimination.

Reno v. American Civil Liberties Union
521 U.S. 844 (1997)

In 1996 Congress passed the Communications Decency Act (CDA) to prohibit indecent material on the Internet. The Court ruled the federal law unconstitutional, because it violated First Amendment guarantees of free speech and press.

Rosenberger v. Rector and Visitors of University of Virginia
515 U.S. 819 (1995)

Officials of the University of Virginia denied financial assistance from the university's Student Activities Fund for the publication of a student-published Christian newspaper. The Supreme Court ruled that the First Amendment rights to free speech and press and free exercise of religion prohibit a state university from discriminating against a religious publication by denying it financial support on equal terms with other student publications.

Santa Fe Independent School District v. Doe
530 U.S. 290 (2000)

Student-led prayers before the football games of a public school in Texas became a constitutional issue. Most students and parents supported the pregame prayer ceremony, but a few students disagreed and their parents filed suit in a federal court to halt the public prayer ceremony, because, they claimed, it violated the First Amendment's prohibition of an establishment of religion. The Supreme Court ruled that student-led prayer at public high school football games violated the establishment clause of the Constitution's First Amendment, applied to the states through the due process clause of the Fourteenth Amendment, because it was endorsed by local public school officials.

Schechter Poultry Corp. v. United States
295 U.S. 495 (1935)

The National Recovery Administration granted President Franklin Roosevelt broad powers to approve codes of fair competition for different industries. When four brothers who owned a poultry company challenged the law, the Court stuck it down because the Constitution's separation of powers principle does not allow Congress to delegate such power to the executive branch. The Court established, as a principle of constitutional law, that in domestic affairs Congress may not delegate broad legislative powers to the President without specifying clear standards to guide the chief executive in using these powers.

Shelley v. Kraemer
334 U.S. 1 (1948)

The Supreme Court ruled that state courts cannot enforce privately made covenants that prohibit nonwhite persons from owning or occupying property. Judicial enforcement of such racially discriminatory agreements violated the equal protection clause of the Fourteenth Amendment and the due process clause of the Fifth Amendment. By invalidating enforcement of privately made covenants, which had the purpose of excluding nonwhites from owning homes or residing in all-white communities, the Court made a significant statement against racial segregation in the United States and for all practical purposes put an end to residential discrimination.

Slaughterhouse Cases
83 U.S. 36 [16 Wall. 36] (1873)

In 1869 the Louisiana legislature passed a law requiring that all butchering in New Orleans be done at the newly formed Cresent City Company, as a measure to control the slaughterhouse industry in the interest of the public health. The Court ruled against the claims of the Butchers' Benevolent Association, formed by local butchers to protest the law, narrowly interpreting the Fourteenth Amendment's privileges and immunities clause to exclude rights of property and labor. This precedent deterred the Court in subsequent cases from including civil liberties guaranteed by the Bill of Rights within the privileges and immunities protected by the Fourteenth Amendment.

Stenberg v. Carhart
530 U.S. 914 (2000)

The Court struck down a Nebraska law that prohibited a practice called "partial birth abortion" because the statute did not provide an exception for cases when the health or life of the mother is in danger. Further, the Court held that the law at issue was written so broadly that it could be used to prohibit abortion procedures other than "partial birth abortion," which would violate the precedent set in *Roe* v. *Wade* (1973) to protect the right of a woman to choose an abortion.

Steward Machine Co. v. Davis
301 U.S. 548 (1937)

The Court ruled that a tax on employers required by the federal Social Security Act is constitutional. Conditions of employment, said the Court, are part of commerce, which Congress can regulate under the commerce clause of the Constitution's Article 1, Section 8. Previously, the Court had ruled that employment was only indirectly related to commerce and therefore could be neither be regulated nor taxed on the basis of the commerce clause. This case expanded the scope of regulation and taxation of private enterprises based on the commerce power of Congress.

Stromberg v. California
283 U.S. 359 (1931)

Yetta Stromberg, a nineteen-year-old camp counselor and member of the Young Communist League, had campers make a replica of Communist Russia's flag and recite a pledge to the flag. When she was arrested for violating a state law banning the display of a red flag, Stromberg argued that the state of California had denied her right to freedom of speech. In siding with Stromberg, the Court invoked the First Amendment right to free speech under the due process clause of the Fourteenth Amendment to invalidate the state statute. The Court also recognized symbolic speech—an action, such as displaying a red flag, that communicates without the use of words—as an instance of constitutionally protected free speech. The Court's decision in *Stromberg* established the incorporation of the First Amendment right to free speech under the Fourteenth Amendment's due process clause, which had been asserted originally, but not applied, in *Gitlow* v. *New York* (1925).

Swann v. Charlotte-Mecklenburg Board of Education
402 U.S. 1 (1971)

School officials at the large public school district of Charlotte-Mecklenburg, North Carolina, had been acting slowly and deceptively in their response to federal court–ordered racial integration of schools. The Supreme Court held that public school officials had "affirmative obligations" to integrate their schools. If they failed to eradicate race-based segregation in schools under their authority, then "judicial authority may be invoked" to achieve racial integration. The Court's unanimous decision signified its strong support for action to achieve the aim of the 1954 decision in *Brown* v. *Board of Education*, which prohibited racial segregation in public schools.

Sweatt v. Painter
339 U.S. 629 (1950)

Under a state law that restricted university admission to whites only, Herman Sweatt was rejected from the University of Texas Law School. After Sweatt asked a state court to order his admission, the university announced a plan to build a separate law school for nonwhite students. The U.S. Supreme Court unanimously decided that the separate facilities proposed by the University of Texas could never be equal to those available to whites and would, therefore, violate the equal protection clause of the Constitution's Fourteenth Amendment. The Court ordered the University of Texas to admit Sweatt, the first time it had ever required a previously all-white school to admit a black student.

Swift and Co. v. United States
196 U.S. 375 (1905)

Five large meat packing companies contested a federal injunction charging that they had violated the Sherman Antitrust Act, a federal law against restraint of trade and suppression of competition. Although they admitted their collusive and monopolistic acts against free competition, the meat packing companies claimed that they were not involved in interstate commerce. Thus, the federal government had no constitutional authority to regulate them under the commerce power of Congress. The Supreme Court ruled against the meat packers by establishing the "stream of commerce" doctrine, which expanded Congress's regulatory power to encompass business activity within a state that is connected to activity crossing state boundaries.

Terry v. Ohio
392 U.S. 1 (1968)

A police officer confronted three men who he believed were preparing to rob a store in downtown Cleveland and frisked them. His search revealed that two of the men had concealed weapons, and the men were convicted on weapons charges. One of the men, John Terry, claimed that his Fourth Amendment rights had been violated because he had been searched without a warrant. The Supreme Court ruled, however, that police may stop and frisk, or search, a suspect's outer clothing for dangerous weapons, without first obtaining a warrant, if it is reasonable under the circumstances to believe that a crime is about to be committed. Thus, the Court established an exception to the standard Fourth Amendment requirement that a search warrant must be obtained from a magistrate before a search is conducted.

Texas v. Johnson
491 U.S. 397 (1989)

During protests outside the Republican Party Convention in Dallas, Texas, Gregory Johnson soaked an American flag in kerosene and set it on fire. Johnson was convicted of violating a Texas law banning desecration of the flag. When Johnson appealed his case, the Court overturned the Texas law, ruling that the act of burning the U.S. flag is a form of symbolic speech protected by the First and Fourteenth Amendments.

United States v. *American Library Association*
539 U.S. 194 (2003)

The Children's Internet Protection Act (CIPA), which regulates Internet access to obscene images in public libraries, is intended to protect the mental health and personal development of children. When the American Library Association challenged this law, the Court ruled that it does not violate First Amendment rights to free speech, because the federal government has the authority to regulate programs in public facilities for the public good.

United States v. *Carolene Products*
304 U.S. 144 (1938)

The issue in this case was relatively insignificant, but Harlan Fiske Stone's opinion for the Court includes in a footnote the "preferred freedoms" doctrine. This doctrine became a standard for incorporating First Amendment political rights of free speech, free press, assembly, and petition under the due process clause of the Fourteenth Amendment in order to protect the rights of vulnerable minorities, such as African Americans, from infringement by state governments. According to this doctrine, all citizens must have the undisputed right to exercise the preferred freedoms in order for a constitutional and representative democracy, such as the United States of America, to function properly.

United States v. *Curtiss-Wright Export Corp.*
299 U.S. 304 (1936)

In 1934, Congress passed a joint resolution giving President Franklin Roosevelt authority to place a ban on U.S. companies selling weapons to the warring nations of Bolivia and Paraguay, in an effort to restore peace. When the Curtiss-Wright Corporation was convicted of violating this embargo by selling armed aircraft to Bolivia, the company claimed that the ban was unconstitutional. The Court ruled in favor of Congress, affirming its authority to delegate broad powers to the President to conduct foreign affairs, including powers that would not be constitutionally permissible under the separation of powers principle in regard to domestic affairs.

United States v. *Darby Lumber Co.*
312 U.S. 100 (1941)

The 1938 Fair Labor Standards Act set minimum wage, maximum hour, and overtime pay standards for workers in businesses involved in interstate commerce. When Darcy Lumber Company declared the act unconstitutional and filed suit, the Court upheld the constitutionality of the federal statute. The Court's ruling strengthened a broad interpretation of Congress's commerce power and enabled the federal government to regulate aspects of the employee-employer relationship.

United States v. *E.C. Knight Co.*
156 U.S. 1 (1895)

In its first interpretation of the Sherman Antitrust Act, the Court ruled against the federal government's claim that the E.C. Knight Company, which controlled more than 90 percent of the production of refined sugar, had established a monopoly that restrained trade. The Court narrowly interpreted Congress's regulatory power under the Constitution's commerce clause of Article 1, Section 8 by holding that production and commerce were different kinds of economic activity and that Congress had no authority over the production of a commodity that took place within the boundaries of a single state. The Court later changed course and supported a broad regulatory power of Congress under the commerce clause.

United States v. *Lopez*
514 U.S. 549 (1995)

In 1990 Congress passed the Gun-Free School Zones Act, which made it a federal crime to knowingly possess a firearm within a school zone. Alfonso Lopez, a twelfth-grade student in San Antonio, Texas, was arrested and convicted for carrying a concealed handgun at school. The Supreme Court ruled that the federal government's commerce power does not extend to the regulation of gun possession by individuals near schools. This matter is left to the discretion of state and local governments under the Constitution's Tenth Amendment.

United States v. *O'Brien*
391 U.S. 367 (1967)

David O'Brien was arrested for burning his draft card during a protest against the Vietnam War, in violation of an amendment to the Selective Service Act that made it a crime for anyone to "destroy or mutilate" a draft registration card. The Court ruled that the public burning of a draft card, as an act of protest against federal government policy, was not a constitutionally protected act of symbolic speech. Rather, the government may restrict this kind of expression to further a substantial government interest, if this restriction is no broader than necessary to carry out the valid public interest.

United States v. *Virginia*
518 U.S. 515 (1996)

A female public high school student filed a complaint with the U.S. Department of Justice to charge the Virginia Military Institute, a state-supported institution of higher education, with illegal sex discrimination in violation of the Fourteenth Amendment's guarantee of equal protection of the laws. VMI was an all-male military school and refused to accept applications for admission from females. The Supreme Court decided that the Fourteenth Amendment's guarantee of equal protection of the laws prohibits a state government from maintaining an all-male military institution of higher education.

United States v. Wong Kim Ark
169 U.S. 649 (1898)

Wong Kim Ark was born in San Francisco in 1873 to parents who remained subjects of the Chinese emperor. When he was refused entry into the United States after visiting China, on the grounds that he was not a citizen, he argued that his birth in the United States made him a natural citizen. The Court ruled that the Fourteenth Amendment guarantees U.S. citizenship to all persons born within the United States, even if their parents are not eligible for U.S. citizenship.

Vernonia School District v. Acton
515 U.S. 646 (1995)

The Vernonia, Oregon, school board decided to institute a policy of giving random drug tests to middle and high school student athletes in order to combat a drug problem in the schools. James Acton's parents refused to sign their son's urinalysis consent form when he wanted to join the seventh-grade football team, claiming it violated the Fourth Amendment protection against unreasonable searches. The Court ruled that random drug testing of public school students participating in interschool athletic programs is not an infringement of Fourth Amendment rights applied to the states through the due process clause of the Fourteenth Amendment.

Wallace v. Jaffree
472 U.S. 38 (1985)

When his children reported that their teachers had led prayers in school, Ishmael Jaffree challenged two Alabama laws, one from 1981 requiring a moment of silence in public schools for "meditation and voluntary prayer" and another from 1982 permitting teachers to lead "willing students" in prayer. The Court ruled that the laws violated the First Amendment's establishment clause applied against the states through the due process clause of the Fourteenth Amendment. The laws' religious intent failed the Lemon test established in *Lemon* v. *Kurtzman* (1971) and was struck down.

Walz v. Tax Commission of the City of New York
397 U.S. 664 (1970)

In this case, the Court upheld an exemption from payment of state property taxes by churches in New York City. Said the Court, this privilege, provided to churches on equal terms with other nonprofit organizations that contribute to the public good, is not a violation of the First Amendment's establishment clause.

Ware v. Hylton
3 U.S. 199 [3 Dall. 199] (1796)

Under the terms of the 1783 Treaty of Paris, which ended the Revolutionary War, U.S. citizens were required to pay debts owed to British creditors. Virginia, however, passed a law exempting its state's citizens from this requirement. The Court ruled that Article 6 of the U.S. Constitution says that a state government cannot violate treaties made by the U.S. government. For the first time, the Court ruled an act of a state government to be unconstitutional.

Webster v. Reproductive Health Services
492 U.S. 490 (1989)

Federal district and appellate courts struck down most provisions of a Missouri law that significantly limited a woman's right to choose an abortion. In a 5–4 decision, the Supreme Court upheld two limitations on abortion enacted by the law and agreed with the lower courts in striking down other parts of the statute. One provision of the state law upheld by the Supreme Court was its prohibition against the use of public employees and facilities in abortions that are not necessary to save a woman's life. The other provision was the requirement that a physician must determine if a fetus carried by a woman for more than twenty weeks is capable of life outside the womb; if so, the physician may not perform an abortion. However, the Court upheld the core provisions of *Roe* v. *Wade* (1973), which protect a woman's right to choose an abortion.

Weeks v. United States
232 U.S. 383 (1914)

Local police and then a U.S. marshal searched the home of Freemont Weeks, without a warrant, and found evidence that he was selling lottery tickets illegally through the mail. The Court reversed Weeks's conviction, and established the exclusionary rule, which requires that evidence obtained in violation of a person's Fourth Amendment rights must be excluded from any legal proceedings against him or her in a federal trial.

Westside Community Board of Education v. Mergens
496 U.S. 226 (1990)

Bridget Mergens wanted to organize a Christian student club at her high school in Omaha, Nebraska, but her principal refused her proposal on the grounds that it would violate the First Amendment's establishment clause. The Court upheld the Equal Access Act of 1984, a federal law that specifies conditions by which public schools are required to permit student religious organizations to use school facilities for their meetings. The Equal Access Act passed the Lemon test set forth in *Lemon* v. *Kurtzman* (1971) to guide decisions about whether or not the First Amendment's establishment clause has been violated.

Whitney v. California
274 U.S. 357 (1927)

Charlotte Anita Whitney was convicted under the California Criminal Syndicalism Act for her activities with the Communist Labor Party. The Court unanimously upheld the act and thereby limited the free speech rights of those who advocated violent overthrow of the government. In a concurring opinion, Justice Louis Brandeis proposed standards for determining when political speech can be constitutionally limited; these standards influenced later Supreme Court decisions that significantly broadened the scope of free speech.

Wickard v. Filburn
317 U.S. 111 (1942)

Roscoe Filburn, a small-scale chicken farmer in Ohio, was penalized for exceeding wheat production quotas set by a federal law, the Agricultural Marketing Agreement Act of 1937. Filburn's defense was that the federal law at issue was an unconstitutional exercise of Congress's power under the commerce clause of the Constitution's Article 1, Section 8. However, the Supreme Court ruled that Congress may regulate agricultural production, as an activity affecting interstate commerce, even if the produce is not meant for sale. This decision represented a very broad expansion of Congress's regulatory power under the commerce clause.

Wolf v. Colorado
338 U.S. 25 (1949)

When police suspected a Colorado doctor of performing abortions in violation of state law, they took the doctor's appointment book without his knowledge, interviewed his patients, and gained enough evidence to convict Wolf. The Court ruled for the first time that Fourth Amendment rights were incorporated under the due process clause of the Fourteenth Amendment and applied to the states. However, the Court declined to require states to exclude evidence seized in violation of Fourth Amendment protections, as required in federal criminal trials, and Wolf's conviction was upheld.

Worcester v. Georgia
31 U.S. 515 [6 Pet. 515] (1832)

Samuel Worcester, a Christian missionary, was arrested for violating a Georgia law prohibiting all white persons from residing on land occupied by the indigenous Cherokee people without the permission of Georgia's governor. He appealed to the Supreme Court, which ruled that the government of Georgia had no authority to regulate the Cherokee territory within its state and ordered the release of Worcester. Georgia ignored this order, asserting its right to regulate Indian lands—an ominous prelude to the forced removal of the Cherokee people from their territory a few years later.

Yates v. United States
354 U.S. 298 (1957)

Oleta O'Connor Yates, a member of the Communist Party of the United States, was arrested for violating the Smith Act, a 1940 law that limited the activities of radical opponents of the U.S. government. The Court ruled that leaders of the U.S. Communist Party had a constitutional right, under the First Amendment, to express themselves publicly and to teach, during its meetings, the party's doctrine of violent political revolution.

Zelman v. Simmons-Harris
536 U.S. 639 (2002)

The Court upheld an Ohio voucher program that supported children attending private religiously affiliated schools, because the government aid was granted directly to the parents for the secular purpose of improving the educational opportunities of their children. Thus, the Court determined, the financial aid was not provided to advance the religious mission of the sectarian schools; had it done so, the program would have violated the First Amendment's establishment clause.

Zobrest v. Catalina Foothills School District
509 U.S. 1 (1993)

The Court ruled that federal funds granted to Arizona public schools through the Individuals with Disabilities Education Act could be used to assist the education of a physically handicapped student in a Roman Catholic high school. This use of public funds in a church-affiliated school did not violate the First Amendment's prohibition of an establishment of religion because the aid went directly to the student for a reasonable secular purpose and did not advance the religious mission of the private school.

Zorach v. Clausen
343 U.S. 306 (1952)

The Court ruled that a New York State law allowing students to be released early from public schools in order to participate in religious instruction outside the public school facilities did not violate the First Amendment's prohibition of an establishment of religion. In his opinion for the Court, Justice William O. Douglas said that an accommodation between religion and the state may be constitutionally permissible under certain conditions, because the First Amendment's establishment clause does not require an absolute separation of church and state.

Further Reading

The U.S. Constitution

Amar, Akhil Reed. *America's Constitution: A Biography.* New York: Random House, 2005.

Amar, Akhil Reed. *The Bill of Rights: Creation and Reconstruction.* New Haven, Conn.: Yale University Press, 1998.

Anastaplo, George. *The Constitution of 1787: A Commentary.* Baltimore: Johns Hopkins University Press, 1989.

Anastaplo, George. *The Amendments to the Constitution: A Commentary.* Baltimore: Johns Hopkins University Press, 1995.

Maier, Pauline. *The Declaration of Independence and the Constitution of the United States.* New York: Bantam, 1998.

Patrick, John J. *The Bill of Rights: A History in Documents.* New York: Oxford University Press, 2003.

Ritchie, Donald A. *Our Constitution.* New York: Oxford University Press, 2005.

The U.S. Supreme Court

Best, Bradley J. *Law Clerks, Support Personnel, and the Decline of Consensual Norms on the United States Supreme Court.* New York: LFB Scholarly Publications, 2002.

Dickson, Del, ed. *The Supreme Court in Conference, 1940–1985.* New York: Oxford University Press, 2001.

Gerber, Scott Douglas, ed. *Seriatim: The Supreme Court before John Marshall.* New York: New York University Press, 1998.

Greenberg, Ellen. *The Supreme Court Explained.* New York: Norton, 1997.

Hall, Kermit L., James W. Ely Jr., and Joel B. Grossman, eds. *The Oxford Companion to the Supreme Court of the United States,* 2nd ed. New York: Oxford University Press, 2005.

Irons, Peter H. *The Courage of Their Convictions: Sixteen Americans Who Fought Their Way to the Supreme Court.* New York: Penguin, 1990.

Irons, Peter H., and Stephanie Guitton, eds. *May It Please the Court: The Most Significant Oral Arguments Made before the Supreme Court Since 1955.* New York: New Press, 1993.

Marcus, Maeva, et al., eds. *The Documentary History of the Supreme Court of the United States, 1789–1800,* 7 vols. New York: Columbia University Press, 1985–2003.

McCloskey, Robert G., and Sanford Levinson. *The American Supreme Court,* 4th ed. Chicago: University of Chicago Press, 2005.

O'Connor, Sandra Day. *The Majesty of the Law: Reflections of a Supreme Court Justice.* New York: Random House, 2003.

Patrick, John J. *The Supreme Court of the United States: A Student Companion,* 3rd ed. New York: Oxford University Press, 2006.

Provine, Doris Marie. *Case Selection in the United States Supreme Court.* Chicago: University of Chicago Press, 1980.

Roosevelt, Kermit. *The Myth of Judicial Activism: Making Sense of Supreme Court Decisions.* New Haven, Conn.: Yale University Press, 2006.

Schwartz, Bernard. *A History of the Supreme Court.* New York: Oxford University Press, 1993.

Semonche, John E. *Charting the Future: The Supreme Court Responds to a Changing Society, 1890–1920.* Westport, Conn.: Greenwood, 1978.

Starr, Kenneth W. *First among Equals: The Supreme Court in American Life.* New York: Warner, 2002.

Ward, Artemus. *Deciding to Leave: The Politics of Retirement from the United States Supreme Court.* Albany: State University of New York Press, 2003.

Woodward, Bob, and Scott Armstrong. *The Brethren: Inside the Supreme Court.* New York: Simon & Schuster, 1979.

The U.S. Supreme Court Justices

Cushman, Clare. *The Supreme Court Justices: Illustrated Biographies,1789–1995,* 2nd ed. Washington, D.C.: Congressional Quarterly Press, 1995.

Friedman, Leon, and Fred L. Israel, eds. *The Justices of the United States Supreme Court, 1789–1995: Their Lives and Major Opinions.* New York: Chelsea House, 1995.

Martin, Fenton S., and Robert U. Goehlert. *How to Research the Supreme Court.* Washington, D.C.: Congressional Quarterly Press, 1992.

Martin, Fenton S., and Robert U. Goehlert. *The U.S. Supreme Court: A Bibliography.* Washington, D.C.: Congressional Quarterly Press, 1990.

Urofsky, Melvin I., ed. *Biographical Encyclopedia of the Supreme Court: The Lives and Legal Philosophies of the Justices.* Washington, D.C.: Congressional Quarterly Press, 2006.

Chapter 1: The Rise of Judicial Review

Clinton, Robert Lowry. *Marbury v. Madison and Judicial Review.* Lawrence: University Press of Kansas, 1989.

Kahn, Paul W. *The Reign of Law: Marbury v. Madison and the Construction of America.* New Haven, Conn.: Yale University Press, 1997.

Nelson, William E. *Marbury v. Madison: The Origins and Legacy of Judicial Review.* Lawrence: University Press of Kansas, 2000.

Chapter 2: The National Bank and Federalism

Gunther, Gerald, ed. *John Marshall's Defense of McCulloch v. Maryland.* Stanford, Calif.: Stanford University Press, 1969.

Hobson, Charles F. *The Great Chief Justice: John Marshall and the Rule of Law.* Lawrence: University Press of Kansas, 1996.

White, G. Edward. *The Marshall Court and Cultural Change, 1815–1835.* New York: Oxford University Press, 1991.

Chapter 3: Steamboats, States' Rights, and the Powers of Congress

Baxter, Maurice G. *Daniel Webster and the Supreme Court.* Amherst: University of Massachusetts Press, 1966.

Baxter, Maurice G. *The Steamboat Monopoly: Gibbons v. Ogden, 1824.* New York: Knopf, 1972.

Newmyer, R. Kent. *John Marshall and the Heroic Age of the Supreme Court.* Baton Rouge: Louisiana State University Press, 2001.

Remini, Robert Vincent. *Daniel Webster: The Man and His Time.* New York: Norton, 1997.

Chapter 4: Denying an Appeal for Freedom

Fehrenbacher, Don E. *The Dred Scott Case: Its Significance in American Law and Politics.* New York: Oxford University Press, 1978.

Finkelman, Paul. *Dred Scott v. Sandford: A Brief History with Documents.* Boston: Bedford, 1997.

Chapter 5: Civil Liberties and the Civil War

Farber, Daniel A. *Lincoln's Constitution.* Chicago: University of Chicago Press, 2003.

Neely, Mark E., Jr. *The Fate of Liberty: Abraham Lincoln and Civil Liberties.* New York: Oxford University Press, 1991.

Chapter 6: Separate but Not Equal

Fireside, Harvey. *Separate and Unequal: Homer Plessy and the Supreme Court Decision that Legalized Racism.* New York: Carroll & Graf, 2005.

Thomas, Brook, ed. *Plessy v. Ferguson: A Brief History with Documents.* Boston: Bedford, 1997.

Chapter 7: The Rights of Labor and the Rights of Women

Gillman, Howard. *The Constitution Besieged: The Rise and Demise of Lochner Era Police Powers Jurisprudence.* Durham, N.C.: Duke University Press, 1993.

Kens, Paul. *Judicial Power and Reform Politics: The Anatomy of Lochner v. New York.* Lawrence: University Press of Kansas, 1990.

Kens, Paul. *Lochner v. New York: Economic Regulation on Trial.* Lawrence: University Press of Kansas, 1998.

Woloch, Nancy. *Muller v. Oregon: A Brief History with Documents.* New York: Bedford, 1996.

Chapter 8: The Latitude and Limits of Free Speech

Fraleigh, Douglas. *Freedom of Speech in the Marketplace of Ideas.* New York: St. Martin's, 1997.

Polenberg, Richard. *Fighting Faiths: The Abrams Case, the Supreme Court, and Free Speech.* Ithaca, N.Y.: Cornell University Press, 1999.

White, G. Edward. *Oliver Wendell Holmes: Sage of the Supreme Court.* New York: Oxford University Press, 2000.

Chapter 9: Affirming the New Deal

Cushman, Barry. *Rethinking the New Deal Court: The Structure of a Constitutional Revolution.* New York: Oxford University Press, 1998.

Leuchtenburg, William Edward. *The Supreme Court Reborn: The Constitutional Revolution in the Age of Roosevelt.* New York: Oxford University Press, 1995.

Chapter 10: The Flag-Salute Cases

Curtis, Michael Kent, ed. *The Constitution and the Flag,* 2 vols. New York: Garland, 1993.

Manwaring, David Roger. *Render unto Caesar: The Flag-Salute Controversy.* Chicago: University of Chicago Press, 1962.

Chapter 11: Internment of Japanese Americans during World War II

Irons, Peter. *Justice at War: The Story of the Japanese American Internment Cases.* Berkeley: University of California Press, 1993.

Smith, Page. *Democracy on Trial: The Japanese American Evacuation and Relocation in World War II.* New York: Simon & Schuster, 1995.

Chapter 12: A Decision to Limit Presidential Power

Marcus, Maeva. *Truman and the Steel Seizure Case: The Limits of Presidential Power.* Durham, N.C.: Duke University Press, 1994.

Westin, Alan F. *The Anatomy of a Constitutional Law Case: Youngstown Sheet and Tube Co. v. Sawyer, the Steel Seizure Decision.* New York: Macmillan, 1958.

Chapter 13: Public School Desegregation

Cottrol, Robert J., Raymond T. Diamond, and Leland B. Ware. *Brown v. Board of Education: Caste, Culture, and the Constitution.* Lawrence: University Press of Kansas, 2003.

Kluger, Richard. *Simple Justice: The History of Brown v. Board of Education and Black America's Struggle for Equality,* rev. ed. New York: Knopf, 2004.

Patterson, James T. *Brown v. Board of Education: A Civil Rights Milestone and Its Troubled Legacy.* New York: Oxford University Press, 2001.

Chapter 14: Establishing Equality in Voting and Representation

Cortner, Richard C. *The Apportionment Cases.* Knoxville: University of Tennessee Press, 1970.

Hasen, Richard L. *The Supreme Court and Election Law: Judging Equality from Baker v. Carr to Bush v. Gore.* New York: New York University Press, 2003.

Chapter 15: Freedom of the Press in a Free Society

Fireside, Harvey. *New York Times v. Sullivan: Affirming Freedom of the Press.* Springfield, N.J.: Enslow, 1999.

Hopkins, W. Wat. *Actual Malice: Twenty-Five Years after Times v. Sullivan.* New York: Praeger, 1989.

Lewis, Anthony. *Make No Law: The Sullivan Case and the First Amendment.* New York: Random House, 1991.

Chapter 16: Finding a Right to Privacy

Alderman, Ellen, and Caroline Kennedy. *The Right to Privacy.* New York: Knopf, 1995.

Johnson, John W. *Griswold v. Connecticut: Birth Control and the Constitutional Right of Privacy.* Lawrence: University Press of Kansas, 2005.

Chapter 17: The Right to Remain Silent

Schmalleger, Frank. *Miranda Revisited: The Case of Dickerson v. U.S. and Suspect Rights Advisements in the United States.* Upper Saddle River, N.J.: Prentice-Hall, 2001.

Stuart, Gary L. *Miranda : The Story of America's Right to Remain Silent.* Tucson: University of Arizona Press, 2004.

Chapter 18: Freedom of Speech in Public Schools

Johnson, John W. *The Struggle for Student Rights: Tinker v. Des Moines and the 1960s.* Lawrence: University Press of Kansas, 1997.

Werhan, Keith. *Freedom of Speech: A Reference Guide to the United States Constitution.* Westport, Conn.: Praeger, 2004.

Chapter 19: Standards for Interpreting the Establishment Clause

Gaustad, Edwin S. *Proclaim Liberty throughout All the Land: A History of Church and State in America.* New York: Oxford University Press, 2003.

Hamburger, Philip. *Separation of Church and State.* Cambridge, Mass.: Harvard University Press, 2002.

Kowalski, Kathiann M. *Lemon v. Kurtzman and the Separation of Church and State Debate: Debating Supreme Court Decisions.* Berkeley Heights, N.J.: Enslow, 2005.

Chapter 20: Abortion, Privacy, and Values in Conflict

Garrow, David J. *Liberty and Sexuality: The Right to Privacy and the Making of Roe v. Wade.* Berkeley: University of California Press, 1998.

Greenhouse, Linda. *Becoming Justice Blackmun: Harry Blackmun's Supreme Court Journey.* New York: Times Books, 2005.

Hull, N. E. H., and Peter Charles Hoffer. *Roe v. Wade and the Abortion Rights Controversy in American History.* Lawrence: University Press of Kansas, 2001.

Chapter 21: Presidential Immunity and the Watergate Crisis

Friedman, Leon, ed. *United States v. Nixon: The President before the Supreme Court.* New York: Chelsea House, 1974.

Herda, D. J. *United States v. Nixon: Watergate and the President.* Springfield, N.J.: Enslow, 1996.

Kutler, Stanley I. *The Wars of Watergate: The Last Crisis of Richard Nixon.* New York: Norton, 1992.

Reeves, Richard. *President Nixon: Alone in the White House.* New York: Simon & Schuster, 2002.

Chapter 22: Affirmative Action and the Boundaries of Discrimination

Ball, Howard. *The Bakke Case: Race, Education, and Affirmative Action.* Lawrence: University Press of Kansas, 2000.

Belz, Herman. *Equality Transformed: A Quarter Century of Affirmative Action.* New Brunswick, N.J.: Transaction, 1991.

Carter, Stephen L. *Reflections of an Affirmative Action Baby.* New York: Basic, 1991.

Rubio, Philip F. *A History of Affirmative Action, 1619–2000.* Jackson: University Press of Mississippi, 2001.

Stohr, Greg. *A Black and White Case: How Affirmative Action Survived Its Greatest Legal Challenge.* Princeton, N.J.: Bloomberg, 2004.

Chapter 23: The Judicial Path to the White House

Banks, Christopher, David B. Cohen, and John C. Green, eds. *The Final Arbiter: The Consequences of Bush v. Gore for Law and Politics.* Albany: State University of New York Press, 2005.

Dionne, E. J., Jr., and William Kristol, eds. *Bush v. Gore: The Court Cases and the Commentary.* Washington, D.C.: Brookings Institution Press, 2001.

Posner, Richard A. *Breaking the Deadlock: The 2000 Election, the Constitution, and the Courts.* Princeton, N.J.: Princeton University Press, 2001.

Websites

American Bar Association

www.abanet.org

Full-text articles on legal issues are provided along with other resources about federal and state courts, judges, and lawyers.

Cornell Legal Information Institute

www.law.cornell.edu

This site of the Cornell University Law School contains all U.S. Supreme Court opinions since May 1990 and 600 opinions on major cases throughout the Court's history. It also includes information on current events and issues involving the courts, judges, and law.

Federal Judicial Center

www.fjc.gov

Provides general information about the federal judiciary, including a history of federal courts, a biographical database of federal judges since 1789, and information on key legislation about the federal judiciary throughout U.S. history.

Federal Judiciary

www.uscourts.gov

Provides news about current events and basic information about the federal judicial system. The site includes information about the structure and functions of the federal courts, with links to the U.S. Supreme Court, U.S. Courts of Appeals, and the U.S. District Courts.

FindLaw

www.findlaw.com

Includes information about the U.S. federal judiciary and the judiciaries of the 50 states. Provides opinions from the Supreme Court, all federal circuits, and the appellate courts of the 50 states. Presents information about current legal events and issues.

H-LAW

www.h-net.org/~law

This online discussion list stresses legal and constitutional history and contemporary issues in the law. It includes book reviews and links to the American Society of Legal History, which sponsors this site.

Jurist: Legal News and Research

http://jurist.law.pitt.edu

This site of the University of Pittsburgh School of Law includes a broad range of current legal news and information about federal and state courts with emphasis on the U.S. Supreme Court. Research and expert commentary about current legal events and issues are provided. Decisions of the Supreme Court are accessible.

Justice Learning

www.justicelearning.org

This site, a collaboration of National Public Radio's "Justice Talking" and the New York Times Learning Network, offers resources for teachers and students on law and justice issues. The site includes an annotated Constitution with historical timelines for each article and amendment.

Landmark Supreme Court Cases

www.landmarkcases.org

This site, a collaboration between Street Law and the Supreme Court Historical Society, includes instructional resources for teachers and students. Includes basic information about key decisions of the Supreme Court along with teaching strategies and lesson plans.

Lexis-Nexis

www.lexisnexis.com

This legal research service offers a broad range of data on historical and current topics. Opinions, briefs, and secondary sources on U.S. Supreme Court cases are available, as are materials pertaining to all federal district courts, U.S. Courts of Appeals, specialized federal courts, and state courts. Through its daily opinion service, immediate access to decisions of all federal and state courts is provided. In addition, primary and secondary sources on current events and legislation are available.

Library of Congress: U.S. Judiciary

www.loc.gov/law/guide/usjudic.html

Provides links to many sites related to the federal judicial branch of government, including those with information about legal history, federal laws, judicial opinions, court rules, and law journals, and legal news.

Oyez: U.S. Supreme Court Multimedia Database

www.oyez.org

This site is a project of Northwestern University and includes information about Supreme Court cases, biographies of Supreme Court justices, and instructional materials for teachers and students.

Supreme Court Historical Society

www.supremecourthistory.org

Provides access to opinions of notable Supreme Court cases and information on the society's programs and publications.

Supreme Court of the United States

www.supremecourtus.gov

This official site of the Court includes information about the history, structure, functions, and rules of the federal judiciary. It presents opinions on all cases that have gone before the Court, oral arguments, the Court's docket, and a guide to visiting the Court.

Westlaw

www.westlaw.com

Provides access to opinions, briefs, oral arguments, and secondary materials related to cases of the U.S. Supreme Court.

Index

Text Credits

p. 20: *Marbury* v. *Madison,* 5 U.S. 137 [1. Cr. 137] (1803).

p. 24: Lipscomb, Andrew Adgate, and Albert Ellery Bergh, eds. *The Writings of Thomas Jefferson,* 20 vols., Washington, D.C., 1903–4, 11:50, 51; 14:303; 14:305; 15:212; 15:277. Leicester Ford, Paul. *The Writings of Thomas Jefferson,* 10 vols., New York, 1892–99, 10:192. Lipscomb, Andrew Adgate, and Albert Ellery Bergh, eds. *The Writings of Thomas Jefferson,* 15:451.

p. 32: *Alexandria Gazette* (July 3, 1819).

p. 40: *Gibbons* v. *Ogden* 22 U.S. 1 [9 Wheat. 1] (1824).

p. 49: Douglass, Frederick. *The Dred Scott Decision* (Rochester, N.Y.: C. P. Dewey, 1857).

p. 57: *The Annals of America: 1858–1865,* vol. 9 (Chicago: Encyclopaedia Britannica, 1968), pp. 268–74.

p. 65: *Plessy* v. *Ferguson* 163 U.S. 537 (1896).

p. 75: Brief for the Defendant in Error, *Muller* v. *Oregon,* Louis D. Brandeis, October Term, 1907. Supreme Court Library, Washington, D.C.

p. 83: *Abrams* v. *United States* 250 U.S. 616 (1919).

p. 92: "Franklin D. Roosevelt, Fireside Chat on the 'Court-Packing' Bill," radio address given March 9, 1937. Found at *www.hpol.org/fdr/chat/.*

p. 102: *West Virginia State Board of Education* v. *Barnette* 319 U.S. 624 (1943).

p. 111: Reprinted with the permission of the Free Press, a division of Simon & Schuster Adult Publishing Group, from the *The Courage of Their Convictions* by Peter Irons. Copyright © 1988 by Peter Irons. All rights reserved. Pp. 53–54, 55, 57–58, 60–62.

p. 119: From *The Supreme Court in Conference, 1940–1985,* edited by Del Dickson. Copyright © 2001 by Oxford University Press, used by permission. Pp. 172–82.

p. 132: *Congressional Record,* 84th Congress, 2nd session. (March 12, 1956), pp. 4460–61.

p. 140: The National Archives, Records of the Supreme Court of the United States, Record Group 267.3.1; Oral Arguments in Cases before the Court, 1955-97, *Baker* v. *Carr* (1962). Available online at *http://www.oyez.org/oyez/resource/case/25/.*

p. 149: "Free Press and Free People," *The New York Times,* March 10, 1964. Copyright © 1964 by the New York Times Co. Reprinted with permission. "New Libel Test," *Evening Star,* March 10, 1964. Copyright © by the Washington Post, reprinted with permission.

p. 156: From *The Supreme Court in Conference, 1940–1985,* edited by Del Dickson. Copyright © 2001 by Oxford University Press, used by permission. Pp. 800–803.

p. 163: The National Archives, Records of the Supreme Court of the United States, Record Group 267.3.1; Oral Arguments in Cases before the Court, 1955-97, *Miranda* v. *Arizona* (1966). Available online at *http://www.oyez.org/oyez/resource/case/251/.*

p. 171: Reprinted with the permission of the Free Press, a division of Simon & Schuster Adult Publishing Group, from the *The Courage of Their Convictions* by Peter Irons. Copyright © 1988 by Peter Irons. All rights reserved. Pp. 245–48.

p. 178: "Safeguarding Religious Freedom," *Washington Post,* June 30, 1971. Copyright © 1971, the Washington Post, reprinted with permission.

p. 188: *Planned Parenthood of Southeastern Pennsylvania v. Robert P. Casey* 1991 U.S. Briefs 744; 1992 U.S. S. Ct. Briefs LEXIS 321, October Term, 1991.

p. 189: *Roe* v. *Wade,* 410 U.S. 113 (1973).

p. 200: Articles of Impeachment Adopted by the House Committee on the Judiciary July 27, 1974.

p. 211: President Lyndon B. Johnson, "To Fulfill These Rights," Commencement address delivered at Howard University, June 4, 1965. Found at *www.lbjlib.utexas.edu/johnson/archives.hom/speeches.hom/650604.asp.*

p. 212: *Grutter* v. *Bollinger* 539 U.S. 306 (2003).

p. 220: Al Gore, "Concession Speech," delivered from Washington, D.C., December 13, 2000. Found at *www.thegreenpapers.com/News/20001213-1.html.*

p. 222: George Bush, "Acceptance Speech," delivered from the Capitol in Austin, Texas, December 13, 2000. Found at *www.thegreenpapers.com/News/20001213-1.html.*

Picture Credits

About the Authors

Kermit L. Hall was president and professor of history at the University at Albany, State University of New York. A scholar of American constitutional, legal, and judicial history, he had previously served as president of Utah State University and as a professor of history and an administrator at many other American universities. He wrote extensively on the American judicial system and served as the editor of *The Oxford Companion to the Supreme Court, American Legal History: Cases and Materials, The Judicial Branch,* and *The Oxford Companion to American Law.* Kermit Hall died on August 13, 2006, just after completing this book.

John J. Patrick is professor emeritus of education at Indiana University and has also been a middle school and high school teacher of history, civics, and government. His many publications include *The Supreme Court of the United States: A Student Companion, The Bill of Rights: A History in Documents, Understanding Democracy, Founding the Republic: A Documentary History, Constitutional Debates on Freedom of Religion,* and *How to Teach the Bill of Rights.* He is also the co-author of several high school and middle school textbooks. Professor Patrick has also been an international civic education consultant and lecturer in several post-communist countries. In recognition of his contributions to international programs, Professor Patrick received Indiana University's John W. Ryan Award in 2002. In 2005, he was the first recipient of the Indiana State Bar Association's Civic Education Award.

About the Annenberg Foundation Trust at Sunnylands

The Annenberg Foundation Trust at Sunnylands was established in 2001 by the Annenberg Foundation to advance public understanding of and appreciation for democracy and to address serious issues facing the country and the world. The Trust convenes:

- leaders of the United States to focus on ways to improve the functioning of the three branches of government, the press, and the public schools;
- educators to determine how to better teach about the Constitution and the fundamental principles of democracy;
- leaders of major social institutions including learned societies to determine how these institutions can better serve the public and the public good;
- scholars addressing ways to improve the well-being of the nation in such areas as media, education, and philanthropy.

The Annenberg Classroom (*www.annenbergclassroom.org*), *www.justicelearning.org,* and a collection of books on the U.S. Constitution, democracy, and related topics, are all projects of the Annenberg Foundation Trust at Sunnylands.

About Justice Learning

Justice Learning, a joint effort with the New York Times Learning Network, is a comprehensive on-line resource on civics education. The website offers balanced radio debates from NPR's *Justice Talking,* topical and age-appropriate articles from the *New York Times,* and a host of primary source materials, timelines, and lesson plans on a wide range of justice issues. Visit on-line at *www.justicelearning.org.*